Second Edition

THE LANGUAGE
OF LEARNING

Vocabulary for College Success

Titles of Related Interest:

Second Edition

THE LANGUAGE
OF LEARNING

Vocabulary for College Success

Jane N. Hopper
California State University,
Irvine

Jo Ann Carter-Wells
California State University,
Fullerton

Wadsworth Publishing Company
Belmont, California
A Division of Wadsworth, Inc.

English Editor: Angela Gantner
Senior Editorial Assistant: Lisa Timbrell
Production: Sara Hunsaker/*Ex Libris*
Designer: Vargas/Williams/Design
Print Buyer: Barbara Britton
Copy Editor: Elliot Simon
Cover: Stephen Rapley
Compositor: Maryland Composition
Printer: Malloy Lithographing, Inc.

 This book is printed on acid-free recycled paper.

International Thomson Publishing
The trademark ITP is used under license.

Printed in the United States of America
1 2 3 4 5 6 7 8 9 10—98 97 96 95 94

Library of Congress Cataloging-in-Publication Data

Hopper, Jane.
    The language of learning : vocabulary for college success / Jane Hopper, Jo Ann Carter-Wells.—2nd ed.
       p.   cm.
    Includes index.
    ISBN 0-534-21384-7
    1. Vocabulary. 2. Learning and scholarship—Terminology.
3. Universities and colleges—Curricula—Terminology. I. Carter-Wells, Jo Ann. II. Title.
PE1683.H67   1994
428.1—dc20   93-23210
                                          CIP

CONTENTS

Chapter 22   Business: Computer Science   354

PART FOUR: APPENDIXES   373

Index   393

PREFACE

This second edition of *The Language of Learning* represents our effort to incorporate our increased experience with students of wider and more diverse backgrounds with suggestions from faculty friends who have worked with the book. In addition, we have responded to suggestions from students who have used the text to improve their vocabularies, and from reviewers who generously contributed ideas to make the book even better.

The first edition was the result of a project that began about fifteen years ago when we were teaching a university vocabulary class. Because that class offered general education credit, students from many majors and many class levels enrolled. The class was set up to improve students' vocabularies in four areas: listening, speaking, reading, and writing. The listening and speaking activities took place in small groups, much like groups used to develop foreign language skills. Reading vocabulary developed through reading materials in the course syllabus that contained excerpts from "classical" works in the various disciplines, such as Adam Smith's *The Wealth of Nations*. Writing vocabulary words were supplied by the students from their own college reading. They selected and defined words that were unknown to them; they wrote sentences and essays using context clues; and we gave feedback. That activity eventually led to the first edition of the text.

Over many semesters we noticed that although the students and the textbooks changed, the words did not vary a great deal. We began to collect words and organize them according to source (academic discipline, fields related to an academic discipline, literature, and so on) and according to the selector (age, year in school, major). We collected thousands of words; some of them appeared many times. A number of those words appeared in the first edition. In this second edition we have changed a few of them in the rewritten reading selections, and added more by including new chapters. While some of the student-selected words may appear too easy at first glance, we have found that a reader can be familiar with a word like *democracy*, for instance, yet still be unable to distinguish that form of government from other forms. Having heard a word or being able to use it in a narrow way does not indicate mastery.

We have learned that the text can be used effectively by a wider audience than we first anticipated. Our original population included a small number of English as a Second Language students. As that population increased, we discovered that the text, with its accompanying audiotapes, proved very useful to those who were working hard to increase their skills in English. We also found that high school students preparing for college entrance, as well as those enrolled in special college/university preparation courses such as the Summer Bridge Program, could profit by using the book. Initially the text was conceived as a tool for freshmen and sophomores who might not have selected a major and whose academic vocabularies had not developed. We discovered, however, that more academically advanced students often have difficulty with the words used in disciplines outside their own. Since today's graduate schools give preference to those who are knowledgeable in a variety of fields, students preparing to take graduate school entrance exams find this text helpful in introducing them to basic concepts in various fields and providing terms that represent those concepts.

Our purpose in writing this book is twofold: to introduce some of the words that our students found essential, and to give students the necessary skills to increase their vocabularies throughout their lives. Fundamental to our purpose is knowledge of the dictionary. Therefore we devote time to its description and use, and we include actual entries. We find that few students are able to use the dictionary efficiently, in part because most vocabulary texts supply definitions rather than requiring students to seek them in a dictionary format. (In a survey of former students, we found that learning to use the dictionary in our class rated high and was "of continuing importance to vocabulary growth.")

We structured the book so that it can be used independently, with context clues and several exercises for each word. We provide a variety of evaluation measures and answer keys for immediate feedback. We cover a number of academic disciplines and include an overview of each discipline to increase student awareness. We emphasize the importance of creating a personalized concept of a word, because we know that even a hard-working, determined student cannot remember irrelevant words. Current research in vocabulary instruction supports these methods.

The book is divided into four sections. Part One provides information useful to the vocabulary student and necessary to the successful completion of the text. Instruction in using context clues has been expanded; instruction in using etymologies has been added in this edition. Part Two introduces general words from our student-supplied pool in a context useful to college students. The new chapter on critical thinking is especially pertinent to today's world and reflects national education goals. Part Three introduces academic words in reading selections about the disciplines. This second edition includes three new disciplines, and four of the reading selections from the first edition have been rewritten. Each word introduced has separate exercises, accompanied by its own dictionary entry. Instructions are repeated frequently, so the units can also stand alone. If students have not mastered a word, the posttests alert them to this and instructions return them to the exercises for more careful study.

The fourth section, the appendixes, includes a segment giving etymologies of the words introduced, for reference purposes and for those who prefer more emphasis on word origins. The second segment provides the pretest answer keys. Additional words for each discipline and the format for student-generated vocabulary lists are provided in the Instructor's Manual. Posttest answer keys remain in the Instructor's Manual, as recommended by several reviewers.

The instructor who prefers to do so can use this text as an adjunct, providing little assistance beyond making sure students understand how to use it, evaluating the posttests, and, perhaps, using the section mastery tests supplied in the Instructor's Manual. An instructor who prefers to give more direction can select the areas to be studied and assign the words to be mastered. The text can be used by individuals, in small groups, or with whole class instruction, depending on the instructor's teaching style and the nature of the group. Our prime hope is that this text will help its users develop the abilities necessary to increase their vocabularies continuously throughout their lives. In this multimedia age, it is clear that we must know the words that carry messages effectively. Whichever medium is employed, knowledge of appropriate words enables the writer to produce a powerful message and assists the reader in making an enlightened interpretation of it.

Acknowledgments

We are indebted not only to the hundreds of students who provided the academic terms over the years and to those who made suggestions for improving the text, but also to those students and faculty who assisted in the development of the reading selections. We would like especially to thank the following for their contributions:

Biology: Shari Aube and Kenneth Goodhue-McWilliams, California State University, Fullerton

Business Administration: James W. Anderson, Fullerton College

Chemistry: Joan Burt, Saddleback Valley Unified School District

Communications: Nicholas King, Jr., California State University, Fullerton

Economics and Accounting: Dennis Leahy, California State University, Fullerton

History: Jerald Hopper, Saddleback Valley Unified School District

Mathematics: Cynthia Skogen and Gerald Gannon, California State University, Fullerton

Music: Diane Herbert, California State University, Fullerton

Political Science: Nguyen Hong Hoang, University of California, Irvine

Special assistance was received from Ron A. Carlyle, Cal-Poly, Pomona; Donald G. Wells, Cal-Poly, Pomona; and Col. David Porter, U.S. Air Force Academy.

The faculty who reviewed our material also assisted in refining our ideas to make this text more meaningful for students in the classroom. We are grateful for the guidance of Happy Miller-Retwaiut, University of

Hawaii; Bettye W. Jones, Virginia State University; Carol Radin, Cazenovia College; and Pat Hargis, Judson College.

Support and encouragement throughout the nuturing and writing stages came from our husbands, Jerald Hopper and Donald Wells; from our families; and from our colleagues both within and outside our field of endeavor.

Jane N. Hopper
Jo Ann Carter-Wells

PART ONE

INTRODUCTION

CHAPTER ONE

HOW TO USE
THIS BOOK

◆

The vocabulary words in this book were selected by college and university students like you. For each discipline, they chose the words they felt were essential to their learning and success as students. These choices of words do not necessarily represent the core vocabulary of a particular discipline, but they are words that are useful when reading a textbook or listening to a lecture in a particular field. Because these student-selected words have been collected by the authors over many years, the words will be more meaningful and useful than those generally found in college-level vocabulary texts. The vocabulary words in this book are used in context in reading selections. This provides interest and also helps you develop knowledge of a specific academic field as well as familiarity with important or key terms. Most of the reading selections were written by faculty and others with expertise in their disciplines. Although the selections were developed to present particular issues or concepts you might encounter in your introductory-level classes, the selections are primarily meant to serve as a vehicle for introducing the student-selected academic vocabulary.

This book is divided into four sections. Part I provides background information that will help you use this book, including dictionary usage, context clues, and verbal analogies. Part II introduces student-selected general vocabulary words focusing on the theme of becoming successful as a college student. Part III presents student-selected academic words from four major schools of study and fifteen separate disciplines. There is also an overview of each discipline that includes what you would typically study, what careers you would be prepared for, and how the textbooks usually are structured. The appendixes contain etymological information for each word featured in the text and answer keys for the pretests.

You can select those chapters and academic areas you wish to study, or complete the ones as directed by your instructor. Before you work with the words, you will be able to identify those in your working, or production, vocabulary (words you know and use) and those in your recognition, or reception, vocabulary (words you recognize but do not actively know or use). The words are then used in reading selections to give you useful information. Pretests will help you find out what you know. Exercises focused toward various levels of thinking will give you practice where you need it. Posttests will let you evaluate your progress.

We have organized the book this way because we have found that students learn and remember best when they become *personally involved* with each new word and use it as often as possible in speech and writing. We have also found that most students *want* to learn, to become knowledgeable, and to demonstrate the extent of their knowledge. It is with this thought in mind that we provide the information in this book, some of which is expressed directly (as in the exercises) and some of which is expressed less directly (as in the chapter reading selections). You will find that some of the exercises have more than one correct answer. They are designed to make you think carefully about the meaning of each word.

You will probably know some of the words introduced. However, we hope that when you have completed this book, you will know and use *all* of the words. What is more important, you will know how to use context clues to help you understand new words. You will also know how to create a concept for a new word so that you can continue to increase your vocabulary throughout your life.

We think that this book can add to your success in your college endeavors, in your personal life, and in your chosen career. To summarize: In this book you will learn how to

- use context clues to understand unknown words
- create concepts for words in order to learn and remember them
- discover where English words come from
- understand and use dictionaries
- reason through verbal analogies
- think imaginatively about etymologies

You will also learn about

- efficient reading and learning strategies
- using your time and energy wisely
- critical thinking
- using resources of the library

In addition, you should learn more about

- various fields of study
- typical information or content in a field of study
- textbook structure
- sources of additional vocabulary words

Finally, and perhaps most importantly, you will learn a process that will enable you to improve your vocabulary effectively, not only during your college career but throughout life.

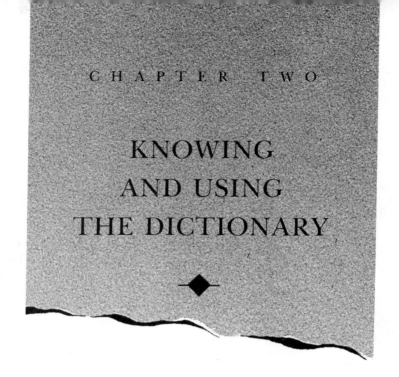

CHAPTER TWO

KNOWING AND USING THE DICTIONARY

◆

Think of the dictionary as a tool. True, it is only one of the tools of the language user, but it is the most fundamental. Like all tools, the dictionary performs better as its user becomes more skilled. Prior to this time you may only have used the dictionary to verify the spelling or to find the meaning of a word. Now, however, you need to become more skillful. You are about to become an expert. You need to be aware of how a dictionary sets out its information and to realize that there are different types of dictionaries that offer different kinds of information in varying degrees of complexity. The brief outline that follows should help you to select the best tool for your job.

TYPES OF DICTIONARIES

Special Dictionaries

There are dictionaries that specialize in the vocabularies specific to the various disciplines, for example, the *Oxford Classical Dictionary* and *Henderson's Dictionary of Biological Terms*. Some are even specific within a discipline, such as the *Dictionary of Middle English Musical Terms*. These dictionaries restrict their entries to words that are used in a field and limit their definitions to those that are pertinent to the field. You may find words in these specialized volumes that are not included in regular dictionaries, even unabridged ones. Use a specialized dictionary when you cannot find the entry you need in a good unabridged volume. There are dictionaries specific to almost every field.

Oxford English Dictionary

Of the general dictionaries, the most complete is the *Oxford English Dictionary* (usually referred to as the *OED*). The second edition of this monumental work is now available in twenty volumes. The first portion of the dictionary was published in 1894, with ten volumes published by 1928. However, when the project might have been complete, it was realized that there were still many English words that had not been included. Updating was begun, and four more volumes were completed by 1986. Thanks to computer technology, the 290,500 main entries are now encorporated into a single alphabet, evenly distributed in the twenty volumes. In addition to the usual information given for an entry—the pronunciation(s), part(s) of speech, etymology (history), and definition(s)—dates and examples of usage over time are provided. For an enlightening view of how language usage changes through the ages, look up a word of your choice.

Unabridged Dictionaries

Next in order of complexity are the unabridged dictionaries. These works list (nearly) all of the words in the language. Volumes are not reprinted at each updating, so new words often are incorporated as addenda in a separate section. These volumes give the word (called a *main entry*) with its derivatives (those words similar to it with different endings), the pronunciation(s), part(s) of speech, and a full array of definitions accompanied by examples of usage where appropriate. The etymology, or history, appears at the base word and is not repeated at main entries that share the same origin. Synonyms are given as well as references to related words.

Not all unabridged dictionaries are of the same quality. Size does not always ensure that a dictionary provides the depth of information you need to be a scholar of words. One way to check the quality of a volume advertised as unabridged is to look up several words, ranging from easy to difficult, and see if full information, including examples of usage, is given. The etymology should be set out in some detail at the entry considered the base entry. Recommended unabridged dictionaries on the market are the Merriam-Webster *Webster's Third New International Dictionary, The Random House Dictionary of the English Language* (second unabridged edition), and *The World Book Dictionary*.

Desk Dictionaries

Next in size and complexity are the desk volumes, in some cases based on an unabridged work but with fewer words and examples of usage. A good desk volume will supply thousands of words, each with its pronunciation(s), part(s) of speech, derivatives, and definition(s). The definitions may not be as extensive as in an unabridged work, and examples of usage and usage notes may be limited. The etymology, however, should be as complete as that shown in the larger work. Desk volumes most suitable for college use are Merriam-Webster *Webster's Tenth New Collegiate Dictionary*, *The American Heritage Dictionary of the English Language* (first, second, and third editions), *Webster's New World Dictionary: College Edition* (third edition), and *Webster's College Dictionary*, published by Random House.

Publishers update desk volume dictionaries regularly. You will want to use one that is no more than ten years old. In another analogy (comparison), we can say that a dictionary is a picture of the language as it exists at a given moment. And language is not a permanent thing but rather changes with use over time. You do not want to rely on an out-of-date "snapshot" as a reference tool.

A word of caution: The name *Webster* is in the public domain and may be used by anyone who produces a dictionary or reference work. Don't be fooled into thinking you are purchasing a quality work merely because it is called Webster's. Before you purchase, look at the work carefully to see if it offers all of the features listed above with reasonable completeness.

Paperback Dictionaries

Next in size and quality are paperback dictionaries. These usually provide information limited to pronunciation(s), part(s) of speech, and selected definitions. A few provide limited etymological information. Because college work requires a full range of definitions, paperback works are not recommended. They seldom include examples of usage or point out special usage problems. Also, as you become more skilled, you will need etymologies to help develop your concepts for the words. Most paperback dictionaries are not adequate tools for the serious college student.

The Thesaurus

Another tool often used by writers is the thesaurus. A thesaurus is a dictionary of synonyms and is labeled such by some publishers. Some thesauri are printed in alphabetical order, while others are grouped according to a classification system devised early in the nineteenth century by Peter Mark Roget. Whichever one you select is a matter of personal preference, but two comments are in order. First, the name *Roget* is in the public domain (like the name *Webster*), so even an inadequate work may carry that title. Second, a thesaurus provides *synonyms only, no definitions.* This means that if you are searching for synonyms of the word *severe,* you must realize that they will be different depending on whether you mean "harsh" (some synonyms of *harsh* are *strict, hard, rigid,* and *inflexible*) or "simple" (some synonyms of *simple* are *plain, ordinary, unadorned,* and *natural*). Words listed as synonyms do not necessarily have identical meanings, but they do have some concept in common. To appreciate this fact, read carefully the synonym studies (also called *synonymies*) that appear in this book and in good dictionaries. While a thesaurus can be valuable when employed correctly, do not try to use one as a substitute for a dictionary.

WHICH DEFINITION IS BEST?

Words by themselves have no meaning but only take on meaning as we attach concepts to them. That is, the word *chair* is only a sound until we have a picture in our minds of "chairness" and attach that picture, or concept, to the sound. If you already have the concept for a word in your mind, it is not too difficult to match the agreed-on word with that concept. Having once seen a table, you need only to be told what it is called, and that word becomes part of your vocabulary. One reason is that a table is a concrete object. It is more difficult to create concepts for abstract things, like faith or regret, particularly if you have never experienced them. To add to the problem, some concepts are varied and extensive. For example, some of the concepts (or definitions) of a simple word like *charge* are "to entrust with a duty," "to blame," "to postpone payment," "to attack violently," "to load (a gun)," "to excite or intensify," and "to fill." There are more verb definitions and even more noun definitions of *charge!* Attaching concepts to words can be very complicated indeed! All of this is not intended to discourage you but is intended to show you how you must form narrow or broad concepts and, in some instances, stretch your imagination to encompass the variety of ideas included within the word.

When you look up an unknown word in the dictionary, your task is to carefully examine the context that surrounds the word, then read all the recorded definitions and select the one that most nearly fits the author's use. If you are not sure of the author's meaning after one reading, read the material again until the likely meaning becomes clear. You cannot be sure you have the author's exact meaning, but you can proceed with thought and logic. So the answer to the question raised above is: *The best definition is the one that best fits the individual author's use.*

DENOTATIONS AND CONNOTATIONS

Although it is your responsibility as a user of language to form concepts for the words you use, you must be careful to not go beyond the definitions listed in the dictionary. A good dictionary will include the variety of agreed-on denotations of a word. *Denotations* are meanings "officially" attached to words. But many words also have *connotations,* or meanings that are suggested by a word and "unofficially" attached to it. Consider the word *work.* Although most dictionaries list many definitions for this word, it is safe to say that each individual attaches even more concepts to it! What do you think of when you think of work? Another example of the differences between denotations and connotations might be found in the word *football.* Denotations from the dictionary refer to games played by kicking and sometimes carrying a ball and include American football, British rugby, and soccer. Connotations of the word *football* may include thoughts of games attended in person or watched on television, so that football can come to mean excitement. Or if the thought of football fills you with boredom or annoyance, these may be the word's connotations for you.

But connotations are not attached to words only by individuals. Some groups of people have generally accepted connotations for certain words. For instance, in some societies the idea of fat has positive connotations. Fat people are considered more attractive, and body fat is a sign of prosperity and wealth. In other societies, fat has a negative connotation. A person who is fat is considered unfashionable, and body fat is thought to be a sign of poor health. Remember then, as you create concepts for new words or attach words to previously established concepts that you must take care to distinguish between the official definitions, or *denotations,* and the unofficial "tag-ons," or *connotations.*

USING THE DICTIONARY

The information on the following pages will help you interpret the dictionary definitions that accompany each of the words you will study so that you can work efficiently in this book.* Dictionaries differ somewhat in the way

---

* Dictionary entries given with the exercises for each word are taken from the text of *The World Book Dictionary* as needed, with the word being introduced given first and other pertinent or necessary words added after. Wherever possible, an etymology is included. If, in the etymology of a word, we are directed to "see etym. under ____," and we feel it would be useful to you, we have added that etymology to this text. Occasionally, the dictionary directs us to a synonym study with the indication "**SYN:** See syn. under ____." If we believe this synonym study might be useful to you in the exercises we provide, we include it also. All rearrangements of *The World Book Dictionary* text are made by special permission of World Book, Inc.

they present material, and the entries here may be slightly different from those in the dictionary you have been using. Look these pages over carefully and return to them if you experience any problems with the dictionary portion of the exercises.

Etymologies

One thing you may not have experienced previously is reading the history of the word, or the *etymology,* which is found between square brackets [   ]. Reading the information between the brackets will tell you the "family tree" of the word. (In the dictionary used here, the etymology appears at the end of the definitions.) Because a great number of English words have Latin and Greek roots, many people find that learning roots (nouns, verbs, or adjectives in the original language) and prefixes (usually prepositions) creates a basic core of knowledge that is useful in analyzing unknown words.

    You can begin creating your core of knowledge in this book by carefully reading the etymology when it is included with the introduced word. Use the information given to strengthen your concept of the word and of other words related to it. (For more information about how to expand your vocabulary by using etymologies, see Chapter 4.) In addition, Appendix A provides all of the Latin and Greek combining forms (prefixes and roots) that are found in the etymologies of the 270 words introduced in this book. In some cases, the origins are other than Latin or Greek, and those prefixes and roots are included also. Use the material in Appendix A to help build concepts based on the family trees of the words.

HOW TO USE THE DICTIONARY
ENTRIES GIVEN IN THIS TEXT

Main Entry Main entries are words or phrases in heavy type that extend into the margin.

sub|li|ma|tion (sub´lə mā´shən), *n.* **1** the act or process of sublimating or subliming; purification: *This direct transition from solid to vapor is called sublimation* (Sears and Zemansky). **2** the resulting product or state, especially, mental elevation or exaltation: *that enthusiastic sublimation which is the source of greatness and energy* (Thomas L. Peacock). **3** the highest stage or purest form of a thing. **4** a chemical sublimate.

Pronunciation and Stress These are found in parentheses following the main-entry word. Be sure to read the pronunciation key carefully. It is printed in the inside cover of this book.

co|vert (*adj.* 1, *n. 3* kō´vərt, kuv´ərt; *adj.* 2,3; *n. 1, 2* kuv´ərt, kō´vərt), *adj., n.* **—*adj.* 1** kept from sight; secret; hidden; disguised: *The children cast covert glances at the box of candy they were told not to touch.* SYN: concealed. See syn. under **secret. 2** *Law.* married and under the authority or protection of her husband. **3** *Rare.* covered; sheltered.
—*n.* 1a a hiding place; shelter. **b** a thicket in which wild animals or birds hide. **2** a covering. **3** = covert cloth.

Parts of Speech   These are abbreviated and italicized following the pronunciation. The parts of speech and their abbreviations are as follows: noun, *n.;* verb, *v.;* transitive verb, *v.t.;* intransitive verb, *v.i.;* pronoun, *pron.;* adjective, *adj.;* adverb, *adv.;* preposition, *prep.;* conjunction, *conj.;* interjection, *interj.*

Inflections   These show any irregular endings. If a noun is made plural in any way except by adding an "s" or if the past tense and present participle of a verb are irregular, the dictionary will show the irregular endings. Comparative forms of adjectives and adverbs are also given.

Definitions   These are the meanings of the entries. Words that have more than one meaning have numbered definitions. When both a number and a letter are given, it means that the numbered definition is followed by one or more definitions that are closely related to it.

Illustrative Sentences and Phrases These are set off from the definition by a colon and help show the actual usage of the word.

Restrictive or Usage Labels   These indicate that a particular word is not part of standard speech or writing or that it has special meaning in certain circumstances. Among the labels used in this dictionary are the following:

aug|ment (*v.* ôg ment′; *n.* ôg′ment), *v., n.* —*v.t.* **1** to make greater in size, number, amount, or degree; enlarge: *The king augmented his power by taking over rights that had belonged to the nobles.* SYN: amplify, swell. See syn. under **increase. 2** to add an augment to. —*v.i.* to become greater; increase; grow; swell: *The sound of traffic augments during the morning rush hour.* —*n.* **1** a prefix or lengthened vowel marking the past tenses of verbs in Greek and Sanskrit. **2** *Obsolete.* increase; augmentation. [< Late Latin *augmentāre* < Latin *augmentum* an increase < *augēre* to increase] —**aug|ment′a|ble,** *adj.* —**aug|ment′er, aug|men′tor,** *n.*

com|pen|di|um (kəm pen′dē əm), *n., pl.* **-di|ums, -di|a** (-dē ə). a short summary of the main points or ideas of a larger work; abridgment; condensation. SYN: abstract, précis, epitome. [< Latin *compendium* a shortening; a weighing together < *com-* in addition + *pendere* weigh]

per|son|i|fy (pər son′ə fī), *v.t.* **-fied, -fy|ing. 1** to be a type of; embody: *Satan personifies evil.* SYN: exemplify. **2** to regard or represent as a person. We often personify the sun and moon, referring to the sun as *he* and the moon as *she.* We personify time and nature when we refer to *Father Time* and *Mother Nature. Greek philosophy has a tendency to personify ideas* (Benjamin Jowett). [probably patterned on French *personnifier* < *personne* person + *-fier* -fy] —**per|son′i|fi′er,** *n.*

sol|vent (sol′vent), *adj., n.* —*adj.* **1** able to pay all one owes: *A bankrupt firm is not solvent.* **2** able to dissolve: *Gasoline is a solvent liquid that removes grease spots.* —*n.* **1** a substance, usually a liquid, that can dissolve other substances: *Water is a solvent of sugar and salt.* **2** a thing that solves, explains, or settles. [< Latin *solvēns, -entis,* present participle of *solvere* loosen (used in *rem solvere* to free one's property and person from debt)] — **sol′vent|ly,** *adv.*

in|dict|ment (in dīt′mənt), *n.* **1** a formal written accusation, especially on the recommendation of a grand jury: *an indictment for murder. When an indictment does come down, the accused individuals will have an opportunity at trial to defend their innocence* (New York Times). *I do not know the method of drawing up an indictment against a whole people* (Edmund Burke). **2** an indicting or being indicted; accusation: *Mr. Bond has written . . . a perfectly stunning indictment of the welfare state* (New Yorker).

sub|sist|ence (səb sis′təns), *n.* **1** the condition or fact of keeping alive; living: *Selling papers was the poor old man's only means of subsistence.* **2** a means of keeping alive; livelihood: *The sea provides a subsistence for fishermen.* **3** continued existence; continuance. **4** *Philosophy.* **a** the individualizing of substance, especially as a particular rational (human) being standing apart from all others but possessing certain rights, powers, and functions in common with all others of the same type. **b** the condition of subsisting. **5** *Obsolete.* the condition or quality of inhering or

- *Archaic*—no longer in general use but found in special contexts such as law or scripture.
- *Foreign language*—such as Latin or French.
- *Obsolete*—words found only in writings of an earlier time or writings that imitate them.
- *Professional terms*—terms pertaining to arts, sciences, or technology.

Run-On Words These are formed by adding suffixes to the main-entry word. They appear in boldface type after the main-entry words from which they are formed. They are not defined because the meaning is clear from the main-entry definitions.

Etymology This traces the word's origin and development to its present use. In this dictionary, etymologies appear in square brackets following entry definitions. Two important symbols are <, meaning "derived from" or "taken from," and +, meaning "and." Some words are *doublets*, and this fact is noted in the etymology. (See Chapter 3 for more about doublets.)

residing (in something). [< Late Latin *subsistentia* < Latin *subsistēns, -entis*, present participle of *subsistere;* see etym. under **subsist**]

de|us ex ma|chi|na (dē′əs eks mak′ə ne), *Latin.* **1** a person, god, or event that comes just in time to solve a difficulty in a story, play, or other literary or dramatic work, especially when the coming is contrived or artificial: *There is … Ferral, a French representative of big business, whom Malraux uses as the novel's deus ex machina* (New Yorker). (*Figurative.*) *Mr. Galbraith rejects the notion that somewhere in Wall Street there was a deus ex machina who somehow engineered the boom and bust* (New York Times). **2** (literally) a god from a machine (referring to a mechanical device used in the ancient Greek and Roman theater by which actors who played the parts of gods were lowered from above the stage to end or resolve the dramatic action).

as|sid|u|ous (ə sij′ů əs), *adj.* working hard and steadily; careful and attentive; diligent: *No error escaped his assiduous attention to detail.* SYN: steady, unremitting, untiring. [< Latin *assiduus* (with English *-ous*) < *assidēre* sit at < *ad-* at + *sedēre* sit] —**as|sid′u|ous|ly,** *adv.* —**as|sid′u-ous|ness,** *n.*

vic|ar (vik′ər), *n.* **1** in the Church of England: **a** the minister of a parish, who is paid a salary by the man to whom the tithes are paid. **b** a person acting as parish priest in place of the actual rector. **2** in the Protestant Episcopal Church: **a** a clergyman in charge of a chapel in a parish. **b** a clergyman acting for a bishop, in a church where the bishop is rector or in a mission. **3** in the Roman Catholic Church: **a** a clergyman who represents the pope or a bishop. **b** the Pope, as the earthly representative of God or Christ. **4** a person acting in place of another, especially in administrative functions; representative; vicegerent. [< Anglo-French *vikere, vicare*, Old French *vicaire*, learned borrowing from Latin *vicārius* (originally) substituted < *vicis* change, alteration. See etym. of doublet **vicarious.**]

vi|car|i|ous (vī kār′ē əs, vi-), *adj.* **1** done or suffered for others: *vicarious work, vicarious punishment.* **2** felt by sharing in the experience of another: *The invalid received vicarious pleasure from reading travel stories.* **3** taking the place of another; doing the work of another: *a vicarious agent.* **4** delegated: *vicarious authority.* **5** based upon the substitution of one person for another: *this vicarious structure of society, based upon what others do for us.* **6** *Physiology.* denoting the performance by or through one organ of functions normally discharged by another, as for example in vicarious menstruation. [< Latin *vicārius* (with English *-ous*) substituted < *vicis* a turn, change, substitution. See etym. of doublet **vicar.**] —**vi|car′i|ous|ly,** *adv.* —**vi|car′i|ous|ness,** *n.*

Definition of *doublet:*

(An asterisk * means that a word has an illustration.)

*dou|blet (dub′lit), *n.* **1** a man's close-fitting jacket, with or without sleeves. Men in Europe wore doublets from the 1400's to the 1600's. **2** a pair of two similar or equal things; couple. **3** one of a pair. **4** one of two or more different words in a language derived from the same original source but coming by different routes. *Example:* 1) *aptitude* and *attitude. Aptitude* came into English as a direct borrowing from Late Latin *aptitudo, aptitudinis.* However this Latin word was taken into Italian in the form *attitudine,* which was later further changed to *attitude* in French, from which it came into English. 2) *fragile* and *frail. Fragile* came into English as a direct borrowing from the Latin *fragilis.* However, the word *fragilis* changed to *frele* (or *fraile*) in French, from which it came into English in the form *frail.* **5** an imitation gem made of two pieces of glass or crystal with a layer of color between them. **6** *Printing, U.S.* a word or phrase set a second time by mistake. **doublets,** two dice thrown that show the same number on each side facing up. [< Old French *doublet* (originally) a "double" fabric < *doubler* to double + *-et* -et]

*doublet
definition 1

Synonyms These are words that have the same, or nearly the same, meaning. A synonym you can use in place of the word defined appears immediately after the definition and is labeled **SYN.** A synonym study that helps you select the best word is labeled —**Syn.**

ac|ces|si|ble (ak ses′ə bəl), *adj.* **1** easy to get at; easy to reach or enter: *tools readily accessible on an open rack. A telephone should be put where it will be accessible.* SYN: convenient. **2** that can be entered or reached: *This rocky island is accessible only by helicopter.* SYN: approachable. **3** that can be obtained: *Not many facts about the kidnaping were accessible.* SYN: available.
accessible to, capable of being influenced by; susceptible to: *An open-minded person is accessible to reason.*
—**ac|ces′si|ble|ness,** *n.* —**ac|ces′si|bly,** *adv.*

eth|i|cal (eth′ə kəl), *adj., n.* —*adj.* **1** having to do with standards of right and wrong; of ethics or morals: *ethical standards.* SYN: See syn. under **moral. 2** morally right: *ethical conduct.* **3** in accordance with formal or professional rules of right and wrong: *It is not considered ethical for a doctor to repeat a patient's confidences.* **4** of or having to do with ethical drugs: *ethical products, an ethical consultant firm.*
—*n.* Usually, **ethicals.** a drug that cannot be obtained without a doctor's prescription; ethical drug: *The proprietary industry is not growing as fast as the ethicals* (Wall Street Journal).
—**eth′i|cal|ly,** *adv.* —**eth′i|cal|ness,** *n.*

— *Syn. adj.* **1 Moral, ethical** mean in agreement with a standard of what is right and good in character or conduct. **Moral** implies conformity to the customary rules and accepted standards of society: *He leads a moral life.* **Ethical** implies conformity to the principles of right conduct expressed in a formal system or code, such as that of a profession or business: *It is not considered ethical for doctors to advertise.*

Usage Notes This dictionary supplies notes to help clarify the use of some often misused words. Usage notes are indicated by a boldface arrow.

Figurative Usage Definitions and illustrative sentences or phrases are labeled "figurative" when the word defined is used out of its usual, matter-of-fact sense.

ad|ja|cent (ə jā′sənt), *adj.* lying near or close, or contiguous (to); neighboring or adjoining; bordering; next: *The house adjacent to ours has been sold.* sʏɴ: abutting. [< Latin *adjacēns, -entis,* present participle of *adjacēre* lie near < *ad-* near + *jacēre* lie²] —**ad|ja′cent|ly,** *adv.*
▶**Adjacent** means lying near or neighboring, but not necessarily touching.

co|he|sive (kō hē′siv), *adj.* **1** sticking together; tending to hold together: *Magnetized iron filings form a cohesive mass.* (*Figurative.*) *The members of a family are a cohesive unit in our society.* (*Figurative.*) *What is important in determining the work output of an industrial group is whether the group is tight-knit and cohesive enough to be properly called a group* (Science News Letter). **2** causing cohesion: *When a substance is heated, the heat energy causes its molecules to move faster. Eventually, the molecules will move so rapidly that their cohesive forces cannot hold them together* (Louis Marick). —**co|he′sive|ly,** *adv.* —**co|he′sive|ness,** *n.*

WORD SOURCES

◆

Words can come from almost any source, and English has borrowed and created at will, giving us a language that is extensive (one estimate is as high as one million words) and varied (it is hard to find an area where we have *not* borrowed or created). In this chapter we give you a very brief history to show how English has developed, and tell you of the interesting origins of several words.

HISTORY OF ENGLISH

English is not as old as some of the languages on earth, but it is related to the oldest languages and belongs to a family of languages called "Indo-European." If you are interested in seeing how many languages belong to this family and how they are related, look in an unabridged dictionary under "Indo-European languages" for a chart. (Some desk volumes also have this information.)

Very early inhabitants of the British Isles, the Celts, furnished us with a few words, such as *plaid* and *heather,* and influenced the speech of some current inhabitants of the islands—the Welsh, some Scots, and some Irish—but the language of these early settlers had almost no effect on the English of today. A much greater influence came from the Germanic tribes of Angles and Saxons that came from the continent of Europe about A.D. 410. Because the Romans had controlled much of the continent for hundreds of years, the language of the Angles and the Saxons had already been affected by Latin, and keep in mind that Latin had been influenced by Greek a great many years before that. Words used today that come from the Angles and the Saxons include *man, wife,* and *house.* During the Anglo-Saxon period, Christianity spread in England, and some religious words were introduced, such as *candle, church,* and *shrine.* At the same time, Vikings were raiding the coasts of England (called *Englalond,* where *Englisc* was spoken) with increasing success. By the eleventh century, the raids had stopped, and the Norsemen (Danes or Vikings) were ruling much of England. Under the Danes, the pronouns *they, their,* and *them* were carried into English from Old Norse, as well as words like *knife, steak, law,* and *husband.*

The next invasion came from the Normans, who lived across the English Channel from the southern coast of England. The Normans were descendants of Vikings who had settled in Normandy about the same time their kin had settled in England. Their language was a blend of Old Norse and Old French; the Old French had been derived from Latin. After this successful invasion of England, the Norman language, French, became the language of the ruling classes for almost 350 years. Despite this, native English survived because the common people continued to use it. A great many words came into the language from French during this period: words from cooking, such as *chef* and *saute;* words from the arts, such as *tapestry* and *design;* and words from polite society, such as *chivalry* and *etiquette.* Borrowings from such intermingled languages resulted in the phenomenon of *doublets.* A language *doublet* is one of two or more words derived from the same original source but coming by different routes. For example, we use the word *chief,* which comes from a Latin word meaning "head," and that Latin word (*caput*) is also the source of *chef.* (You may notice that some of the words introduced in the exercises are *doublets.* A complete definition appears in the material explaining how to use the dictionary entries at the end of Chapter 2.)

During the Renaissance we borrowed again from Latin. This time the borrowings came directly from the older Latin authors, for literary use, instead of by word of mouth as they had in the earlier borrowings of Latin. As travel and trade increased, words were taken from languages around the world. Words from the field of music, such as *stanza, andante,* and *tempo,* were borrowed from Italian; words like *cargo, cigar,* and *vanilla* were borrowed from Spanish; words having to do with the number system, *algebra, cipher,* and *zero,* were taken from Arabic; American Indian words borrowed include *moccasin, raccoon,* and *hickory.* And more, too, from many sources!

You realize that this brief history can give only a few of the borrowings. More information about word origins is revealed as you read the etymologies of words. And English is growing still! It is said to be the richest language in the world.

CHAPTER THREE

CREATING WORDS

In addition to borrowing words from other languages, we create words as we need them. For example, we "blend" breakfast and lunch to form *brunch* and smoke and fog to form *smog*. We "compound" words by putting them together to label new concepts like *downtime* and *spinout,* and we make new words from the first letters of other words, as in the acronyms *scuba* (*s*elf-*c*ontained *u*nderwater *b*reathing *a*pparatus) and *radar* (*ra*dio *d*etecting *a*nd *r*anging). Business creates trademark words such as *Xerox* and *Kleenex,* and we use them in a much more general way. Words, words, everywhere! You can see why the language is so rich!

Other words come from literature, classical myths, places, and real people. We borrow these words because new concepts have been introduced or defined in written works, and we need the terms to label those concepts. Then, too, people and places become identified with certain characteristics or objects and become labels for those concepts.

WORDS FROM LITERATURE

Odyssey The Greek writer Homer wrote an epic poem, *The Odyssey,* describing a long and difficult journey of the Greek hero Odysseus to Ithaca at the conclusion of the Trojan War. Now any long wandering or series of adventurous journeys may be called an "odyssey." (It no longer has a capital letter; it is "naturalized.")

Robot Karel Capek, a Czech author and playwright, wrote *R.U.R.* (Rossum's Universal Robots) about machines used to function in place of men. The Czech word *robot* means "worker," but the English translation of the play in 1923 retained the original word and it soon became widely used.

Quixotic (kwik sot'ik) A Spanish novel in two parts that was intended to make fun of contemporary (early 1600s) chivalric romances (books) introduced *quixotic* into English. Miguel de Cervantes created *Don Quixote* (kē hō' tē), a lean elderly man who thought he was a knight and set out on his equally lean horse to right the wrongs of the world. Today the word means romantic, without regard to practicality. (This story also exists as a musical production titled "Man of La Mancha.")

Pandemonium Literature has also given us some "place" words. One of them, *pandemonium,* was created by John Milton in his *Paradise Lost* as the name of the capital of hell and means, literally, "all demons." Now, you may know, it means "a wild uproar."

Utopia   Another place named is *utopia*, created by Thomas More in 1516 in his Latin essay describing an ideally perfect community. Translated literally it means "no place," and today it retains a similar meaning, that is, something ideal and nonexistent.

Some other words from written works are *scrooge, gargantuan,* and *yahoo.*

WORDS FROM CLASSICAL MYTHS

Aegis (ē' jis)   *Aegis* was the name of a shield associated with the Greek god Zeus and in later mythology was represented as a goatskin hanging over the shoulder of the Greek goddess Athena. Since it was a form of protection for them, it came to mean "protection," and today we say that someone supported or protected by a powerful person or business is "under the *aegis* of" that entity.

Herculean   Today, *herculean* describes a task requiring great strength or someone who has great strength and courage. Hercules was the Roman name for the strong and courageous hero who completed numerous difficult tasks (we hear of "the twelve labors" particularly) and who was the only man in mythology to make the full transition from mortal to god.

Nemesis   In Greek and Roman myth, a goddess named Nemesis was "the unrelenting avenger of human faults." That is, she saw to it that you got the punishment you deserved. These days you may hear the word used to describe someone, such as a policeman or lawyer, as the *nemesis* of criminals.

Tantalize   According to Greek myth, Tantalus was a Lydian king who took advantage of his friendship with the gods, eventually making them very angry. As punishment, he was condemned to the everlasting torment of continual hunger and thirst. He was made to stand in the river Hades with water up to his neck, but it receded when he stooped to drink. Just out of reach, over his head, hung luscious fruits. A *tantalus* today is a stand in which liquor decanters are visible but not available unless one has the key. *Tantalize* is a verb, meaning to tease or torment by presenting something desirable to the view but keeping it continually out of reach.

Protean   Proteus was a minor Greek god represented as a wise old man and servant of Poseidon (called Neptune by the Romans—the god of the sea). People, and even gods, would seek advice and favors of him, but he was able to elude them by changing himself from one shape to another.

Today we might use the word *protean* to describe an actor who is capable of assuming different characters or to describe anything extremely variable. Some other words from classical myths are *panic, erotic, echo,* and *atlas.*

WORDS FROM PLACES

Stoic   Stoics were ancient Greek philosophers who first met near the Painted *Portico* (*Stoa* Poikile) of the marketplace in Athens. Their founder, Zeno, taught uncomplaining submission to the vicissitudes of life. Today, someone able to preserve complete indifference to pleasure, pain, or catastrophe is called a *stoic,* or we may say that he meets life's changes with *stoicism.*

Sybarite   A *sybarite* is someone who cares very much for luxury and pleasure—a voluptuary. The term comes from inhabitants of the ancient Greek colony of Sybaris, in southern Italy. The fabulous luxury and sensuousness of the colony were known throughout the ancient world. Legend has it that the people of Sybaris taught their horses to dance to the music of flutes or pipes. They were overcome in battle when their enemies discovered the fact and played music during an attack, causing great confusion and defeat.

Laconic   When Laconia, a district in ancient Greece, was under attack, its enemy declared "If we come to your city we will level it to the ground." The only Laconian reply was *"If."* This habit of terseness gave the name of the area to our adjective *laconic,* which today describes someone blunt and brief in speech.

Solecism   A *solecism* is a blunder or provincialism in writing or speech and takes its name from the Greek colony of Soloi. Located across the Mediterranean Sea from Athens (the capital and considered seat of learning and correct behavior), inhabitants developed a Greek dialect of their own. Visiting Athenians were shocked by the crude, substandard speech they heard and named such errors after the area.

Denim   This heavy, coarse, cotton cloth with a diagonal weave has become one of the most popular fabrics in the world. Most of us wouldn't be without our *denims.* The word comes from the town of Nîmes, France, where a durable, twilled fabric with a pronounced diagonal rib called "serge d'Nîmes" was produced. Before long, that special fabric was called *denim.*

Some other words that come from places are *tuxedo, turquoise, jersey, hamburger,* and *spa.*

WORDS FROM PEOPLE

Gerrymander Elbridge Gerry (1744–1814) was a signer of the Declaration of Independence, congressman, governor of Massachusetts, and vice president of the United States. While governor of Massachusetts, he signed a bill into law designed to ensure continuing majorities for his political party. One of the districts so created was used in a political cartoon where the artist added wings, teeth, and claws. Someone suggested that it looked like a salamander, to which a political opponent is said to have replied, "A Gerrymander, you mean!" Today, *gerrymander* is a verb or a noun. The U.S. Supreme Court has ruled legislative districts must contain roughly equal numbers of people, but legislators are permitted to draw district lines. Wherever the lines are drawn, someone is sure to cry *"Gerrymander!"*

Quisling This is a rather recent "people word" that came into the language in the 1940s. It refers to Vidkum Quisling (1887–1945), a Norwegian facist, who admired Nazi Germany and helped it in its conquest of his homeland during World War II. He served as the Nazi's puppet ruler of Norway until the end of the war, when he was tried, convicted of high treason, and executed. And so, a political traitor, particularly one who serves in a puppet government, is known as a *quisling*.

Maverick Samuel A. Maverick (1803–70) was a Texas politician and a cattleman who declined to brand his calves. Whether this was due to carelessness or laziness is not recorded, but rounding up and branding cattle is a difficult job at best, and given the vast expanse of Texas range lands, it becomes a task of extraordinary proportions. Those who expended the necessary effort found that Maverick's cattle were as good as branded, since they were the ones without a brand! If, on occasion, they branded a stray, or a *maverick,* as their own, who is to blame them? Today the word has extended meanings. One of them describes a person who refuses to affiliate or who breaks with a regular political party as a *maverick.*

Dunce A *dunce* is someone who is dull witted or stupid and may be pictured as sitting in a corner of the school room with a *dunce* cap. But the word stems from someone who was not considered dull witted. John Duns Scottus (d. 1308) was one of the most brilliant thinkers of the Middle Ages. However, after his death his followers held firmly (and loudly) to the doctrines he had endorsed, even in the face of more "modern" thought. Their opponents referred to them as stupid enemies of learning and progress or "Dunsmen," which soon became *dunce.*

Martinet A person who enforces very strict discipline on those under him is labeled a *martinet.* The word comes from Jean Martinet (d. 1672) who served as inspector general of the infantry for Louis XIV of France. Excessively strict, demanding ways made his name synonymous with sharp, military discipline. Martinet was killed at the siege of Duisberg in 1672, accidentally shot by his own artillery.

Many words come from real people. Some others are *fahrenheit, volt, diesel, boycott, guillotine,* and *sadism.*

You can understand from this quick overview that language begins and evolves in diverse ways. Words begin, grow and change, and even die, depending on people's use, or disuse, of them. You have just read of some of the many ways words may begin. Then they may change—in pronunciation, spelling, and meaning—not just once but several times. And sometimes when the times change and we no longer need to express certain concepts, words fall out of use and become obsolete. (For example, according to the Oxford English Dictionary, *auripotent,* or "rich in gold," hasn't been used in a written work since 1560.) If it were not for written language and record books, these words would be forgotten. Think of the words that must have come and gone in prehistoric times! But that's another story.

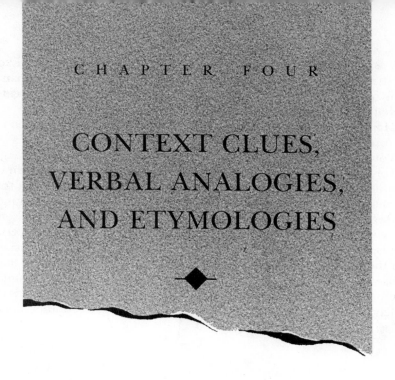

CHAPTER FOUR

CONTEXT CLUES, VERBAL ANALOGIES, AND ETYMOLOGIES

USING CONTEXT CLUES

Context clues are probably the most commonly used means of understanding unknown or partially known words. To use context clues effectively, you must try to understand the writer's point of view and his style as well as considering the subject matter of the written work. For example, the mournful tone of Edgar Allan Poe is unlike the brisk tone set by Rudyard Kipling. The vocabulary and sentence patterns used by Charles Dickens are different from those used by Ernest Hemingway. But the importance of style and vocabulary extend beyond literature. If you are reading a biology book and come to an unknown word, your guess about its meaning would be different from the guess you would make if you were reading an auto repair manual. Your use of the context clues will be influenced by your knowledge of the subject matter and your understanding of just how the author is trying to transmit his message to you.

In trying to grasp the meaning of an unknown word, you must look at all the other elements of the written work. Not all sentences give enough context clues to indicate the meaning of the unknown word, but you must use whatever clues are given. In the sentence

He had an obsequious manner,

the meaning of the word *obsequious* is not clear. It could refer to mood: Is he happy or sad? It could refer to style: Is he formal or informal? It could refer to conduct: Is he bold or shy? There are many possibilities. You cannot be sure from the sentence just what obsequious means, but you do know that it refers to some characteristic of a person. Other clues about the person would have to come from other sentences. If the sentence is changed to

> His obsequious manner made his superiors take advantage of him and made his comrades scornful,

you are now able to detect the negative qualities of the word and get a better picture of the person described.

TYPES OF CONTEXT CLUES

Context clues may be expressed in many ways. They may appear as *examples,* as in the sentence

> She dressed in a tawdry fashion, using cheap laces, glass beads, and poor-quality clothing.

(The examples given reveal the meaning of *tawdry,* which is "showy and cheap.")

Or context clues may *restate* or *reinforce,* as in

> He was a stentorian man, with a voice so loud that the neighbors complained.

(The meaning of *stentorian* is "very loud or powerful in sound" which is described in the sentence.)

Context clues may indicate *contrast,* as in

> John had sworn fealty to his master, so all were surprised when he refused to obey the order.

(The surprise felt by "all" came because what occurred was the opposite of what they expected. *Fealty* has to do with loyalty and faithfulness, so John's refusal to obey an order was in contrast to their expectation.)

Another type of context clue is one of *general information,* or *experience,* where your knowledge and experience help you get the meaning of the unknown word. Take the following sentence:

> Jake is a debonair bachelor, enjoying the southern California good life.

You can use experience (if you have it) or your knowledge of southern California life-styles and of the life a bachelor is supposed to lead to deduce that *debonair* means "lighthearted and carefree." If you have no experience or knowledge to assist in determining the meaning of an unknown word, you should guess the meaning and continue reading, searching for context clues in the sentences that follow.

In addition to these meaning, or *semantic*, clues, *graphic* clues often are supplied. Occasionally the meaning of the word will be given, set off by commas or dashes, for example:

Origami, the oriental art of paper folding, can be an interesting pastime.

In other cases, a capital letter may give you a clue that the word used is a proper noun rather than a common noun and so has special meaning, as in

Charles Bradlaugh was the most formidable atheist on the Secularist platform.

This sentence suggests that there was a political party (indicated by the word *platform*) called "Secularist" (indicated by the capital letter) to which an atheist named Charles Bradlaugh belonged.

As a reader, then, you must look for meaning in all of the words, using whatever background information you possess. As a writer, you owe it to your readers to supply enough context clues to show them clearly your meaning. In this book you will use context clues both ways. In the reading selections you must pick up every available hint, and in writing your own sentences, you must give enough clues to show that you understand—and are practicing—the meanings of the words. A good dictionary will show an early definition of *clue* (also spelled clew) to be "a ball of thread or yarn to be unwound to serve as a guide through a labyrinth or maze." The *Oxford English Dictionary* includes examples of usage, one of which is meaningful to us as readers and writers: "I will give you a clue of thread, and by that perhaps you may find your way out again" (Kingsley, 1855). Be sure you use the context clues given to you by the writers, and be sure you give them to your readers!

CONTEXT CLUE EXERCISES

To give yourself some practice using context clues, complete the following three exercises:

1. Try to define these words. Do not look them up in a dictionary.
   a. moiety
   b. eschew
   c. penultimate
   You can see that without any context to give clues, it is very hard to determine the meaning of a word.

2. Now try to define the same words after some context clues are supplied.
   a. John inherited the *moiety* of his grandfather's estate, while his sister inherited the other half.
      Meaning of *moiety* in this sentence: _____
   b. Convincing reports of the dangers of tobacco have led many smokers to *eschew* cigarettes.
      Meaning of *eschew* in this sentence: _____
   c. "Y" is the *penultimate* letter of the English alphabet.
      Meaning of *penultimate* in this sentence: _____

ANSWERS TO EXERCISE 2

In sentence *a, moiety* means "half." If John's sister inherited "the other half," John inherited the first half. *Moiety* can also mean "component" or "part," so you must use context clues to decide which meaning best fits the author's intent.

    Eschew, in sentence *b,* means "to avoid habitually," or "to shun." Reports of the health hazards of smoking have made some smokers give up the habit.

    Penultimate, in sentence *c,* means "next to last." You know that "z" is the last letter, so "y" is the next to last.

3. In the following sentences, a real word has been replaced by a nonsense word. Using the context clues supplied in each sentence, try to determine the meaning of the underlined nonsense word.
   a. The city council said today that a small chemical spill that occurred Tuesday probably would not glubblub the local water supply.
      Meaning of glubblub in this sentence: _____
   b. Mrs. Smith was found to be a dependable parent and so was awarded dreplam of the children.
      Meaning of dreplam in this sentence: _____
   c. If you want to succeed on this diet, you will have to give up chiduks such as pasta, bread, and breakfast cereal.
      Meaning of chiduks in this sentence: _____

ANSWERS TO EXERCISE 3

You can see that the meaning of glubblub in sentence *a* has something to do with damage. A better word for damage done to a water supply is pollution, so the verb that fits here is *pollute*.

    Sentence *b* gives you only one choice: Mrs. Smith gets *custody* of the children.

    Sentence *c* gives you examples of *carbohydrates*. If you have heard or read much about dieting, you probably know about these.

USING VERBAL ANALOGIES

An analogy is a resemblance, or a similarity. For instance, we say that the heart is a pump because there are certain similarities between the two entities; thus we make an analogy between a heart and a pump. In another analogy we say that an atom is a miniature solar system. This comparison helps us realize the great distances between the component parts of the atom, and thus the analogy is used to improve our understanding. It is essential that we recognize just what the resemblance is between the two items in an analogy; we must understand their relationship.

Although an analogy is a comparison, the meaning of *analogy* is somewhat different; the concept is more specific. A comparison may include differences as well as similarities. An analogy is concerned only with similarities and, frequently, with a *single* similarity. To return to one of our examples: We know that an atom is not really very much like the solar system. It would be a waste of time to compare them carefully, and yet we can gain understanding of the atom's structure if the analogy is presented to us.

In addition to general analogies, words may be set out in what are called "verbal analogies." *Verbal analogies* are words, set up in pairs, that have some kind of relationship. For example, the words *hot* and *cold* are opposites, and realizing this relationship, you would be able to select two more words that are also opposites; if given a word such as *up,* you could supply *down* to complete the analogy. Written in standard form, this analogy would look like this:

hot : cold :: up : _____

a. warm   b. down   c. fall   d. temperature

You would, of course, select "b. down" from the supplied alternatives. Another way of setting out this verbal analogy is like this:

hot : cold :: _____ : _____

a. warm : hot   b. up : down   c. fall : down   d. water : wet

You would again select *b* as the correct answer, because it has the same *relationship* as the first two words. They, too, are opposites. A third way of setting out this verbal analogy would be like this:

hot : up :: cold : _____

a. warm   b. down   c. fall   d. temperature

Again the answer is *b,* and the relationship is the same, but the analogy is set up between the first word *(hot)* and the third word *(cold),* and then the second word *(up)* and the fourth word *(down).* Now you *might* see this relationship as one of description or analogy. (Yes, it's true. The relationship in a verbal analogy may be *analogy.*) When something is hot, we think of it as up (temperature), and when something is cold, we think of it as down.

This relationship gives you the same answer, *b.* As you can imagine, there are a great many possible relationships.

IMPORTANCE OF VERBAL ANALOGIES

Understanding verbal analogies is important to you as a student. Being able to see relationships will strengthen your ability to reason, which is an essential skill. In addition to increasing your general reasoning ability, you will want to understand verbal analogies in order to do well on tests that are used to evaluate your verbal skills. The ability to complete verbal analogies is learned. The less experience you have had, the more you will need to practice. Perhaps you can think of it as a mental tennis game. Practice will improve your score!

VERBAL ANALOGY EXERCISES

Some of the exercises in this book ask you to complete verbal analogies. To give yourself some practice, complete the following activities. (Answers follow each segment of the activity.)

Complete the following verbal analogies by placing the correct words in the blanks. In the first five verbal analogies, you need to add only one word to complete the relationship set up by the words in columns 1 and 2. Use the words supplied after number 5, labeled "column 4."

1		**2**		**3**		**4**
1. early	:	late	::	ahead	:	_____
2. fast	:	slow	::	run	:	_____
3. front	:	back	::	street	:	_____
4. light	:	dark	::	day	:	_____
5. past	:	future	::	before	:	_____

column 4—after, alley, behind, crawl, night

The first segment is fairly easy. In number 1, *early* and *late* are *opposite* elements of time that can also be expressed as the opposites, *ahead* and *behind.* In number 2, the relationship is again one of *opposites,* so the word in the blank should be *crawl.* The relationship in number 3 is that of *position.* A *street* is in *front,* and an *alley* is in *back.* Number 4 sets out a relationship of *characteristics: Light* is a characteristic of *day,* while *dark* is a characteristic of *night.* (If you think of these as opposites, this will give you the right answer, too, but you should be aware of the *characteristic* relationship.) Number 5 sets out a *sequence. Past* evolves into *future,* while *before* evolves into *after.* You might think of these as opposites also, but you should know that *sequence* is a possible relationship in verbal analogies.

In this second group, numbers 6 through 10, you must supply words in columns 3 and 4 that have the same relationship as the words in columns 1 and 2. Use the words supplied after number 10, labeled "column 3" and "column 4."

	1		2		3		4
6.	honey	:	bee	::	_____	:	_____
7.	go in	:	go out	::	_____	:	_____
8.	day	:	night	::	_____	:	_____
9.	bottom	:	top	::	_____	:	_____
10.	food	:	body	::	_____	:	_____

column 3—fuel, enter, below, book, dawn

column 4—above, writer, twilight, leave, engine

After practice on the first segment, the second segment should not be too difficult. In number 6, the relationship between *honey* and *bee* is that of *creation* and *creator*. Fill in columns 3 and 4 with *book* and *writer*. *You must not reverse these.* The relationship must be consistent from one pair to the other pair. The relationship in number 7 is *definition*. *Go in* defines *enter* and *go out* defines *leave*. In number 8, the relationship is of *sequence*. The beginning of *day* is *dawn*, and the beginning of *night* is *twilight*. Number 9 sets out a *position* relationship: *Bottom* is *below*, while *top* is *above*. *Food* is used by the *body* to produce energy, much like *fuel* is used by an *engine*, so the relationship in number 10 is *similar use*.

In the third group, 11 through 15, you must supply words in columns 2, 3, and 4. Using only the words supplied for the columns indicated, you must create an analogy on each line that has the same relationship for each pair of words.

	1		2		3		4
11.	ink	:	_____	::	_____	:	_____
12.	play	:	_____	::	_____	:	_____
13.	iron	:	_____	::	_____	:	_____
14.	knife	:	_____	::	_____	:	_____
15.	sand	:	_____	::	_____	:	_____

column 2—desert, pen, toy, cut, steel

column 3—gun, sand, paint, work, wax

column 4—brush, tool, candle, shoot, glass

In this last segment, you had many choices so you needed to think through all the possibilities before you made a final decision. The answers to number 11 are *pen*, *paint*, and *brush*. The relationship is *medium and implement;* we use ink in a pen and paint with a brush. In number 12, the answers are *toy*, *work*, and *tool*, showing the primary *function* of the object given. Number 13 deals with a *refinement process: Iron* is a raw product that can be refined into *steel*, while *sand* can be processed into *glass*. A *functional* relationship exists in number 14: A *knife cuts*, and a *gun shoots*. Using the only remaining words, we fill in number 15 with *desert, wax,* and *candle.* Do you see the relationship? It is *general–specific. Sand* is a general term, and *desert* is a specific kind of sand. *Wax* is a general term, and *candle* is a specific form of wax.

USING ETYMOLOGIES

The etymology of a word offers you a look at its history or as we called it previously, its "family tree." You can use this information to create categories and thereby increase your word knowledge by association. However you need to remember that words are only symbols for concepts, and to realize that different languages, used by people in other times and other places, might represent concepts in ways other than you expect to use them. Even words in current use may represent concepts that are different from those applied in English. One example is the French word *ciel* which means "heaven," "sky," "canopy," and "roof." Certainly there is no single word in English that encompasses all these concepts, and to understand the relationship between what we consider to be different concepts, you must exercise your imagination. In fact, working with etymologies is a creative, imaginative activity.

You must read the etymology of each word carefully. When you note the meaning of a root or prefix, try to select an easy word to serve as a "seed word" in your memory. For example, in looking up the word *deposition* (the giving of testimony under oath), a careful reading of the etymology shows that the word comes from Latin. *De* means "down" and *pos* means "to put or place." It comes from the Latin verb *ponere,* which has the forms *pon-, pos-,* and *posit-.* (Compare this with irregular English verbs that also have other forms, such as *sing, sang, sung* or *eat, ate, eaten,* and so on.) You might use *deposit* as your seed word, since it is easy to remember. (You might think to yourself, "When I make a deposit, I put money in the bank.") Then let us say you come on the following sentence:

> The author's granddaughter selected Oxford's Bodleian Library as the *repository* for his works.*

You would know that the word had something to do with "putting or placing," and by adding other clues from the reading, you could deduce the meaning of the word and of the sentence.

If you are noting the meaning of a prefix, you need to be aware that they *assimilate* or vary, depending on the root to which they are attached. For example, the Latin prefix *co (com),* meaning "with, together," combines

---

* The granddaughter of English poet Percy Bysshe Shelley actually did donate his works to the Bodleian Library at Oxford University, even though some of those writings caused his expulsion from the school.

variously to form such words, among many others, as "*co*exist," "*col*lect," "*com*mand," "*con*duct," and "*cor*rect." As you gain experience working with etymologies you will become familiar with the ways the various prefixes assimilate.

ETYMOLOGY EXERCISES

A few of the exercises in this book ask you to use whatever background knowledge you possess and to stretch your imagination to match words that share a common etymology with their meanings. If reading and using the etymologies of words is new to you, these exercises may feel like guessing games. Remember, however, that as you practice you will improve. Guessing is a reasonable way to begin if you check your answers against the answer keys and analyze your errors.

Assume you are reading a book on art and come on the following sentence:

> A monochromatic color scheme that uses only gradations of one color creates quite a different feeling for the viewer.

To be sure you understand the meaning of *gradation,* you look it up in the dictionary and note the etymological information:

gra|da|tion (grā dā′shən), *n.* **1a** a change by steps or stages; gradual change: *Our acts show gradation between right and wrong. She sometimes contemplated a little sorrowfully the gradation from her former simplicity to her present sophistication.* **b** the fact or condition of including or being arranged in a series of degrees: *a variety of forms exhibiting gradation.* **2** Often, **gradations.** one of the steps, stages, or degrees in a series: *There are many gradations between poverty and wealth. The rainbow shows gradations of color besides the six main colors.* **3** the act or process of grading. **4** = ablaut. **5** *Geology.* the process by which the surface of the earth is leveled off, or the bed of a stream is brought to equilibrium, through the action of wind, ice, water, etc. **6** *Obsolete.* an advancing, step by step; gradual progress. [< Latin *gradātiō, -ōnis* < *gradus, -ūs* step, degree; see etym. under **grade**]

from **grade:**
[< Middle French *grade,* learned borrowing from Latin *gradus, -ūs* step, degree, related to *gradī* to walk, go]

You see that the word comes from the Latin *gradus* (step or degree), and is related to *gradi* (walk or go). Now see if you can follow the procedure outlined earlier, stretch your imagination, and match up the following words and definitions. (A suggested procedure and the answers follow this exercise.)

_____	a. congress	aa. to break a law or command; to sin against
_____	b. digress	bb. to go back; to move in a backward direction
_____	c. egress	cc. a formal meeting of representatives
_____	d. ingress	dd. to turn aside from the main subject in talking or writing
_____	e. regress	ee. a way of going in; entrance
_____	f. transgress	ff. a way out; exit

Your seed word might be *graduation,* since that is easy to remember and can be personalized by thinking of a graduation ceremony (yours or someone else's) when you "walked down the aisle and received a degree." If you stretch your imagination you will see that all of the words have to do with stepping, walking, or going—either literally or figuratively. At present you may be unfamiliar with the prefixes. But a look at Appendix A of this text can assist you. However, if you relate these prefixes to those in other words you know, you might reason as follows:

> "If I consent, I go along with somebody, and I do know that a congress is a legislative body. I can imagine the members of the group walking toward a meeting with other members. *Con* means 'with,' and *gress* means 'step' or 'go.' To *redo* something means to do it again. Therefore *regress* must mean to go back or to walk through it again."

Proceeding along this line of thinking you should match up the words and definitions as follows:

cc a; *dd* b; *ff* c; *ee* d; *bb* e; *aa* f

Now try another exercise.

You continue to read the art book and come on the following sentence:

> Thus an artist's perception or insight into reality or his own personal experiences can be presented using a variety of techniques.

Since your instructor has been emphasizing the artist's *perception,* you decide to investigate the word in the dictionary and find the etymological information:

per|cep|tion (per sep'shen), *n.* **1** the act of perceiving: *His perception of the change came in a flash.* **syn**: insight, apprehension, discernment, comprehension. **2** the power of perceiving: *a keen perception. Defect in manners is usually the defect of fine perceptions* (Emerson). **3** understanding that is the result of perceiving; percept: *He had a clear perception of what was wrong, and soon fixed it.* **4** *Psychology.* the study of the complex process by which patterns of environmental energies become known as objects, events, people, and other aspects of the world. [< Latin *perceptiō, -ōnis* < *percipere* perceive]

per|ceive (per sēv'), *v.,* **-ceived, -ceiv|ing.** — *v.t.* **1** to be aware of through the senses; see, hear, taste, smell, or feel: *Did you perceive the colors of that bird? We perceived a little girl coming toward us* (Frederick Marryat). **syn**: See syn. under **see. 2** to take in with the mind; observe: *I soon perceived that I could not make him change his mind. I plainly perceive some objections remain* (Edmund Burke). **syn**: understand, comprehend. See syn. under **see.** — *v.i.* to grasp or take in something with the senses or mind. [< Old North French *perceivre* < Latin *percipere* < *per-* thoroughly + *capere* to grasp] — **per|ceiv'er,** *n.*

You see that the word comes from the Latin *per* (thoroughly) plus *capere* (to grasp). (Perception comes from *ca*pere. What does that suggest?) Now follow the procedure outlined earlier, stretch your imagination, and match the words with the definitions.

_____ a. capable   aa. to leave out; exclude
_____ b. capture   bb. a beginning or originating

_____ c. except   cc. having fitness, power, or ability
_____ d. inception   dd. to take by force or trickery; seize
_____ e. intercept   ee. to take or seize on the way from one place
                          to another

What is your seed word? Write it here. _____ Be sure to personalize it in some way. You may have thought something like this as you worked your way through the words:

> "To be *capable* of something, my brain has to grasp it. If I *capture* someone or something, I probably have to take it by force. If I give away some of my audiotapes, I might give all *except* one of them, which I picture myself grabbing back. *Inception* is harder to imagine, but at the beginning of something, someone has to grab an idea out of the air or out of the corner of her brain. *Intercept* begins like *interrupt*, which means 'to break in,' so I can picture someone seizing something as it moves from place to place."

ANSWERS

The answers are, *cc* a; *dd* b; *aa* c; *bb* d; *ee* e

As with any other exercise, physical or mental, you will become more skillful at working with etymologies the more you practice. Eventually you may build a word-form "bank" that you can combine with your use of context clues to increase greatly your success with unknown words.

ESSENTIALS
FOR COLLEGE
SUCCESS

EFFICIENT READING
AND LEARNING
STRATEGIES

◆

VOCABULARY SELF-EVALUATION

The following words will be introduced in this reading selection. Place a check mark (√) in front of any that you know thoroughly and use in your speech and writing. Place a question mark (?) in front of any that you recognize but do not use yourself.

_____ adhere	_____ deleterious	_____ linguistic
_____ articulate	_____ diligent	_____ optimum
_____ assimilate	_____ discern	_____ procrastinate
_____ cogent	_____ erudite	_____ proximity
_____ competence	_____ impediment	_____ retrieval

LEARNING TO READ CRITICALLY AND STUDY EFFECTIVELY

Succeeding in college requires more than just making good grades in high school and doing well on college entrance examinations. The academic environment in college is much different from that in high school, and therefore more efficient reading and learning strategies are crucial for success in college. Such strategies can help you approach learning systematically; as a consequence, you should become more successful and confident as a college student.

TAKING NOTES FROM LECTURES

Probably the most important activity of a student is to organize and retain information, or academic content, presented in a variety of formats. In many classes you will receive the majority of information from an erudite[1] professor in a scholarly lecture presentation. The professor is usually an expert in his field and knowledgeable about his subject, and therefore efficient note-taking strategies are essential. You will need to be diligent[2] in listening to the professor and in organizing key information and ideas using a system that will provide for fast retrieval[3] and recall. You are usually required to know the information presented in the lecture and demonstrate your knowledge later on some type of examination.

We also know from learning theory that reviewing your lecture notes within twenty-four hours after the lecture will help you retain the information longer. Often students procrastinate[4] and delay reviewing their notes. Because of the prin-

ciple of proactive interference in memory, it is more difficult to relearn old information because it has not been transferred to your long-term memory through reinforcement techniques such as recitation and regular review.

READING FROM TEXT AND THINKING CRITICALLY

Reading is a complex psychological and linguistic[5] process that incorporates prior knowledge, background, and experience. College reading, also known as "constructive reading," is an active process that requires you to relate what you learn to what you may already know.

Learning to discern[6] key ideas is an important skill when reading a textbook. Other crucial elements in learning from texts are recognizing the textbook structure, identifying important details, and relating the content to information you received in the lecture.

The optimum[7] learning situation is one in which the classroom lecture corresponds to the textbook chapters you have been assigned to read. Not every course is structured this way, however, and strategies that help you link information from a variety of sources—lecture, textbook reading, guest speakers, field trips, labs, and so on—will be most valuable.

Learning to be a critical thinker by analyzing the author's ideas, comparing and contrasting information in each paragraph, and making judgments on what you read will help you assimilate[8] ideas more effectively. A number of note-taking and textbook-mastery systems have been developed to help you organize course information. Or you may be able to develop your own systems once you have analyzed both your needs and the lecture and reading requirements. Most colleges and universities offer courses in academic reading and learning for this purpose.

PREPARING FOR AND TAKING EXAMINATIONS

There will be many opportunities for you to demonstrate your competence[9] in a particular course. Occasionally you will need to clearly articulate[10] your ideas in an oral discussion or classroom presentation. Most often you will take written examinations. Many of these are the objective type, which include multiple-choice, true-false, short completion, and matching-item questions. At other times you will be tested in a subjective, or essay, format. Most essay examinations require that you can present your ideas about a topic with the vocabulary or terminology appropriate to the particular field of study. You will also need to present a cogent[11] argument in your essay response to demonstrate your comprehensive knowledge of the issues related to the topic.

MANAGING TIME EFFICIENTLY

One of the most important strategies for the contemporary student is managing time efficiently. Most students today are combining their educations with jobs and therefore have multiple responsibilities. These additional responsibilities can create an impediment[12] to achieving success in college.

Analyzing your time demands and then developing an efficient time-management system that you adhere[13] to on a regular basis can make you feel more in control of your life.

A large number of students are commuters who do not live in proximity[14] to either their college campus or work location. For these students, commuting time would be an important factor to include in any time-management system and to consider when planning classes and study time.

Finally, devoting too much time to either school or work could be deleterious[15] to your health. Many students neither take care of themselves properly nor allow time for relaxing and exercising. Be sure to provide time on a regular basis for such activities, as this is one more way to help you develop the necessary strategies for success in the academic environment. ◆

PRETEST

Select words from this list and write them in the blanks to complete the sentences.

adhere	deleterious	linguistic
articulate	diligent	optimum
assimilate	discern	procrastinate
cogent	erudite	proximity
competence	impediment	retrieval

1. When you show how qualified you are, you are demonstrating your _____.

2. It is difficult to _____ new information when you are sleepy or ill.

3. A learned or scholarly teacher is one who is _____.

4. College and adult reading is a complex _____ process that demands sophisticated thinking skills on the part of the reader.

5. Having an apartment across the street from school is an example of living in _____ to campus.

6. A student who is hard working and persistent can be described as _____.

7. Closely following a daily schedule that you have developed means that you are about to _____ to it.

8. A persevering student is one who can overcome the _____ to learning that can occasionally occur.

9. The _____ of important information from class lectures requires an efficient note-taking system.

10. It is not unusual to _____ when studying for an exam until the day before it is scheduled.

11. It is difficult to _____ the most important ideas in a class when you have had no previous experience with the subject.

12. Poor dietary habits and lack of sufficient sleep could prove to be _____ to your health.

13. Learning to _____ your ideas is important in classes that require student participation and interaction through group discussions and oral presentations.

14. A(n) _____ argument presented in an essay exam is one that is both valid and convincing.

15. The _____ arrangement is one that is the most favorable, such as a lecture that corresponds to the assigned readings.

    Answers to this pretest are in Appendix B.
    Unless your instructor tells you to do otherwise, complete the exercises for each word that you missed on the pretest. The words, with their meanings and exercises, are in alphabetical order. The superscript numbers indicate where the words appeared in the reading selection so that you can refer to them when necessary. There are several types of exercises, but for each word you will be asked to write a sentence using context clues. (See Chapter 4 if you need information about how to create context clues.) You are also asked to perform some activity that will help you make your concept of the word personal. *Complete this activity thoughtfully, for creating a personalized concept of the word will help you remember it in the future.*
    Answers to all the exercises are at the end of the exercise segment.

EXERCISES

Adhere[13]

ad|here (ad hir′), *v.i.,* **-hered, -her|ing. 1** to stick fast; remain attached (to): *Mud adheres to your shoes. Paint adheres best to a clean, dry surface.* SYN: cling. See syn. under **stick²**. **2** to hold closely or firmly (to): *He adheres to his ideas even when they are proved wrong. We adhered to our plan in spite of the storm.* SYN: cleave, persevere. **3** to be devoted or attached (to); be a follower or upholder; give allegiance (to a party, leader, or belief): *Many people adhere to the church of their parents.* **4** *Obsolete.* to agree. [< Latin *adhaerēre* stick to < *ad-* to + *haerēre* cling] —**ad|her′er,** *n.*

1. Which of the numbered dictionary definitions of *adhere* best fits the word's use in the reading selection? _____

2. If you *adhere* to an idea, you probably
   _____ a. clarify a point.   _____ c. become attached to it.
   _____ b. reject it.   _____ d. discern its parts.

3. What might you most likely *adhere* to?
   _____ a. a schedule   _____ c. a chair or couch
   _____ b. food   _____ d. glue

4. Describe the time-management system that you *adhere* to on a regular basis. If you do not have one, do you plan on developing one? If so, what kind?

   _____

   _____

5. Write a sentence correctly using *adhere.* (Be sure to include context clues to show you understand the meaning of the word.)

   _____

   _____

Articulate[10]

ar|tic|u|late (*adj., n.* är tik′yə lit; *v.* är tik′yə lāt), *adj., v.,* **-lat|ed, -lat|ing,** *n.* —*adj.* **1** spoken in distinct syllables or words: *A baby cries and gurgles but does not use articulate speech.* SYN: clear, intelligible. **2** able to put one's thoughts into words easily and clearly: *Julia is the most articulate of the sisters.* **3** made up of distinct parts; distinct. **4** having joints; jointed; segmented. *The backbone is an articulate structure.*
—*v.t.* **1** to speak distinctly; express in clear sounds and words: *The speaker was careful to articulate his words so that everyone in the room could understand him.* SYN: enunciate. **2** to unite by joints: *The two bones are articulated like a hinge.* —*v.i.* **1** to express oneself in words: *Radio and television announcers are trained to articulate clearly.* SYN: enunciate. **2** to fit together in a joint: *After his knee was injured, he was lame because the bones did not articulate well.*
—*n.* any invertebrate having the body and limbs composed of jointed segments. [< Latin *articulātus,* past participle of *articulāre* (probably) divide into single joints < *articulus* article] —**ar|tic′u|late|ly,** *adv.* —**ar|tic′u|late|ness,** *n.* —**ar|tic′u|la′tor,** *n.*

1. If you *articulate* an idea, you
   _____ a. present it clearly.   _____ c. speak distinctly.
   _____ b. clarify a point.   _____ d. ignore it.

2. Which professionals need to be able to clearly *articulate* their ideas on a daily basis?
   _____ a. actors   _____ c. artists
   _____ b. lawyers   _____ d. teachers

3. Select the synonym(s) of *articulate*.
   _____ a. stress   _____ c. declare
   _____ b. express   _____ d. speak

4. Write a sentence correctly using *articulate*. (Be sure to include context clues to show you understand the meaning of the word.)

   _____

   _____

5. In what learning situation was it especially important that you *articulate* your ideas correctly? What can you do to better *articulate* your ideas not only in the classroom but in everyday life as well?

   _____

   _____

Assimilate[8]

as|sim|i|late (ə sim′ə lāt), *v.*, **-lat|ed, -lat|ing**, *n.*
— *v.t.* **1a** to change (food) into living tissues; digest: *The human body will not assimilate sawdust.* **b** *Figurative.* to take in and make a part of oneself; absorb: *She reads so much that she does not assimilate it all.* **SYN:** See syn. under **absorb. 2** to make like the people of a nation or other group in customs, viewpoint, character, or other attribute: *We have assimilated immigrants from many lands. By living a long time with the Indians, he was assimilated to them in his thinking and actions.* **SYN:** incorporate. **3** to make (a speech sound, usually a consonant) more like the sound which follows or precedes. **SYN:** adapt. Consonants are frequently assimilated to neighboring consonants; *ads-* becomes *ass-; comr-, corr-; disf-, diff-.* See also **assimilation,** def. 4.
— *v.i.* **1a** to be changed into living tissue; be digested: *The woody fibers of plants will not assimilate into the human body.* **b** *Figurative.* to be taken into oneself; absorb: *After he has watched television all day, nothing will assimilate through his senses.* **2** to become like the people of a nation, or other group in customs, viewpoint, character or other attribute: *Many immigrants assimilate readily in this country.* **3** to become like.
— *n. Obsolete.* that which is like.
[< Latin *assimilāre* (with English *-ate*[1]), variant of *assimulāre* compare < *ad-* to + *simulāre* imitate]
— **as|sim′i|la′tor,** *n.*

1. Which of the numbered and lettered dictionary definitions of *assimilate* best fits the word's use in the reading selection? _____

2. Who might need to *assimilate* information?
   _____ a. a professor preparing a lecture
   _____ b. a politician coordinating an election strategy
   _____ c. a student reviewing before an exam
   _____ d. a weightlifter eating lunch

3. Select the synonym(s) of *assimilate*.
   _____ a. adapt   _____ c. absorb
   _____ b. differentiate _____ d. convert

4. What are some strategies that you as a good student can do to best *assimilate* information learned in a class?

_____

_____

5. Write a sentence correctly using *assimilate*. (Be sure to include context clues to show you understand the meaning of the word.)

_____

_____

Cogent[11]

co|gent (kō′jənt), *adj.* **1** having the power to convince; forceful or convincing: *The lawyer used cogent arguments to persuade the jury that his client was innocent.* SYN: potent, compelling. See syn. under **valid**. **2** constraining; impelling; powerful: *The French Emperor . . . determined to insist in cogent terms* (Alexander Kinglake). [< Latin *cogēns, -entis*, present participle of *cogere* compel < *co-* together + *agere* drive] —**co′gent|ly**, *adv.*

1. The etymology of *cogent* shows that the word comes from the Latin words *co* (together) and *agere* (drive). Use this information, your background knowledge, and your imagination to match the following:

   _____ a. exigent   aa. to subject to smoke or fumes in order to exterminate vermin or insects

   _____ b. litigate   bb. able to move in a quick and easy fashion; active

   _____ c. fumigate   cc. requiring immediate attention or remedy; urgent

   _____ d. agile   dd. to subject to legal proceedings

   _____ e. navigate   ee. to control the course of a ship or aircraft

2. Select the synonym(s) of *cogent*.

   _____ a. impelling   _____ c. concur

   _____ b. valid   _____ d. convincing

3. Who would need to be able to present a *cogent* argument?

   _____ a. a student on an examination

   _____ b. a racecar driver

   _____ c. a politician defending new legislation

   _____ d. a lawyer during courtroom proceedings

4. Write a sentence correctly using *cogent*. (Be sure to include context clues to show you understand the meaning of the word.)

_____

_____

5. In what class did you present a *cogent* argument or position either on an examination or in class discussion? If you have not yet had the opportunity, in what situation do you think you will need to do so?

_____

_____

Competence[9]

com|pe|tence (kom′pe tens), *n.* **1** the quality or condition of being competent; ability; fitness; capacity: *No one doubted the guide's competence. The madwoman lacked the competence to manage her own affairs.* **2** enough money to provide a comfortable living: *He still thought how fine it would be to take one's ease with a rod by the lake ... now that his work was behind him and* he had his competence (Atlantic). **3** *Law.* legal power or authority. **4** *Geology.* the ability of a stream to carry and transport solid particles, pebbles, boulders, etc., measured by the size of the largest piece it can move. **5** *Embryology.* the ability of an embryonic tissue to react to various stimuli which can influence its development in particular directions.

1. Someone who has demonstrated *competence* would probably be
   _____ a. a world-class gymnast.
   _____ b. a college dropout.
   _____ c. a president of a nation.
   _____ d. a nationally known doctor.

2. Select the synonym(s) of *competence*.
   _____ a. ability   _____ c. diligence
   _____ b. capacity   _____ d. clarification

3. In which of the following sentences is *competence* used correctly?
   _____ a. The student demonstrated his competence when he received an A in his seminar class.
   _____ b. It is important to have competence when you eat apple pie.
   _____ c. The president displayed competence when negotiating with the congressional representatives.
   _____ d. The lawyer lacked competence when he won the difficult court case.

4. How can you demonstrate your *competence* on an essay examination? Have you ever felt concerned that you did not have the *competence* to perform a task? When?

_____

_____

5. Write a sentence correctly using *competence*. (Be sure to include context clues to show you understand the meaning of the word.)

_____

_____

Deleterious[15]

del|e|te|ri|ous (del´ə tir´ē əs), *adj.* causing harm; injurious: *'Tis pity wine should be so deleterious* (Byron). *The deleterious genetic effects [of radiation] would persist for hundreds of generations* (Bulletin of Atomic Scientists). syn: harmful, noxious, pernicious. [< New Latin *deleterius* (with English *-ous*) < Greek *dēlētērios* < *dēlētēr* destroyer < *dēléesthai* hurt, injure] —**del´e|te´ri|ous|ly,** *adv.* —**del´e|te´ri|ous|ness,** *n.*

1. Complete the verbal analogy.
   adherence : cling :: *deleterious* : _____
   - a. assimilate   c. hurt
   - b. complete   d. discern

2. What might be *deleterious* to your health?
   - _____ a. eating too much
   - _____ b. driving during the night
   - _____ c. studying for an exam
   - _____ d. not getting enough sleep

3. Select the synonym(s) of *deleterious.*
   - _____ a. closeness   _____ c. disadvantageous
   - _____ b. harmful   _____ d. procrastinate

4. Write a sentence correctly using *deleterious.* (Be sure to include context clues to show you understand the meaning of the word.)

   _____

   _____

5. What activities might you or other students engage in that would be *deleterious* to your health? How could these be corrected?

   _____

   _____

Diligent[2]

dil|i|gent (dil´ə jənt), *adj.* **1** hard-working; industrious: *The diligent student kept on working until he had finished his homework.* syn: assiduous. See syn. under **busy. 2** careful and steady: *The detective made a diligent search for clues.* [< Latin *dīligēns, -entis,* present participle of *dīligere* value highly, love < *dis-* apart + *legere* choose] —**dil´i|gent|ly,** *adv.*

1. Which of the following could correctly be called *diligent?*
   - _____ a. a successful businessman
   - _____ b. an incompetent policeman
   - _____ c. a serious student
   - _____ d. a student who drops out of school

2. Select the synonym(s) of *diligent*.
   _____ a. hardworking _____ c. illiterate
   _____ b. lethargic _____ d. assiduous

3. Which of the numbered dictionary definitions of *diligent* best fits the word's use in the reading selection? _____

4. In what situations have you had to be *diligent*? Classroom/school? Personal relationship? Job? Why?

   _____

   _____

5. Write a sentence correctly using *diligent*. (Be sure to include context clues to show you understand the meaning of the word.)

   _____

   _____

Discern[6]

dis|cern (də zėrn′, -sėrn′), *v.t.* to perceive; see clearly; distinguish or recognize: *Through the fog I could just discern a car coming toward me. When there are many conflicting opinions, it is hard to discern the truth. Not till the hours of light return, All we have built do we discern* (Matthew Arnold). — *v.i.* to distinguish; make a distinction; discriminate: *The Philosopher whose discoveries now dazzle us could not once discern between his right hand and his left* (William Ellery Channing). [< Old French *discerner* distinguish, separate, learned borrowing from Latin *discernere* < *dis-* off, away + *cernere* distinguish, separate] — **dis|cern′er**, *n.*

1. Complete the verbal analogy.
   linguistic : language :: *discern* : _____
   a. recognize   c. reclaim
   b. determine   d. defer

2. Select the synonym(s) of *discern*.
   _____ a. determine _____ c. discharge
   _____ b. discuss _____ d. discriminate

3. The etymology of *discern* shows that the word comes from the Latin words *dis* (off, away) and *cernere* (distinguish, separate). Use this information, your background knowledge, and your imagination to match up the following:
   _____ a. decree   aa. insecurity or instability
   _____ b. hypocrisy   bb. to engage or involve the mind or interest of
   _____ c. criterion   cc. insincerity
   _____ d. concern   dd. an authoritative order having the force of law
   _____ e. incertitude   ee. a standard, rule, or test on which a judgment or decision can be based

4. Write a sentence correctly using *discern*. (Be sure to include context clues to show you understand the meaning of the word.)

_____

_____

5. In what classes was it difficult for you to *discern* information? What did you or can you do in such a situation?

_____

_____

Erudite[1]

er|u|dite (er′ù dīt, -yù-), *adj.* having much knowledge; scholarly; learned: *an erudite teacher, an erudite book.* [< Latin *ērudītus,* past participle of *ērudīre* instruct < *ex-* away, out of + *rudis* rude, unskilled] —**er′u|dite′ly,** *adv.* —**er′u|dite′ness,** *n.*

1. Select the synonym(s) of *erudite*.
   _____ a. cultivated _____ c. learned
   _____ b. ignorant _____ d. scholarly

2. Complete the verbal analogy.
   ignorant : learned :: *erudite* : _____
   a. lazy   c. adhere
   b. keen   d. illiterate

3. In which of the following sentences can *erudite* correctly be placed in the blank?
   _____ a. The math professor presented information in an _____ manner.
   _____ b. He selected an _____ present for his mother at Christmas.
   _____ c. As the tutor discussed the science problem, the student looked _____.
   _____ d. The student received an _____ book as a graduation gift.

4. Describe a person whom you've met who is *erudite*. Would you consider yourself to be *erudite?* Why or why not?

_____

_____

5. Write a sentence correctly using *erudite*. (Be sure to include context clues to show you understand the meaning of the word.)

_____

_____

Impediment[12]

im|ped|i|ment (im ped′ə mənt), *n.* **1** a hindrance; obstruction: *As an impediment to South American tourism, the expensiveness of getting to some places is being given serious study* (Newsweek). **2** some physical defect, especially a defect in speech: *Stuttering is a speech impediment. They bring unto him one that was deaf, and had an impediment in his speech* (Mark 7:32). **3** *Law.* a bar to the making of a valid marriage contract. [< Latin *impedīmentum* < *impedīre*; see etym. under **impede**]

1. Select the synonym(s) of *impediment.*
   _____ a. disadvantage   _____ c. exemption
   _____ b. competence   _____ d. obstruction

2. What could be an *impediment* for a college student?
   _____ a. living on the campus grounds
   _____ b. receiving high SAT or ACT scores
   _____ c. not knowing the vocabulary used in the classes
   _____ d. not having enough money for books

3. Complete the verbal analogy.
   competence : ability :: *impediment* : _____
   a. clarify   c. defer
   b. discern   d. hindrance

4. Write a sentence correctly using *impediment.* (Be sure to include context clues to show you understand the meaning of the word.)

   _____

   _____

5. What is an *impediment* to learning and receiving a degree that most students face? Finances? Working? Career decisions? Discuss what might be an *impediment* for you and how you plan to avoid or overcome it.

   _____

   _____

Linguistic[5]

lin|guis|tic (ling gwis′tik), *adj.* having to do with language or the study of languages. —**lin|guis′ti-cal|ly,** *adv.*

1. Who would most likely need to develop *linguistic* talents for their jobs?
   _____ a. an international politician
   _____ b. an administrator of an ethnically diverse school district
   _____ c. a postman
   _____ d. the ruler of a country

2. If you take a class where you do *linguistic* analysis, you would probably study
   _____ a. the political characteristics of various cultural groups.
   _____ b. the history and structure of language.
   _____ c. issues related to health issues in society.
   _____ d. basic units of language—phonemes and morphemes.

3. Select the synonym(s) of *linguistic*.
   _____ a. speech   _____ c. diligence
   _____ b. correctness   _____ d. language

4. How would a knowledge of *linguistic* differences help you as a student? As a citizen?

   _____

   _____

5. Write a sentence correctly using *linguistic*. (Be sure to include context clues to show you understand the meaning of the word.)

   _____

   _____

Optimum[7]

op|ti|mum (op′tə məm), *n., pl.* **-mums, -ma** (-mə) *adj.* —*n.* **1** the best or most favorable point, degree, or amount, for the purpose. **2** *Biology.* the degree or amount of heat, light, food, moisture, or other condition, most favorable for the reproduction or other vital process of an organism: *There is usually for each species a rather narrow range, the optimum, in which the organism lives most effectively* (Harbaugh and Goodrich). —*adj.* best or most favorable: *An optimum population is one of a size and quality best fitted to* achieve some social goal (Emory S. Bogardus). [< Latin *optimum,* neuter of *optimus;* see etym. under **optimism**]

from **optimism:**

[< French *optimisme* < New Latin *optimum* the greatest good (in Leibniz′ philosophy); the best, neuter of Latin *optimus,* superlative of *bonus* good]

1. Complete the verbal analogy.
   procrastinate : delay :: *optimum* : _____
   a. cheerful   c. favorable
   b. learned   d. freedom

2. The etymology of *optimum* (see at *optimism*) shows that the word comes from the Latin words *optimum* (the greatest good) and *optimus* (the best). Use this information, your background knowledge, and your imagination to match the following:
   _____ a. copious   aa. to develop to the utmost
   _____ b. optimist   bb. horn of plenty
   _____ c. cornucopia   cc. characterized by great wealth; rich
   _____ d. opulent   dd. a person who looks on the bright side of things
   _____ e. optimize   ee. large in quantity; abundant

3. Use *optimum* in two sentences: one as a noun and one as an adjective. (See the dictionary entry if necessary.)

_____

_____

4. Write a sentence correctly using *optimum*. (Be sure to include context clues to show you understand the meaning of the word.)

_____

_____

5. What would you describe as an *optimum* learning situation for yourself? What type of instruction do you prefer? Why?

_____

_____

Procrastinate[4]

pro|cras|ti|nate (prō kras′tə nāt), *v.i., v.t.,* **-nat-ed, -nat|ing.** to put things off until later; delay, especially repeatedly: *to procrastinate until an opportunity is lost.* SYN: defer, postpone. [< Latin *prōcrāstināre* (with English *-ate¹*) < *prō-* forward + *crāstinus* belonging to tomorrow < *crās* tomorrow] **—pro|cras′ti|na′tor,** *n.*

1. If you *procrastinate,* you might
   _____ a. hurry to complete an assignment.
   _____ b. postpone a decision.
   _____ c. act diligently.
   _____ d. wait to do something.
2. Select the synonym(s) of *procrastinate.*
   _____ a. defer   _____ c. determine
   _____ b. decide   _____ d. delay
3. Complete the verbal analogy.
   retrieval : reclamation :: *procrastinate* : _____
   a. continue   c. postpone
   b. hinder   d. retain
4. When do you usually *procrastinate?* Before an exam? Doing homework? Deciding on classes to take? Looking for a job? List a few examples.

_____

_____

5. Write a sentence correctly using *procrastinate.* (Be sure to include context clues to show you understand the meaning of the word.)

_____

_____

Proximity[14]

prox|im|i|ty (prok sim′ə tē), *n.* nearness; close-ness: *She and her cat enjoy their proximity to the fire. Marriages in proximity of blood are amongst us forbidden* (John Florio). [< Latin *proximitās < proximus* nearest]

1. In which sentence(s) is *proximity* used correctly?
   _____ a. She lived in proximity to her job.
   _____ b. He needed proximity to complete the assignment.
   _____ c. Mary's aunt represents proximity in kinship.
   _____ d. Having proximity is important when completing an examination.

2. Select the synonym(s) of *proximity*.
   _____ a. closeness _____ c. condition
   _____ b. relativity _____ d. nearness in kinship

3. Select the antonym(s) of *proximity*.
   _____ a. retrieval _____ c. distance
   _____ b. separation _____ d. difference

4. Write a sentence correctly using *proximity*. (Be sure to include context clues to show you understand the meaning of the word.)

   _____

   _____

5. Why might it be important for a student to have *proximity* to his college campus? Do you live in *proximity* to your campus? How does this affect your life as a student? If you work, do you have *proximity* to either school or home?

   _____

   _____

Retrieval[3]

re|triev|al (ri trē′vəl), *n.* **1** the act of retrieving; recovery: *data storage and retrieval.* **2** the possibility of recovery.
re|trieve (ri trēv′), *v.,* **-trieved, -triev|ing,** *n.*
—*v.t.* **1** to get again; recover: *to retrieve a lost pocketbook, to retrieve information from the storage of a computer.* **SYN:** See syn. under **recover.** **2** to bring back to a former or better condition; restore: *to retrieve one's fortunes.* **3a** to make good; make amends for; repair: *to retrieve a mistake, to retrieve a loss or defeat.* **b** to rescue; save: *to retrieve the nations sitting in darkness from eternal perdition* (William H. Prescott). **4** to find and bring to a person: *Some dogs can be trained to retrieve game.* —*v.i.* to find and bring back killed or wounded game.
—*n.* the act of retrieving; recovery, or possibility of recovery.
[< Old French *retruev-,* stem of *retrouver < re-* again + *trouver* to find] —**re|triev′a|ble,** *adj.*
—**re|triev′a|bly,** *adv.*

1. Complete the verbal analogy.
   erudite : scholarly :: *retrieval* : _____
   a. destroy   c. refer
   b. release   d. return

2. Which of the numbered and lettered dictionary definitions of *retrieval* best fits the word's use in the reading selection? _____

3. Select the synonym(s) of *retrieval*.
    _____ a. recovery   _____ c. cancellation
    _____ b. reclamation   _____ d. revelation

4. What are some study strategies that you have developed to help you in fast *retrieval* of course information when preparing for an examination?

    _____

    _____

5. Write a sentence correctly using *retrieval*. (Be sure to include context clues to show you understand the meaning of the word.)

    _____

    _____

ANSWERS TO CHAPTER 5 EXERCISES

Adhere: **1.** 1 **2.** c **3.** a, d
Articulate: **1.** a, c **2.** a, b, d **3.** b, d
Assimilate: **1.** 1b **2.** a, b, c **3.** a, c
Cogent: **1.** cc, dd, aa, bb, ee **2.** a, b, d **3.** a, c, d
Competence: **1.** a, c, d **2.** a, b **3.** a, c
Deleterious: **1.** c (characteristic) **2.** a, d **3.** b
Diligent: **1.** a, c **2.** a, d **3.** 1
Discern: **1.** a (synonym) **2.** d **3.** dd, cc, ee, bb, aa
Erudite: **1.** c, d **2.** d (antonym) **3.** a, d
Impediment: **1.** d **2.** c, d **3.** d (synonym)
Linguistic: **1.** a, b, d **2.** b, d **3.** a, d
Optimum: **1.** c (synonym) **2.** ee, dd, bb, cc, aa
Procrastinate: **1.** b, d **2.** a, d **3.** c (synonym)
Proximity: **1.** a, c **2.** a, d **3.** b, c
Retrieval: **1.** d (synonym) **2.** 1 **3.** a

If you missed any of the items in the exercises, return to the exercise and to the dictionary definitions to see where you went wrong. Remember: If you get something right, you only affirm that you knew it. If you get something wrong and understand why, *you have learned something.*

POSTTEST

Fill in the blanks with the words from this list.

adhere	deleterious	linguistic
articulate	diligent	optimum
assimilate	discern	procrastinate
cogent	erudite	proximity
competence	impediment	retrieval

1. _____ is the act of recovery.

2. *Defer* and *postpone* are synonyms of _____ .

3. _____ means "having to do with language."

4. *Scholarly* and *learned* are characteristics of a(n) _____ teacher.

5. To _____ something is to perceive, distinguish, or recognize it.

6. Something that is harmful, or injurious, is said to be _____ .

7. A(n) _____ argument is one that is convincing and forceful.

8. _____ means "to absorb, or take in and make a part of oneself."

9. *Cling* and *stick* are synonyms of _____ .

10. _____ means "to speak distinctly, or to express in clear sounds and words."

11. Ability, fitness, and capacity are indicators of a level of _____ .

12. A(n) _____ is something that is a hindrance, or obstacle.

13. Hardworking and industrious are characteristics of a(n) _____ student.

14. A(n) _____ condition means that it is the best, or most favorable.

15. _____ means "nearness and closeness."

Answers to this posttest are in the Instructor's Manual.

If you missed any of the words, you may need to return to the exercises and to the dictionary entries to see why your concepts for some words are incomplete.

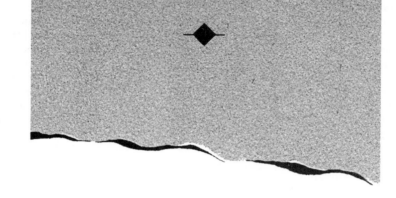

C H A P T E R S I X

CRITICAL THINKING

◆

VOCABULARY SELF-EVALUATION

The following words will be introduced in this reading selection. Place a check mark (√) in front of any that you know thoroughly and use in your speech and writing. Place a question mark (?) in front of any that you recognize but do not use yourself.

_____ assumption	_____ implicit	_____ monitor
_____ critique	_____ inference	_____ proclivity
_____ deduction	_____ inquiry	_____ quest
_____ explicit	_____ intrinsic	_____ schema
_____ generic	_____ literacy	_____ synthesis

LEARNING TO THINK CRITICALLY
FOR THE 21ST CENTURY

As our society approaches the next century there are renewed concerns about the level of literacy[1] of the general population. National assessments of the effectiveness of education reveal low levels of reasoning skills in large numbers of students. These results are echoed in complaints from employers about the level at which college graduates read, write, compute, and employ critical thinking as employees. As a result of these concerns and complaints, critical thinking has become the focus of schools, and efforts are being made to teach the required skills at every grade level.

Those who are unfamiliar with critical thinking may associate it with the generic[2] term, and define it as criticizing or finding fault with material. While these activities do require some of the abilities intrinsic[3] to critical thinking and may be formalized in a written critique,[4] they do not require the range of skills needed to think critically. In addition, they do not demand the attitudes and dispositions needed by an effective critical thinker.

As a serious student you will want to increase your critical thinking ability in order to be more employable and more successful in your life. What are the qualities and abilities that you must develop in order to be a critical thinker? If critical thinking is defined as the ability to reason well within the framework of a given situation or problem, then you must improve your ability to reason well. In your quest[5] to become a successful student, qualified employee, and contributing citizen, you will need to develop the following abilities and attitudes.

First you must develop the interdependent skills of inquiry[6] and analysis. You must learn to gather pertinent information and to examine it thoroughly, with particular attention to the credibility of the ideas presented and the relationships among them. Next you must develop the ability to evaluate the arguments and conclusions being presented. Your evaluation must be based on explicit[7] standards and criteria so that others will be able to understand the basis of your judgment.

A third essential skill you must acquire to be a critical thinker is that of making inferences.[8] In any real-life situation, some information will be unavailable. The thinker may not even realize which factors are missing. As a result, conclusions must be drawn, and judgments made, based on logic and prior experience. If, for example, you see water dripping from your ceiling and it is raining outside, you make the inference that the roof is leaking. If it is not raining, your inference may center on leaking pipes or some other factor. Two types of reasoning that can be employed to make inferences are induction* and deduction.[9] Induction begins with individual facts and observations and, after sufficient evidence is gathered, moves to a general rule. Deduction begins with a general rule and applies that rule to a particular case. As a critical thinker you will use these processes as complements to one another as you work to reason through situations and problems.

The fourth skill necessary to become a critical thinker is that of recognizing assumptions.[10] These unstated notions probably underlie all thoughts, and must be detected before you can evaluate material effectively. Note that these implicit[11] ideas are present in yourself also, and you must be aware of them in order to be a critical thinker. A simple statement such as "I'll see you here tomorrow" is full of assumptions. The speaker assumes that

---

* *Induction* is introduced in Chapter 9.

the person to whom the remark is directed is willing and able to be present tomorrow, that some occurrence will not prevent the speaker from meeting with the friend again, and that the meeting place will be in existence the next day. The final critical thinking skill you must develop is that of integrating information through synthesis[12] to create new knowledge and understanding. (Some critical thinking theorists see this factor as a link to creative thinking.)

These five abilities, when developed and practiced interactively, can help you be a critical thinker if they are supplemented by sufficient background knowledge. A well-informed thinker has experiences and information on a given topic, organized into a mental category known as a schema[13] (plural, schemata). This prior knowledge (background information) forms your world view, which creates the frame of reference that helps you interpret the situation or problem at hand and enables you to employ the skills of critical thinking.

What attitudes and dispositions must you possess to be a critical thinker? First, you must be open to other people's ideas, even if they conflict with your own, and you must be willing to apply the critical thinking process in your daily life. Next, you must be willing to recognize your own biases and proclivities,[14] as well as those of others, and to set them aside whenever possible. Then you must be persistent and must not be discouraged by obstacles or difficulties when they arise; you must have confidence in your own knowledge and abilities. Finally, you must monitor[15] your own thinking processes and self-correct when necessary. That is, you must learn from your own mistakes. With these abilities and attitudes, and with the determination to employ them on a regular basis, you can increase your chances of success in all areas of your life. You can be a critical thinker. ◆

PRETEST

Select words from this list and write them in the blanks to complete the sentences.

assumption	implicit	monitor
critique	inference	proclivity
deduction	inquiry	quest
explicit	intrinsic	schema
generic	literacy	synthesis

1. Something meant but not stated is _____.

2. A book review may take the form of a(n) _____.

3. A(n) _____ is a question.

4. Something clearly expressed is _____.

5. A synonym for _____ is "pursuit."

6. Something essential is _____.

7. If you take something for granted without proof, it is a(n)

_____.

8. _____ means having to do with class or group.

9. A combination of parts into a whole is a(n) _____ .

10. A(n) _____ is a diagram or outline.

11. To presume, based on some evidence, is to make a(n) _____ .

12. Reasoning from general to particular is _____ .

13. The ability to write is part of _____ .

14. A(n) _____ is a tendency.

15. To check and listen is to _____ .

Answers to this pretest are in Appendix B.

Unless your instructor tells you to do otherwise, complete the exercises for each word you missed on the pretest. The words, with their meanings and exercises, are in alphabetical order. The superscript numbers indicate where the words appeared in the reading selection so that you can refer to them when necessary. There are several types of exercises, but for each word you will be asked to write a sentence using context clues. (See Chapter 4 if you need information about how to create context clues.) You are also asked to perform some activity that will help you make your concept of the word personal. *Complete this activity thoughtfully, for creating a personalized concept of the word will help you remember it in the future.*

Answers to all the exercises are at the end of the exercise segment.

EXERCISES

Assumption[10]

as|sump|tion (ə sump′shən), *n.* **1** a thing assumed: *His assumption that he would win the prize proved incorrect. Every assertion of fact or system of facts rests on assumptions, avowed or implied* (John E. Owen). **syn:** supposition, hypothesis, premise, conjecture. **2** unpleasant boldness; arrogance; presumption: *The reporter's assumption in always thrusting himself forward made him disliked.* **3** the act of assuming: *The President's assumption of authority takes place upon his inauguration.* [< Latin *assūmptiō, -ōnis* < *assūmere* assume]

as|sume (ə süm′), *v.,* **-sumed, -sum|ing.** —*v.t.* **1** to take for granted without actual proof; suppose: *He assumed that the train would be on time.* **syn:** presume. **2** to take upon oneself; undertake (an office or responsibility): *to assume leadership. He assumed the responsibility for planning the picnic.* **3** to take on; put on: *The problem has assumed a new form.* **4** to pretend: *Although he saw the accident, he assumed ignorance of it.* **syn:** feign, simulate. See syn. under **pretend. 5** to claim for oneself; appropriate; usurp: *The king's wicked brother tried to assume the throne.* **6** to adopt: *to assume a new partner.* —*v.i.* to be arrogant; claim more than is due; presume. [< Latin *assūmere* < *ad-* to + *sūmere* take] —**as-sum′a|ble,** *adj.* —**as|sum′a|bly,** *adv.* —**as-sum′er,** *n.*

1. In which of the following sentences can *assumption* correctly be placed in the blank?

_____ a. John's _____ that we agree with his statement is correct.

_____ b. The election was delayed, so there was also a delay in Mr. Chang's _____ of his position as mayor.

_____ c. Our government is founded on the _____ that elected officials will represent the wishes of those citizens who elect them to office.

_____ d. Fidel Castro's _____ of power came after the overthrow of the Cuban dictator, Batista.

2. Check any synonym of *assumption*.

_____ a. invention   _____ c. supposition   _____ e. association
_____ b. premise   _____ d. decision   _____ f. hypothesis

3. Match the following sentence with a similar statement below: "The statement in this speech is an *assumption*."

_____ a. His statement is supported by extensive proof.
_____ b. The remark has been made many times before.
_____ c. His statement adds important information to the field.
_____ d. The speaker's remark is unsupported by fact.

4. Write a sentence correctly using *assumption*. (Be sure to include context clues to show you understand the meaning of the word.)

_____

_____

5. If you say to your friend, "Next time you come to dinner at my house we'll have roast beef," you make *assumptions*. What are some of them?

_____

_____

Critique[4]

cri|tique (kri tēk′), *n., v.* **-tiqued, -tiqu|ing.** — *n.*
1 a critical essay or review: *Some newspapers have critiques of new books. This provocative essay of close to three hundred pages is a critique of France today and yesterday—an angry inquiry into what happened to the fibre of the nation and that of its Frenchmen* (New Yorker). **2** the act or art of criticizing; criticism.
— *v.t.* to write a critique on; criticize; review: *He rules lightly, exercising his control largely by critiquing the editors monthly reports* (Time).
[< French *critique* < Greek *kritikē* (*téchnē*) the critical (art), feminine of *kritikós;* see etym. under **critic**]

1. Which of the following might correctly be called a *critique?*

_____ a. a book review
_____ b. an essay pointing out problems
_____ c. a commentary on the works of a poet
_____ d. a book of maps with descriptions of points of attraction

CRITICAL THINKING

2. Check any appropriate response to the following statement: "In his *critique* of the music, Leo discussed the ways that it did not fit standard forms."

   _____ a. It seems that Leo liked the music very much.

   _____ b. Leo sang along with the music, even though he didn't know the words.

   _____ c. Music doesn't have to fit a standard form to be enjoyable.

   _____ d. The music was really different, wasn't it?

3. Which of the following would be necessary to a well-done *critique*?

   _____ a. careful analysis of the work

   _____ b. personal acquaintance with the author or creator

   _____ c. knowledge of other works of similar type

   _____ d. only negative comments

4. Imagine that your assignment is to *critique* a piece of music or literature, recognizing good and bad points. What work would you *critique*?

   _____

   _____

   What is one good point? _____

   One bad point? _____

5. Write a sentence correctly using *critique*. (Be sure to use context clues to show you understand the meaning of the word.)

   _____

   _____

Deduction[9]

de|duc|tion (di duk′shən), *n.* **1** the act of taking away; subtraction: *No deduction from one's pay is made for absence due to illness.* **syn:** reduction. **2** an amount deducted: *There was a deduction of $50 from the bill for damage caused by the movers.* **syn:** rebate, discount. **3** a reaching of conclusions by reasoning; inference. A person using deduction reasons from general laws to particular cases. *Example:* All animals die; this cat is an animal; therefore, this cat will die. **4** a thing deduced; conclusion: *Sherlock Holmes reached his clever deductions by careful study of the facts.*

▶**Deduction, induction** are names of opposite processes of reasoning, the two ways in which we think. *Deduction* applies to the process by which one starts with a general principle that is accepted as true, applies it to a particular case, and arrives at a conclusion that is true if the starting principle was true, as in *All female mammals secrete milk; this is a female mammal; therefore, this will secrete milk.* Induction applies to the process by which one collects many particular cases, finds out by experiment what is common to all of them, and forms a general rule or principle which is probably true, as in *Every female mammal I have tested secreted milk; probably all female mammals secrete milk.*

1. In which of the following sentences can *deduction* correctly be placed in the blank?

   _____ a. Careful gathering of information is _____.

   _____ b. To reproduce something, to create it again, is

   _____.

   _____ c. The social security _____ from my paycheck has increased recently.

_____ d. If I reason from the general rule to the specific case, I
use _____ .

2. Check any synonym of *deduction*.
   _____ a. insertion   _____ c. rebate   _____ e. intuition
   _____ b. remainder   _____ d. discount   _____ f. reduction

3. Check any appropriate response to the following statement: "Some
   business expenses are allowed *deductions* from your taxable income."
   _____ a. I think it is cheating to take expenses off my taxes.
   _____ b. I read the instruction book carefully, so I know what I can
   take off.
   _____ c. That's good. It's hard to make a profit these days.
   _____ d. I keep careful records, so I can fill out the forms accurately.

4. Complete the following reasoning, using *deduction:*
   All of the members of the men's basketball team are over six feet tall.
   Juan is a member of the men's basketball team.
   Therefore, _____

5. Write a sentence correctly using *deduction*. (Be sure to use context clues
   to show you understand the meaning of the word.)

   _____

   _____

Explicit[7]

ex|plic|it (ek splis′it), *adj.* **1** clearly expressed;
distinctly stated; definite: *He gave such explicit
directions that everyone understood them.* **syn:**
precise, exact, unequivocal. **2** not reserved;
frank; outspoken. [< Latin *explicitus,* variant past
participle of *explicāre* unfold, explain < *ex-* un- +
plicāre to fold] — **ex|plic′it|ly,** *adv.* — **ex|plic′it-
ness,** *n.*

1. In which of the following sentences can *explicit* correctly be placed in
   the blank?
   _____ a. His _____ statements made his points clear to
   us.
   _____ b. When asked to explain her actions, Maria refused to be
   _____ .
   _____ c. Jamal was _____ : he left nothing unsaid.
   _____ d. Sometimes being too _____ can be tiresome.

2. Which of the following would be a characteristic of something *explicit?*
   _____ a. unexplained   _____ c. comprehensible   _____ e. clear
   _____ b. distinct   _____ d. equivocal   _____ f. plainly stated

3. The etymology of *explicit* shows that it comes from the Latin *ex* (out)
   and *plicare* (to fold). Use that information, your imagination, and your
   background knowledge to match the following.

_____ a. complicate   aa. to copy exactly
_____ b. perplex   bb. to make hard to understand
_____ c. plait   cc. to trouble with doubt; puzzle
_____ d. replicate   dd. a braid of hair and ribbon

4. Write a sentence correctly using *explicit*. (Be sure to use context clues to show you understand the meaning of the word.)

5. What information would you like to make *explicit* to the dean of your school or the president of your college?

Generic[2]

ge|ner|ic (jə ner′ik), *adj., n.* — *adj.* **1** having to do with or characteristic of a genus, kind, or class: *Cats and lions show generic differences. ... a philanthropist in the generic sense of one who loves mankind* (Thomas Lask). **2** having to do with a class or group of similar things; general; not specific or special: *"Liquid" is a generic term, but "milk" is a specific term.* **SYN:** inclusive. **3** not registered as a trademark: *Drugs are always cheaper if ordered by the generic rather* than the proprietary trade names (Harper's). — *n.* **1** a generic term: ... *waterways with the generics creek and run, elevations with generics such as hill, mount, and knob* (Eugene Green). **2** a generic drug: *Indigents should purchase low-cost generics instead of more costly brand-name drugs* (Science News). [< Latin *genus, -eris* kind (see etym. under **genus**) + English *-ic*] — **ge|ner′i|cal|ly,** *adv.*

1. Select the *generic* term in each of the following pairs.
   _____ a. automobile c. tree   _____ e. flower g. Kleenex
   _____ b. Ford   d. pine   _____ f. rose   h. facial tissue

2. In which of the following sentences can *generic* correctly be placed in the blank?
   _____ a. Although we may not be able to cure common colds, we often treat them with _____ drugs.
   _____ b. The _____ term for Sears or Bloomingdale's is "department store."
   _____ c. Geraldo is _____ and often gives his friends expensive gifts.
   _____ d. The word "zipper" was once a trade name but is now a _____ term.

3. Which of the numbered dictionary definitions of *generic* best fits the word's use in the reading selection? _____

4. Have you ever purchased *generic* products at a store? _____ If so, what was your purchase? _____ What is one reason to purchase a *generic* rather than a brand name?

5. Write a sentence correctly using *generic*. (Be sure to use context clues to show you understand the meaning of the word.)

_____

_____

Implicit[11]

im|plic|it (im plis'it), *adj.* **1** meant, but not clearly expressed or distinctly stated; implied: *He gave us implicit consent to take the apples, for he smiled when he saw us do it. Her silence gave implicit consent.* SYN: tacit. **2** without doubting, hesitating, or asking questions; absolute: *He has implicit confidence in his friends. A soldier must give implicit obedience to his officers.* SYN: unquestioning, unreserved. **3** involved as a necessary part or condition; contained (in): *The oak tree is implicit in the acorn.* **4** *Psychology.* involving activity that cannot easily be observed, such as a glandular or muscular reaction: *implicit behavior, an implicit response.* **5** *Obsolete.* entangled; entwined: *Th' humble shrub, And bush with frizzled hair implicit* (Milton). [< Latin *implicitus,* variant past participle of *implicāre;* see etym. under **implicate**] — **im|plic'it|ness,** *n.*

1. If something is *implicit,* it

   _____ a. is clearly stated.

   _____ b. is easily observed.

   _____ c. is suggested.

   _____ d. applies without being spoken.

   _____ e. has been thoroughly worked out.

   _____ f. is contained in something else.

2. Place an "s" in front of any synonym and an "a" in front of any antonym of *implicit*.

   _____ a. unreserved   _____ c. tacit   _____ e. unquestioning

   _____ b. obvious   _____ d. implied   _____ f. expressed

3. Which of the numbered dictionary definitions of *implicit* best fits the word's use in the reading selection? _____

4. Some people have *implicit* faith in a parent or a friend. In whom do you have *implicit* trust? _____

5. Write a sentence correctly using *implicit*. (Be sure to use context clues to show you understand the meaning of the word.)

_____

_____

Inference[8]

in|fer|ence (in'fər əns), *n.* **1** the act or process of inferring: *to form a judgment by inference from known facts. What happened is only a matter of inference; no one saw the accident.* SYN: deduction, illation, presumption, assumption, surmise. **2** that which is inferred; conclusion: *to make rash inferences. What inference do you draw from smelling smoke?* SYN: deduction, illation, presumption, assumption, surmise.

in|fer (in fėr'), *v.,* **-ferred, -fer|ring.** — *v.t.* **1** to find out by reasoning; come to believe after thinking; conclude: *People inferred that so able a governor would make a good President.* SYN: gather, deduce. See syn. under **conclude.** **2** to be a sign or hint of; suggest indirectly; indicate; imply: *Ragged clothing infers poverty.* **3** *Obsolete.* **a** to bring on; cause: *Who ... fled fast away, afeard Of villainy to be to her inferred* (Edmund Spenser). **b** to adduce; allege: *Full well hath Clifford play'd the orator, Inferring arguments of mighty force* (Shakespeare). — *v.i.* to draw inferences. [< Latin *īnferre* introduce, inflict, bring in or on (in Late Latin, adduce) < *in-* in + *ferre* bring]

1. Which of the following might require *inference?*
   _____ a. a decision that is based on complete information
   _____ b. a scientist who has limited evidence but carries out experiments
   _____ c. a jury deciding guilt or innocence
   _____ d. an article that is not clearly written

2. Select any synonym of *inference.*
   _____ a. presumption _____ c. surmise _____ e. illation
   _____ b. exaggeration _____ d. misjudgment _____ f. suspicion

3. If I make an *inference,* I
   _____ a. guess that something is so.
   _____ b. have complete evidence to support a decision.
   _____ c. made a judgment based on some evidence.
   _____ d. lie about what I know.

4. Imagine that one Saturday morning you are in the check-out line at the grocery store. The young woman in front of you is buying soda pop, potato chips, hot dogs, buns, pickles, and marshmallows. What *inference* might you make about her activities that afternoon? _____

   _____

   _____

5. Write a sentence correctly using *inference.* (Be sure to use context clues to show you understand the meaning of the word.)

   _____

   _____

Inquiry[6]

in|quir|y (in kwīr′ē, in′kwər-), *n., pl.* **-quir|ies.**
1 the act of inquiring; asking: *Inquiry of the operator will get you the right telephone number.* **SYN:** interrogation. **2** a search for information, knowledge, or truth: *The research and inquiry into the whereabouts of the old treasure took years of work.* **SYN:** search, research, examination. See syn. under **investigation. 3** a question: *The guide answered all our inquiries.* Also, **enquiry.**

in|quire (in kwīr′), *v.,* **-quired, -quir|ing. — v.t.**
1 to try to find out by questions; ask: *to inquire a person's name. The detective went from house to house, inquiring whether anyone had seen the* lost boy. **SYN:** See syn. under **ask. 2** *Obsolete.* to search for: *Well known to me the palace you inquire* (Alexander Pope). Also, **enquire. — v.i. 1** to try to find out something by questions; ask: *If you lose your way, inquire at a service station.* **2** to make a search for information, knowledge, or truth: *The man read many old documents while inquiring into the history of the town.* **SYN:** search, seek.
inquire after, to ask how (a person) is; ask about one's welfare or health: *Everyone has been inquiring after you during your illness.* [< Latin *inquīrere* < *in-* into + *quaerere* ask] **— in|quir′er,** *n.* **— in|quir′ing|ly,** *adv.*

1. In which of the following sentences can *inquiry* correctly be placed in the blank?
   _____ a. In our philosophy class we are making an _____ into the nature of truth.
   _____ b. The information desk at the student center has at least one _____ every day for directions to the health center.
   _____ c. Mr. Johnson wrote a letter of _____ to the school.

_____ d. _____ is an important part of the scientific method.

2. Place an "s" in front of any synonym and an "a" in front of any antonym of *inquiry*.

_____ a. response   _____ c. interrogation   _____ e. reply

_____ b. search   _____ d. research   _____ f. examination

3. If you engage in *inquiry,* you

_____ a. want to find the truth.

_____ b. may ask many questions.

_____ c. want to increase your knowledge.

_____ d. write down everything you know.

4. Write a sentence correctly using *inquiry.* (Be sure to use context clues to show you understand the meaning of the word.) _____

_____

_____

5. If you were going to conduct an *inquiry* into a job you are interested in, what is the first question you would ask? _____

_____

Intrinsic[3]

in|trin|sic (in trin′sik), *adj.* **1** belonging to a thing by its very nature; essential; inherent: *The intrinsic value of a dollar bill is the cost of the paper it's printed on.* **syn:** innate, ingrained. **2** *Anatomy.* originating or being inside the part on which it acts: *the intrinsic muscles of the larynx.* [< Middle French *intrinsèque* < Old French, learned borrowing from Medieval Latin *intrinsecus* internal < Latin *intrīnsecus* inwardly] —**in|trin′si|cal|ly,** *adv.* —**in|trin′si|cal|ness,** *n.*

1. Place an "s" by any synonym and an "a" by any antonym of *intrinsic*.

_____ a. extraneous   _____ c. incidental   _____ e. inherent

_____ b. innate   _____ d. ingrained   _____ f. essential

2. In which of the following sentences can *intrinsic* correctly be placed in the blank?

_____ a. There is often a difference between our _____ feelings and our social expression of them.

_____ b. Kindness has _____ merit and serves as its own reward.

_____ c. _____ enzymes are produced by many organs of the body.

_____ d. The _____ value of a rose is greater than its cost.

3. Select any appropriate response to the following statement: "I think Romona has characteristics *intrinsic* to a successful artist."

_____ a. I agree. She is very creative.

_____ b. Yes. A few more lessons and she should draw quite well.

_____ c. She makes unusual use of color and texture.

_____ d. Her original drawings show talent.

CRITICAL THINKING

4. What qualities do you think are *intrinsic* to the successful student?

_____

5. Write a sentence correctly using *intrinsic*. (Be sure to include context clues to show you understand the meaning of the word.)

_____

_____

Literacy[1]

lit|er|a|cy (lit′ər ə sē), *n.* the ability to read and write; quality or state of being literate.

lit|er|ate (lit′ər it), *adj., n.* — *adj.* 1 able to read and write: *The literate person can find out from books what the person who cannot read must find out for himself or be told.* 2 acquainted with literature; educated; literary. SYN: lettered.

— *n.* 1 a person who can read and write: *The number of literates in the United States has been increasing until most can now read and write.* 2 an educated person. [< Latin *litterātus* < *littera* letter (in the plural, literature, learning)] — **lit′er|ate|ly**, *adv.* — **lit′er|ate-ness**, *n.*

1. Select any appropriate response to the following statement: "I believe the *literacy* level of students today is very low."
   - _____ a. Not in my school. We can all read and write well.
   - _____ b. I agree, not one young person on my street can drive a car safely.
   - _____ c. If we had more orchestra and chorus teachers, students would be more literate.
   - _____ d. But colleges and universities are full of students who not only read and write well but also know literature.

2. Which of the following would be important to determine in any discussion of *literacy?*
   - _____ a. how the term is to be defined
   - _____ b. the level of reading and writing skill required
   - _____ c. the ways that the skills are to be tested
   - _____ d. the level of literary knowledge required

3. If you are known for your *literacy*, you
   - _____ a. can play a musical instrument.
   - _____ b. can discuss books on different topics.
   - _____ c. can discuss movies and television programs.
   - _____ d. are athletic.

4. What is your level of *literacy?* That is, in what languages can you read and write? _____ With what type(s) of literature are you most familiar? _____

_____

5. Write a sentence correctly using *literacy*. (Be sure to include context clues to show you understand the meaning of the word.)

_____

_____

Monitor[15]

mon‖i‖tor (mon′ə tər), *n., v.* —*n.* **1** a pupil in school with special duties, such as helping to keep order and taking attendance: *Several of the older boys in school serve as monitors on the playground.* **2** a person who gives advice or warning: *The Teamsters Union, which has been battling to rid itself of court-appointed monitors* (Wall Street Journal). **3** something that reminds or gives warning: *Conscience ... a most importunate monitor, paying no respect to persons and making cowards of us all* (Frederick Marryat). **4** a low, armored warship having one or more revolving turrets, each with one or two heavy guns. It was used chiefly in the late 1800's. **5** any one of a family of large, carnivorous lizards of Africa, southern Asia, Australia, Indonesia, New Guinea, and the Solomon Islands. Monitors are from 4 to 10 feet long, have a forked tongue and the habit of swallowing their prey without chewing it, and exhibit other snakelike characteristics. They are the only living genus of their family, the dragon lizard or dragon of Komodo being the most familiar, and are known to have lived in America from the fossils found in Wyoming. *All of the zoo's tenants were at their best, but the ... giant lizards or monitors virtually stole the show* (New York Times). **6** a receiver or other device used for checking and listening to radio or television transmissions, telephone messages, or other electronic signals as they are recorded or broadcast: *When a monitor or headphone connection is provided, it will be "live" even during recording* (Roy J. Hoopes).
—*v.t., v.i.* **1a** to check and listen to (radio or television transmissions, telephone messages, or other electronic signals) by using a monitor, specially to check the quality, wave frequency, or the like. **b** to listen to (broadcasts or telephone messages) for censorship, military significance, or other surveillance: *He noted that agency investigators have been monitoring broadcasts and telecasts since last fall* (Wall Street Journal). **2** *Physics.* to test the intensity of radiations, especially of radiations produced by radioactivity. **3** to check in order to control something: *Hearing aids now play a life-saving role in the operating room by monitoring the breathing of unconscious surgical patients* (Science News Letter).
[< Latin *monitor, -ōris* < *monēre* to admonish, warn]

1. In which of the following sentences can *monitor* correctly be placed in the blank?

   _____ a. When I was in grade school, I often worked as hall _____.

   _____ b. If you pick up this receiver, you can _____ Mario's phone calls.

   _____ c. The _____, a ship with armored sides, was built for use during the U.S. Civil War.

   _____ d. I find Mai's _____ voice very boring and dull.

2. The etymology of *monitor* shows that it comes from the Latin *monere* (to warn). Use that information, your imagination, and your background knowledge to match the following:

   _____ a. admonish   aa. to display in order to frighten

   _____ b. demonstrate   bb. to order to come before a court

   _____ c. monument   cc. to warn so one may improve

   _____ d. premonition   dd. something to keep a memory alive

   _____ e. summon   ee. a warning in advance

3. Which of the numbered and lettered dictionary definitions of *monitor* best fits the word's use in the reading selection? _____

4. When you were a child, what forbidden or dangerous behavior did your parents or caregivers have to *monitor* most closely?

   _____

   _____

5. Write a sentence correctly using *monitor*. (Be sure to include context clues to show that you understand the meaning of the word.)

   _____

   _____

CRITICAL THINKING

Proclivity[14]

pro|cliv|i|ty (prō kliv′ə tē), *n., pl.* **-ties**. tendency; inclination; predisposition; leaning; propensity: *The old woman had a proclivity for finding fault. There are many spots in Florida that attract people with a proclivity for uncrowded but urbane resort life* (New Yorker). **SYN:** bias, bent. [< Latin *prōclivitās* < *prōclīvis* prone to; (literally) sloping, inclining < *prō-* forward + *clīvus* a slope, related to *clīnāre* to bend. Compare etym. under **acclivity.**]

(Note: The etymology of this word provides a physical description that supports its meaning. A "forward slope" makes us "lean" in a specific direction.)

1. In which of the following sentences can *proclivity* correctly be placed in the blank?
   - _____ a. Juan dislikes avocados. In fact, he has a _____ for them.
   - _____ b. My aunt has a _____ for scolding all of us.
   - _____ c. My _____ for expecting honesty from everyone sometimes leads to disappointment.
   - _____ d. Cindy has a _____ for falling asleep in psychology lectures.

2. Select any appropriate response to the following statement: "Kelley's *proclivities* make her a successful student."
   - _____ a. She certainly works hard at her studies.
   - _____ b. Her good grades are the result of luck.
   - _____ c. Her parents probably didn't bring her up right.
   - _____ d. She uses her time well, attends every class, and always does her homework.

3. Which of the following describe *proclivity?*
   - _____ a. tendency   _____ c. predisposition   _____ e. responsibility
   - _____ b. proneness   _____ d. possibility   _____ f. inclination

4. For what academic subject(s) do you have a *proclivity?*

   _____

5. Write a sentence correctly using *proclivity.* (Be sure to use context clues to show that you understand the meaning of the word.)

   _____

   _____

Quest[5]

quest (kwest), *n., v.* — *n.* **1** a search or hunt: *She went to the library in quest of something to read.* **SYN:** pursuit. **2a** an expedition of knights: *There sat Arthur on the dais-throne, And those that had gone out upon the quest, Wasted and worn ... stood before the King* (Tennyson). **b** the knights in such an expedition. **c** the object sought for. **3a** = inquest. **b** a jury of inquest. — *v.t.* to search or seek for; hunt. — *v.i.* **1** to go about in search of something; search or seek: *This sense of man's balanced greatness and fallibility in the search for truth has made ours a profoundly questing civilization* (Adlai Stevenson). **2** of hunting dogs: **a** to search for game. **b** to bark when in sight of game; bay: *Who cry out for him yet as hounds that quest, And roar as on their quarry* (Algernon Charles Swinburne). [< Old French *queste* < Vulgar Latin *quaesita* < Latin *quaerere* seek]

1. In which of the following sentences can *quest* correctly be placed in the blank?

    _____ a. When you apply for that job, they will _____ your name and address.

    _____ b. In south county, several scientists are on a _____ for dinosaur fossils.

    _____ c. Much of the world today is _____ing for a lasting peace.

    _____ d. We took an automobile trip in _____ of amusement.

2. If you go on a *quest,*

    _____ a. you are searching for something in particular.

    _____ b. there is a chance that you will not find what you seek.

    _____ c. it may take you a very long time.

    _____ d. you will probably give up easily.

3. The etymology of *quest* shows that it comes from the Latin *quaerere* (to seek). Use that information, your imagination, and your background knowledge to match the following:

    _____ a. acquire   aa. beautifully made or designed

    _____ b. conquer   bb. to demand; insist upon

    _____ c. exquisite   cc. something gained by overcoming

    _____ d. inquire   dd. to gain possession of

    _____ e. require   ee. to look into; investigate

4. If you had unlimited time and money, what *quest* would you undertake?

_____

5. Write a sentence correctly using *quest.* (Be sure to use context clues to show you understand the meaning of the word.)

_____

_____

Schema[13]

sche|ma (skē′mə), *n., pl.* **-ma|ta** (-mə tə). **1** a diagram, plan, or scheme: *What Dr. Donaldson found was a perfectly good schema which ... put the arbitrary zero at body temperature, with "warm" as its label* (New Yorker). **2** a draft of decrees to be issued by an ecumenical council: *This schema consisted of ... such topics as the principles of liturgical renewal, the eucharistic mystery, the sacraments and sacramentals* (New Yorker). **3** (in Kantian philosophy) any one of certain forms or rules of the "productive imagination" through which the understanding is able to apply its "categories" to the manifold of sense perception in the process of realizing knowledge or experience. [< Latin *schēma* < Greek *schêma, -atos* figure, appearance. See etym. of doublet **scheme.**]

1. If you have a *schema* for some topic, you

    _____ a. have organized information into categories.

    _____ b. always have thought carefully about the topic.

    _____ c. may rearrange the information when new information comes to your attention.

    _____ d. may have included some inaccurate information.

CRITICAL THINKING

2. In which of the following sentences can *schema(ta)* correctly be placed in the blank?

_____ a. The developmental psychologist Jean Piaget said that children establish _____ that are changed over time.

_____ b. George and Barry _____ed to fool the teacher and get out of class.

_____ c. We create _____ about people, which may lead to bias and prejudice.

_____ d. My _____ for the perfect garden includes roses of all kinds.

3. Complete the following verbal analogy.
sunshine : warm :: *schema* : _____

_____ a. organized   _____ c. memorable
_____ b. complete   _____ d. scholarly

4. Write a sentence correctly using *schema*. (Be sure to include context clues to show you understand the meaning of the word.)

_____

_____

5. *Schema* theory of memory states that we organize information into categories that are arranged in sets and subsets. Write several items that are in your *schema* for "school." _____

_____

Synthesis[12]

syn|the|sis (sin′thə sis), *n., pl.* **-ses** (-sēz). **1a** the combination of parts or elements into a whole: *in the opinion of several competent critics the best synthesis of Baudelaire that had appeared in English* (London Times). *I cannot believe that we can achieve a synthesis between Thomas Aquinas and Marx* (Gyorgy Lukas). **b** a body of things put together thus. An idea or concept may be a synthesis of several other ideas. *The happiest synthesis of the divine, the scholar and the gentleman* (Samuel Taylor Coleridge). **2** the formation of a compound or a complex substance by the chemical union of various elements or by the combination of simpler compounds. Alcohol, ammonia, and rubber can be artificially produced by synthesis. *A total synthesis implies that in theory a substance has been elaborated from its elements, in this case carbon, hydrogen and oxygen* (A. J. Birch). **3** *Philosophy, Logic.* **a** the combination or unification of particular phenomena, observed or hypothesized, into a general body or abstract whole. **b** according to Immanuel Kant, the action of the understanding in combining and unifying the isolated data of sensation into a cognizable whole. **c** according to Thomas Hobbes, Isaac Newton, and others, deductive reasoning. [< Latin *synthesis* a collection, set; the composition (of a medication) < Greek *sýnthesis* composition (logical, mathematical) < *syntithénai* to combine < *syn-* together + *tithénai* put, place. Compare etym. under **thesis**.]

1. In which of the following sentences can *synthesis* correctly be placed in the blank?

_____ a. My friend has a list of bad things his parents have told him he must not do. He calls it his _____.

_____ b. The Disney movie *Fantasia* is a _____ of movement and music.

_____ c. I believe that the ideas presently being promoted by the government are not new, but only a _____ of ideas from previous administrations.

_____ d. Nylon does not grow naturally, like cotton, but is a _____ of chemicals.

2. If you create a *synthesis,* you might
   _____ a. make something new and different out of separate elements.
   _____ b. have a good idea, but not act on it.
   _____ c. produce a work of art that wins a prize.
   _____ d. experiment to see how things can fit together in a different way.

3. Which of the numbered and lettered dictionary definitions of *synthesis* best fits the word's use in the reading selection? _____

4. A buffet table is made up of different foods, put together, perhaps in an unusual way. Yet it is not a *synthesis.* How is an arrangement of food on a table different from a *synthesis?* _____

_____

5. Write a sentence correctly using *synthesis.* (Be sure to use context clues to show you understand the meaning of the word.)

_____

_____

ANSWERS TO CHAPTER 6 EXERCISES

Assumption: 1. a, b, c, d 2. b, c, f 3. d
Critique: 1. a, b, c 2. c, d 3. a, c
Deduction: 1. c, d 2. c, d, f 3. b, c, d
Explicit: 1. a, b, c, d 2. b, c, e, f 3. bb, cc, dd, aa
Generic: 1. a, c, e, h 2. a, b, d 3. adj. 2
Implicit: 1. c, d, f 2. s, a, s, s, s, a 3. 1
Inference: 1. b, c, d 2. a, c, e 3. c
Inquiry: 1. a, b, c, d 2. a, s, s, s, a, s 3. a, b, c
Intrinsic: 1. a, s, a, s, s, s 2. a, b, c, d 3. a, c, d
Literacy: 1. a, d 2. a, b, c, d 3. b
Monitor: 1. a, b, c 2. cc, aa, dd, ee, bb 3. v. 3
Proclivity: 1. b, c, d 2. a, d 3. a, b, c, f
Quest: 1. b, c, d 2. a, b, c 3. dd, cc, aa, ee, bb
Schema: 1. a, c, d 2. a, c, d 3. a (characteristic)
Synthesis: 1. b, c, d 2. a, c, d 3. 1b

If you missed any of the items in the exercises, return to the exercise and to the dictionary definition to see where you went wrong. Remember: If you get something right, you only affirm that you know it. If you get something wrong and understand why, *you have learned something.*

POSTTEST

Fill in the blanks with words from this list.

assumption   implicit   monitor
critique   inference   proclivity
deduction   inquiry   quest
explicit   intrinsic   schema
generic   literacy   synthesis

1. Chemical union to form a compound is _____.
2. "Conjecture" is a synonym of _____.
3. A(n) _____ is an ecumenical council's draft of decrees.
4. To review is to _____.
5. King Arthur's knights were on a _____ for the holy grail.
6. The act of taking away is called _____.
7. The definition of _____ is "propensity."
8. A synonym of _____ is "unequivocal."
9. A(n) _____ is a large carnivorous lizard.
10. _____ means having to do with the characteristics of a genus.
11. _____ has to do with being educated.
12. Something not easily observed is _____.
13. A synonym of _____ is "surmise."
14. Something originating inside the part on which it acts is _____.
15. "Interrogation" is a synonym of _____.

Answers to this posttest are in the Instructor's Manual.
    If you missed any of the words, you may need to return to the exercises and to the dictionary definitions to see why your concepts for some words are incomplete.

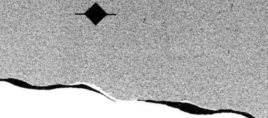

CHAPTER SEVEN

LIBRARY RESOURCES AND THEIR USE

◆

VOCABULARY SELF-EVALUATION

The following words will be introduced in this reading selection. Place a check mark (√) in front of any that you know thoroughly and use in your speech and writing. Place a question mark (?) in front of any that you recognize but do not use yourself.

_____ abstract	_____ assiduous	_____ formidable
_____ accessible	_____ avid	_____ myriad
_____ adjacent	_____ compendium	_____ plagiarize
_____ adjunct	_____ copious	_____ replicate
_____ ancillary	_____ expedite	_____ stringent

LEARNING TO USE THE LIBRARY

The purpose of a college or university is to provide education beyond high school. It may prepare students for a profession as well as give them a broader basis of, and appreciation for, knowledge. In order to carry out these functions, many institutions furnish ancillary[1] services in addition to the traditional lecture, laboratory, practice, and evaluation. For example, colleges may provide mental and physical health centers, tutoring and job placement services, special assistance for the handicapped, and so on. But the service most essential to the assiduous[2] student, and to the entire college community, is the library. Knowing how to use the library efficiently can greatly increase your chances of academic success.

LIBRARY ORGANIZATION

Even if you have used libraries previously, the college library can be a formidable[3] place. Yet while each library has its own arrangement, it also has certain standard features. There will be a central catalog, located in a prominent position, that serves as a compendium[4] of the entire collection. This catalog may be divided into sections according to author, title, and subject (and labeled as such) or unified into a single, alphabetical whole. More and more libraries are using computers to make the extent of their collections known to users. Instead of searching through the card catalog for materials written by an author or about a given subject, you need only put the necessary information into the computer terminal, and the titles in the collection, with the location of each, will be shown on the screen. Data may be called up using title, author, subject, or key terms.

At the time of this writing, most community and public school libraries in the United States use a classification (organization) system called the Dewey Decimal System, while colleges, universities, and (of course) the Library of Congress use a system called the Library of Congress Classification System. Each is based on the same principle, that is, of arranging materials according to subject matter. Things about the same topic are labeled alike and clustered together on the shelves. If you are accustomed to the Dewey system, you will immediately notice the differences in the call numbers with the Library of Congress system, but this should not keep you from locating the materials you need. Watch for the signs that indicate the floors and areas where the books are shelved. Signs will also tell you where to find the reserve room, the reference room, and periodicals.

Reserve Room

The reserve room houses special-assignment materials. Instructors frequently assign adjunct[5] readings and will place a few copies "on reserve." The avid[6] student will check these materials out promptly. If the professor does not tell you the identifying number of the material, you can find it in the nearby printout by looking up the class and instructor. Then you can give the identifier to the library clerk, who will retrieve the material from the shelves. Materials in the reserve room have more stringent[7] time limits placed on them than most other library materials. Frequently they may be checked out for as few as two hours.

Reference Room and Periodicals

In the reference room are myriad[8] reference works, such as almanacs, atlases, encyclopedias, dictionaries, technical books, and so on. Also included are indexes and abstracts,[9] which lead you to articles in periodicals and other publications. Often the works abstracted will not be available in the library, but if the data given indicate the material is useful, you can send for it. Once you know which periodical(s) you need, you can look in the printout of the holdings, usually to be found adjacent[10] to the periodical section. The list of holdings may also be on a computer or on microform, with a microform reader nearby. Many libraries keep the most recent periodicals on shelves, easily accessible[11] to readers, while back issues are on microform, usually in another area. Make a note of the call numbers in the printout and follow the maps and signs to the correct location. Microform (microcard, microfilm, or any other reduced-size) machines will be available and will permit you to read, and sometimes copy, the reduced-size material.

Interlibrary Loan

Occasionally the books and periodicals, as well as the abstract sources mentioned earlier, will not be housed in your college library, but in most cases they are still available to you. Most libraries are part of a system of libraries—other college libraries, a state or regional library system, and so forth—and can request the material you need from the larger collection. This is called interlibrary loan. Your school may also have a special name for this process, but the general term will communicate your need to the librarian. You will have to fill out a form, taking care to include all the necessary information to expedite[12] your request. You may also be able to use a system wherein you supply key terms referring to your subject, and the library, through its computer network, can search for works that relate to your topic. You can understand that these procedures take time, and so it is important to begin the research for a paper or project early.

USING THE MATERIAL

If you are using library materials to prepare a paper, be sure to take copious[13] notes or to replicate[14] the needed pages on a copy machine. Record the bibliographic material (the author, title, edition, publisher, place, and date of publication) carefully. You won't want to begin work, discover data are missing, and then have to locate your sources again! One important piece of advice: Do not plagiarize.[15] If you wish to use information directly from a source, quote it directly and give credit to the author. It is understandable to want to "borrow" a few words and ideas when there are so many before you, but *do* resist the temptation. It is academic dishonesty and, if it is discovered, may lead to an F on the submitted paper or to dismissal from the class. (Rules governing academic dishonesty are usually clearly set out in the college catalog so that students can be aware of them.) The library is full of a wide variety of information that can be used to stimulate your thoughts so that you can create a fine piece of writing of your own. ◆

PRETEST

Select words from this list and write them in the blanks to complete the sentences.

abstract	assiduous	formidable
accessible	avid	myriad
adjacent	compendium	plagiarize
adjunct	copious	replicate
ancillary	expedite	stringent

1. An abridgment of a larger work is a(n) _____.

2. A synonym for *innumerable* is _____.

3. A(n) _____ person is extremely eager.

4. If you are steady and untiring, you are _____.

5. To take the ideas or writings of another and use as one's own is to _____.

6. _____ is a synonym for *convenient*.

7. If you reproduce something exactly, you _____ it.

8. Something added but nonessential is a(n) _____.

9. A(n) _____ rule is a strict rule.

10. If something is close or nearby, it is _____.

11. Something _____ contains more than enough.

12. Something _____ is concerned with concepts rather than actual particulars.

13. A thing hard to deal with is _____.

14. Something that assists is _____.

15. If you make something easy, you _____ it.

Answers to this pretest are in Appendix B.

Unless your instructor tells you to do otherwise, complete the exercises for each word you missed on the pretest. The words, with their meanings and exercises, are in alphabetical order. The superscript numbers indicate where the words appeared in the reading selection so that you can refer to them when necessary. There are several types of exercises, but for each word you will be asked to write a sentence using context clues. (See Chapter 4 if you need information about how to create context clues.) You are also asked to perform some activity that will help you make your concept of the word personal. *Complete this activity thoughtfully, for creating a personalized concept of the word will help you remember it in the future.*

Answers to all the exercises are at the end of the exercise segment.

EXERCISES

Abstract[9]

ab|stract (*adj.* ab′strakt, ab strakt′; *v. 1, 3, 4* ab-strakt′; *v. 2, n.* ab′strakt), *adj., v., n.* —*adj.*
1 thought of apart from any particular object, real thing, or actual instance; not concrete: *Sweetness is abstract; a lump of sugar is concrete. Truth is an abstract concept.* **2** expressing or naming a quality, idea, or other concept, rather than a particular object or concrete thing: *Honesty is an abstract noun.* See also **abstract noun, abstract number**. **3** hard to understand; difficult; abstruse: *The atomic theory of matter is so abstract that it can be fully understood only by advanced students.* syn: profound. **4** concerned with ideas or concepts rather than actual particulars or instances; not practical or applied; ideal or theoretical: *abstract reasoning, abstract mathematics.* syn: visionary. **5** not representing any actual object or concrete thing; having little or no resemblance to real or material things, especially in art that avoids the use of ordinary conventional designs and the representation of material things, animals, or persons: *We saw many abstract paintings in the Museum of Modern Art. The interest of an abstract picture is exclusively decorative* (London Times). syn: nonrepresentational, nonobjective.
—*v.t.* **1** to think of (a quality, such as color, weight, or truth) apart from any object or real thing having that quality or any actual instance: *We can abstract the idea of redness from the color of all red objects.* **2** to make an abstract of; summarize: *Try to abstract this story for a book report.* syn: abridge. **3a** to take away; remove: *Iron is abstracted from ore.* syn: extract. **b** to take away secretly, slyly, or dishonestly; steal, purloin. **4** to withdraw (the attention); divert. syn: detach, disengage.
—*n.* **1** a brief statement of the main ideas or important points of an article, book, case in court, or other printed material; summary: *The students will write brief summaries of scientific treatises, earning $2.50 for each such abstract* (Wall Street Journal). syn: abridgment, digest, compendium. **2** an abstract of title. *Abbr:* abs. **3** a work of abstract art; abstraction: *a geometric abstract in red and yellow.* **4** an abstract idea or term; abstraction: *the abstract called capitalism.*
in the abstract, in theory rather than in practice: *10 percent of society understands in the abstract the meaning of "freedom"* (Maclean's).
[< Latin *abstractus,* past participle of *abstrahere* draw away < *abs-* away + *trahere* draw] —**abstract′er, ab|strac′tor,** *n.* —**ab′stract|ly,** *adv.* —**ab′stract|ness,** *n.*

1. In which of the following sentences can *abstract* correctly be placed in the blank?

   _____ a. Mary read the entire article and then wrote an _____ of it.

   _____ b. Many modern artists create _____ paintings.

   _____ c. Please _____ the main points of the story and hand them in.

   _____ d. Concrete is too expensive, so we have decided to cover the driveway with _____ .

2. Place an "s" before any synonym and an "a" before any antonym of *abstract*.

   _____ a. digest   _____ d. abridgment

   _____ b. concrete   _____ e. summary

   _____ c. difficult   _____ f. representational

3. Which of the numbered and lettered dictionary definitions of *abstract* best fits the word's use in the reading selection? _____

4. What is your favorite candy bar? What is one of its *abstract* qualities?

   _____

   _____

   _____

5. Write a sentence correctly using *abstract*. (Be sure to include context clues to show you understand the meaning of the word.)

_____

_____

Accessible[11]

ac|ces|si|ble (ak ses′ə bəl), *adj.* **1** easy to get at; easy to reach or enter: *tools readily accessible on an open rack. A telephone should be put where it will be accessible.* SYN: convenient. **2** that can be entered or reached: *This rocky island is accessible only by helicopter.* SYN: approachable. **3** that can be obtained: *Not many facts about the kidnaping were accessible.* SYN: available.
accessible to, capable of being influenced by; susceptible to: *An open-minded person is accessible to reason.*
—**ac|ces′si|ble|ness,** *n.* —**ac|ces′si|bly,** *adv.*

1. If an object is *accessible*, it is
   _____ a. useful.   _____ d. portable.
   _____ b. easy to reach.   _____ e. hard to find.
   _____ c. convenient.   _____ f. in great demand.

2. Check any appropriate response to the following statement:
   "The counselor's office is *accessible* to students in the Learning Center."
   _____ a. They must not enter that office.
   _____ b. I'm happy they have made it so easy for the students.
   _____ c. Too bad it couldn't be better arranged.
   _____ d. How convenient!

3. Complete the verbal analogy.
   access : verb :: *accessible* : _____
   a. noun   d. adverb
   b. verb   e. conjunction
   c. adjective

4. Are you able to park your car (or bike) so that it is *accessible?* Where do you put it?

   _____

   _____

5. Write a sentence correctly using *accessible*. (Be sure to include context clues to show you understand the meaning of the word.)

   _____

   _____

   _____

Adjacent[10]

ad|ja|cent (ə jā′sənt), *adj.* lying near or close, or contiguous (to); neighboring or adjoining; bordering; next: *The house adjacent to ours has been sold.* **SYN:** abutting. [< Latin *adjacēns, -entis,* present participle of *adjacēre* lie near < *ad-* near + *jacēre* lie[2]] —**ad|ja′cent|ly,** *adv.*
►**Adjacent** means lying near or neighboring, but not necessarily touching.

1. In which sentence(s) can *adjacent* correctly be placed in the blank?
   _____ a. The horse stood in a field _____ to the highway.
   _____ b. Bring that _____ set of tools into the garage.
   _____ c. John's car was parked in the lot _____ to the school.
   _____ d. We plan to paint the front wall white and the _____ wall brown.

2. Which of the following might be *adjacent*?
   _____ a. a driveway and a street
   _____ b. the sun and the moon
   _____ c. a couch and a chair
   _____ d. a house and a garden

3. Things that are *adjacent* must
   _____ a. be near one another.
   _____ b. be touching.
   _____ c. be similar in nature.
   _____ d. be contiguous.

4. Write a sentence correctly using *adjacent*. (Be sure to include context clues to show you understand the meaning of the word.)

   _____

   _____

5. Name an object that is *adjacent* to the chair in which you are sitting.

   _____

   _____

Adjunct[5]

ad|junct (aj′ungkt), *n., adj.* —*n.* **1** something added that is less important or not necessary, but helpful: *A spare tire is a more important adjunct to a car than a radio.* **SYN:** accessory, auxiliary. **2** an assistant to, or associate of, a more important person. **3** a word or phrase that qualifies or modifies one of the essential elements of a sentence. Adjectives, adjectival phrases, adverbs, adverbial phrases, and some nouns used in a modifying or qualitative position are adjuncts. In "The tired man walked down the village street," *tired* is an adjunct to the subject *man, down the street* is an adjunct to the verb *walked,* and *village* is an adjunct to *street.* **4** *Logic.* a nonessential property or attribute.
—*adj.* **1** subordinate: *adjunct arteries.* **2** accompanying: *adjunct military forces.*
[< Latin *adjūnctus,* past participle of *adjungere* join to < *ad-* to + *jungere* join] —**ad′junct|ly,** *adv.*

1. In which of the following sentences is *adjunct* used correctly?
   _____ a. In the phrase "a beautiful sunset," beautiful is an adjunct.
   _____ b. Sue is taking Biology I and an adjunct class called "Reading Biology Textbooks."
   _____ c. Now semiretired, George works as Adjunct Professor of Psychology.
   _____ d. All they have for sale at that garage sale is a bunch of adjunct.

2. Check anything that might be an *adjunct.*
   _____ a. a class _____ d. a textbook
   _____ b. a teacher _____ e. a support group
   _____ c. an adjective _____ f. life

3. Which of the numbered dictionary definitions of *adjunct* best fits the word's use in the reading selection? _____

4. What is your favorite *adjunct* to your daily diet?

   _____

   _____

5. Write a sentence correctly using *adjunct.* (Be sure to include context clues to show you understand the meaning of the word.)

   _____

   _____

Ancillary[1]

an|cil|lar|y (an′sə ler′ē), *adj., n., pl.* **-lar|ies.**
—*adj.* **1** subordinate; dependent; subservient. **SYN:** subsidiary. **2** assisting; auxiliary: *an ancillary engine in a sailboat.* **SYN:** accessory.
—*n. British.* **1** a subordinate part; accessory. **SYN:** subsidiary. **2** an assistant; helper. **SYN:** accessory.
[< Latin *ancillāris* < *ancilla* handmaid]

(Note: *Ancillary* and *adjunct* are very much alike. In fact, the dictionary gives each of them the synonym *accessory,* gives *adjunct* the synonym *auxiliary,* and uses *auxiliary* as a definition of *ancillary.* The words have in common the meaning of something secondary, rather than primary, in importance. To distinguish between them, it helps to look at the etymology of each word. *Adjunct* is something "added," or "joined," while *ancillary* comes from a word meaning "helper, or handmaiden." In some cases, these two words can be used interchangeably; but in other instances, where shades of meaning are important, one of them will fit the context better than the other.)

1. Check any appropriate response to the following statement:
   "John works in an *ancillary* position in the factory office."
   _____ a. He must be the president of the company.
   _____ b. Perhaps he can work his way up.
   _____ c. How wonderful to be on top!
   _____ d. I'm sure he makes a fine assistant.

2. Check any statement that describes something *ancillary*.

_____ a. of primary importance

_____ b. giving assistance

_____ c. of secondary importance

_____ d. independent

3. Complete the verbal analogy.

church : churches :: *ancillary* : _____

a. ancillarys   c. ancillarae

b. ancillaries   d. ancillaris

4. Write a sentence correctly using *ancillary*. (Be sure to include context clues to show you understand the meaning of the word.)

_____

_____

5. What *ancillary* services do you use at your school? At work?

_____

_____

Assiduous[2]

as|sid|u|ous (ə sij′ù əs), *adj.* working hard and steadily; careful and attentive; diligent: *No error escaped his assiduous attention to detail.* **SYN:** steady, unremitting, untiring. [< Latin *assiduus* (with English *-ous*) < *assidēre* sit at < *ad-* at + *sedēre* sit] —**as|sid′u|ous|ly,** *adv.* —**as|sid′u-ous|ness,** *n.*

1. Check any appropriate response to the following sentence:
"Mark is well known for his *assiduous* study habits."

_____ a. He'd better get his act together or he'll flunk.

_____ b. No wonder he gets good grades.

_____ c. Maybe he would do better if he liked what he is studying.

_____ d. I know. He works hard.

2. If someone is *assiduous,* he or she

_____ a. works if he or she feels like it.

_____ b. works carefully.

_____ c. is steady.

_____ d. keeps at the task.

3. Place an "s" by any synonym and an "a" by any antonym of *assiduous*.

_____ a. careless   _____ d. untiring

_____ b. unremitting   _____ e. lazy

_____ c. diligent   _____ f. steady

4. Have you ever been *assiduous?* When? What were you doing?

_____

_____

5. Write a sentence correctly using *assiduous*. (Be sure to include context clues to show you understand the meaning of the word.)

_____

_____

Avid[6]

av|id (av'id), *adj.* extremely eager; greatly desir-
ous; greedy: *The dictator had an avid desire for
power. The miser was avid for gold.* SYN: keen,
craving, covetous. [< Latin *avidus* < *avēre* desire
eagerly] —**av'id|ly**, *adv.*

1. If you had a friend who was *avid*, you might
   _____ a. tell him to take it easy.
   _____ b. have her divide the last piece of cake.
   _____ c. expect him to let you win at games.
   _____ d. find out she likes to win.
2. Which of the following might be *avid*?
   _____ a. a leader   _____ d. a town
   _____ b. a student   _____ e. weather
   _____ c. a child   _____ f. a tree
3. A person who is *avid* is
   _____ a. eager.   _____ d. greedy.
   _____ b. generous.   _____ e. craving.
   _____ c. covetous.   _____ f. disinterested.
4. Write a sentence correctly using *avid*. (Be sure to include context clues to show you understand the meaning of the word.)

_____

_____

5. Is there anything for which you are *avid*? Describe it.

_____

_____

Compendium[4]

com|pen|di|um (kəm pen'dē əm), *n., pl.* **-di|ums,
-di|a** (-dē ə). a short summary of the main points
or ideas of a larger work; abridgment; condensation. SYN: abstract, précis, epitome. [< Latin *compendium* a shortening; a weighing together <
com- in addition + *pendere* weigh]

1. In which of the following sentences might *compendium* correctly be placed in the blank?
   _____ a. The instructor asked the students to make a
   _____ of the class textbook.

_____ b. A _____ of the novel could be found on the back cover.

_____ c. Only the main points of the book are found in this _____ .

_____ d. A _____ must contain every detail of the work.

2. Check any appropriate response to the following sentence:
   "Have you seen the *compendium* of Jefferson Parker's new book?"
   _____ a. Yes. We went to that movie last night.
   _____ b. I don't want to read it. I want to read the whole book.
   _____ c. Yes. I saw it in the book review section of the newspaper.
   _____ d. Yes, but it is longer than the book itself.

3. Complete the verbal analogy.
   wheel : round :: *compendium* : _____
   a. summary   d. short
   b. large   e. work
   c. abstract   f. précis

4. If you were to create a *compendium* of the happy times of your life, what are some of the things that you would include?

   _____

   _____

   _____

5. Write a sentence correctly using *compendium*. (Be sure to include context clues to show you understand the meaning of the word.)

   _____

   _____

Copious[13]

co|pi|ous (kō′pē əs), *adj.* **1** more than enough; plentiful; abundant: *copious tears. There was a copious supply of wheat in the grain elevators.* **SYN:** overflowing, ample. **2a** containing much matter; full of information. **b** containing many words; profuse; diffuse. **3** *Obsolete.* having or yielding an abundant supply. [< Latin *cōpiōsus* < *cōpia* plenty < *cōpis* well supplied < *co-* with + *ops* resources] — **co′pi|ous|ly**, *adv.* — **cō′pi|ous|ness**, *n.*

1. Check any appropriate response to the following sentence:
   "Mary eats *copious* amounts of vegetables on her new diet."
   _____ a. She is likely to get very fat.
   _____ b. She probably gets lots of vitamins and minerals.
   _____ c. I'm going to tell her to eat more vegetables than that!
   _____ d. I like vegetables, so I may try that diet, too.

2. If something is *copious,* it is

_____ a. abundant. _____ d. ample.

_____ b. full. _____ e. simple.

_____ c. limited. _____ f. profuse.

3. Which of the numbered dictionary definitions of *copious* best fits the word's use in the reading selection? _____

4. Write a sentence correctly using *copious.* (Be sure to include context clues to show you understand the meaning of the word.)

_____

_____

5. Think of your bedroom. Is there a *copious* amount of anything there? What is it?

_____

_____

Expedite[12]

ex|pe|dite (eks′pe dīt), *v.,* **-dit|ed, -dit|ing,** *adj.*
— *v.t.* **1** to make easy and quick; help forward; hurry along; speed up: *Airplanes expedite travel. The telephone expedites business. If everyone will help, it will expedite matters.* **SYN:** accelerate, hasten, quicken. **2** to do quickly: *The manager had the ability to expedite all tasks assigned him.* **3** to issue officially; dispatch.
— *adj.* **1** (of a place, road, or way) clear of obstacles or impediments. **2** (of an action or motion) unrestricted; unembarrassed; easy; free. **3** (of persons) ready for action; prompt; alert; ready.

4 (of contrivances or instruments) ready for immediate use; conveniently serviceable; handy. **5** (of an action or process, a means, or remedy) prompt; speedy; expeditious.
[< Latin *expedītus,* past participle of *expedīre;* see etym. under **expedient**]

from **expedient:**

[< Latin *expediēns, -entis,* present participle of *expedīre* to free from a net, set right < *ex-* out + *pēs, pedis* foot]

1. In which of the following sentences is *expedite* used correctly?

_____ a. The company will do well to hire John; he is an expedite worker.

_____ b. A new highway across the foothills would expedite the flow of traffic to the beach.

_____ c. The large budget for the navy will expedite its shipbuilding program.

_____ d. You can expedite your raise in pay by doing all of your work carefully.

2. Place an "s" by any synonym and an "a" by any antonym of *expedite.*

_____ a. hinder _____ d. delay

_____ b. accelerate _____ e. hasten

_____ c. quicken _____ f. dispatch

3. Which of the numbered dictionary definitions of *expedite* best fits the word's use in the reading selection? _____

4. If you had the power to *expedite* one thing in your life, what would it be?

_____

_____

5. Write a sentence correctly using *expedite*. (Be sure to include context clues to show you understand the meaning of the word.)

_____

_____

Formidable[3]

for|mi|da|ble (fôr′mə də bəl), *adj.* hard to overcome; hard to deal with; to be dreaded: *a formidable opponent. A long examination is more formidable than a short test.* SYN: appalling, fearful. [< Latin *formīdābilis* < *formīdāre* dread < *formīdō* terror, dread] —**for′mi|da|ble|ness**, *n.*
for|mi|da|bly (fôr′mə də blē), *adv.* in a formidable manner

1. If you have a *formidable* task to perform,
   _____ a. you can do it easily.
   _____ b. you may not want to do it.
   _____ c. you can do it with some extra effort.
   _____ d. no one can do it.

2. Check any appropriate response to the following sentence:
   "Driving a large truck would be a *formidable* task for Jim."
   _____ a. It should be easy for him to earn his living that way.
   _____ b. Those things would be hard for me to handle, too.
   _____ c. Oh, he's just lazy.
   _____ d. Since his accident he doesn't even like to drive a car!

3. Complete the verbal analogy.
   national : nation :: *formidable* : _____
   a. formidability   c. formidably
   b. formulation   d. formidableness

4. Write a sentence correctly using *formidable*. (Be sure to include context clues to show you understand the meaning of the word.)

_____

_____

5. Is there anything in your life that is *formidable*? Taking tests? A trip to the dentist? Going on a blind date? Explain.

_____

_____

Myriad[8]

myr|i|ad (mir′ē əd), *n., adj.* —*n.* **1** a very great number: *There are myriads of stars. The grove bloomed with myriads of wild roses* (Francis Parkman). **2** ten thousand.
—*adj.* **1** countless; innumerable: *the City's moon-lit spires and myriad lamps* (Shelley). **2** ten thousand. **3** having innumerable aspects or phases: *the myriad mind of Shakespeare or Da Vinci.*
[< Late Latin *myrias, -adis* < Greek *mȳriás, -ados* ten thousand, countless]

(Note: As a noun, *myriad* is usually used with *of* and often used in the plural.)

1. In which of the following sentences is *myriad* used correctly?
   _____ a. Sue has myriad problems, but she is usually cheerful.
   _____ b. I think my cat has myriads of fleas!
   _____ c. John's virtues are myriad, and his faults are few.
   _____ d. The valley is filled with myriads of colorful flowers.

2. Check any characteristic of the word *myriad*.
   _____ a. It means a very great number.
   _____ b. The plural is formed by adding an "s."
   _____ c. It has a noun and an adjective form.
   _____ d. It can function as a verb.

3. Which of the numbered dictionary definitions of *myriad* best fits the word's use in the reading selection? _____

4. There are *myriads* of books to be read. If you had the time, which ones would you read?

   _____

   _____

5. Write a sentence correctly using *myriad*. (Be sure to include context clues to show you understand the meaning of the word.)

   _____

   _____

Plagiarize[15]

pla|gia|rize (plā′jə rīz), *v.,* **-rized, -riz|ing.** — *v.t.* to take and use as one's own (the thoughts, writings, or inventions of another), especially, to take and use (a passage, plot, or the like) from the work of another writer: *I could not help plagiarizing Miss Hannah More's first line* (Harriet Beecher Stowe).
— *v.i.* to take ideas, passages, or the like, and represent them as one's own: *He even had doubts whether in 'The Silent Places,' he had been plagiarizing, more or less unconsciously, from Henry James's 'Great Good Place'* (H. G. Wells). — **pla′gia|riz′er,** *n.*
pla|gia|rism (plā′jə riz əm), *n.* **1** the act of plagiarizing: *If an author is once detected in borrowing, he will be suspected of plagiarism ever after* (William Hazlitt). **2** something plagiarized; an idea, expression, plot, or the like, taken from another and used as one's own. [< Latin *plagiārius* literary thief, kidnaper; earlier, plunderer (< *plaga* snare, net) + English *-ism*]

1. In which of the following sentences is *plagiarize* used correctly?
   _____ a. Sam and Joe plagiarized a small office of the Bank of America.

_____ b. Bill discovered that someone had plagiarized his book and sold it to a publisher.

_____ c. Mark Twain was once accused of plagiarizing Bret Harte.

_____ d. To avoid plagiarizing, you must give credit to any source from which you copy.

2. If you *plagiarize* something,

_____ a. you use someone else's written word or ideas without giving credit.

_____ b. you commit literary theft.

_____ c. you are being dishonest.

_____ d. the instructor may give you an F.

3. Check any appropriate response to the following sentence: "You do not *plagiarize* if you copy from the encyclopedia."

_____ a. Yes, you do! You must give credit even if you copy from that work.

_____ b. You can't take an idea from another source and present it as your own.

_____ c. It is okay to plagiarize if you don't get caught.

_____ d. Something like the encyclopedia belongs to everybody.

4. Write a sentence correctly using *plagiarize*. (Be sure you include context clues to show you understand the meaning of the word.)

_____

_____

5. Have you ever been tempted to *plagiarize?* What topic were you writing about?

_____

_____

Replicate[14]

rep|li|cate (*adj., n.* rep′lə kit; *v.* rep′lə kāt), *adj., n., v.,* **-cat|ed, -cat|ing.** —*adj.* **1** exactly reproduced; duplicated. **2** folded back on itself: *a replicate leaf.*
—*n.* any exact reproduction or duplicate.
—*v.t.* **1** to copy exactly; reproduce; duplicate. **2** to say in reply. **3** to fold or bend back. —*v.i.* **1** to reproduce oneself or itself: *When the cell reproduces by the process of division known as mitosis, these homologous chromosomes replicate and separate,* so that each of the two daughter cells has a full complement of 46 chromosomes (Scientific American). **2** to fold or bend back.
[< Latin *replicātus,* past participle of *replicāre* fold back; see etym. under **reply**]

from **reply:**

[< Old French *replier* < Latin *replicāre* unroll, fold back < *re-* back + *-plicāre* to fold]

1. In which of the following sentences can *replicate* correctly be placed in the blank?

_____ a. Taking great care, the scientist was able to _____ the experiment.

_____ b. If you _____ that page, we will have an exact copy.

_____ c. It is not unusual for some kinds of leaves to

_____ .

_____ d. The TV movie "The Thorn Birds" was able to

_____ the novel.

2. How might you *replicate* something?
   _____ a. by carefully repeating each step
   _____ b. by using a Xerox machine
   _____ c. by making a general outline
   _____ d. by tracing every part on another sheet of paper

3. Which of the numbered dictionary definitions of *replicate* best fits the word's use in the reading selection? _____

4. What was the last thing you had to *replicate*? How did you do it?

_____

_____

5. Write a sentence correctly using *replicate*. (Be sure to include context clues to show you understand the meaning of the word.)

_____

_____

Stringent[7]

strin|gent (strin′jənt), *adj.* **1** strict; severe: *stringent laws against speeding.* SYN: rigid, rigorous, exacting, binding. **2** lacking ready money; tight: *a stringent market for mortgage loans.* **3** convincing; forcible; cogent: *stringent arguments.* [< Latin *stringēns, -entis,* present participle of *stringere* bind, draw tight] —**strin′gent|ly,** *adv.*

1. In which of the following sentences is *stringent* used correctly?
   _____ a. The country must now follow stringent economic policies.
   _____ b. Joe cut his face while shaving and applied a stringent.
   _____ c. Some parents have stringent rules for their children.
   _____ d. His stringent comments made the information clear to all.

2. Place an "s" by any synonym and an "a" by any antonym of *stringent*.
   _____ a. lenient   _____ e. rigid
   _____ b. strict   _____ f. binding
   _____ c. mild   _____ g. severe
   _____ d. easygoing   _____ h. forcible

3. Which of the numbered dictionary definitions of *stringent* best fits the word's use in the reading selection? _____

4. Write a sentence correctly using *stringent*. (Be sure to include context clues to show you understand the meaning of the word.)

_____

_____

5. What *stringent* rule or law annoys you the most?

_____

_____

ANSWERS TO CHAPTER 7 EXERCISES

Abstract: **1.** a, b, c **2.** s, a, s, s, s, a **3.** *n.* 1
Accessible: **1.** b, c **2.** b, d **3.** c (part of speech)
Adjacent: **1.** a, c, d **2.** a, c, d **3.** a, d
Adjunct: **1.** a, b, c **2.** a, b, c, d, e **3.** *n.* 1
Ancillary: **1.** b, d **2.** b, c **3.** b (plural)
Assiduous: **1.** b, d **2.** b, c, d **3.** a, s, s, s, a, s
Avid: **1.** a, d **2.** a, b, c **3.** a, c, d, e
Compendium: **1.** a, b, c **2.** b, c **3.** d (characteristic)
Copious: **1.** b, d **2.** a, b, d, f **3.** 1
Expedite: **1.** b, c, d **2.** a, s, s, a, s, s **3.** *v.t.* 1
Formidable: **1.** b, c **2.** b, d **3.** d (noun form)
Myriad: **1.** a, b, c, d **2.** a, b, c **3.** *adj.* 1
Plagiarize: **1.** b, c, d **2.** a, b, c, d **3.** a, b
Replicate: **1.** a, b, c **2.** a, b, d **3.** *v.t.* 1
Stringent: **1.** a, c, d **2.** a, s, a, a, s, s, s, s **3.** 1

If you missed any of the items in the exercises, return to the exercise and to the dictionary definition to see where you went wrong. Remember: If you get something right, you only affirm that you knew it. If you get something wrong and understand why, *you have learned something.*

POSTTEST

Fill in the blanks with the words from this list.

abstract	assiduous	formidable
accessible	avid	myriad
adjacent	compendium	plagiarize
adjunct	copious	replicate
ancillary	expedite	stringent

1. A summary of a longer work is a(n) _____.
2. Something rigid, or severe, is _____.

3. _____ means "expressing a quality rather than a particular object."

4. To _____ is to commit literary theft.

5. _____ means "a very great number."

6. To copy exactly is to _____.

7. Something available is _____.

8. Something _____ is to be dreaded.

9. _____ means "keen, or craving."

10. _____ means "overflowing."

11. A thing subservient or dependent is _____.

12. _____ means "adjoining."

13. Something useful but not necessary is _____.

14. To do quickly is to _____.

15. To be _____ is to be diligent.

Answers to this posttest are in the Instructor's Manual.

If you missed any of the words, you may need to return to the exercises and to the dictionary entries to see why your concepts for some words are incomplete.

PART THREE

FIELDS OF STUDY

SCIENCES

SOCIAL SCIENCES

HUMANITIES

BUSINESS

CHAPTER EIGHT

SCIENCES: BIOLOGY

◆

OVERVIEW

Biology is concerned with the relationship between structure and function in living systems. Biology has helped to solve problems in medicine, environmental resources, agriculture, and human ecology.

Emphases within the biological sciences include botany, zoology, microbiology, ecology, genetics, marine and medical biology, animal physiology, and neurobiology.

A wide range of job opportunities is available for students with a biology degree, including work as a public health microbiologist, laboratory technician, museum curator, science librarian, plant physiologist, forest ecologist, recreation specialist, park naturalist/ranger, entomologist, and fish and game warden. Biological training can also prepare students for advanced degrees leading to employment as research biologists, college and university professors, and medical and health professionals.

The introductory textbooks in biology are both expository and descriptive in that they explain broad concepts and generalizations as well as statements, ideas, and problems. Biology manuals are structured according to process analysis, with explanations of experimental procedures. There is usually visual reinforcement of concepts, provided through illustrations, photographs, charts, tables, classification systems, and structural formulas.

The vocabulary in biology is primarily specialized, with terminology unique to the field. Such terms as chloroplast, mitosis, *and* metabolism *represent processes, structures, procedures, and theories within the field of biology and are usually Latin or Greek in etymology.*

VOCABULARY SELF-EVALUATION

The following words will be introduced in this reading selection. Place a check mark (√) in front of any that you know thoroughly and use in your speech or writing. Place a question mark (?) in front of any that you recognize but do not use yourself.

_____ chloroplast	_____ eucaryote	_____ osmosis
_____ chromosome	_____ meiosis	_____ permeable
_____ cytokinesis	_____ metabolism	_____ photosynthesis
_____ cytoplasm	_____ mitosis	_____ procaryote
_____ diffusion	_____ organelle	_____ symbiosis

INSIGHTS INTO BIOLOGY

What does biology mean to you? Do you immediately picture a frog with its unidentified insides protruding onto a dissecting tray? Or perhaps your eyes burn in memory of time spent looking at yeast cells divide under a microscope. Although these experiences are part of biology, the field consists of much more. Biology is the study of life, and the smallest unit of life is the cell. Cells vary in size, shape, and function but exhibit similar traits that characterize them as cells.

Two types of cells make up all contemporary organisms. According to cell type, they are called either procaryotes[1] or eucaryotes.[2] All cells have a plasma membrane, a phospholipid (fatlike) bilayer, that is differentially permeable[3] to ions, water, and other molecules. In addition to the plasma membrane, both types of cells have deoxyribonucleic acid (DNA) and ribosomes.* Eucaryotes, the more complex cells, have a visible nucleus, which is a membrane-bound organelle[4] that contains the DNA. This genetic material carries the necessary information to synthesize all the organic materials a cell needs for growth and reproduction.

* Ribosome—small organelle composed of protein and ribonucleic acid; the site of protein synthesis.

Although the nucleus is responsible for a cell's function and replication, it is in the cytoplasm[5] of the cell that most of a cell's activity takes place. The cytoplasm consists of everything other than the plasma membrane and the nucleus, and includes several organelles, such as mitochondria,† Golgi bodies,‡ and endoplasmic reticulum,§ which are responsible for a cell's function and replication. Thus the cell is the basic foundation for all biological studies.

Although both plant and animal cells have the structures just listed, there are some differences between them. Animal cells lack cell walls, whereas plant cells have a relatively thick cell wall external to the outer membrane. Plants also contain organelles called *plastids,* one of which is the chloroplast[6] that carries out photosynthesis,[7] converting water and carbon dioxide to water.

Many college courses, such as genetics, physiology, microbiology, and molecular biology, concentrate on the study of cells and their functions. Cellular biologists seek to understand the basic chemical processes of protein synthesis, osmosis,[8] and diffusion[9] that allow cells to perform those various functions that ultimately maintain the organism's metabolism.[10] Cell membranes that are permeable allow the movement of water through them via the process of osmosis. And substances move within cells by the process of diffusion, which is the movement of suspended or dissolved particles from a more concentrated to a less concentrated region as a result of the random movement of individual particles.

When eucaryotic cells divide, they do so by the process of mitosis.[11] In this process, which produces new cells identical to the old cells, the cell duplicates all of its chromosomes[12] and evenly distributes them into the daughter nuclei. Then the cytoplasm divides to form two separate cells in a process called cytokinesis.[13] A similar but more complicated process is meiosis.[14] This process, carried out by sexually reproducing organisms, reduces the chromosome number by half so that when the sperm and egg unite during fertilization the chromosome number of the offspring is the same as that of the parents.

An exciting topic in cellular biology is genetic engineering, a technique that alters the genetic makeup of cells by selective removal, insertion, or modification of nucleotide sequences (units of nucleic acid). One successful application of genetic engineering in agriculture involves nitrogen fixation. Gaseous nitrogen is abundant in the atmosphere but is useless to plants in that form. However, certain bacteria are capable of fixing nitrogen (changing it to a form that plants can use) by working with plants in a relationship called symbiosis.[15] Together they convert the gas to nitrogen-containing compounds that plants can take up from the soil. Gene-splicing techniques make it possible to increase nitrogen fixation, thereby increasing the protein content of the plants. This scientific advance in agriculture, if used extensively, could provide great improvement in worldwide human nutrition.

As you can see, biology isn't just concerned with formaldehyde-scented organs of lower vertebrates or the reproductive cycle of fungi. Biology is a field that looks at all living things and their interactions in the world around us. ◆

---

† Mitochondria—organelles bound by a double membrane in which energy is captured in the form of ATP in the course of cellular respiration.

‡ Golgi bodies—organelles consisting of stacks of membranes that modify, store, and route products of the endoplasmic reticulum.

§ Endoplasmic reticulum—extensive system of double membranes present in most cells, dividing the cytoplasm into compartments and channels; often coated with ribosomes.

BIOLOGY PRETEST

Select words from this list and write them in the blanks to complete the sentences.

chloroplast	eucaryote	osmosis
chromosome	meiosis	permeable
cytokinesis	metabolism	photosynthesis
cytoplasm	mitosis	procaryote
diffusion	organelle	symbiosis

1. A cell or organism having at least one visible nucleus is a(n) _____.

2. _____ is the mixing together, or spreading into each other, of the atoms and molecules of different substances.

3. The cellular process of _____ results in products identical to the parent cell.

4. A(n) _____ is a minute, specialized part of a cell that carries out particular functions within the cell, such as providing energy for the cell's activities.

5. The tendency of a fluid of lower concentration to pass through a semi-permeable membrane into a solution of higher concentration is known as _____.

6. A membrane that permits molecules to pass through its openings is said to be _____.

7. An important function of _____ is reduction of chromosome number.

8. The sum of chemical processes, such as energy production occurring within a living unit, is called _____.

9. A cell without a membrane-bound nucleus is a(n) _____ cell.

10. _____s carry the genetic information of a cell.

11. An organelle that is exclusive to plants is a(n) _____.

12. _____, the conversion of light energy to chemical energy, takes place within special cellular organelles.

13. _____ is a living together of two unlike organisms.

14. All cells have _____, which is the living matter of a cell, excluding the nucleus.

15. In the process of _____, the cytoplasm of the parent cell is divided and packaged into two identical new parts.

Answers to this pretest are in Appendix B.

Unless your instructor tells you to do otherwise, complete the exercises for each word that you missed on the pretest. The words, with their meanings and exercises, are in alphabetical order. The superscript numbers indicate where the words appeared in the reading selection so that you can refer to them when necessary. There are several types of exercises, and more than one answer may be correct. For each word you will be asked to write a sentence using context clues. (See Chapter 4 if you need information about how to create context clues.) You are also asked to perform some activity that will help you make your concept of the word personal. *Complete this activity thoughtfully, for creating a personalized concept of the word will help you remember it in the future.*

Answers to all the exercises are at the end of the exercise segment.

BIOLOGY EXERCISES

Chloroplast[6]

chlo|ro|plast (klôr'e plast, klōr'-), *n.* a tiny body in the cells of green plants that contains chlorophyll: *The green color of stems is usually due to chloroplasts in the cortical cells just beneath the epidermis* (Fred W. Emerson). See picture under **cell.** [< *chloro-* + *-plast*]

from **cell:**

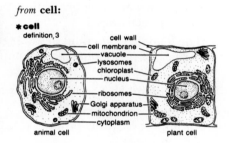

1. In which of the following sentences can *chloroplast* correctly be placed in the blank?
   _____ a. _____(s) are common to plant and animal cells.
   _____ b. Animal cells have _____(s) that are larger than those in plant cells.
   _____ c. An electron microscope will reveal that a cell's _____(s) contain chlorophyll.
   _____ d. A _____ is located outside the cell wall of a plant.

2. Check any of the following that is a characteristic of a *chloroplast*.
   _____ a. red in color   _____ d. found in plant cells
   _____ b. contains chlorophyll _____ e. similar to a nucleus
   _____ c. usually in pairs   _____ f. found in all eucaryotic cells

3. The etymology of *chloroplast* shows that it comes from the Greek forms *chloros* (pale green) and *plassein* (to form, mold). Use this information, your background knowledge, and your imagination to match the following:

_____ a. plaster   aa. protoplasm; substance that makes up the body of the cell, excepting the nucleus

_____ b. plastic   bb. condition in plants in which green plants are yellow

_____ c. plastid   cc. a greenish-yellow, bad-smelling, poisonous gas

_____ d. plasma   dd. small mass of protoplasm in a plant cell

_____ e. chlorine   ee. substance that can be molded or shaped

_____ f. chlorosis   ff. a sticky mixture that dries as it hardens

4. Write a sentence correctly using *chloroplast*. (Be sure to include context clues to show you understand the meaning of the word.)

_____

_____

5. In which type of cell is the *chloroplast* located? _____ Draw a circle around it in the drawings of the cells included with the dictionary entry.

Chromosome[12]

chro|mo|some (krō′mə sōm), *n.* any one of the rod-shaped bodies found in the nucleus of a cell that appear when the cell divides. Chromosomes are derived from the parents and carry the genes that determine heredity, controlling the development of the organism and determining its nature. They are of a definite number for each species and occur in pairs in most organisms, except in their germ cells. The genetic material in each chromosome is a long polynucleotide strand, usually of deoxyribonucleic acid but sometimes of ribonucleic acid, set in a protein matrix. *The human embryo develops into a person . . . because the material carried in its chromosomes, its constellation of genes, initiates and guides a marvelously coordinated sequence of reactions that leads inevitably, under normal conditions, to the differentiation and growth of a human being* (Atlantic). [< German *Chromosom* < Greek *chrôma* color + *sôma* body]

1. Select any of the following that is characteristic of *chromosomes*.

_____ a. sometimes in pairs   _____ d. carry genetic information

_____ b. outside nucleus of cell   _____ e. rod-shaped when cell divides

_____ c. green in color   _____ f. each species has the same number

2. In which of the following sentences can *chromosome* correctly be placed in the blank?

_____ a. Organisms receive their _____(s) from their parents.

_____ b. Germ cells (egg and sperm cells) contain pairs of _____ .

_____ c. _____(s) are generally composed of deoxyribonucleic acid.

_____ d. A _____ is a polynucleotide strand of genetic material.

3. Complete the verbal analogy.
   vegetables : garden :: *chromosomes* : _____
   a. nucleus   b. DNA   c. colored body   d. heredity

4. Your *chromosomes* carry the genetic information that determines your characteristics. What eye color did the genes on your *chromosomes* give you?

   _____

5. Write a sentence correctly using *chromosome*. (Be sure to include context clues to show you understand the meaning of the word.)

   _____

   _____

Cytokinesis[13]

cy|to|ki|ne|sis (sī'tō ki nē'sis, -kī-), *n.* the changes occurring in the cytoplasm of a cell during mitosis, meiosis, and fertilization.

1. In which of the following sentences can *cytokinesis* be correctly placed in the blank?
   _____ a. In _____, the cytoplasm of the parent cell is divided into two parts, each containing one of the nuclei.
   _____ b. _____ usually begins during telophase of mitosis.
   _____ c. _____ is the fusion of two gametes and their nuclei.
   _____ d. In our own species, _____ takes place in the reproductive organs.

2. Complete the verbal analogy.
   organelle : specialized structure :: *cytokinesis* : _____
   a. bacteria production   c. osmosis
   b. cell division   d. mutation

3. Where does *cytokinesis* takes place?
   _____ a. membrane   _____ c. cell wall
   _____ b. nucleus   _____ d. cytoplasm

4. How are cytoplasm and *cytokinesis* related? (See the dictionary entry if necessary.)

   _____

   _____

5. Write a sentence correctly using *cytokinesis*. (Be sure to include context clues to show you understand the meaning of the word.)

   _____

   _____

Cytoplasm[5]

cy|to|plasm (sī′tə plaz əm), *n.* the living sub-
stance or protoplasm of a cell outside of the nucleus: *The main body of the cell, its cytoplasm,
corresponds to the factory area where workers
are manufacturing the specified product from in-
coming raw materials* (Scientific American). See
picture under **cell**.

from **cell:**

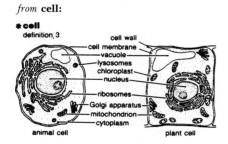

1. Where is the *cytoplasm* located?
   _____ a. outside the cell wall   _____ c. within the cell
   _____ b. within organelles   _____ d. inside the nucleus

2. Select the synonym(s) of *cytoplasm*.
   _____ a. living matter   _____ c. diffusion
   _____ b. gaseous substance   _____ d. inorganic compound

3. In which of the following sentences is *cytoplasm* used correctly?
   _____ a. Cytoplasm is the net movement of water through a mem-
   brane separating two solutions.
   _____ b. All cells have a cytoplasm, which contains a large variety of
   molecules.
   _____ c. The process by which plants manufacture their food is called
   cytoplasm.
   _____ d. The process of glycolysis takes place in the cell fluid, or cyto-
   plasm.

4. Write a sentence correctly using *cytoplasm*. (Be sure to include context
   clues to show you understand the meaning of the word.)

   _____

   _____

5. How is the *cytoplasm* different from the membrane of a cell?

   _____

   _____

Diffusion[9]

dif|fu|sion (di fyü′zhən), *n.* **1** the act or fact of
diffusing; a spreading or scattering widely: *The
invention of printing greatly increased the diffusion of knowledge. The spreading of patterns
and traits from one group or area to another is
known as cultural diffusion.* **2** a being widely
spread or scattered; diffused condition. **3a** a mixing together of the atoms or molecules of substances by spreading into one another: *the
diffusion of gases, liquids, or solids. An example
of a new relation is found in the combination of
diffusion and heat flow* (R. O. Davies). **b** the
scattering of light resulting from its being reflected from a rough surface. See **scatter**. **4** the
use of too many words; wordiness.

1. Which of the numbered dictionary definitions of *diffusion* best fits the
   word's use in the reading selection? _____

2. In which of the following sentences is *diffusion* used correctly?

_____ a. The loss of water vapor from a plant body is known as diffusion.

_____ b. Even distribution of molecules is a net result of the process of diffusion.

_____ c. The movement of water in diffusion is through membranes that are selectively permeable.

_____ d. Movement from a region of greater concentration to one of lesser concentration is a characteristic of diffusion.

3. Choose an appropriate synonym for *diffusion*.

_____ a. control   _____ c. spread

_____ b. recede   _____ d. clot

4. What is the difference between osmosis and *diffusion*? (See the reading selection if necessary.)

_____

_____

5. Write a sentence correctly using *diffusion*. (Be sure to include context clues to show you understand the meaning of the word.)

_____

_____

Eucaryote[2]

eu|car|y|ote (yü kar′ē ōt), *n.* a cell or organism having a visible nucleus or nuclei: *If the first eucaryotes arose 1.2 to 1.4 billion years ago, there would be about half this time available for the evolution of soft-bodied multicellular organisms, since the first fossil animal skeletons were deposited around 600 million years ago at the beginning of the Cambrian period* (Scientific American). Also, **eukaryote**. [< *eu-* good, true + Greek *káryon* nut, kernel]

1. What is the unique characteristic of a *eucaryote*?

_____ a. invisible nucleus   _____ c. visible nucleus

_____ b. no membrane   _____ d. living matter

2. What part of *eucaryote* tells you that it has a "good," or "true," nucleus?

_____ a. cary

_____ b. eu

_____ c. ote

3. In which of the following sentences can *eucaryote* be correctly placed in the blank?

_____ a. _____ is a cell which has a true nucleus and inner membrane structure, or organelle.

_____ b. Plants use _____, water, and sunlight to make their food.

_____ c. A _____ is the smallest indivisible particle of all matter.

_____ d. A _____ is usually smaller than a prokaryote.

4. Describe the characteristics of a *eucaryote* in your own words. Then check the dictionary entry to see if your concept was correct.

_____

_____

5. Write a sentence correctly using *eucaryote*. (Be sure to include context clues to show you understand the meaning of the word.)

_____

_____

Meiosis[14]

*mei|o|sis¹ (mī ō′sis), *n., pl.* **-ses** (-sēz). **1** *Biology.* the process by which the number of chromosomes in reproductive cells of sexually reproducing organisms is reduced to half the original number, resulting in the production of gametes or spores; reduction division. Meiosis consists essentially of two cell divisions. In the first, the homologous chromosomes separate equally into the two new cells so that each contains the haploid number, or half the diploid number. In the second cell division, the pairs of chromosomes split, one of each kind of chromosome going to the four new cells. Thus each new cell again contains the haploid number of chromosomes. See picture below. **2** = litotes. Also, **miosis**. [< New Latin *meiosis* < Greek *meiōsis* a lessening < *meioûn* lessen < *meíōn* less]

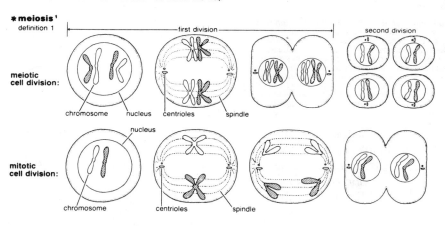

1. Select any characteristic of *meiosis*.
   _____ a. has two cell-division stages
   _____ b. occurs in sexually reproducing organisms
   _____ c. end result is two identical cells
   _____ d. end result is cells with haploid number of chromosomes

2. The etymology of *meiosis* shows that it comes from the Greek *meiosis* (a lessening) and *melon* (less). Use this information, your background knowledge, and your imagination to match the following:

_____ a. mince   aa. a number from which another is to be sub-
tracted

_____ b. diminish   bb. smaller, less important; lesser

_____ c. minuend   cc. to cut or chop up into very small pieces

_____ d. minor   dd. to make smaller in size or amount; lessen;
reduce

3. Complete the verbal analogy.
   location : place :: *meiosis* : _____
   a. diploid number   c. reproductive cells
   b. reduction division   d. chromosome pairs

4. Write a sentence correctly using *meiosis*. (Be sure to include context clues to show you understand the meaning of the word.)

   _____

   _____

5. How many cells are produced as the end product of cell *meiosis*? _____ How many are produced as the end product of mitosis? _____ Check the drawing supplied with the definition, if necessary.

Metabolism[10]

me|tab|o|lism (mə tab′ə liz əm), *n.* **1** the process by which all living things turn food into energy and living tissue. In metabolism food is broken down to produce energy, which is then used by the body to build up new cells and tissues, provide heat, and engage in physical activity. Growth and action depend on metabolism. *Only living matter is able to carry on metabolism* (A. M. Winchester). **2** the metamorphosis of an insect. [< Greek *metabolē* change + English *-ism*]

1. In which of the following sentences can *metabolism* be correctly placed in the blank?

   _____ a. _____ provides another method for studying photosynthesis.

   _____ b. The part of the earth where life exists is called

   _____ .

   _____ c. _____ is simply the sum total of all of the chemical activities of a living system.

   _____ d. The heart and lungs are important in maintaining the high rate of _____ of both birds and mammals.

2. Select the characteristics of *metabolism*.

   _____ a. energy production   _____ c. cell division

   _____ b. genetic change   _____ d. food conversion

3. The etymology of *metabolism* shows that the word comes from the Greek *metabole* (change). Use this information, your background knowledge, and your imagination to match the following:

—— a. catabolism   aa. brief story used to teach some moral lesson or truth

—— b. parole   bb. exaggerated statement used for effect and not meant to be taken literally

—— c. parable   cc. conference, or talk, to discuss terms or matters in dispute

—— d. hyperbole   dd. process of breaking down living tissues into simpler substances or waste matter, thereby producing energy

—— e. parley   ee. conditional release from prison before the full term is served

4. How can you characterize your own personal rate of *metabolism?* Fast? Slow? Why do you think so?

_____

_____

5. Write a sentence correctly using *metabolism.* (Be sure to include context clues to show you understand the meaning of the word.)

_____

_____

Mitosis[11]

mi|to|sis (mi tō′sis, mī-), *n. Biology.* the process by which a cell of a plant or animal divides to form two new cells, each containing the same number of chromosomes as the original cell; cell division. Mitosis is typically divided into four stages: *prophase,* in which the chromatin of the nucleus forms into a thread that separates into segments or chromosomes, each of which in turn separates longitudinally into two parts; *metaphase,* in which the nuclear membrane disappears and the chromosomes line up near the middle of the cell; *anaphase,* in which one chromosome of each pair moves toward each end of the cell; and *telophase,* in which the chromosomes lose their threadlike shape and again become chromatin, two new nuclear membranes form around the chromatin, and the cytoplasm draws together in the middle, divides, and two new cells exist. [< New Latin *mitosis* < Greek *mitos* thread + English *-osis*]

1. Complete the verbal analogy.
   bacterium : tiny organism :: *mitosis* : _____
   a. alteration   c. cell division
   b. environmental changes   d. gradual development

2. If an original cell has four chromosomes, how many does each of the new cells created during *mitosis* have?
   —— a. two   —— c. six
   —— b. four   —— d. eight

3. In which of the following sentences can *mitosis* be correctly placed in the blank?
   —— a. Darwin's theory of _____ was concerned with hereditary changes.

_____ b. In _____ the nuclear membrane breaks down, and after the chromosomes are divided equally, two new nuclei are formed.

_____ c. The conversion of light into energy is the result of _____.

_____ d. _____ is the means or process by which organisms grow.

4. Write a sentence correctly using *mitosis*. (Be sure to include context clues to show you understand the meaning of the word.)

_____

_____

5. What are the four stages of *mitosis?* (Consult the dictionary entry if necessary.)

_____

_____

Organelle[4]

or|gan|elle (ôr′gə nel′), *n. Biology.* a minute specialized part of a cell, such as a vacuole in protozoans, analogous in function to an organ of higher animals.

1. Complete the verbal analogy.
   membrane : layer of animal tissue : *organelle* : _____
   a. chromosomes   c. fatty acid hormone
   b. organic substance   d. specialized structure

2. Which of the following are some functions of an *organelle?*
   _____ a. create mutations
   _____ b. make enzymes and other proteins
   _____ c. produce bacteria
   _____ d. provide energy for the cell's activities

3. In which of the following sentences is *organelle* correctly used?
   _____ a. An organelle provides energy for the cell's activities and makes enzymes and other proteins.
   _____ b. At the time of cell division, the organelle changes its appearance.
   _____ c. An organelle is the means by which an organism obtains the oxygen required by its cells and rids itself of carbon dioxide.
   _____ d. In an organelle, energy-rich molecules using oxygen are broken down and provide the energy for the cell's activities.

4. Write a sentence correctly using *organelle*. (Be sure to include context clues to show you understand the meaning of the word.)

_____

_____

5. What organ in the human body do you think is comparable to an *organelle?* Explain.

_____

_____

Osmosis[8]

os|mo|sis (oz mō′sis, os-), *n.* **1** the tendency of two fluids of different strengths that are separated by something porous to go through it and become mixed. Osmosis is the chief means by which the body absorbs food and by which fluid in the tissues moves into the blood vessels. Osmosis is specifically the tendency of a fluid of lower concentration to pass through a semipermeable membrane into a solution of higher concentration. **2** *Chemistry.* the diffusion or spreading of fluids through a membrane or partition till they are mixed. **3** *Figurative.* a gradual, often unconscious, absorbing or understanding of facts, theories, ideas, and the like: *to learn French by osmosis. A hilarious round of sport and pleasure which could only be described as the broadest education by osmosis* (Harper's). [Grecized variant (as in *endosmosis*) of *osmose* < French < Greek *ōsmós* a thrust]

1. Which of the numbered dictionary definitions of *osmosis* best fits the word's use in the reading selection? _____

2. If a friend said he received his education through *osmosis,* he meant that he
   _____ a. paid for it.   _____ c. used telecommunication.
   _____ b. studied diligently.   _____ d. unconsciously learned.

3. Select a synonym for *osmosis.*
   _____ a. modification   _____ c. reduction
   _____ b. mixture   _____ d. differentiation

4. Describe a function or activity in the body that is accomplished through *osmosis.* (See the dictionary entry if necessary.)

_____

_____

5. Write a sentence correctly using *osmosis.* (Be sure to include context clues to show you understand the meaning of the word.)

_____

_____

Permeable[3]

per|me|a|ble (pèr′mē ə bəl), *adj.* that can be permeated; allowing the passage or diffusion of liquids or gases through it: *permeable cell walls. A sponge is permeable by water.* **syn:** pervious. [< Latin *permeābilis* < *permeāre;* see etym. under **permeate**] —**per′me|a|ble|ness,** *n.* —**per′me|a|bly,** *adv.*

1. In which of the following sentences can *permeable* correctly be placed in the blank?
   _____ a. A balloon is made of material that is _____ by gases.

_____ b. Most cotton cloth is _____ by water.

_____ c. _____ cells permit the passage of some liquids.

_____ d. A _____ cell wall would block the passage of gases and liquids.

2. Check any one of the following that is *permeable* to liquids.

_____ a. overcoat   _____ c. silk dress   _____ e. necktie

_____ b. rubber boots   _____ d. bathing suit   _____ f. denim trousers

3. Which statement below matches the following sentence?

"The plasma membrane of a cell is *permeable* to ions, water, and other molecules."

_____ a. The plasma membrane of a cell has openings so molecules can enter.

_____ b. The membrane of a cell permits only gases to pass through it.

_____ c. Ions, water, and other molecules are permeable by cell membranes.

_____ d. Several kinds of molecules can pass through the plasma membrane of a cell.

4. If you put an uncapped pen in the pocket of your shirt or blouse, you will discover that the material is _____ by ink. (You do not need to try this in order to fill in the blank correctly!)

5. Write a sentence correctly using *permeable*. (Be sure to include context clues to show you understand the meaning of the word.)

_____

_____

Photosynthesis[7]

pho|to|syn|the|sis (fō'tə sin'thə sis), *n.* **1** the process by which plant cells make carbohydrates from carbon dioxide and water in the presence of chlorophyll and light, and release oxygen as a by-product: *Photosynthesis, called by some the most important chemical reaction occurring in nature, takes place only in plants containing certain pigments, principally chlorophyll* (Harbaugh and Goodrich). **2** the process by which chemical compounds are synthesized by means of light or other forms of radiant energy.

1. In which of the following sentences is *photosynthesis* used correctly?

_____ a. Bacteria reproduce using the process of photosynthesis.

_____ b. The sun obtains its energy from photosynthesis.

_____ c. Chlorophyll is a key compound in the process of photosynthesis.

_____ d. A by-product of photosynthesis is the release of oxygen.

2. Which of the following derive energy from the process of *photosynthesis*?

_____ a. animals   _____ c. humans

_____ b. green plants   _____ d. algae

3. What is a by-product of *photosynthesis?*

_____ a. cell division　　_____ c. carbon dioxide
_____ b. carbohydrates　　_____ d. oxygen

4. Write a sentence correctly using *photosynthesis.* (Be sure to include context clues to show you understand the meaning of the word.)

_____

_____

5. Why is *photosynthesis* so important? What do you think is the relationship of *photosynthesis* to the food chain?

_____

_____

Procaryote[1]

pro|car|y|ote (prō kar′ē ōt), *n.* a cell or organism without a visible nucleus or nuclei: *Procaryotes were found in the Beck Spring Dolomite in association with the primitive eucaryotes* (Scientific American). Also, **prokaryote.** [< *pro-*[2] + Greek *káryon* nut, kernel]

1. In which of the following sentences can *procaryote* correctly be placed in the blank?

_____ a. The process by which _____(s) divide is called mitosis.

_____ b. Most _____(s) are small, single-celled organisms.

_____ c. A _____ has a membrane that is permeable by several ions.

_____ d. Most plant cells are _____(s).

2. Check any characteristic of a *procaryote.*

_____ a. plasma membrane　　_____ c. organelles
_____ b. plastids　　_____ d. genetic information

3. Check any statement below that closely matches the following sentence: "The genetic material of a *procaryotic* cell is concentrated in a region called the nucleoid, but no membrane separates it from the rest of the cell."

_____ a. Genetic material in a procaryote is found throughout the nucleus.

_____ b. In addition to a nucleus, the procaryotic cell has a nucleoid region.

_____ c. The membrane separating the genetic material of a procaryote from the rest of the cell is called a nucleoid.

_____ d. The DNA of a procaryote is in a special region but not in the nucleus.

4. Write a sentence correctly using *procaryote*. (Be sure to use context clues to show you understand the meaning of the word.)

_____

_____

5. Bacteria are *procaryotes*. Write one thing that bacteria do. (If you know of none, consult the reading selection.) _____

Symbiosis[15]

sym|bi|o|sis (sim′bī ō′sis, -bē-), *n., pl.* **-ses** (-sēz). **1** *Biology.* **a** the association or living together of two unlike organisms for the benefit of each other. Symbiosis is the opposite of *parasitism,* in which one organism feeds on the body of the other. Most lichens, which are composed of an alga and a fungus, are examples of symbiosis; the alga provides the food, and the fungus provides water and protection. *Symbiosis covers those associations where neither is harmed, and* one or both benefit (David Park). **b** any association or living together of two unlike organisms, as in commensalism or parasitism. **2** *Figurative.* a mutually beneficial relationship: *Newsmen support the committees because the committees feed the newsmen: they live together in happy symbiosis* (Daniel J. Boorstin). [< New Latin *symbiosis* < Greek *symbíōsis* < *symbioûn* live together < *sýmbios* (one) living together (with another); partner < *syn-* together + *bios* life]

(Note: Some biologists refer to any "living together" relationship between unlike organisms as *symbiosis*. If both organisms profit, it is called a *mutualism;* if one profits and the other loses more than it gains, it is termed *parasitism;* if one gains and the other is unaffected, it is a *commensalism*.)

1. Check any appropriate response to the following statement: "Horticulturalists have long been aware of the *symbiosis* between pine trees and fungi."
   _____ a. They grow better if they are kept apart.
   _____ b. Pine trees are both beautiful and useful.
   _____ c. They are more successful together than they are separately.
   _____ d. Probably the best-known fungi are mushrooms.

2. In which of the following sentences can *symbiosis* correctly be placed in the blank?
   _____ a. There is _____ between some plants and some bacteria.
   _____ b. The relationship between flowering plants and insects that pollinate them is a _____.
   _____ c. There is _____ between dogs and cats.
   _____ d. The relationship between humans and some animals is _____.

3. The etymology of *symbiosis* shows that it comes from the Greek *syn* (together) and *bios* (life). Use that information, your imagination, and your background knowledge to match the following:
   _____ a. aerobe   aa. minute life form; microorganism
   _____ b. antibiotic   bb. requires oxygen to live
   _____ c. biographer   cc. inhibits growth of microorganisms
   _____ d. biology   dd. writes a life story
   _____ e. microbe   ee. science of life and life processes

4. You have *symbioses* with many other organisms, especially if you consider dictionary definitions 1 and 2. Who is your favorite symbiont (partner in *symbiosis*)? _____

5. Write a sentence correctly using *symbiosis*. (Be sure to use context clues to show you understand the meaning of the word.)

_____

_____

ANSWERS TO CHAPTER 8 EXERCISES

Chloroplast: 1. c 2. b, d 3. ff, ee, dd, aa, cc, bb
Chromosome: 1. a, d, e 2. a, c, d 3. a (location)
Cytokinesis: 1. a, b 2. b (definition) 3. d
Cytoplasm: 1. c 2. a 3. b, d
Diffusion: 1. 3a 2. b, d 3. c
Eucaryote: 1. c 2. b 3. a, d
Meiosis: 1. a, b, d 2. cc, dd, aa, bb 3. b (synonym)
Metabolism: 1. c, d 2. a, d 3. dd, ee, aa, bb, cc
Mitosis: 1. c (definition) 2. b 3. b, d
Organelle: 1. d (definition) 2. b, d 3. a, d
Osmosis: 1. 1 2. d 3. b
Permeable: 1. b, c 2. a, c, d, e, f 3. d
Photosynthesis: 1. c, d 2. b, d 3. d
Procaryote: 1. b, c 2. a, d 3. d
Symbiosis: 1. c 2. a, b, d 3. bb, cc, dd, ee, aa

BIOLOGY POSTTEST

Fill in the blanks with the words from this list.

chloroplast	eucaryote	osmosis
chromosome	meiosis	permeable
cytokinesis	metabolism	photosynthesis
cytoplasm	mitosis	procaryote
diffusion	organelle	symbiosis

1. Having a visible nucleus is a characteristic of a(n) _____.

2. The mixture of two fluids by passing through a membrane is a description of _____.

3. _____ literally means "living together."

4. A(n) _____ contains chlorophyll.

5. If liquids or gases can pass through it, a substance is _____.

6. A(n) _____ cell lacks a visible nucleus or nuclei.

7. _____(s) carry the genes that determine heredity.

8. The change occurring in the cytoplasm of a cell is called

_____.

9. _____ is the living substance of a cell, outside of the nucleus.

10. The process by which plant cells make carbohydrates from carbon dioxide and water in the presence of chlorophyll and light and release oxygen as a by-product is called _____.

11. Cell division is known as _____.

12. _____ includes the process by which all living things turn food into energy and living tissue.

13. The process that reduces chromosome number is _____.

14. A specialized cell part is called a(n) _____.

15. Spreading or scattering widely is a characteristic of the process of _____.

   Answers to this posttest are in the Instructor's Manual.
   If you missed any of the words, you may need to return to the exercises and to the dictionary entries to see why your concepts for some words are incomplete.

CHAPTER NINE

SCIENCES: CHEMISTRY

◆

OVERVIEW

Chemistry deals with the characteristics of simple substances (elements), the changes that take place when they combine to form other substances, and the laws of their behavior under various conditions. Research in chemistry has led to many advances in modern life through improvements in agriculture, drugs and medicines, the management of energy, and the production of consumer goods.

Four common fields of specialization in chemistry are analytical, inorganic, organic, and physical chemistry. Some specific course emphases include agricultural chemistry, biochemistry, clinical chemistry, forensic chemistry, and spectroscopy.

Students who receive degrees in chemistry can pursue careers in a variety of fields, including food processing, secondary education, technical sales, chemical patent law, forensic sciences, and environmental law. An emphasis in biochemistry is useful for students preparing for admission to the health professions—dentistry, medicine, pharmacology, or veterinary medicine. An emphasis on biochemistry is also valuable for students interested in graduate work in molecular biology, medical technology, or clinical chemistry.

Introductory chemistry textbooks are a combination of expository and process analysis. They explain broad concepts or generalizations, and there may be examples and illustrations in the form of charts, diagrams, and tables. Lab manuals are presented in an instructional format, with procedures for experiments and chemical analyses.

The vocabulary in chemistry usually consists of specialized terminology to represent substances, reactions, procedures, and so on and includes such terms as distillation, solvent, *and* induction.

VOCABULARY SELF-EVALUATION

The following words will be introduced in this reading selection. Place a check mark (√) in front of any that you know thoroughly and use in your speech and writing. Place a question mark (?) in front of any that you recognize but do not use yourself.

_____ alchemy	_____ equilibrium	_____ miscible
_____ amorphous	_____ evaporation	_____ solute
_____ aqueous	_____ induction	_____ solvent
_____ condensation	_____ kinetic	_____ sublimation
_____ distillation	_____ liquefaction	_____ viscosity

SOME PHYSICAL PROPERTIES OF MATTER

Chemistry is the branch of science that deals with the nature and composition of matter and the changes that matter undergoes. Although it has been a science in the modern sense for only two or three hundred years, historians generally agree that man's earliest involvement with changes in the composition of matter occurred when primitive man discovered fire and was thus able to change wood to gas and ash. Using fire, man was able to turn soil into pottery, to extract metals from soil, and to combine metals by smelting.

In the Middle Ages, the study of metals and their ability to combine became the "science" of alchemy.[1] The alchemist, observing the seemingly magical ability of metals to combine and change, became

overly ambitious. He hoped to solve many problems of health and nature, to create gold and silver from base metals, and to produce precious stones from glass or quartz.

THE STUDY OF GASES

However, by the seventeenth century, scientists were better able to understand the physical properties of matter. Using a reasoning process called induction,[2] they collected evidence from specific cases and formed general rules. Evidence concerning odor, color, melting point, boiling point, and state (solid, liquid, or gas) could be observed without changing one substance to another substance. A number of discoveries were made through the study of gases, which could be easily and cheaply produced in the laboratory. Their weights and volumes could be measured with simple equipment, and because many gases are elements, the simplest form of matter, accurate general rules could be formed. Some of these "gas scientists" believed that matter was made up of tiny particles called atoms, even though the particles could not be seen. By experiment the scientists were able to determine that gas will expand to occupy any container into which it is placed and, unless contained, will escape into the atmosphere. Gas has both potential and kinetic[3] energy. (Energy is defined as the capacity or the ability to do work.) Both pressure and temperature affect the volume of gas. (Think, for example, of a balloon full of air. We can change the amount of space the air occupies by heating, cooling, or compressing the balloon.) When a gas is cooled to a specific temperature and compressed by a specific amount of pressure, it undergoes liquefaction.[4] The combination of temperature and pressure needed to produce this state differs according to the substances that make up the gas.

THE LIQUID STATE

Early studies of liquids revealed that some mix completely with others. These are said to be highly miscible.[5] (Liquids that will not mix are immiscible.) Liquids will also dissolve some solids. For example, water will dissolve salt. In such an aqueous[6] solution, the salt is called the solute[7] and the water is called the solvent.[8] Solutions have special properties. They do not "settle out," they can be filtered without being changed, and the solute is evenly distributed in the solvent. In our saltwater solution, for instance, the salt does not settle out of the water, it cannot be filtered out, and the water is as salty at the top of the container as it is at the bottom. The salt can be separated from the water again using a procedure called distillation.[9] If the molecules in a liquid have enough kinetic energy, they escape the attractive forces of the other liquid molecules and become gas, a process called evaporation.[10] The reverse of this process, called condensation,[11] occurs when the gas molecules return to the liquid state. When the number of molecules changing from liquid to gas is equal to the number of molecules changing from gas to liquid, a state of equilibrium[12] exists. Most substances change state in a progression from gas, to liquid, to solid, or the reverse: from solid, to liquid, to gas. In some cases, however, solid substances go directly from the solid state to the gaseous state without becoming a liquid, a process called sublimation.[13] Dry ice, which is solid carbon dioxide, is an example of a solid that sublimates.

Another observable characteristic of a liquid is its resistance to flow, or its viscosity.[14] Oil is more viscous than water, water more viscous than gasoline. We now know that viscosity is determined by differences in the attractions between molecules in the particular liquid.

THE SOLID STATE

Changes in solids could also be observed by early scientists, but there was no way to determine the reason for these changes. Later studies showed that solids exist in two principle types. One is the crystalline solid in which the molecules or atoms are in an ordered arrangement called a crystalline lattice. The second is an amorphous[15] solid in which the molecules or atoms are clumped together in a disordered fashion. A snowflake (a water crystal) is an example of a crystalline solid; common window glass is an example of an amorphous solid.

The changes discussed above are physical changes and do not involve changes in the molecules of the substances. If the molecules were to change—if, for instance, the water changed into its elements of hydrogen and oxygen—this would be a chemical change. Important to the understanding of both kinds of change is knowledge of atomic theory. Modern chemists know a great deal about the atom, the basic building block of nature, and about its composition, how it exists in elements and compounds, and how it undergoes changes. This knowledge has made modern living more comfortable through improvements in agricultural productivity, advances in drugs and medicines, the management of energy, and the production of an ever-wider variety of consumer goods. It is safe to say that the chemistry of today is as important to modern life as fire was to early man. ◆

CHEMISTRY PRETEST

Select words from this list and write them in the blanks to complete the sentences.

alchemy	equilibrium	miscible
amorphous	evaporation	solute
aqueous	induction	solvent
condensation	kinetic	sublimation
distillation	liquefaction	viscosity

1. Something ＿＿＿＿＿＿ is made with water.
2. Reasoning from particular to general is called ＿＿＿＿＿＿.
3. Water and oil are not ＿＿＿＿＿＿.
4. The highest stage of something is ＿＿＿＿＿＿.
5. A(n) ＿＿＿＿＿＿ is dissolved in a liquid.
6. The science of the Middle Ages was ＿＿＿＿＿＿.
7. The process of changing a vapor to liquid is ＿＿＿＿＿＿.
8. In ＿＿＿＿＿＿, opposing forces exactly balance.
9. Resistance of fluid to the motion of molecules is ＿＿＿＿＿＿.
10. ＿＿＿＿＿＿ means "able to dissolve."
11. Something uncrystallized is ＿＿＿＿＿＿.
12. ＿＿＿＿＿＿ has to do with motion.
13. Applying pressure and cooling to a gas results in ＿＿＿＿＿＿.
14. Changing a liquid into vapor is ＿＿＿＿＿＿.
15. ＿＿＿＿＿＿ is a process of refinement.

Answers to this pretest are in Appendix B.
   Unless your instructor tells you to do otherwise, complete the exercises for each word you missed on the pretest. The words, with their meanings and exercises, are in alphabetical order. The superscript numbers indicate

where the words appeared in the reading selection so that you can refer to them when necessary. There are several types of exercises, but for each word you will be asked to write a sentence using context clues. (See Chapter 4 if you need information about how to create context clues.) You are also asked to perform some activity that will help you make your concept of the word personal. *Complete this activity thoughtfully, for creating a personalized concept of the word will help you remember it in the future.*

Answers to all the exercises are at the end of the exercise segment.

CHEMISTRY EXERCISES

Alchemy[1]

al|che|my (al′kə mē), *n.* **1** a combination of chemistry, magic, and philosophy, studied in the Middle Ages. Alchemy tried to find or prepare a substance which would turn cheaper metals into gold and silver and which would also cure any ailment and prolong human life. *In its fullest sense alchemy was a philosophical system containing a complex and mobile core of rudimentary science and elaborated with astrology, religion, mysticism, magic, theosophy and many other constituents. Alchemy dealt not only with the* mysteries of matter but also with those of creation and life; it sought to harmonize the human individual with the universe surrounding him (Scientific American). **2** *Figurative.* a magical or mysterious power or process of transforming one thing into another: *the lovely alchemy of spring.* [< Old French *alkemie,* learned borrowing from Medieval Latin *alchimia* < Arabic *alkīmiyā′* < Late Greek *chymeiā* art of alloying metals < Greek *chȳma* ingot < *cheîn* pour]

1. In which of the following sentences can *alchemy* correctly be placed in the blank?

   _____ a. Someone who believed in the promises of _____ might be cheated.

   _____ b. _____ is a modern science.

   _____ c. The solution to many of life's problems can be solved by _____ .

   _____ d. _____ was related to magic.

2. If you practiced *alchemy* during the Middle Ages

   _____ a. you might be honest but mistaken.

   _____ b. you might be trying to cheat people.

   _____ c. you might conduct careful "experiments."

   _____ d. you might have understood atomic theory.

3. Which of the numbered dictionary definitions of *alchemy* best fits the word's use in the reading selection? _____

4. Write a sentence correctly using *alchemy.* (Be sure to include context clues to show you understand the meaning of the word.)

   _____

   _____

   _____

SCIENCES: CHEMISTRY

5. Why do you think people might believe in *alchemy?*

_____

_____

Amorphous[15]

a|mor|phous (ə môr′fəs), *adj.* **1a** having no definite form; shapeless; formless: *The ghost was an amorphous being that drifted with mist.* **b** *Biology.* without the definite shape or organization found in most higher animals or plants: *An ameba is amorphous.* **c** *Geology.* occurring in a continuous mass, without stratification or cleavage. **2** of no particular type or pattern; anomalous; unclassifiable. **3** not consisting of crystals; uncrystallized; noncrystalline: *Glass is amorphous; sugar is crystalline.* [< Greek *ámorphos* (with English *-ous*) < *a-* without + *morphē* shape] — a|mor′phous|ly, *adv.* — a|mor′phous|ness, *n.*

1. Place an "s" by any synonym of *amorphous.*
   - _____ a. crystalline   _____ d. uncrystallized
   - _____ b. formless   _____ e. shapeless
   - _____ c. anomalous   _____ f. shaped

2. Which of the following would be *amorphous?*
   - _____ a. a cloud   _____ d. smoke
   - _____ b. an ameba (amoeba)   _____ e. sugar
   - _____ c. a snowflake   _____ f. glass

3. Which of the numbered and lettered dictionary definitions of *amorphous* best fits its use in the reading selection? _____

4. Unless you have special equipment, you cannot see *amorphous* matter in the sense that a chemist uses the word. You do, however, see objects that are *amorphous.* When you say the word, what do you think of?

_____

_____

5. Write a sentence correctly using *amorphous.* (Be sure to include context clues to show you understand the meaning of the word.)

_____

_____

Aqueous[6]

a|que|ous (ā′kwē əs, ak′wē-), *adj.* **1** of water: *aqueous vapor.* **2** containing water; made with water: *The druggist put the medicine in an aqueous solution.* **3** like water; watery: *Aqueous matter ran from the sore.* **4** produced by the action of water. Aqueous rocks are formed of the sediment carried and deposited by water. —a′que-ous|ly, *adv.* —a′que|ous|ness, *n.*

1. Check any appropriate response to the following statement:
   "An *aqueous* solution may contain many dissolved substances."
   _____ a. That helps to explain how water can become polluted.
   _____ b. That's because it is an acid.
   _____ c. Stirring will remove the substances.
   _____ d. Water solutions are very common.

2. Complete the verbal analogy.
   aqueousness : *aqueous* :: _____ : _____
   a. adj. : n.   c. n. : v.
   b. adv. : adj.   d. n. : adj.

3. Which of the numbered dictionary definitions of *aqueous* best fits the word's use in the reading selection? _____

4. Write a sentence correctly using *aqueous*. (Be sure to include context clues to show you understand the meaning of the word.)

   _____

   _____

5. What is your favorite *aqueous* solution?

   _____

   _____

Condensation[11]

con|den|sa|tion (kon′den sā′shən), *n.* **1** the act of condensing: (*Figurative.*) *He* [*Goldsmith*] *was a great and perhaps unequalled master of the arts of selection and condensation* (Macaulay). **2** the state of being condensed. **3** a condensed mass. *A cloud is a condensation of water vapor in the atmosphere.* **4** the act or process of changing a gas or vapor into a liquid by cooling: *the condensation of steam into water. Condensation begins first on solid surfaces because these get colder than the general mass of air* (Thomas A. Blair). **5** *Chemistry.* a reaction in which two or more molecules unite to form a larger, more dense, and more complex molecule, often with the separation of water or some other simple substance: *the condensation of milk by removing most of the water from it.* **6** *Physics.* **a** an increase in density and pressure in a medium, such as air, due to the passing of a sound wave or other compression wave. **b** the region in which this occurs. **7** *Psychoanalysis.* the process by which images characterized by a common effect are grouped so as to form a single or composite image, as in dreams.

con|dense (kən dens′), *v.,* **-densed, -dens|ing.** —*v.t.* **1** to make denser or more compact. **SYN:** compress, contract. **2** to increase the strength of; concentrate: *Light is condensed by means of lenses.* **3** *Figurative.* to put into fewer words; say briefly: *A long story can sometimes be condensed into a few sentences.* **SYN:** reduce, shorten. **4** to change (a gas or vapor) to a liquid. **5** *Chemistry.* to cause to undergo condensation: *Milk is condensed by removing much of the water from it.* —*v.i.* **1** to become denser or more compact: *Each* [*theory*] *starts from the notion that stars condense from the matter scattered thinly through interstellar space* (W. H. Marshall). **2** to change from a gas or vapor to a liquid. *If steam touches cold surfaces, it condenses into water. If it is cloudy, rainy, or foggy, the water vapor in the air is condensing* (Beauchamp, Mayfield, and West). **3** *Chemistry.* to undergo condensation. [< Latin *condēnsāre* < *com-* together + *dēnsus* thick] —**con|den′sa|ble, con|den′si|ble,** *adj.*

1. In which of the following sentences can *condensation* correctly be placed in the blank?
   _____ a. Sometimes a magazine will print the _____ of a novel.

_____ b. Vapor can change to liquid in the process of
_____ .

_____ c. Joe is not very tall; he is the _____ of his father.

_____ d. Canned milk is a _____ of regular milk.

2. Which of the following might undergo *condensation?*

_____ a. a gas   _____ d. a person

_____ b. a book   _____ e. a liquid

_____ c. an idea   _____ f. air

3. Which of the numbered and lettered dictionary definitions of *condensation* best fits the word's use in the reading selection? _____

4. You probably observe the result of *condensation* regularly. Can you say where? (Perhaps on the outside of a cold bottle or can of pop or beer.)

_____

_____

5. Write a sentence correctly using *condensation.* (Be sure to include context clues to show you understand the meaning of the word.)

_____

_____

Distillation[9]

✱**dis|til|la|tion** (dis'tə lā'shən), *n.* **1** the act of distilling: *the distillation of water to purify it.* (*Figurative.*) Ordinarily, decisions which must be made when life and death are at stake require a profundity of reflection, a weighing of factors, and the eventual distillation of a choice (Atlantic). **2** the process of distilling; heating a liquid or solid in a retort, still, etc., and condensing the vapor given off by cooling it in order to purify and condense the thing heated: *Distillation is important both in the laboratory and in industry* (William N. Jones). **3** something distilled; extract; the refined or concentrated essence: (*Figurative.*) "Lover Man," written in 1941, [is] recorded by him for the first time on this disk with a simple, direct persuasiveness that can only be the distillation of 25 years of playing it in every conceivable fashion (New York Times).

dis|till (dis til'), *v.,* -tilled, -till|ing. — *v.t.* **1** to make (a liquid or other substance) pure by turning it into a vapor and then cooling it into a liquid form again: *to distill water for drinking.* **2** to obtain by distilling; refine: *Gasoline is distilled from crude oil. Alcoholic liquor is distilled from mash made from grain.* **3** *Figurative.* to get out the essential principle; extract: *A jury must distill the truth from the testimony of witnesses.* **4** to give off in drops: *These flowers distill a sweet nectar.* SYN: exude. **5** to let fall in drops: *The sky distills the dew.* — *v.i.* **1** to fall in drops; drip; trickle: *Tears distilled slowly from her eyes.* **2** to undergo distillation. [< Late Latin *distīllāre,* for *dēstīllāre* < Latin *dē-* down + *stīlla* drop]

1. Which of the following might be the result of *distillation?*

_____ a. a sandy beach   _____ c. perfume

_____ b. purified water   _____ d. liquor

2. Complete the verbal analogy.

fire : warmth :: *distillation* : _____

a. purification   c. heat

b. process   d. chemistry

3. Which of the numbered dictionary definitions of *distillation* best fits the word's use in the reading selection? _____

4. Write a sentence correctly using *distillation*. (Be sure to include context clues to show you understand the meaning of the word.)

_____

_____

5. The *distillation* of seawater for drinking purposes is possible. Do you think it should be widely practiced?

_____

_____

Equilibrium[12]

e|qui|lib|ri|um (ē′kwə lib′rē əm), *n., pl.* **-ri|ums, -ri|a** (-rē ə). **1** balance; condition in which opposing forces exactly balance or equal each other: *The acrobat in the circus maintained equilibrium on a tightrope. Scales are in equilibrium when the weights on each side are equal.* **2** the state of a chemical system when no further change occurs in it. **3** *Figurative.* balance between powers of any kind; equality of importance or effect among the various parts of any complex unity: *After a time which varies from a few to many years an equilibrium is established between parasite and host, so that both continue to survive* (Fenner and Day). **4** mental poise: *My mother does not let quarrels between my brother and me upset her equilibrium.* sʏɴ: stability. [< Latin *aequilībrium* < *aequus* equal + *lībra* balance]

1. In which of the following sentences can *equilibrium* correctly be placed in the blank?
   _____ a. In chemical _____, the rates of reaction between two solutions are the same.
   _____ b. I admire Mary's emotional _____.
   _____ c. _____ appears to be the absence of change.
   _____ d. In chemical _____, there is no movement of molecules.

2. Which of the following describe *equilibrium?*
   _____ a. unchanging   _____ d. balanced
   _____ b. stable   _____ e. unstable
   _____ c. equality   _____ f. varied

3. Which of the numbered dictionary definitions of *equilibrium* best fits the word's use in the reading selection? _____

4. Have you achieved a state of mental *equilibrium?* How? If not, how might you achieve it?

_____

_____

5. Write a sentence correctly using *equilibrium*. (Be sure to include context clues to show you understand the meaning of the word.)

_____

_____

Evaporation[10]

e|vap|o|ra|tion (i vap′ə rā′shən), *n.* **1** the act or process of changing a liquid or a solid into vapor; an evaporating: *Wet clothes on a line become dry by evaporation of the water in them.* **2** the state of being changed into vapor. **3** the removal of water or other liquid. **4a** the product of the evaporating process. **b** the amount evaporated. **5** *Figurative.* disappearance.
e|vap|o|rate (i vap′ə rāt), *v.,* **-rat|ed, -rat|ing.**
— *v.i.* **1** to turn into vapor; change from a liquid or solid into a vapor: *Boiling water evaporates rapidly. Some solids, such as moth balls and dry* ice, *evaporate without melting.* **syn:** volatilize, vaporize. **2** to give off moisture. **3** *Figurative.* to vanish; disappear: *His good resolutions evaporated after New Year.* **syn:** dissipate.
— *v.t.* **1** to remove water or other liquid from, for example by heat, in order to dry or to reduce to a more concentrated state: *Heat is used to evaporate milk.* **2** to cause to change from a liquid (or less often, solid) into a vapor; drive off in the form of vapor: *Heat evaporates water.*
[< Latin *ēvapōrāre* (with English *-ate*[1]) < *ex-* out + *vapor* vapor, steam]

1. Check any appropriate response to the following statement:
   "During *evaporation,* molecules escape from a liquid."
   _____ a. They become a gas.
   _____ b. You have to pour them out of the container.
   _____ c. It is the chemical opposite of condensation.
   _____ d. The rate of evaporation can change with temperature.

2. Complete the verbal analogy.
   fishing : fish :: *evaporation* : _____
   a. change   c. liquid
   b. vapor   d. vanish

3. Which of the numbered and lettered dictionary definitions of *evaporation* best fits the word's use in the reading selection? _____

4. Write a sentence correctly using *evaporation*. (Be sure to include context clues to show you understand the meaning of the word.)

   _____

   _____

5. Are you aware of experiencing the process of *evaporation?* Describe the way your body is cooled in hot weather. Think about it the next time you perspire.

   _____

   _____

Induction[2]

in|duc|tion (in duk′shən), *n.* **1a** the process by which an object having electrical or magnetic properties produces similar properties in a nearby object, usually without direct contact; inductance: *Induction can give a conductor a permanent charge ... until it leaks off or is otherwise dissipated* (Scientific American). **b** a tendency exhibited by currents of electricity to resist change. **2a** reasoning from particular facts to a general rule or principle. **b** a conclusion reached in this way: *Every induction is a speculation and it guesses at a unity which the facts present but do not strictly imply* (J. Bronowski). **3a** the act of inducting; act or ceremony of installing a person in office; installation. **b** *U.S.* enrollment in military service. **4** the act of bringing into existence or operation; producing; causing; inducing: *induction of a hypnotic state.* **5** the taking of the explosive mixture or air into the cylinder of an internal-combustion engine. **6** *Embryology.* the change in form or shape caused by the action of one tissue of an embryo on adjacent tissues or parts. **7** *Archaic.* an introductory statement in a literary work; a preface or prelude.
► See **deduction** for usage note.

from **deduction:**

►**Deduction, induction** are names of opposite processes of reasoning, the two ways in which we think. *Deduction* applies to the process by which one starts with a general principle that is accepted as true, applies it to a particular case, and arrives at a conclusion that is true if the starting principle was true, as in *All female mammals secrete milk; this is a female mammal; therefore, this will secrete milk. Induction* applies to the process by which one collects many particular cases, finds out by experiment what is common to all of them, and forms a general rule or principle which is probably true, as in *Every female mammal I have tested secreted milk; probably all female mammals secrete milk.*

1. Check any appropriate response to the following statement:
"He solved the problem by using *induction*."
_____ a. Guesswork is sometimes the best way.
_____ b. He established a general rule first.
_____ c. He worked from individual items to a general rule.
_____ d. Do you mean it was a chance discovery?

2. Which of the following might be interested in *induction?*
_____ a. a waiter   _____ d. an army recruiter
_____ b. a hairdresser _____ e. a detective
_____ c. a hypnotist   _____ f. a mechanic

3. Which of the numbered and lettered dictionary definitions of *induction* best fits the word's use in the reading selection? _____

4. *Induction* and *deduction* as reasoning processes are often confused. (Sir Arthur Conan Doyle added to this confusion in one of his Sherlock Holmes stories, "The Sign of the Four," with a chapter called "The Science of Deduction." Many people conclude from this that crime detection is carried out by *deduction*, rather than *induction*.) Take this opportunity to clarify for yourself the concepts of and differences between the two.

_____

_____

5. Write a sentence correctly using *induction*. (Be sure to include context clues to show you understand the meaning of the word.)

_____

_____

Kinetic[3]

ki|net|ic (ki net′ik), *adj.* **1** of or having to do with motion. **2** caused by or resulting from motion. **3** of or having to do with kinetic art; involving motion or the suggestion of motion produced especially by mechanical parts, colors, and lights. [< Greek *kīnētikós* < *kīneîn* to move] — **ki|net′i|cal|ly,** *adv.*

1. Complete the verbal analogy.
   attempt : try :: *kinetic* : _____
   a. motion   c. process
   b. energy   d. chemistry

2. Check any appropriate response to the following statement:
"Tom is interested in *kinetic* theory."
_____ a. He is taking dance lessons.
_____ b. Perhaps he should run a restaurant.
_____ c. No wonder he is studying chemistry.
_____ d. Do you think he will run for political office?

3. Which of the numbered dictionary definitions of *kinetic* best fits the word's use in the reading selection? _____

4. Write a sentence correctly using *kinetic*. (Be sure to include context clues to show you understand the meaning of the word.)

_____

_____

5. The word *kinetic* comes from the same Greek root as *cinema*. Do you know how pictures appear to move?

_____

_____

Liquefaction[4]

liq|ue|fac|tion (lik′wə fak′shən), *n.* **1** the process of changing into a liquid, especially of changing a gas by the application of pressure and cooling. **2** liquefied condition.
liq|ue|fy (lik′wə fī), *v.t., v.i.,* **-fied, -fy|ing.** to change into a liquid; make or become liquid: *Liquefied air is extremely cold.* [< Middle French *liquéfier,* learned borrowing from Latin *liquefacere* < *liquēre* be fluid + *facere* make] —**liq′ue|fi′a-ble,** *adj.* —**liq′ue|fi′er,** *n.*

1. In which of the following sentences can *liquefaction* correctly be placed in the blank?
_____ a. _____ occurs when a gas is cooled to a specific temperature and compressed by a specific pressure.
_____ b. The combination of temperature and pressure needed for the _____ of a gas differs depending on the substances that make up the gas.
_____ c. _____ occurs when the attractive forces between molecules overcome the forces of kinetic motion.
_____ d. _____ is the formation of a gas.

2. The etymology of *liquefaction* (see at *liquefy*) shows that the word comes from Latin words, *liquere* (to be fluid) and *facere* (to make). Use this information, your background knowledge, and your imagination to match the following:
_____ a. benefaction   aa. the liquid in which food is canned
_____ b. liquor   bb. to make by hand or machine
_____ c. malefactor   cc. fulfillment of desires
_____ d. manufacture   dd. a criminal; evil doer
_____ e. satisfaction   ee. kindly or generous action

3. Complete the verbal analogy.
    rose : flower :: *liquefaction* : _____
    a. liquefy   c. process
    b. Latin   d. pressure

4. You might have to make use of products that have undergone *liquefaction*. Liquefied gas fire extinguishers should be used on fires that involve combustible liquids such as cooking grease, gasoline, or oil, and on fires that involve motors, switches, or other electrical equipment. Where else might you see or use liquefied gas?

    _____

    _____

5. Write a sentence correctly using *liquefaction*. (Be sure to include context clues to show you understand the meaning of the word.)

    _____

    _____

Miscible[5]

mis|ci|ble (mis′ə bəl), *adj.* that can be mixed:
Water is not miscible with oil. [< Latin *miscēre*
mix + English *-ible*]

1. Check any appropriate reply to the following statement:
    "Oil and kerosene are *miscible* liquids."
    _____ a. I notice the price has gone down lately.
    _____ b. But oil and water are not.
    _____ c. Water and alcohol also mix.
    _____ d. Engines would miss them, all right!

2. Which statement(s) match(es) the following statement?
    "Two liquids that are infinitely soluble are said to be completely *miscible*."
    _____ a. Some liquids are partially miscible.
    _____ b. Any amount of water will dissolve in any amount of methyl alcohol.
    _____ c. Gasoline and oil are insoluble in water.
    _____ d. Gasoline and water are immiscible.

3. Complete the verbal analogy.
    opposition : cooperation :: *miscible* : _____
    a. mixable   c. soluble
    b. liquids   d. immiscible

4. Write a sentence correctly using *miscible*. (Be sure to include context clues to show you understand the meaning of the word.)

    _____

    _____

SCIENCES: CHEMISTRY

5. What *miscible* liquids make up your favorite beverage? Chocolate syrup and milk? Water and Kool-aid? Other?

_____

_____

Solute[7]

sol|ute (sol′yüt, sō′lüt), *n., adj.* —*n.* a solid, gas, or liquid that is dissolved in a liquid to make a solution: *Salt is a solute in seawater. Stems . . . act as channels through which water and solutes reach the leaves* (Fred W. Emerson).
—*adj.* **1** dissolved; in solution. **2** *Botany.* not adhering; free.
[< Latin *solūtus*, past participle of *solvere* dissolve, loosen]

1. Which of the following might be a *solute*?

   _____ a. sugar   _____ d. salt

   _____ b. carbon dioxide   _____ e. oxygen

   _____ c. milk   _____ f. pepper

2. Which statement(s) match(es) the following statement?
   "One of the *solutes* in champagne is carbon dioxide."

   _____ a. Champagne contains water and alcohol.

   _____ b. Champagne is a solution containing a dissolved gas.

   _____ c. Champagne is an aqueous solution.

   _____ d. One of the solutes in champagne is sugar.

3. Complete the verbal analogy.
   branch : tree :: *solute* : _____

   a. solution   c. gas

   b. dissolve   d. solid

4. Do you add any *solute* to coffee or tea?

_____

_____

5. Write a sentence correctly using *solute*. (Be sure to include context clues to show you understand the meaning of the word.)

_____

_____

Solvent[8]

sol|vent (sol′vənt), *adj., n.* —*adj.* **1** able to pay all one owes: *A bankrupt firm is not solvent.* **2** able to dissolve: *Gasoline is a solvent liquid that removes grease spots.*
—*n.* **1** a substance, usually a liquid, that can dissolve other substances: *Water is a solvent of sugar and salt.* **2** a thing that solves, explains, or settles.
[< Latin *solvēns, -entis*, present participle of *solvere* loosen (used in *rem solvere* to free one's property and person from debt)] —**sol′vent|ly,** *adv.*

1. In which of the following sentences is *solvent* used correctly?
   _____ a. A solvent is a medium, usually a liquid, that dissolves another substance.
   _____ b. Water is a good solvent for many salts.
   _____ c. Through chemistry, many of the world's problems are solvent.
   _____ d. No solvent has been found for current banking problems.

2. Which of the following might be a *solvent*?
   _____ a. cold water   _____ d. sand
   _____ b. coffee   _____ e. alcohol
   _____ c. gasoline   _____ f. hot water

3. Which of the numbered dictionary definitions of *solvent* best fits the word's use in the reading selection? _____

4. Write a sentence correctly using *solvent*. (Be sure to include context clues to show you understand the meaning of the word.)

   _____

   _____

5. List at least five ways you use that most popular *solvent,* water.

   _____

   _____

Sublimation[13]

sub|li|ma|tion (sub´lə mā′shən), *n.* 1 the act or process of sublimating or subliming; purification: *This direct transition from solid to vapor is called sublimation* (Sears and Zemansky). 2 the resulting product or state, especially, mental elevation or exaltation: *that enthusiastic sublimation which is the source of greatness and energy* (Thomas L. Peacock). 3 the highest stage or purest form of a thing. 4 a chemical sublimate.
sub|lime (sə blīm′), *adj., n., v.,* **-limed, -lim|ing.**
—*adj.* 1 noble; grand; majestic; lofty: *Mountain scenery is often sublime.* 2 exalted; excellent; eminent; supreme: *sublime devotion. How sublime a thing it is To suffer and be strong* (Longfellow). 3 expressing lofty ideas in a grand manner: *sublime poetry.* **4a** of lofty bearing or appearance: *In his simplicity sublime* (Tennyson). **b** *Obsolete.* haughty; proud. 5 *Archaic.* set or raised aloft. 6 *Obsolete.* elated.
—*n.* 1 something that is lofty, noble, exalted, or majestic: *the sublime in literature and art. No, never need an American look beyond his own country for the sublime and beautiful of natural*

scenery (Washington Irving). 2 the highest degree or example (of): *Your upward gaze at me now is the very sublime of faith, truth, and devotion* (Charlotte Brontë).
—*v.t.* 1 to make higher or nobler; make sublime: *A judicious use of metaphors wonderfully raises, sublimes and adorns oratory* (Oliver Goldsmith). **2a** to heat (a solid substance) and condense the vapor given off; purify; refine. **b** to cause to be given off by this or a similar process. —*v.i.* 1 to pass off as a vapor and condense as a solid without going through the liquid state; become purified or refined. 2 to be changed into a gas directly from the solid state.
from the sublime to the ridiculous, from one extreme to the other: *His writing is very uneven, running the gamut from the sublime to the ridiculous.*
[< Latin *sublīmis* (originally) sloping up (to the lintel) < *sub-* up + *līmen, -inis* threshold] —**sub|lime′ly,** *adv.* —**sub|lime′ness,** *n.* —**sub|lim′er,** *n.*

1. Check any appropriate response to the following statement: "The vaporization of a solid is called *sublimation.*"
   _____ a. There is no liquid stage.
   _____ b. The solid must go directly into the gaseous stage.
   _____ c. The solid becomes a liquid solution.
   _____ d. This process does not occur in all solids.

SCIENCES: CHEMISTRY

2. Which statement(s) match(es) the following statement?
   "Naphthalene (mothballs) will undergo *sublimation*."
   _____ a. Mothballs melt to a sticky liquid.
   _____ b. Mothballs change from solid to gas.
   _____ c. The alchemists purified sulfur and arsenic by this process.
   _____ d. Mothballs are made of naphthalene.

3. Which of the numbered dictionary definitions of *sublimation* best fits the word's use in the reading selection? _____

4. Have you ever seen the chemical process of *sublimation*? (If you have not seen dry ice, make it a point to see some.)

   _____

   _____

5. Write a sentence correctly using *sublimation*. (Be sure to include context clues to show you understand the meaning of the word.)

   _____

   _____

Viscosity[14]

vis|cos|i|ty (vis kos′ə tē), *n., pl.* **-ties. 1** the condition or quality of being viscous. **2** *Physics.* **a** the resistance of a fluid to the motion of its molecules among themselves. **b** the ability of a solid or semisolid to change its shape gradually under stress.
vis|cose¹ (vis′kōs), *n., adj.* **—n.** a thick, sticky substance made by treating cellulose with caustic soda and carbon disulfide. Viscose is used in manufacturing rayon and cellophane, for sizing, and for other purposes.
— adj. having to do with or made from viscose. [< Latin *viscum* birdlime + English *-ose²* (because it is a syruplike material)]

1. In which of the following sentences can *viscosity* correctly be placed in the blank?
   _____ a. _____ is the syruplike quality of a liquid.
   _____ b. If a liquid is cooled, _____ increases.
   _____ c. A fluid that has low _____ flows readily.
   _____ d. Oil has higher _____ than water.

2. Place an "h" by substances with high *viscosity* and an "l" by substances with low *viscosity*.
   _____ a. mustard   _____ d. milk
   _____ b. tar   _____ e. soda pop
   _____ c. hot tea   _____ f. whipped cream

3. Complete the verbal analogy.
   warmth : fire :: *viscosity* : _____
   a. liquid state   c. resistance
   b. molecule attractions   d. coldness

4. Write a sentence correctly using *viscosity*. (Be sure to include context clues to show you understand the meaning of the word.)

   _____

   _____

5. List some occasions when you deal with the *viscosity* of a liquid. For example, when you try to get ketchup out of a bottle.

_____

_____

ANSWERS TO CHAPTER 9 EXERCISES

Alchemy: 1. a, d 2. a, b, c 3. 1
Amorphous: 1. b, c, d, e 2. a, b, d, f 3. 3
Aqueous: 1. a, d 2. d (parts of speech) 3. 2
Condensation: 1. a, b, d 2. a, b, c, e, f 3. 4
Distillation: 1. b, c, d 2. a (cause-effect) 3. 2
Equilibrium: 1. a, b, c 2. a, b, c, d 3. 2
Evaporation: 1. a, c, d 2. b (product) 3. 1
Induction: 1. c 2. c, d, e, f 3. 2a
Kinetic: 1. a (synonym) 2. c 3. 2
Liquefaction: 1. a, b, c 2. ee, aa, dd, bb, cc 3. c (specific-general)
Miscible: 1. b, c 2. b 3. d (antonym)
Solute: 1. a, b, c, d, e 2. b 3. a (part-whole)
Solvent: 1. a, b, d 2. a, b, c, e, f 3. *n.* 1
Sublimation: 1. a, b, d 2. b 3. 1
Viscosity: 1. a, b, c, d 2. h, h, l, l, l, h 3. b (effect-cause)

If you missed any of the items in the exercises, return to the exercise and to the dictionary definition to see where you went wrong. Remember: If you get something right, you only affirm that you knew it. If you get something wrong and understand why, *you have learned something*.

CHEMISTRY POSTTEST

Fill in the blanks with the words from this list.

alchemy	equilibrium	miscible
amorphous	evaporation	solute
aqueous	induction	solvent
condensation	kinetic	sublimation
distillation	liquefaction	viscosity

1. _____ is the ability of a solid to change shape gradually.

2. In _____, no chemical change occurs.

3. A liquefied condition is _____.

4. A(n) _____ is an extract.

5. _____ is the removal of water.

6. A cloud is an example of _____.

7. _____ means "without stratification."

8. Another word for installation is _____.

9. Something suggesting motion is _____.

10. _____ means purification.

11. Liquids that are highly soluble are completely _____.

12. Something being dissolved is a(n) _____.

13. _____ has to do with water.

14. A thing that solves or explains is a(n) _____.

15. _____ is from the Greek meaning "the art of alloying metals."

Answers to this posttest are in the Instructor's Manual.

If you missed any of the words, you may need to return to the exercises and to the dictionary entries to see why your concepts for some words are incomplete.

CHAPTER TEN

SCIENCES:
MATHEMATICS

◆

OVERVIEW

Mathematics is the study of numbers, measurements, and space. It is the science dealing with the measurement, properties, and relationships of quantities as expressed in numbers or symbols. The study of mathematics provides powerful intellectual tools that have contributed to advances in science and technology.

Curriculum offerings in mathematics include courses in calculus, trigonometry, analytic and plane geometry, probability and statistics, linear and abstract algebra, operations research, matrix analysis, linear programming, and differential equations. Coursework in mathematics prepares students for careers in applied mathematics, probability and statistics, or in teaching at the elementary or secondary levels. Computer science majors usually are required to take mathematics courses as part of their program also.

Introductory mathematics textbooks provide a combination of expository, problem-solution, and instructional material. They present theoretical concepts and accompanying examples, as well as problem sets with instructions on finding the problem solutions. Texts may contain historical notes and charts, as well as tables and figures that visually represent concepts.

The vocabulary in mathematics consists mainly of general vocabulary terms that have a specific meaning within the context of mathematics. Examples of such terms are range, function, *and* integral. *Specialized vocabulary unique to mathematics contains terms such as* calculus, decimal, *and* integer.

VOCABULARY SELF-EVALUATION

The following words will be introduced in this reading selection. Place a check mark (√) in front of any that you know thoroughly and use in your speech and writing. Place a question mark (?) in front of any that you recognize but do not use yourself.

_____ composite	_____ factor	_____ postulate
_____ congruent	_____ function	_____ prime
_____ derivative	_____ hypotenuse	_____ range
_____ domain	_____ integral	_____ theorem
_____ exponent	_____ inverse	_____ variable

THEOREMS IN MATHEMATICS

Mathematics is the study of numbers, forms, or arrangements and their associated relationships. Thus mathematics is a form of reasoning, and mathematicians work from a set of fundamental rules or assumptions, also known as axioms,* that are accepted as true. A theorem[1] is another element in a mathematical system, since it is a statement that has been proved based on the assumed truth of the axiom(s) on which it was developed. Each of the following fields within mathematics—number theory, algebra, geometry, and calculus—contain theorems that have been proved through a logical deductive process, that is, through various levels of reasoning with statements and their proofs.

NUMBER THEORY

Number theory is a branch of mathematics concerned with properties of numbers.

One collection of often-studied numbers is that of natural numbers; that is, 1, 2, 3, and so on. Interest in numbers is as old as civilization itself, and number theory grew out of the inexact sciences of numerology and astrology. Greek mathematicians, such as Eratosthenes and Euclid, were especially interested in investigating the properties of natural numbers.

One classification of natural numbers is even and odd numbers, and another classification consists of prime[2] and composite[3] numbers. A prime number is a natural number greater than 1 that has exactly two divisors, itself and 1, namely, 2, 3, 5, 7, 11, and so on. The fourth-century B.C. mathematician Euclid proved that the number of prime numbers is infinite. A composite number, on the other hand, is a natural number greater than 1 that is not a prime number and thus has more than two divisors, such as 4 (which is divisible by 1, 2, and 4).

The fundamental theorem of arith-

---

* _Axiom_ is introduced as word number 3 in Chapter 21.

metic states that any natural number greater than 1 is prime or can be expressed as a product of prime numbers. This fundamental theorem also relates to the concept of the factor[4] of a number, that is, a composite number is a product of prime factors. For example, the prime factors of the composite number 21 would be 3 and 7, since both 3 and 7 are prime numbers and $21 = 3 \cdot 7$. For 30, it would be 2, 3, and 5, since they are prime numbers and $30 = 2 \cdot 3 \cdot 5$.

The early Greek mathematician Eratosthenes designed a technique called the "sieve of Eratosthenes" for finding primes smaller than some given number. And in 1640 the French mathematician Pierre de Fermat developed a test for primes that is still used today. In 1876, the English mathematician E. Lucas developed a test to discover a certain type of prime number. The test was refined in 1930 by the American D. H. Lehmer. It was used in 1986 in a large computer to discover a prime number that was so large it contained over 65,000 digits!

Finally, another concept in number theory concerns real numbers and integers. Integers are whole numbers, and real numbers include a decimal (44 is an integer, while 4.4 is a real number). Both real numbers and integers can be written in scientific notation, which expresses numbers in multiples of 10 to an exponent.[5] An exponent is a number placed at the upper right of a number to show how many times it is to be used as a factor. For example, 5,642 can be expressed in scientific notation as 5.642×10^3 or 56.42×10^2; the superscripts 3 and 2 to the right of 10 are both exponents.

ALGEBRA

Algebra is one of the chief branches of mathematics and is basic to more advanced study in higher mathematics, statistics, and computer technology. In algebra, symbols, usually letters of the alphabet such as x and y, represent numbers or members of a specified set of numbers. Such a symbol is also called a variable.[6]

Many early civilizations, such as the Chinese, Persians, Indians, and Babylonians, used a rudimentary form of algebra. A Greek mathematician, Diophantus (c. A.D. 200), has been called the "father of algebra" for his use of quadratic equations and symbols for unknown quantities. The Hindus, Arabs, Italians, and French (including René Descartes) have also contributed to the development of algebra. The term *algebra* is an Arabic word meaning "reduction" in the sense of solving an equation.

An example of an algebraic expression is $x - 3$, with x as the variable assigned to represent any element of the set N. The set N is therefore called the domain[7] of the variable. In an algebraic equation with two variables, such as in $x + y = 6$, x is the first variable and y is the second variable. The name given to the replacement set for y is called the range.[8]

When two variables are related so that for each value assumed by one there is a value determined for the other, this is known as a function.[9] An example of a function would be $y = 6x + 2$, with the value of y depending on the value of x. As different replacements are made for x, y will have a different value.

Finally, an example of a theorem in algebra that has been proved by application of logic to certain axioms is: If x and y are numbers greater than zero and $x > y$, then $y - x$ is a negative number. An application of this theorem would be the following: x is 10 and y is 5, then $5 - 10$ is a negative number, in this case, -5.

GEOMETRY

Geometry is the mathematical study of the shapes and sizes of figures. The term *geometry* comes from the Greek words *geo* (earth) and *metr* (measure). There is evidence that the Egyptians and Babylonians used a type of geometry in architecture, engineering, and astronomy. Early Greek mathematicians, including Thales of Miletus, Pythagoras, Euclid, and Archimedes, developed elementary geometry to a higher degree. The first book on analytic geometry, published in 1637 by the French mathematician René Descartes, showed a relationship between geometric figures and algebraic equations.

Geometry is based on assumptions (also known as axioms or postulates)[10] that are accepted as true without proof. Geometry is designated Euclidean if the postulates of Euclid (from his book *Elements*) are involved, and non-Euclidean if a change has been made in one or more of these postulates. An example of a Euclidean postulate is Postulate 1: A line can be drawn from any point to any other point.

Other geometric concepts include that of congruent and similar figures. Geometric figures are said to be congruent[11] when they have the same size and shape and are symbolized by $\cong$. On the other hand, the symbol $\sim$ is used to represent similar figures, those that have the same shape (see Figures 1 and 2).

Finally, a famous theorem in geometry

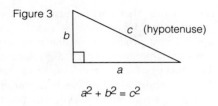

Figure 3

b c (hypotenuse)

a

$$a^2 + b^2 = c^2$$

is that proposed by Pythagorus (c. 500 B.C.) and concerns the triangle. This theorem states that the sum of the squares of the lengths of the sides of a right triangle is equal to the square of the length of the hypotenuse[12] (see Figure 3).

CALCULUS

Calculus is an important tool in higher mathematics as well as in business, computer science, engineering, the physical sciences, and many other fields. The development of calculus in the 1660s marks a turning point in the history of mathematics. Both Isaac Newton and Gottfried Leibniz, working independently, in two different countries and on totally separate problems, developed calculus at about the same time.

Calculus is divided into two main branches of study: differential calculus and integral calculus. Differential calculus studies small, subtle changes, while integral calculus studies total change. The entities involved in calculus are functions. In differential calculus, functions are differentiated to obtain new functions called derivatives.[13] A derivative can be defined as the instantaneous rate of change of a function with respect to a variable through obtaining the slope of the line tangent to the graph of the function at that point.

In integral calculus, functions are integrated to obtain new functions called integrals.[14] By evaluating an integral at the endpoints of an interval in the domain of the function, we sometimes obtain the area of the region between the graph of the function and the horizontal axis on

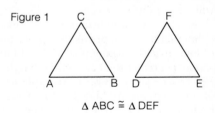

Figure 1

$\triangle$ ABC $\cong$ $\triangle$ DEF

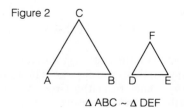

Figure 2

$\triangle$ ABC $\sim$ $\triangle$ DEF

that interval. Integrals are often used in finding areas and volumes.

Differentiation and integration are inverse[15] operations, since integrating a function then differentiating the resulting integral yields the same function back again. For example, if $f(x)$ is $3x^2 - 6x + 5$, differentiation yields the new function $6x - 6$, while integrating $6x - 6$ can bring one back to $3x^2 - 6x + 5$. Prior to the development of calculus, the methods for finding tangent lines and areas were very different. Thus it was truly remarkable to find the derivative and the integral to be related. Newton was the first one in history to exploit this inverse relationship, but it was Newton's teacher Isaac Barrow who discovered and proved the amazing theorem that differentiation and integration are inverse operations in the fundamental theorem of calculus. The formal realization of this relationship can be said to mark the true birth of calculus. ◆

MATHEMATICS PRETEST

Select words from this list and write them in the blanks to complete the sentences.

composite	factor	postulate
congruent	function	prime
derivative	hypotenuse	range
domain	integral	theorem
exponent	inverse	variable

1. Correspondence between two sets of elements is sometimes called a(n) _____ .

2. A superscript number written above and to the right of a quantity to show how many times the quantity is to be used as a factor is a(n) _____ .

3. A(n) _____ number has no common integral divisor but one and the number itself.

4. _____ is the instantaneous rate of change of a function with respect to its variable.

5. _____ refers to a quantity that can assume any of the values in a given set of values or a symbol representing this quantity.

6. Something taken for granted or assumed as a basis for reasoning is a(n) _____ .

7. The set of all the values a given function may take on is called the _____ .

8. _____ refers to an operation that cancels what another operation does.

9. The number ten is a(n) _____ number, since it is a number exactly divisible by some whole number other than itself or 1.

10. A(n) _____ is a statement that can be proved or that has been proved.

11. Any one of the numbers or expressions that produce a given number or quantity when multiplied together is a(n) _____.

12. _____ is the set of all numbers that can be assigned to the algebraic variable x in an equation with two variables.

13. The side of a right triangle opposite the right angle is a(n) _____.

14. Triangles with the same size and shape are said to be _____.

15. The result of an integration in calculus is a(n) _____.

Answers to this pretest are in Appendix B.

Unless your instructor tells you to do otherwise, complete the exercises for each word that you missed on the pretest. The words, with their meanings and exercises, are in alphabetical order. The superscript numbers indicate where the words appeared in the reading selection so that you can refer to them when necessary. There are several types of exercises, but for each word you will be asked to write a sentence using context clues. (See Chapter 4 if you need information about how to create context clues.) You are also asked to perform some activity that will help you make your concept of the word personal. *Complete this activity thoughtfully, for creating a personalized concept of the word will help you remember it in the future.*

Answers to all the exercises are at the end of the exercise segment.

MATHEMATICS EXERCISES

Composite[3]

com|pos|ite (kəm poz′it), *adj., n.* —*adj.* **1** made up of various parts; compound: *The photographer made a composite picture by putting together parts of several others.* **2** belonging to the composite family.
—*n.* **1** any composite thing: *English is a composite of many languages.* SYN: combination, compound, complex. **2** a composite plant. **3** = composite number.

[< Latin *compositus*, past participle of *compōnere* < *com-* together + *pōnere* put. See etym. of doublet **compost, compote.**] —**com|pos′ite|ly,** *adv.* —**com|pos′ite|ness,** *n.*
composite number, a number exactly divisible by some whole number other than itself or one. 4, 6, and 9 are composite numbers; 2, 3, 5, and 7 are prime numbers.

1. Complete the verbal analogy.
   prime : first :: *composite* : _____
   a. premier   c. complication
   b. posterior   d. combination

2. The etymology of *composite* shows that the word comes from the Latin *componere* (*com* means "together" and *ponere* means "to put"). Use this

information, your imagination, and your background knowledge to match the following:

_____ a. impose   aa. to put between; insert

_____ b. preposition   bb. to put out of office or a position of authority, especially a high office such as that of a king

_____ c. repository   cc. to put (a burden, tax, or punishment) on something

_____ d. interpose   dd. a place or container where things are stored or kept

_____ e. depose   ee. a word that shows certain relations between other words

3. In which of the following sentences is *composite* used correctly?

_____ a. A mosaic is a composite of small pieces of glass.

_____ b. The numbers 3, 7, and 11 are composite numbers.

_____ c. This poem is like a composite of images describing a beautiful sunset.

_____ d. The numbers 15, 25, and 40 are composite numbers.

4. Write a sentence correctly using *composite*. (Be sure to include context clues to show you understand the meaning of the word.)

_____

_____

5. List five numbers that are *composite* numbers. How are they different from prime numbers? Explain.

_____

_____

_____

Congruent[11]

con|gru|ent (kong′grù ənt), *adj.* **1** *Geometry.* exactly coinciding: *Congruent triangles have the same size and shape.* **2** *Algebra.* producing the same remainder when divided by a given number. **3** in harmony; agreeing. **syn:** harmonious, accordant, congruous. [< Latin *congruēns, -entis,* present participle of *congruere* agree, correspond with] — **con′gru|ent|ly,** *adv.*

1. Select the synonym(s) of *congruent*.

     a. accordant   c. opposing

     b. harmonious   d. dissimilar

2. Which of the numbered dictionary definitions of *congruent* best fits the word's use in the reading selection? _____

3. Which of the following is an example of a *congruent* figure?

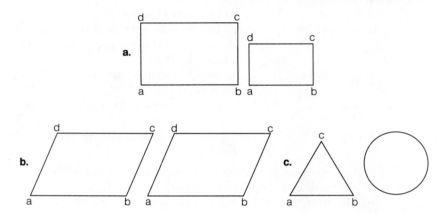

4. With whom do you experience *congruent* attitudes, perceptions of the world, or life goals? Explain.

_____

_____

5. Write a sentence correctly using *congruent*. (Be sure to include context clues to show you understand the meaning of the word.)

_____

_____

Derivative[13]

de|riv|a|tive (di riv′ə tiv), *adj., n.* —*adj.* **1** not original; derived: *derivative poetry.* **2** of derivation; derivational.
—*n.* **1** something derived: *Many medicines are derivatives of roots and herbs. They spoke a derivative of the Malay language* (Harper's). **2** a word formed by adding a prefix or suffix to another word. *Quickness* and *quickly* are derivatives of *quick.* **3** a chemical substance obtained from another by modification or by partial substitution of components: *Acetic acid is a derivative of alcohol.* **4** *Mathematics.* **a** the instantaneous rate of change of a function with respect to its variable. **b** a function derived from another in differential calculus; differential coefficient. —**de|riv′a|tive|ly,** *adv.* —**de|riv′a|tive|ness,** *n.*

de|rive (di rīv′), *v.,* -**rived,** -**riv|ing.** —*v.t.* **1** to obtain from a source or origin; get; receive: *He derives much pleasure from reading adventure stories.* **2** to trace (a word, custom, or title) from or to a source or origin: *The word "December" is derived from the Latin word "decem," which means "ten."* **3** to obtain by reasoning; deduce. **4** to obtain (a chemical substance) from another by substituting a different element. **5** *Obsolete.* to lead; bring; direct.
—*v.i.* to come from a source or origin; originate: *This story derives from an old legend.*
[< Old French *deriver,* learned borrowing from Latin *dērīvāre* lead off, draw off (water) < *dē*- off + *rīvus* stream] —**de|riv′er,** *n.*

1. In which of the following sentences is *derivative* used correctly?

_____ a. A derivative is the center line to which parts of a structure or body are referred.

    b. The inverse operation of multiplication yields a derivative.

    c. The derivative of a function tells how the dependent variable tends to change with respect to the independent variable.

    d. A derivative is the focus of study in differential calculus.

2. Which of the numbered dictionary definitions of *derivative* (as a noun) best fits the word's use in the reading selection? _____

3. Besides the mathematical meaning related to calculus, *derivative* can also mean "a word formed by adding a prefix or suffix to another word" (definition #2). Select the derivatives of *happy*.

    a. unhappy   c. happily

    b. happiness   d. happier

4. Write a sentence correctly using *derivative*. (Be sure to include context clues to show you understand the meaning of the word.)

_____

_____

5. *Derivative* in the specialized field of mathematics is the "instantaneous rate of change of a function with respect to its variable." In a general context, *derivative* means "something derived" or "obtained from a source of origin" (from *derive*). What, then, might be a *derivative* of oil?

_____

_____

Domain[7]

do|main (dō mān′), *n.* **1** the lands under the rule of one ruler or government: *Great Britain is a large island domain under the Crown of England.* **SYN**: realm, dominion. **2** land owned by one person; estate. **SYN**: manor. **3** *Law.* the absolute ownership of land. **4** *Figurative.* field of thought or action; sphere: *the domain of science, the domain of religion. Edison was a leader in the domain of invention.* **SYN**: province. **5** a region within a ferroelectric or ferromagnetic crystal, spontaneously polarized in a single direction. A crystal contains many domains polarized in a variety of directions, offsetting one another's energy. When domains are placed in a magnetic field, those favorably directed in respect to the field tend to grow at the expense of those unfavorably directed. **6** *Mathematics.* the set of all numbers which can be assigned to the algebraic variable x in an equation with two variables. Since the members of such a set may serve as replacements for the variable in a given relation, the set is sometimes called *replacement set.* [< French *domaine* < Old French *demaine,* earlier *demeine,* learned borrowing from Latin *dominium* < *dominus* lord, master < *domus* house. See etym. of doublet **demesne.**]

1. Select the synonym(s) of *domain*.

    a. axis   c. function

    b. realm   d. province

2. The etymology of *domain* shows that the word comes from the Latin *dominus* (lord or master) and *domus* (house). Use this information, your imagination, and your background knowledge to match the following:

_____ a. dominate

aa. power or right of governing and controlling; rule; control

_____ b. domicile

bb. political theory that if one country falls to an expansionist power, the next countries will inevitably fall in turn

_____ c. predominate

cc. to control or rule by strength or power

_____ d. domino

dd. to be greater in power, strength, influence, or numbers

_____ e. dominion

ee. dwelling place, house, home; residence

3. Which of the numbered dictionary definitions of *domain* best fits the word's use in the reading selection? _____

4. *Domain* in the context of mathematics refers to the set of all numbers that can be assigned to the algebraic variable *x* in an equation of two variables. *Domain* in the figurative sense can mean "field of thought or action" or "sphere." In this reading selection, Isaac Barrow was a leader in the *domain* of calculus because of his discovery of integration and differentiation as inverse operations. In what *domain* would you like to be known as a leader in your lifetime?

_____

_____

5. Write a sentence correctly using *domain*. (Be sure to include context clues to show you understand the meaning of the word.)

_____

_____

Exponent[5]

✱ex|po|nent (ek spō′nent), *n.* **1** a person or thing that explains or interprets. **2** a person or thing that stands as an example, type, or symbol of something: *Abraham Lincoln is a famous exponent of self-education.* **3** a person who argues for a policy, program, etc.; advocate. **4** *Algebra.* a small number written above and to the right of a symbol or quantity to show how many times the symbol or quantity is to be used as a factor; index. *Examples:* $2^2 = 2 \times 2$; $a^3 = a \times a \times a$. [< Latin *expōnēns, -entis*, present participle of *expōnere*; see etym. under **expound**]

$$a^2 = a \times a$$

✱exponent
definition 4

$$2^4 = 2 \times 2 \times 2 \times 2$$

$$2^3a^2 = 2 \times 2 \times 2 \times a \times a$$

from **expound:**

[< Anglo-French *espoundre*, Old French *espondre* < Latin *expōnere* < *ex-* forth + *pōnere* put.

1. Which of the following are examples of an *exponent?*

_____ a. $b(a + c)$ _____ c. 4^3b^2

_____ b. 3^2 _____ d. $3xy + 5bc$

2. Which of the numbered dictionary definitions of *exponent* best fits the word's use in the reading selection? _____

3. Identify the synonym(s) of *exponent*.
   _____ a. advocate   _____ c. prime
   _____ b. index   _____ d. symbol

4. Write a sentence correctly using *exponent*. (Be sure to include context clues to show you understand the meaning of the word.)

   _____

   _____

   _____

5. Have you ever been an *exponent* of a political cause either on your campus, in your community, or at work? Explain.

   _____

   _____

   _____

   _____

Factor⁴

fac|tor (fak′tər), *n., v.* — *n.* **1** any one of the causes that help to bring about a result; one element in a situation: *Ability, industry, and health are factors of his success in school. Endurance is an important factor of success in sports.* **2** any one of the numbers or expressions which produce a given number or quantity when multiplied together: *5 and 2 are factors of 10.* **3a** a person who does business for another; an agent; commission merchant. **b** an agent managing a trading post: [*He*] *so impressed Hudson's Bay officials in London that he was transferred out of Labrador to Montreal as the company's chief factor* (Maclean's). **4** *Biology.* a gene: *The terms gene, factor, and determiner will be used as synonyms to designate the units responsible for the transmission of hereditary characters* (Harbaugh and Goodrich). **5** *Scottish.* a person who manages an estate; steward; bailiff. **6** *Law.* a person appointed to manage property that is forfeited or taken away. **7** an agent or company that lends money to a firm which has not yet collected its bills. When the bills are collected, the firm pays the factor a commission on the bills paid and interest on the loan.
— *v.t.* **1** to separate or resolve into factors; factorize. **2** to buy and collect the receivable accounts of (a business).
— *v.i.* to be a factor; act or serve as a factor.
[< Latin *factor, -ōris* doer < *facere* make, do. See etym. of doublet **faitour**.]

1. Select the synonym(s) of *factor*.
   _____ a. determiner   _____ c. agent
   _____ b. composite   _____ d. cause

2. Which of the numbered dictionary definitions of *factor* best fits the word's use in the reading selection? _____

3. The etymology of *factor* shows that the word comes from the Latin *facere* (to make or do). Use this information, your imagination, and your background knowledge to match the following:

_____	a. malefactor	aa.	an exact copy or likeness; perfect reproduction
_____	b. faction	bb.	a criminal; evil doer
_____	c. facsimile	cc.	a person who has given money or kindly help
_____	d. benefactor	dd.	anything made by human skill or work, especially a tool or weapon
_____	e. artifact	ee.	a group of people in a political party, church, club, or other body or organization who stand up for their side or act together for some common purpose against a larger group

4. What are the *factors* of the following numbers: 10, 20, 30? Why? Explain.

_____

_____

5. Write a sentence correctly using *factor*. (Be sure to include context clues to show you understand the meaning of the word.)

_____

_____

Function[9]

func|tion (fungk′shən), *n., v.* —*n.* **1a** proper work; normal action or use; purpose: *The function of the stomach is to help digest food. The great general functions of plant parts ... are conduction, support, storage, protection, and secretion* (Fred W. Emerson). **b** a duty or office; employment. **SYN:** province, task. **2** a formal public or social gathering for some purpose: *The hotel ballroom is often used for weddings, anniversaries, and other functions. He ... set out to attend the last gathering of the season at Valleys House, a function ... almost perfectly political* (John Galsworthy). **3a** *Mathematics.* a quantity whose value depends on the value given to one or more related quantities: *The area of a circle is a function of its radius; as the radius increases so does the area.* **b** anything likened to a mathematical function. **4** *Grammar.* the way in which a word or phrase is used in a sentence. —*v.i.* to work; act; perform a function or one's functions: *One of the older students can function as teacher. This old fountain pen does not function very well.* **SYN:** operate. [< Latin *fūnctiō, -ōnis* < *fungī* perform]

1. Select the synonym(s) of *function*.

   _____ a. operate   _____ c. provide
   _____ b. object   _____ d. task

2. Which of the numbered dictionary definitions of *function* best fits the word's use in the reading selection? _____

3. The etymology of *function* shows that the word comes from the Latin *functio* and *fungi* (perform). Use this information, your imagination, and your background knowledge to match the following:

_____	a. defunct	aa.	person who has certain duties to perform; an official
_____	b. functionalism	bb.	of such a nature that one instance or portion may be replaced by another in respect of function, office or use

_____ c. perfunctory   cc. done merely for the sake of getting rid of the duty; mechanical; indifferent

_____ d. functionary   dd. regard for the function and purpose of something as the primary factor in regulating its design

_____ e. fungible   ee. no longer in existence; dead; extinct

4. Write a sentence correctly using *function*. (Be sure to include context clues to show you understand the meaning of the word.)

_____

_____

5. Why is a *function* also called a "rule of correspondence between two sets"? Give an example. (Use the dictionary entry and context in the reading selection.)

_____

_____

_____

Hypotenuse[12]

*hy|pot|e|nuse (hī pot′ə nüs, -nyüs; hi-), *n.* the side of a right triangle opposite the right angle. Also, **hypothenuse**. [< Late Latin *hypotēnūsa* < Greek *hypoteínousa* stretching under, subtending, feminine present participle of *hypoteínein* < *hypo-* under + *teínein* stretch]

*hypotenuse

1. To what theorem does a *hypotenuse* relate?
   _____ a. Euclidean
   _____ b. Hippocrates
   _____ c. Pythagorean

2. The etymology of *hypotenuse* shows that the word comes from the Greek *hypo* (under) and *teinein* (to stretch). Use this information, your imagination, and your background knowledge to match the following:

_____ a. tendon   aa. to stretch out by pressure from within; swell out; expand

_____ b. contend   bb. to claim falsely

_____ c. pretend   cc. to continue or prolong in time, space, or direction

_____ d. extend   dd. to work hard against difficulties; to fight or struggle

_____ e. distend   ee. a tough, strong band or cord of tissue that joins a muscle to a bone or some other part and transmits the force of the muscle to that part

SCIENCES: MATHEMATICS

3. In which geometric figure would you find a *hypotenuse?*

_____ a. rectangle   _____ c. circle

_____ b. right triangle   _____ d. square

4. Draw a geometric figure that includes a *hypotenuse.* Label the part that is the *hypotenuse.*

_____

_____

5. Write a sentence correctly using *hypotenuse.* (Be sure to include context clues to show you understand the meaning of the word.)

_____

_____

_____

Integral[14]

in|te|gral (in'tə grəl, in teg'rəl), *adj., n.*
—adj. 1 necessary to make something complete; essential: *Steel is an integral part of a modern skyscraper.* **2** entire; complete. **SYN:** unbroken. **3** made up of parts that together constitute a whole. **4** *Mathematics.* **a** having to do with an integer or whole number; not fractional. **b** of or involving integrals.

—n. 1 a whole; a whole number. **2** *Mathematics.* **a** the result of an integration in calculus; the quantity of which a given function is the differential or differential coefficient. **b** an expression from which a given function, equation, or system of equations can be derived by differentiating. [< Late Latin *integrālis* < Latin *integer;* see etym. under **integer**] **—in'te|gral|ly,** *adv.*

1. Complete the verbal analogy.

derivative : differential calculus :: *integral* : _____

a. differential calculus   c. derivatives

b. functions   d. integral calculus

2. Which of the numbered dictionary definitions of *integral* (as a noun) best fits the word's use in the reading selection? _____

3. An *integral* can often be used to find

_____ a. areas.   _____ c. volumes.

_____ b. changes.   _____ d. speed.

4. Write a sentence correctly using *integral.* (Be sure to include context clues to show you understand the meaning of the word.)

_____

_____

_____

5. How are a derivative and an *integral* related? (See the reading selection and dictionary entry.)

_____

_____

Inverse[15]

in|verse (in vèrs', in'vèrs), *adj., n., v.,* **-versed, -vers|ing.** —*adj.* **1** exactly opposite; reversed in position, direction, or tendency; opposite in nature or effect: *DCBA is the inverse order of ABCD. The reigning taste was so bad, that the success of a writer was in inverse proportion to his labor, and to his desire of excellence* (Macaulay). **2** turned upside down; inverted: *I saw a tower builded on a lake, Mock'd by its inverse shadow* (Thomas Hood). **3** *Mathematics.* of or having to do with an inverse or an inverse function: *an inverse operation, inverse elements.* —*n.* **1** something reversed: *The inverse of ¾ is 4/3.* **2** the direct opposite: *Evil is the inverse of good.* **3** *Mathematics.* **a** an operation which cancels what another operation does: *The inverse of addition is subtraction.* **b** = inverse function. **c** either one of two elements in a set that by combining in a binary operation yield the identity element of the set. —*v.t.* to invert; reverse. [< Latin *inversus,* past participle of *invertere;* see etym. under **invert**] —**in|verse'ly,** *adv.*

from **invert:**

[< Latin *invertere* < *in-* in, on + *vertere* to turn]

1. Complete the following statement:
   "The *inverse* of addition is _____."
   _____ a. replication   _____ c. multiplication
   _____ b. subtraction   _____ d. division

2. The etymology of *inverse* shows that the word comes from the Latin *invertere* (to turn). Use this information, your imagination, and your background knowledge to match the following:
   _____ a. transverse   aa. go back; return
   _____ b. versatile   bb. abnormal condition characterized by feeling of whirling in space; dizziness; giddiness
   _____ c. revert   cc. turn aside
   _____ d. vertigo   dd. able to do many things well
   _____ e. divert   ee. lying or passing across

3. Which of the numbered dictionary definitions of *inverse* (as a noun) best fits the word's use in the reading selection? _____

4. Why are differentiation and integration called *inverse* operations? (See the reading selection if necessary.)

   _____

   _____

5. Write a sentence correctly using *inverse*. (Be sure to include context clues to show you understand the meaning of the word.)

   _____

   _____

Postulate[10]

pos|tu|late (*n.* pos'chə lit; *v.* pos'chə lāt), *n., v.,* **-lat|ed, -lat|ing.** —*n.* something taken for granted or assumed as a basis for reasoning; fundamental principle; necessary condition: *One postulate in geometry is that a straight line is the shortest distance between any two points. The underlying postulate ... was that knowledge is good and that those who advance knowledge need no further justification for their existence* (Bertrand Russell). **SYN:** hypothesis. —*v.t.* **1** to assume without proof as a basis of reasoning; take for granted; require as a fundamental principle or necessary condition: *Geometry postulates certain things as a basis for its reasoning.* **2** to require; demand; claim. [< New Latin *postulatum* < Latin *postulāre* to demand] —**pos'tu|la'tion,** *n.*

1. Select the synonym(s) of *postulate*.

    _____ a. hypothesis   _____ c. conclusion

    _____ b. delay   _____ d. claim

2. Which two of the following would *most* likely use a *postulate* in their professions?

    _____ a. a businessperson   _____ c. a mathematician

    _____ b. a church official   _____ d. a truck driver

3. In which of the following sentences is *postulate* used correctly?

    _____ a. A postulate was presented to the research group after extensive study and experimentation.

    _____ b. At the Sunday service, the minister discussed the postulate that each human being has a soul.

    _____ c. Based on the evidence presented in court, the lawyer outlined a postulate in defense of her client.

    _____ d. The early mathematicians developed a postulate in geometry that is still used today.

4. Write a sentence correctly using *postulate*. (Be sure to include context clues to show you understand the meaning of the word.)

    _____

    _____

5. What is the relationship between *postulate* and theorem? (Check the reading selection if necessary.)

    _____

    _____

Prime[2]

*prime[1] (prīm), *adj., n.* —*adj.* **1** first in rank or importance; chief: *His prime object was to get enough to eat. The community's prime need is a new school.* SYN: principal. **2** *Figurative.* first in time or order; primary; fundamental; original: *the prime causes of war.* SYN: primordial. **3** first in quality; first-rate; excellent: *prime interest rates, a prime cut of meat.* **4** having no common integral divisor but 1 and the number itself: *7, 11, and 13 are prime numbers.* **5** having no common integral divisor but 1: *2 is prime to 9.* **6** ranking high or highest in some scale or rating system: *prime borrowers, prime time on television.* **7** (of beef and veal) being the best grade of meat; having red flesh that is firm, flavorful, and somewhat fatty. [partly < Latin *prīmus* first, partly < Old French *prime,* learned borrowing from Latin] —*n.* **1** the best time; best condition: *A man of forty is in the prime of life.* **2** the best part. **3** *Figurative.* the first part; beginning: *We see how quickly sundry arts mechanical were found out, in the very prime of the world* (Richard Hooker). **4** springtime: *And brought him presents, flowers, if it were prime, Or mellow fruit if it were harvest time* (Edmund Spenser). **5** early manhood or womanhood; youth: *They were now in the happy prime of youth* (Hawthorne). **6** Also, **Prime.** the second of the seven canonical hours, or the service for it, originally fixed for the first hour of the day (beginning at 6 A.M.). **7** = prime number. **8a** one of the equal parts into which a unit is divided, especially one of the sixty minutes in a degree. **b** the mark indicating such a part, also used to distinguish one letter, quantity, etc., from another. B′ is read "B prime." **9** *Music.* **a** the same tone or note in another octave. **b** the octave or octaves between two such tones or notes. **c** the tonic or keynote. **10** the first defensive position in fencing. **11** = prime rate: *Banks hiked their best corporate interest rate to 20%, their ninth increase in the prime since the first of the year* (Time). [Old English *prīm* (noun definition 6); later, the first period (of the day) < Late Latin *prīma* the first service < Latin *prīma* (*hōra*) first hour (of the Roman day)] —**prime′ness,** *n.*

1. Which of the numbered dictionary definitions of *prime* best fits the word's use in the reading selection? _____

2. Select the synonym(s) of *prime*.
   _____ a. best   _____ c. chief
   _____ b. last   _____ d. composite

3. The etymology of *prime* shows that the word comes from the Latin *prima* (first). Use this information, your imagination, and your background knowledge to match the following:

   _____ a. primeval

   aa. the condition or fact of being the first born among the children of the same parents

   _____ b. primer

   bb. first in rank or importance

   _____ c. premier

   cc. any of the highest order of mammals, including human beings, apes, monkeys, and lemurs

   _____ d. primogeniture

   dd. of or having to do with the first age or ages, especially of the world

   _____ e. primate

   ee. the first book in reading

4. List five numbers that are *prime* numbers. List five numbers that are *not prime* numbers. What is the difference?

   _____

   _____

5. Write a sentence correctly using *prime* (as a noun). (Be sure to include context clues to show you understand the meaning of the word.)

   _____

   _____

Range[8]

range (rānj), *n., v.,* **ranged, rang|ing,** *adj.* —*n.*
1 the distance between certain limits; extent: *a range of colors to choose from, range of prices from 5 cents to 25 dollars, the average daily range of temperature, vocal range, a limited range of ideas.* **2a** the distance a gun can shoot or a projectile, laser, radio, or other apparatus can operate: *to be within range of the enemy. The useful range of these hand-held radio's is about three miles.* **b** the distance from a gun, launching pad, radio transmitter, or other place or device, of an object aimed at or used: *to set the sights of a howitzer for a range of 1,000 yards. That camera lens is set for a range of three feet to infinity.* **3** the greatest distance an aircraft, rocket, or the like, can travel on a single load of fuel. **4** a place to practice shooting: *a missile range.* **5** land for grazing. **6** the act of wandering or moving about. **7** a row or line of mountains: *the Green Mountain range of the Appalachian system. Mount Rainier is in the Cascade Range.* **8** a row, line, or series: *The library has ranges of books in perfect order.* **9** a line of direction: *The two barns are in direct range with the house.* **10** a rank, class, or order: *The cohesion of the nation was greatest in the lowest ranges* (William Stubbs). **11** the district in which certain plants or animals live or naturally occur: *the reindeer, who is even less Arctic in his range than the musk ox* (Elisha K. Kane). **12** a stove for cooking: *Gas and electric ranges have replaced the coal and wood range.* **13** *Mathematics.* **a** the set of all the values a given function may take on. **b** = domain. **14** *Statistics.* the difference between the smallest and the greatest values which a variable bears in frequency distribution: *The range of this variation is unusually small.* **15a** *U.S.* a row of townships, each six miles square, between two meridians six miles apart. **b** *Canadian.* a subdivision of a township; concession: *A real ghost roams about township 14, range 15* (Neepawa, Manitoba, Star). **16** *Surveying.* a line extended so as to intersect a transit line. **17** the part of an animal hide near the tail. [probably < verb]

— v.i. **1** to extend between certain limits: *prices ranging from $5 to $10.* **2** to wander; rove; roam: *to range through the woods. Our talk ranged over all that had happened on our vacation.* **3** to run in a line; extend: *a boundary ranging from east to west.* **4** to be found; occur: *a plant ranging from Canada to Mexico.* **5** (of a gun, radio, laser, or other device) to have a particular range. **6** to find the distance or direction of something. **7** to take up or have a position in a line or other arrangement. **8** to search an area: *The eye ranged over an immense extent of wilderness* (Washington Irving).
— v.t. **1** to wander over: *Buffalo once ranged these plains.* **2** to put in a row or rows: *Range the books by size.* **3** to put in groups or classes; classify. **4** to put in a line on someone's side: *Loyal citizens ranged themselves with the king.* **5** to make straight or even: *to range lines of type.* **6a** to find the proper elevation for (a gun). **b** to give the proper elevation to (a gun). **7** to direct (a telescope) upon an object; train.
— adj. of or on land for grazing: *a range pony, range cattle.*

[< Old French *ranger* to array < *rang;* see etym. under **rank**[1]]
— Syn. n. **1 Range, scope, compass** mean the extent of what something can do or take in. **Range** emphasizes the extent (and variety) that can be covered or included by something in operation or action, such as the mind, the eye, a machine, or a force: *The car was out of my range of vision.* **Scope** emphasizes the limits beyond which the understanding, view, application, or the like, cannot extend: *Some technical terms are outside the scope of this dictionary.* **Compass** also emphasizes limits, but implies more definite ones that are likely to be permanent: *Supernatural phenomena are beyond the compass of reason or science.*

from **rank**[1]:

[< Old French *rang,* earlier *reng* < Germanic (compare Old High German *hring* circle, ring). Compare etym. under **ranch**.]

1. Select the synonym(s) of *range.*

   _____ a. occur   _____ c. derivative

   _____ b. retraction   _____ d. extent

2. Which of the numbered dictionary definitions of *range* as a noun best fits the word's use in the reading selection? _____

3. The etymology of *range* shows that the word comes from the Old French *ranger* (to array) and from the Old High German *hring* (circle or ring). Use this information, your imagination, and your background knowledge to match the following:

   _____ a. rank   aa. a row or line, usually soldiers, placed side by side

   _____ b. derange   bb. sheet of ice for skating

   _____ c. rink   cc. to disturb the order of arrangement of; throw into confusion

   _____ d. ringhals   dd. to put in the proper, or any desired, order

   _____ e. arrange   ee. South African species of cobra having a narrow hood and ring of color around the neck

4. Write a sentence correctly using *range.* (Be sure to include context clues to show you understand the meaning of the word.)

   _____

   _____

5. If the cost of a two-seater sports car varies from $15,000 to $25,000, what would be the *range* in price for this car? What is the *range* of your abilities in your college classes? How would you describe this *range*?

   _____

   _____

CHAPTER TEN

Theorem[1]

the|o|rem (thē′ər əm, thir′əm), *n.* **1** *Mathematics.*
a a statement that is to be proved or that has
been proved. *Example:* In an isosceles triangle
the angles opposite the equal sides are equal.
b a rule or statement of relations that can be expressed by an equation or formula: *Geometrical
theorems grew out of empirical methods* (Herbert
Spencer). **2** any statement or rule that can be
proved to be true. **3** a kind of picture produced
by painting through one or more colored stencils,
made especially in the 1800's. [< Latin *theōrēma*
< Greek *theōrēma, -atos* < *theōreîn* to consider;
see etym. under **theory**]

from **theory:**

[< Late Latin *theōria* < Greek *theōriā* a looking
at, thing looked at < *theōreîn* to consider, look at
< *theōrós* spectator < *théā* a sight + *horán* see]

1. The etymology of *theorem* shows that the word comes from the Latin
   theorema and the Greek *theorema* (to consider) as well as from the Greek
   theoros (spectator). (Also see *theory*.) Use this information, your imagination, and your background knowledge to match the following:

   _____ a. intuition

   _____ b. theater

   _____ c. spectacle

   _____ d. contemplation

   _____ e. theoretical

   aa. planned or worked out in the mind;
   not from experience

   bb. act of looking at, or thinking about,
   something for a long time

   cc. place where plays or motion pictures
   are shown

   dd. immediate perception or understanding of truths, facts, or events
   without reasoning

   ee. thing to look at; sight

2. What are some characteristics of a *theorem?*

   _____ a. expressed by equation   _____ c. has been proved
   or formula

   _____ b. cannot be proved   _____ d. rule or statement

3. Which of the numbered dictionary definitions of *theorem* best fits the
   word's use in the reading selection? _____

4. What is the fundamental *theorem* of calculus as discussed in the reading
   selection?

   _____

   _____

5. Write a sentence correctly using *theorem*. (Be sure to include context
   clues to show you understand the meaning of the word.)

   _____

   _____

   _____

Variable[6]

var|i|a|ble (vãr′ē ə bəl), *adj., n.* —*adj.* **1** apt to change; changeable; uncertain: *variable winds. The weather is more variable in New York than it is in California.* syn: unsteady, unstable, fluctuating, wavering, mutable. **2** likely to shift from one opinion or course of action to another; inconsistent: *a variable frame of mind.* syn: fickle. **3** that can be varied, changed, or modified: *Adjustable curtain rods are of variable length.* syn: alterable. **4** *Biology.* deviating, as from the normal or recognized species, variety, or structure. **5** likely to increase or decrease in size, number, amount, or degree; not remaining the same or uniform: *a constant or variable ratio. The so-called variable costs—prices for story rights, producer, director,* scriptwriter, and stars—are, if you want a good product, the least amenable to trimming (Sunday Times).
—*n.* **1** a thing or quality that varies: *Temperature and rainfall are variables.* syn: inconstant. **2** *Mathematics.* **a** a quantity that can assume any of the values in a given set of values. **b** a symbol representing this quantity. **3** a shifting wind. **4** = variable star.
the variables, the region between the northeast and the southeast trade winds: *The meeting of the two opposite currents [of wind] here produces the intermediate space called the . . . variables* (Arthur Young).
—**var′i|a|ble|ness,** *n.*

1. Select the synonym(s) of *variable.*
   _____ a. actual number   _____ c. symbol
   _____ b. constant   _____ d. inconstant

2. Which of the numbered dictionary definitions of *variable* (as a noun) best fits the word's use in the reading selection? _____

3. In which of the following sentences can *variable* correctly be placed in the blank?
   _____ a. A _____ is a symbol that is used to represent a quantity.
   _____ b. A _____ is a rule of correspondence between two sets.
   _____ c. To prove the theorem, we need a preliminary theorem called a _____ .
   _____ d. X is a _____ in the following equation: $x = 13 - y.$

4. Write a sentence correctly using *variable.* (Be sure to include context clues to show you understand the meaning of the word.)

   _____

   _____

5. Write an equation using the *variables* x and y. Show it to your instructor or one of your classmates for verification.

   _____

   _____

ANSWERS TO CHAPTER 10 EXERCISES

Composite: **1.** d (synonym) **2.** cc, ee, dd, aa, bb **3.** a, c, d
Congruent: **1.** a, b **2.** 1 **3.** b
Derivative: **1.** c, d **2.** 4ab **3.** a, b, c, d
Domain: **1.** b, d **2.** cc, ee, dd, bb, aa **3.** 6
Exponent: **1.** b, c **2.** 4 **3.** a, b, d
Factor: **1.** a, c, d **2.** 2 **3.** bb, ee, aa, cc, dd
Function: **1.** a, d **2.** 3a **3.** ee, dd, cc, aa, bb
Hypotenuse: **1.** c **2.** ee, dd, bb, cc, aa **3.** b
Integral: **1.** d (field of study) **2.** 2a **3.** a, c
Inverse: **1.** b **2.** ee, dd, aa, bb, cc **3.** 3a
Postulate: **1.** a, d **2.** b, c **3.** b, d
Prime: **1.** 4 **2.** a, c **3.** dd, ee, bb, aa, cc
Range: **1.** a, d **2.** 13a **3.** aa, cc, bb, ee, dd
Theorem: **1.** dd, cc, ee, bb, aa **2.** a, c, d **3.** 1b
Variable: **1.** c, d **2.** 2 **3.** a, d

If you missed any of the items in the exercises, return to the exercise and to the dictionary definitions to see where you went wrong. Remember: If you get something right, you only affirm that you knew it. If you get something wrong and understand why, *you have learned something.*

MATHEMATICS POSTTEST

Fill in the blanks with the words from this list.

composite	factor	postulate
congruent	function	prime
derivative	hypotenuse	range
domain	integral	theorem
exponent	inverse	variable

1. A(n) _____ is a fundamental principle or necessary condition.

2. The number 13 is an example of a(n) _____ number.

3. A(n) _____ is the instantaneous rate of change of a function with respect to its variable.

4. *X* is an example of a(n) _____ .

5. *Combination* and *compound* are synonyms of _____ .

6. The _____ between 50 and 75 is 25.

7. The _____ of multiplication is division.

8. The number 5 is a(n) _____ in 3^5.

9. A(n) _____ is the set of all numbers that can be assigned to x in an equation with two variables.

10. The number 3 is a(n) _____ of 9.

11. A(n) _____ is the result of an integration in calculus.

12. A statement that can be proved or that has been proved is a(n) _____.

13. *Harmonious* and *accordant* are synonyms of _____.

14. A(n) _____ is a quantity whose value depends on the value given to one or more related quantities.

15. The Pythagorean theorem shows a relationship between the sides of the right triangle and the _____.

Answers to this posttest are in the Instructor's Manual.

If you missed any of the words, you may need to return to the exercises and to the dictionary entries to see why your concepts for some words are incomplete.

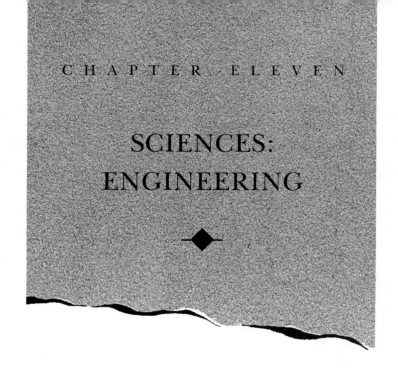

CHAPTER ELEVEN

SCIENCES:
ENGINEERING

◆

OVERVIEW

The field of engineering is very broad and includes the primary categories of aerospace engineering, chemical engineering, civil engineering, electrical and computer engineering, industrial and manufacturing engineering and mechanical engineering. Within the civil engineering emphasis are the fields of structural, geotechnical, hydraulic, environmental, construction, and architectural engineering. One of the most rapidly growing areas within the field of civil engineering is environmental engineering because it is concerned with the quality of our environment. Specifically, environmental engineering focuses on the design and supervision of systems to provide safe drinking water and to prevent and control pollution in the air, soil, and water. Most environmental engineering programs are scientific and/or applied in nature and link the theoretical and empirical to the practical.

Areas of study within environmental engineering include air pollution, groundwater pollution and remediation, domestic and industrial wastewater treatment, drinking water, solid waste disposal, and water reuse and recycling.

Students who major in this field may work in both the public and the private sectors and for such agencies as the U.S. Environmental Protection Agency, the Department of Health and Human Services, and the Army Corps of Engineers. They may also work for local and state air resource and water quality control boards. Environmental engineers may design domestic or industrial waste water treatment plants and landfills, enforce air pollution and drinking water regulations, prepare environmental

147

impact reports, and conduct laboratory analyses. They may also conduct research in such areas as disinfection of drinking water, volatile synthetic organic chemicals in groundwater, or remediation methods of polluted groundwater.

Most introductory textbooks are both expository and descriptive in that they explain broad concepts and generalizations as well as statements, ideas, and problems. Laboratory manuals are structured according to process analysis, with explanations of various procedures. There usually is reinforcement of concepts and design solutions provided through illustrations, photography, charts, tables, and formulas.

The vocabulary in engineering is a combination of general and specialized vocabulary. There are general-use words such as pollution and reservoir that also have a specialized meaning within the context of engineering. Then there are specialized terms such as turbidity and sedimentation that reflect concepts unique to the study of engineering. Since modern civil engineering relies heavily on computer-assisted design (CAD), additional classroom materials would include various types of software programs and related laboratory activities.

VOCABULARY SELF-EVALUATION

The following words will be introduced in this reading selection. Place a check mark (√) in front of any that you know thoroughly and use in your speech and writing. Place a question mark (?) in front of any that you recognize but do not use yourself.

_____ aeration	_____ filtration	_____ precipitation
_____ aqueduct	_____ hydrologic	_____ reservoir
_____ aquifer	_____ palatable	_____ sedimentation
_____ chlorination	_____ percolation	_____ transpiration
_____ coagulation	_____ potable	_____ turbidity

POTABLE WATER: ITS SOURCES, TREATMENT, AND DISTRIBUTION

Water is a very precious resource in our environment. Human beings need potable[1] water, that is, water suitable for drinking, for survival. It must be free from pollution caused by harmful contaminants. We receive fresh raw water in a continuous process of movement of water from the earth to the clouds and back again.

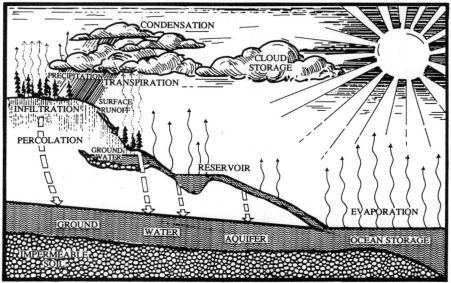

ILLUSTRATION OF THE HYDROLOGIC CYCLE

This fresh raw water delivery system is called the hydrologic[2] cycle (see illustration). There are two primary ways in which water moves from the earth to the sky. One process is called evaporation, whereby water vapor rises from the ocean into the air and is held there by moving air masses or cloud storage. The other is through transpiration,[3] in which water from the soil is taken up by the roots of trees, shrubs, grasses, and other plants and then passed off as moisture into the air from the surfaces of the leaves.

Water can return to the earth as precipitation,[4] which is one of the primary sources of fresh raw water. This precipitation results when the water vapor that was stored in the atmosphere forms tiny droplets of water or minute ice crystals (condensation), which, via precipitation, is then deposited on the earth in the form of rain, snow, dew, sleet, ice, or hail. Some of the precipitation is used by plants and returned to the air by transpiration. Some

of the water may move downward through the pores in the soil in a process called percolation.[5] This percolated water eventually reaches the groundwater aquifer,[6] which consists of a porous, permeable material such as sand, rock, or gravel. When the soil is saturated, that is, can hold no more water, additional precipitation becomes surface runoff and moves over the land, eventually emptying into a lake or an ocean. Water vapor from the ocean returns to the air through evaporation, thus completing the water cycle.

We can obtain some of this fresh raw water for our drinking purposes. Most often an aqueduct,[7] or open channel, is used to transport water from a mountain lake to the city to be used for drinking. However, before we can drink this raw water we need to make sure that it is safe for human consumption. The primary purpose of water treatment is to provide a continuous supply of good drinking water. This water needs to be free of harmful contaminants while also being palatable,[8] that is, pleasing to the taste. Thus, most groundwater or surface-water sources require some type of treatment prior to human consumption.

Surface water, in particular, needs complete treatment before it can be used for drinking. Surface water often carries disease-causing organisms and may contain domestic and industrial wastes. In addition, there may be turbidity,[9] or suspended (floating) matter, which makes the water cloudy and muddy, along with algae, which must be removed through proper treatment. A water treatment system involves many processes and methods for making water safe and appealing to customers. Usually the first major water treatment process used at a treatment plant is aeration,[10] or the mixing of air into the water. This process removes certain dissolved gases in the water. It also increases the dissolved oxygen content, which improves the water's taste. Coagulation[11] is a treatment process that adds a chemical to the water that causes the very small suspended particles to be attracted to one another. This is followed by flocculation, a step that uses mild turbulence to cause these very small particles to come together and create larger particles called floc. During the next treatment process, called sedimentation,[12] these larger particles are settled out by gravity in a settling basin for removal as sludge. The processes of coagulation, flocculation, and sedimentation remove the suspended solids and thus make the water more aesthetically pleasing to the consumer.

Even after sedimentation, some extremely fine particles, which may include harmful microorganisms, still remain. For this reason filtration[13] to remove the remaining harmful particles always follows the sedimentation process. This is accomplished by passing the water through a porous substance such as sand. Although sedimentation and filtration may remove most of the bacteria and viruses, they do not remove all of these potentially harmful organisms. Other processes, such as the addition of chlorine to the water through chlorination,[14] are used to disinfect the water, that is, to kill disease-causing organisms. After the water has been properly treated in accordance with various state and national regulations, it can be distributed to the public.

To deliver the treated water properly to the consumer requires an extensive system of pumps, pipes, and storage. Storage of water is a very important part of this distribution process. Covered reservoirs[15] and water tanks that collect and store water are used in these distribution systems to equalize the rate of flow of the water and to maintain adequate pressure under periods of high consumer demand. These storage facilities are also used for emergency situations such as fires and power failures. Storage tanks can be located above, on, or below the ground.

Finally, it is essential that the quality of the raw water source to be used for drinking be fairly good from its origin, because water treatment is a minimal process. Water treatment removes only suspended materials, such as dirt and microorganisms, and disinfects the water. Water that contains heavy metals or toxic organics cannot be used as a raw water source because these pollutants cannot be removed through the ordinary treatment processes just described. However, these contaminants can be removed through sophisticated and very expensive processes not normally employed at a conventional water treatment plant. It is obvious, then, that we need to protect our raw water sources—lakes, rivers, groundwater—since unpolluted sources are a necessary element for our survival on this planet. ◆

ENGINEERING PRETEST

Select words from this list and write them in the blanks to complete the sentences.

aeration	filtration	precipitation
aqueduct	hydrologic	reservoir
aquifer	palatable	sedimentation
chlorination	percolation	transpiration
coagulation	potable	turbidity

1. The process of exposure to chemical action with oxygen is called _____.

2. The _____ cycle refers to the water cycle within our atmosphere.

3. The action or fact of depositing water into a tank so that the suspended solids can settle to the bottom is called _____.

4. _____ causes water to be cloudy or muddy.

5. Fit for drinking, or drinkable, means being _____.

6. The process or act of thickening, or changing from liquid to a thickened mass, is called _____.

7. A(n) _____ is a stratum of earth or porous soil that contains water.

8. _____ is the act or process of seepage down through the soil.

9. A(n) _____ is a place where water is collected and stored for use.

10. A(n) _____ is an artificial channel or large pipe for bringing water from a distance.

11. The act or fact of depositing moisture in the form of rain, snow, sleet, ice, or hail is called _____.

12. Something that is agreeable to the taste, or pleasing, would be _____.

13. The process of disinfection, or sterilization with a greenish-yellow, bad-smelling, poisonous chemical, is called _____.

14. _____ is the action or process of sending moisture in the form of vapor through a plant membrane or a surface of the foliage.

15. _____ is the process of removing impurities from drinking water by passing water through a porous substance such as sand.

Answers to this pretest are in Appendix B.

Unless your instructor tells you to do otherwise, complete the exercises for each word you missed on the pretest. The words, with their meanings and exercises, are in alphabetical order. The superscript numbers indicate where the words appeared in the reading selection so that you can refer to them when necessary. There are several types of exercises, but for each word you will be asked to write a sentence using context clues. (See Chapter 4 if you need information about how to create context clues.) You are also asked to perform some activity that will help you make your concept of the word personal. *Complete this activity thoughtfully, for creating a personalized concept of the word will help you remember it in the future.*

Answers to all the exercises are at the end of the exercise segment.

ENGINEERING EXERCISES

Aeration[10]

aer|ate (ār′āt), *v.t.*, **-at|ed, -at|ing. 1** to expose to and mix with air: *Water in some reservoirs is aerated and purified by spraying it high into the air.* **2** to fill with a gas; charge or mix with gas, often under pressure: *Soda water is water that has been aerated with carbon dioxide.* **3** to expose to chemical action with oxygen: *Blood is aerated in the lungs.* **4** to expose to air. [< aer- + -ate[1]] —**aer|a′tion,** *n.* —**aer′a|tor,** *n.*

1. Complete the verbal analogy.
   hydrologic : water :: *aeration* : _____
   a. space   c. land
   b. ocean   d. air

2. The etymology of *aeration* shows that the word comes from the Latin *aer* (air). Use this information, your imagination, and your background knowledge to match the following:

   _____ a. aerobics   aa. related to vehicles or travel in space

   _____ b. aerosol   bb. instrument for measuring the weight of air

   _____ c. aerospace   cc. substance distributed from a pressurized container

   _____ d. aerometer   dd. physical conditioning with vigorous exercise and dance routines

3. Which of the following could be affected by *aeration?*
   _____ a. air   _____ c. blood
   _____ b. soil   _____ d. liquid

4. What would be one of the effects of *aeration* on the soil in someone's yard, such as in your garden or on your lawn? Why would farmers want to use *aeration* processes?

_____

_____

5. Write a sentence correctly using *aeration*. (Be sure to include context clues to show you understand the meaning of the word.)

_____

_____

Aqueduct[7]

✶aq|ue|duct (ak′wə dukt), *n.* **1** an artificial channel or large pipe for bringing water from a distance. **2** the structure that supports such a channel or pipe. **3** a similar structure by which a canal is carried over a stream, river, or other obstruction. **4** *Anatomy.* a canal or channel in the body, especially a small one in the head. [< Latin *aquae-ductus* < *aqua* water *ductus, -ūs* a leading < *ducere* to lead]

✶aqueduct
definition 1

1. Which of the numbered dictionary definitions of *aqueduct* best fits the word's use in the reading selection? _____

2. What other discipline(s) have specialized meanings for *aqueduct?*
   _____ a. mathematics
   _____ b. psychology
   _____ c. anatomy

3. The etymology of *aqueduct* shows that the word comes from the Latin *aqua* (water) and *ductus* (leading). Use this information, your imagination, and your background knowledge to match the following:
   _____ a. aquarium   aa. furnishing results or profits
   _____ b. aqualung   bb. guide or manage
   _____ c. conduct   cc. tank or bowl to hold fish
   _____ d. productive   dd. scuba

4. Write a sentence correctly using *aqueduct*. (Be sure to include context clues to show you understand the meaning of the word.)

_____

_____

5. What is the relationship between an *aqueduct* and a *reservoir?* (You may need to write your sentence after you have worked with the word *reservoir.*)

_____

_____

Aquifer[6]

aq|ui|fer (ak'wə fər), *n.* **1** *Geology.* a stratum of earth or porous rock that contains water: *Like surface streams, water in the aquifers flows underground from the source to discharge points —either wells, swamps, springs, or lakes* (Newsweek). See picture under **artesian well.** **2** anything that carries water. [< Latin *aqui-* (< *aqua* water) *ferre* to carry]

1. Where is the location of an *aquifer?*
   - _____ a. on the ground
   - _____ b. above the ground
   - _____ c. below the ground

2. In which of the following sentences can *aquifer* be correctly placed in the blank?
   - _____ a. A geologist might study the porous rock in the _____ .
   - _____ b. The _____ in the elderly woman's car was filled with liquid.
   - _____ c. The young boy tossed the _____ into the ocean after playing with it.
   - _____ d. After disinfection, water from the _____ was pumped into the covered reservoir.

3. An *aquifer* is discussed in what part of the reading selection?
   - _____ a. distribution
   - _____ b. treatment
   - _____ c. source/hydrologic cycle

4. If you were an environmental engineer, why would you want to protect an *aquifer?*

   _____

   _____

5. Write a sentence correctly using *aquifer.* (Be sure to include context clues to show you understand the meaning of the word.)

   _____

   _____

Chlorination[14]

chlo|rin|ate (klôr'ə nāt, klōr'-), *v.t.,* **-at|ed, -at|ing.** **1** to combine with chlorine. **2** to treat with chlorine: **a** to disinfect or sterilize (water or sewage) by the use of chlorine: *to chlorinate water in a swimming pool.* **b** to treat (gold or silver ore) with chlorine, to extract the precious metal; chloridize. —**chlo′rin|a′tion,** *n.* —**chlo′rin|a′tor,** *n.*

1. What is the purpose of *chlorination* in the water treatment process?
   _____ a. to remove sediment
   _____ b. to create floc
   _____ c. to disinfect the water

2. Complete the following verbal analogy.
   antibiotics : pathogens :: *chlorination* : _____
   a. sediment   c. oxygen
   b. aquifer   d. bacteria

3. What are some other purposes of the *chlorination* process?
   _____ a. to convert into chloride
   _____ b. to sterilize water
   _____ c. to extract precious metals

4. Why would one utilize *chlorination* in a backyard swimming pool or in a community swimming pool? Have you ever smelled water that had recently had a *chlorination* treatment? How did it smell or affect you?

   _____

   _____

   _____

5. Write a sentence correctly using *chlorination*. (Be sure to use context clues to show you understand the meaning of the word.)

   _____

   _____

Coagulation[11]

co|ag|u|la|tion (kō ag′yə lā′shən), *n.* **1** the act or process of coagulating. If coagulation of the blood does not take place in a cut or wound, the injured person may bleed to death. **2** a coagulated mass; clot.

co|ag|u|late (*v.* kō ag′yə lāt; *adj.* kō ag′yə lit, -lāt), *v.,* **-lat|ed, -lat|ing,** *adj.* —*v.t., v.i.* **1** to change from liquid to a thickened mass; thicken: *Cooking coagulates the white of egg. Blood from a cut coagulates.* syn: curdle, clot, congeal. **2** *Obsolete.* to form into a solidified cake or mass. —*adj. Obsolete.* coagulated.
[< Latin *coāgulāre* (with English -ate¹) < *coāgulum* means of curdling < *co-* together + *agere* drive]

1. Check any appropriate response to the following statement. (You may need to consult the reading selection again to answer this question.) "*Coagulation* is necessary in the water treatment process."
   _____ a. Very small particles need to be formed into larger particles.
   _____ b. Gravity needs to settle out suspended particles.
   _____ c. Water needs to be pleasing to the taste.
   _____ d. Air and water must be mixed together.

2. Select the words that relate to the *coagulation* process.

_____ a. adjust   _____ c. breathe

_____ b. clot   _____ d. congeal

3. What are some characteristics of the *coagulation* process?

_____ a. melting   _____ c. clumping

_____ b. thickening   _____ d. settling

4. Write a sentence correctly using *coagulation*. (Be sure to include context clues to show you understand the meaning of the word.)

_____

_____

5. How does *coagulation* apply to the medical field?

_____

_____

Filtration[13]

fil|trate (fil′trāt), *n., v.,* **-trat|ed, -trat|ing.** — *n.* the liquid that has been passed through a filter. [< verb]
— *v.t., v.i.* to pass through a filter.
[< Medieval Latin *filtrum* filter + English *-ate*[1]]
— **fil|tra′tion,** *n.*

1. What parts of our body utilize a *filtration* process?

_____ a. kidney

_____ b. lungs

_____ c. mouth

2. Select the synonym(s) of *filtration*.

_____ a. turbidity   _____ c. penetration

_____ b. diffusion   _____ d. transpiration

3. Check all the following statements that apply to the *filtration* process as discussed in the reading selection.

_____ a. It disinfects the water before it goes into the aquifer.

_____ b. It removes the suspended solids that haven't already been removed.

_____ c. It follows the sedimentation process.

_____ d. It helps to remove dissolved metals.

4. Write a sentence correctly using *filtration*. (Be sure to use context clues to show you understand the meaning of the word.)

_____

_____

5. What are some other examples of *filtration* that might occur in your home or in your car?

_____

_____

_____

Hydrologic[2]

hy|dro|log|ic (hī'drə loj'ik), *adj.* of or having to do with hydrology. — **hy'dro|log'i|cal|ly,** *adv.*
hy|dro|log|i|cal (hī'drə loj'ə kəl), *adj.* = hydrologic.
hydrologic cycle, = water cycle.
hy|drol|o|gy (hī drol'ə jē), *n.* the science that deals with water, with special reference to its properties, laws, and geographical distribution. [< New Latin *hydrologia* < Greek *hýdōr, -atos* water + *-logiā* -logy] — **hy|drol'o|gist,** *n.*

1. Complete the verbal analogy.
   aeration : air :: *hydrologic* : _____
   a. water   c. matter
   b. space   d. land

2. The etymology of *hydrologic* as it is derived from hydrology shows that the word comes from the Greek *hydor* (water) and *logia* (study). Use this information, your imagination, and your background knowledge to match the following:
   _____ a. hydrophobia   aa. water cure
   _____ b. hydroponics   bb. fear of water
   _____ c. hydrophone   cc. growth of plants without soil
   _____ d. hydropathy   dd. instrument to detect the flow of water in a pipe

3. Some of the elements or components of the *hydrologic* cycle are
   _____ a. coagulation   _____ c. transpiration
   _____ b. chlorination   _____ d. precipitation

4. What parts of the *hydrologic* cycle were you familiar with before you read the reading selection?

   _____

   What might be the most interesting or fascinating element or activity in the *hydrologic* cycle to you? Why?

   _____

   _____

5. Write a sentence correctly using *hydrologic*. (Be sure to include context clues to show you understand the meaning of the word.)

_____

_____

Palatable[8]

pal|at|a|ble (pal′ə tə bəl), *adj.* **1** agreeable to the taste; pleasing: *That was a most palatable lunch.* SYN: savory. **2** *Figurative.* agreeable to the mind or feelings; acceptable: *His eloquence was distinguished by a bold, uncompromising, truth-telling spirit, whether the words might prove palatable or bitter to his audience* (John L. Motley). —**pal′at|a-ble|ness**, *n.* —**pal′at|a|bly**, *adv.*

1. Select the synonym(s) of *palatable*.
   _____ a. adaptable _____ c. irritable
   _____ b. savory _____ d. pleasing

2. Complete the verbal analogy.
   visual : eye :: *palatable* : _____
   a. mouth c. nose
   b. eyes d. hands

3. In which of the following sentences is *palatable* used correctly?
   _____ a. The sour fruit was palatable to the young boy, so he spit it out.
   _____ b. He needed to modify his normally gruff tone of voice so that it would be more palatable to the audience.
   _____ c. The chef at the restaurant prepared a palatable dinner, which we enjoyed.
   _____ d. The ambassador wrote a peace treaty that was a palatable solution to the conflict between the two countries.

4. Write a sentence correctly using *palatable*. (Be sure to include context clues to show you understand the meaning of the word.)

_____

_____

5. What foods do you find most *palatable*?

_____

Are there certain types of food (ethnic, spicy, mild, etc.) that are more *palatable* to you than others? What are they?

_____

_____

_____

Percolation[5]

per|co|late (pėr′kə lāt), v., -lat|ed, -lat|ing, n.
— v.i. 1 to drip or drain through small holes or spaces: *Let the coffee percolate for seven minutes.* 2 *Slang, Figurative.* to act efficiently. — v.t. 1 to filter through; permeate: *Water percolates sand.* (*Figurative.*) *relief payments percolate the economy.* **SYN:** filter, ooze, trickle. 2 to cause (a liquid or particles) to pass through; filter; sift. 3 to make (coffee) in a percolator.
— *n.* a liquid that has been percolated. [< Latin *percōlāre* (with English *-ate¹*) < *per-* through + *cōlāre* to filter through < *cōlum* strainer]
per|co|la|tion (pėr′kə lā′shən), n. the act or process of percolating.

1. Complete the verbal analogy.
   palatable : adjective :: *percolation* : _____
   a. verb   c. adverb
   b. noun   d. conjunction

2. *Percolation* is part of the following process(es):
   _____ a. water treatment   _____ c. hydrologic cycle
   _____ b. water distribution   _____ d. all of them

3. Select the synonym(s) of *percolation.*
   _____ a. disinfecting   _____ c. breathing
   _____ b. trickling   _____ d. oozing

4. What are some other examples of *percolation* that you can think of that are related to our environment or that may occur in your home? Why would they be considered examples of *percolation?*

   _____

   _____

5. Write a sentence correctly using *percolation.* (Be sure to include context clues to show you understand the meaning of the word.)

   _____

   _____

Potable[1]

po|ta|ble (pō′tə bəl), adj., n. —*adj.* fit for drinking; drinkable: *In dozens of places where the water was not potable, they set up purifying systems* (Newsweek).
—*n.* Usually, **potables, a** anything drinkable: *He bought eatables and potables.* **b** alcoholic liquor. [< Late Latin *pōtābilis* < Latin *pōtāre* to drink]
—**po′ta|ble|ness,** n.

1. Check any appropriate response to the following statement:
   "We visited a country with *potable* water."
   _____ a. It was so muddy that we couldn't drink it.
   _____ b. The water was stored in covered reservoirs.
   _____ c. We were able to drink the water.
   _____ d. The water had been treated so that it was safe to drink.

SCIENCES: ENGINEERING

2. What are some examples of *potables?*

   _____ a. water   _____ c. juice

   _____ b. fruit   _____ d. alcohol

3. Complete the verbal analogy.

palatable : pleasing :: *potable* : _____

a. clear   c. free

b. safe   d. clean

4. Write a sentence correctly using *potable.* (Be sure to include context clues to show you understand the meaning of the word.)

_____

_____

5. Have you ever traveled to another country that did not have *potable* water? Where and when?

_____

What did you/would you do instead of drinking the water?

_____

_____

Precipitation[4]

pre|cip|i|ta|tion (pri sip′ə tā′shən), *n.* **1** the act or condition of precipitating; throwing down or falling headlong: *the tragic precipitation of the climbers over the side of the mountain.* **2** the action of hastening or hurrying. **3** *Figurative.* the act or fact of bringing on suddenly: *the precipitation of a quarrel, the precipitation of war without warning.* **4** *Figurative.* unwise or rash rapidity; sudden haste. **5a** the process of separating a substance from a solution as a solid. **b** the substance separated out from a solution as a solid; precipitate. **6a** the act or fact of depositing moisture in the form of rain, snow, sleet, ice, or hail: *In steppe lands and arid regions, evaporation is greater than precipitation* (R. N. Elston). **b** something that is precipitated, such as rain, dew, or snow. **c** the amount that is precipitated. **7** = materialization (in spiritualism).

1. *Precipitation* is part of which water system according to the reading selection?

   _____ a. treatment

   _____ b. delivery/distribution

   _____ c. source/hydrologic cycle

2. Which of the following is *not* an example of *precipitation?*

   _____ a. sleet   _____ c. thunder

   _____ b. snow   _____ d. rain

3. In which of the following sentences can *precipitation* correctly be placed in the blank?

   _____ a. The _____ of the rocks into the roadway missed the cars.

   _____ b. This year the snowfall _____ exceeded all previous records.

_____ c. The couple was unable to recollect any reason for the _____ of their argument.

_____ d. He was concerned about her _____ , since it was wet.

4. What is your favorite form of *precipitation?* In what season of the year would this form of *precipitation* most likely occur?

_____

_____

5. Write a sentence correctly using *precipitation.* (Be sure to use context clues to show you understand the meaning of the word.)

_____

_____

Reservoir[15]

res|er|voir (rez′ər vwär, -vwôr, -vôr), *n.* **1** a place where water is collected and stored for use, especially an artificial basin created by the damming of a river: *This reservoir supplies the entire city.* **2** anything to hold a liquid: *an oil reservoir for an engine. A fountain pen has an ink reservoir.* **3** *Figurative.* a place where anything is collected and stored: *Her mind was a reservoir of facts.* **4** *Figurative.* a great supply: *a reservoir of manpower. There exists in the world today a gigantic reservoir of good will toward us, the* American people (Wendell Willkie). **5** *Biology.* **a** a part of an animal or plant in which some fluid or secretion is collected or retained. **b** an organism that carries a disease germ or virus to which it is immune: *They hope that the laboratories will soon identify the animal carriers—the reservoirs —and the insects—vectors—that transmit the disease* (New York Times). [< French *réservoir* < Old French *reserver* to reserve]

1. In which of the following sentences is *reservoir* used correctly?

_____ a. The design of a new automobile necessarily includes a gas reservoir.

_____ b. The reservoir needs to be protected from pollutants.

_____ c. A reservoir of talent exists among the members of the younger generation.

_____ d. The settling basin is linked to the reservoir.

2. Select the synonym(s) of *reservoir.*

_____ a. supply _____ c. treatment

_____ b. storage _____ d. reserve

3. Complete the verbal analogy.

precipitation : moisture :: *reservoir* : _____

a. soil b. air c. water

4. Write a sentence correctly using *reservoir.* (Be sure to use context clues to show you understand the meaning of the word.)

_____

_____

_____

5. Have you ever gone swimming or boating in a lake that was also a *reservoir*? Which one? Was the *reservoir* contained by a dam at one end?

_____

_____

Sedimentation[12]

sed|i|men|ta|tion (sed′ə men tā′shən), *n.* the action or fact of depositing sediment.

sed|i|ment (sed′ə mənt), *n., v. —n.* **1** any matter that settles to the bottom of a liquid; dregs. sʏɴ: lees. **2** *Geology.* earth, stones, or other matter suspended in or deposited by water, wind, or ice: *When the Nile overflows, it deposits sediment on the land it covers.*
—v.t., v.i. to deposit as or form sediment.
[< Latin *sedimentum* < *sedēre* to settle; sit]

1. Complete the verbal analogy.
   percolation : filter :: *sedimentation* : _____
   a. deposit   c. diffuse
   b. disinfect   d. aerate

2. What are some examples of the natural *sedimentation* process in a lake or river?
   _____ a. silt   _____ c. dissolved ions (sodium or chloride)
   _____ b. mud   _____ d. clay

3. *Sedimentation* has a specialized meaning in what field(s) of knowledge?
   _____ a. geology
   _____ b. geography
   _____ c. hydraulics

4. What are some potential problems that result from *sedimentation* build-up in a lake? In a backyard pool?

_____

_____

5. Write a sentence correctly using *sedimentation*. (Be sure to include context clues to show you understand the meaning of the word.)

_____

_____

Transpiration[3]

tran|spi|ra|tion (tran′spə rā′shən), *n.* the action or process of transpiring, especially moisture in the form of vapor through a membrane or surface, as from the human body or from leaves or other parts of plants.

tran|spire (tran spīr′), *v.,* **-spired, -spir|ing.** *—v.i.* **1** to take place; happen; occur: *I heard later* what transpired at the meeting. **2** *Figurative.* to leak out; become known. **3** to pass off or send off moisture in the form of vapor through a membrane or surface, as from the human body or from leaves. *—v.t.* to pass off or send off in the form of a vapor or liquid, as waste matter through the skin or moisture through the leaves of a plant. [< Middle French *transpirer* < Latin *trāns-* through + *spīrāre* breathe]

1. *Transpiration* is a form of
   _____ a. light   _____ c. air
   _____ b. vapor   _____ d. heat

2. The etymology of *transpiration* shows that the word comes from the Latin *trans* (through) and *spirare* (breathe). Use this information, your imagination, and your background knowledge to match the following:
   _____ a. spiritual   aa. interchange; change position or order
   _____ b. spiracle   bb. remove from one place to another
   _____ c. transplant   cc. small respiratory opening or vent
   _____ d. transpose   dd. relative to the supernatural or to sacred matters

3. Which of the following might be said of *transpiration*?
   _____ a. Transpiration naturally occurs in leaves or other plants.
   _____ b. Transpiration sends off moisture into the air in the form of vapor.
   _____ c. Humans are unable to participate in the transpiration process.
   _____ d. Breathing is a form of transpiration.

4. Write a sentence correctly using *transpiration*. (Be sure to include context clues to show you understand the meaning of the word.)

   _____

   _____

5. What other forms of life besides plants experience *transpiration* as part of their life cycle? _____
   What activity or process in human beings does *transpiration* relate to?

   _____

   _____

   _____

Turbidity[9]

tur|bid|i|ty (tėr bid′ə tē), *n.* the condition of being turbid: *Water beetles provide clues to the acidity and turbidity of water* (New Scientist).

tur|bid (tėr′bid), *adj.* **1** not clear; cloudy; muddy: *a turbid river.* **2** thick; dense; dark: *turbid air or smoke.* **3** *Figurative.* confused or disordered: *a turbid imagination. Clear writers, like fountains, do not seem so deep as they are; the turbid look the most profound* (Walter S. Landor). [< Latin *turbidus* < *turba* turmoil, crowd] —**tur′bid|ly,** *adv.* —**tur′bid|ness,** *n.*

1. What are some characteristics of *turbidity*?
   _____ a. clear   _____ c. muddy
   _____ b. cloudy   _____ d. even

2. Which of the following could experience *turbidity?*
   _____ a. the mind   _____ c. land
   _____ b. air   _____ d. a river

3. What are some reasons to remove *turbidity* from the water system?
   _____ a. to make the water aesthetic, or pleasing, to the consumer
   _____ b. it may result in cloudy water
   _____ c. it may conceal disease-causing microorganisms
   _____ d. to allow vapor to return to the air

4. Does water (such as in your household tap or in a lake or pond) with the physical characteristic of *turbidity* bother you?

   _____

   What would you do if you found a water source with obvious *turbidity?* Would you drink it or swim in it?

   _____

   Why or why not?

   _____

   _____

5. Write a sentence correctly using *turbidity.* (Be sure to use context clues to show you know the meaning of the word.)

   _____

   _____

ANSWERS TO CHAPTER 11 EXERCISES

Aeration: **1.** d (requirement)   **2.** dd, cc, aa, bb   **3.** b, c, d
Aqueduct: **1.** l   **2.** c   **3.** cc, dd, bb, aa
Aquifer: **1.** c   **2.** a, d   **3.** c
Chlorination: **1.** c   **2.** d (purpose)   **3.** b, c
Coagulation: **1.** a, b   **2.** b, d   **3.** b, c
Filtration: **1.** a, b   **2.** b, c   **3.** b, c
Hydrologic: **1.** a (process)   **2.** bb, cc, dd, aa   **3.** c, d
Palatable: **1.** a, b, d   **2.** a (sense/location)   **3.** b, c, d
Percolation: **1.** b (part of speech)   **2.** a   **3.** b, d
Potable: **1.** c, d   **2.** a, c, d   **3.** b (characteristic)
Precipitation: **1.** c   **2.** c   **3.** a, b, c
Reservoir: **1.** a, b, c   **2.** a, b, d   **3.** c (content)
Sedimentation: **1.** a (purpose)   **2.** a, b, d   **3.** b
Transpiration: **1.** b   **2.** dd, cc, bb, aa   **3.** a, b
Turbidity: **1.** b, c   **2.** a, b, d   **3.** a, c

If you missed any of the items in the exercises, return to the exercise and to the dictionary definitions to see where you went wrong. Remember: If you get something right, you only affirm that you knew it. If you get something wrong and understand why, *you have learned something*.

ENGINEERING POSTTEST

Fill in the blanks with the words from this list.

aeration	filtration	precipitation
aqueduct	hydrologic	reservoir
aquifer	palatable	sedimentation
chlorination	percolation	transpiration
coagulation	potable	turbidity

1. *Clotting* and *congealing* are synonyms for _____.
2. A process that uses a very strong chemical to disinfect the water is called _____.
3. Snow, sleet, and rain are examples of _____.
4. A(n) _____ is designed for the storage of water.
5. _____ is the process of exposing something to chemical action with oxygen or air.

6. Silt, mud, and clay are examples of the _____ process in a lake or river.

7. _____ is part of the hydrologic cycle that refers to movement of water through the earth.

8. *Cloudy* and *muddy* are characteristics of _____.

9. *Diffusion* and *penetration* are synonyms for _____.

10. _____ sends off moisture into the air in the form of vapor.

11. Transpiration and precipitation are parts of the _____ cycle.

12. *Savory* and *pleasing* are synonyms for _____.

13. A(n) _____ is a conduit, channel, or pipe that moves water over a distance.

14. Water that is drinkable is described as being _____.

15. A(n) _____ is an underground source of natural raw water.

Answers to this posttest are in the Instructor's Manual.

If you missed any of the words, you may need to return to the exercises and to the dictionary entries to see why your concepts for some words are incomplete.

CHAPTER TWELVE

SOCIAL SCIENCES: ECONOMICS

◆

OVERVIEW

Economics employs systematic analysis to study the way in which societies are organized to produce the goods and services that are the underpinnings of their communities. Issues studied in economics include inflation, shortages, unemployment, price setting, regulation, foreign trade, determination of wages, government policies, and growth and income distribution.

Some areas of concentration within economics are international trade and development; economic history and comparative systems; labor and manpower economics; econometrics and systems; public finance and planning; land, resource, and urban economics; industrial organization; transportation and public utilities; economics and social welfare; and economic projecting and planning.

A degree in economics can prepare students for employment in national and multinational corporations, financial institutions, unions, and at all levels of government and agribusiness. It can also serve as preparation for advanced studies in economics, business, law, and public administration. Some activities of an economist are statistical forecasting, cost analysis, marketing research, evaluation of social programs, and strategic pricing.

Economics textbooks are structured in a variety of ways. They can be expository, with presentations of broad concepts and generalizations. They may include real-world examples and problems linked with the theory and ideas in the text. There may be supplemental material, such as graphs, tables, and biographical data of leaders in the field. Finally, some textbooks include a form of argumentation and discussion of the pros and cons of various issues.

The vocabulary in economics is a combination of general and specialized terminology. There are general vocabulary words, such as price, efficiency, *and* trust, *that also have a specialized meaning within the context of economics. There are also specialized terms such as* cartel *and* mercantilism, *as well as compound nouns, such as* capital transaction, income effect, *and* export subsidies, *that reflect concepts unique to the study of economics.*

VOCABULARY SELF-EVALUATION

The following words will be introduced in this reading selection. Place a check mark (√) in front of any that you know thoroughly and use in your speech or writing. Place a question mark (?) in front of any that you recognize but do not use yourself.

_____ aggregate	_____ expenditure	_____ oligopoly
_____ capitalism	_____ externality	_____ recession
_____ cartel	_____ fiscal	_____ revenue
_____ consumption	_____ inflationary	_____ sector
_____ entrepreneur	_____ monopoly	_____ tariff

MICROECONOMICS AND MACROECONOMICS

Economics is the science of how people produce goods and services and how they distribute and use them. The study of economics is divided into two basic categories: microeconomics and macroeconomics. Microeconomics is concerned with the economic decisions made by individual people or firms, while macroeconomics deals with the economy as a whole.

The economy itself is also divided into two parts: the private sector[1] and the public sector. The private sector is concerned mostly with microeconomic issues, while the public sector, the government, is concerned with macroeconomic issues. An individual firm uses microeconomic principles to make decisions based on its own self-interest. A firm must make decisions on what to produce, how to produce it, and how much to produce in order to maximize its operating profit. These decisions are affected by the market in which the firm operates. Free competition produces competitive markets. Examples of markets other than a perfect competition market include monopoly,[2] oligopoly,[3] and cartel.[4]

Many firms would like to become a monopoly. A monopoly is desirable because this structure allows the monopolist, the single seller of a good or item with no close substitute, to have a great influence on the price of the good produced. An oligopoly is a market condition where a few large companies produce a similar product and thus dominate the market. Oligopolies and monopolies tend to exist where research and development costs are high. The U.S. automobile industry is an example of an oligopoly. While monopolies are generally not allowed to exist in the United States, there are a few natural monopolies. Most utilities, those that perform a public service such as the gas and electric companies, are natural monopolies regulated by the government. Artificial monopolies are those that result from deliberate efforts to eliminate any competition.

Another market condition not permitted to exist in the United States is the cartel. A cartel exists when several firms divide the market among themselves and then restrict output in order to maintain high prices. OPEC (Organization of Petroleum Exporting Countries) is the best known example of a cartel. Many Middle Eastern countries have joined together to restrict the output of oil and set a high price for each barrel, thus controlling the market worldwide and creating an immense profit for themselves.

The public sector, on the other hand, focuses on macroeconomics to deal with the aggregate,[5] or total, economy. Although the main motivation of capitalism[6] is self-interest, ideally those in the public sector are not seeking personal gain from their positions. The government in a capitalist economy seeks to maintain a stable economy while discouraging those activities that are harmful to the economy or society as a whole. The public sector accomplishes this through both public finance policies and regulation.

Although the economy is dynamic and constantly changing, the public sector tries to maintain as stable an economy as possible. A volatile economy plagued by the unemployment and idle factories caused by a recession[7] or the increasing price levels of inflationary[8] periods does not stimulate new business activity. The government seeks to avoid these and other problems associated with various business cycles through the use of fiscal[9] policy. Fiscal policy involves the government's use of its spending and taxing powers to influence the economy. One form of taxation is the tariff[10] on imported goods for the purpose of generating additional monies, or in some cases, to discourage the importation of certain goods that may be inhibiting the sale and/or production of U.S.-made goods.

The public sector also uses regulation to maintain the economy. In order for the country's entrepreneurs,[11] or independent businessmen, to undertake new business activity, a competitive environment must be maintained. This is the reason for the public sector's prohibition and regulation of most monopolies and cartels.

Many economic issues also have a social side. Some business activities can produce an externality,[12] which is the side effect of economic production. Pollution caused by a manufacturing process is an example of a negative externality. It is also an indirect cost of production. The government may decide to use the fiscal instrument of taxation if the natural resources used in the production of the good are not fully reflected in its selling price. Placing a tax on the good increases its price so as to reflect the true cost of production. Because of the law of supply and demand, the price increase will usually result in decreased consumption[13] of the good. This taxation process, then, could be used to correct for a negative externality such as pollution.

For example, Company X produces

aluminum widgets in a major U.S. city. Aluminum is heavily used in the manufacturing process and causes an enormous air pollution problem. Because of this problem, the government decides to place a tax on the widget in order to provide funds for dealing with the air pollution in the city. The tax on the widget will make it more expensive and will reduce consumer demand. With a reduction in demand will come a reduction in production along with decreased pollution. The money from the tax, or the revenue[14] collected, may be spent by the government, then, on further research into industrial air pollution problems. This expenditure[15] of funds collected through the taxation of a good/product with a negative externality (air pollution) would be another component of the public sector's fiscal policy.

Finally, even though the issues may be varied and complex, understanding the dimensions and dynamics of economics is vital to the future growth and development of our country. ◆

ECONOMICS PRETEST

Select words from this list and write them in the blanks to complete the sentences.

aggregate	expenditure	oligopoly
capitalism	externality	recession
cartel	fiscal	revenue
consumption	inflationary	sector
entrepreneur	monopoly	tariff

1. Any clearly defined section or division of the economy can also be characterized as a(n) _____.

2. A(n) _____ is the exclusive control of a commodity or service.

3. The condition in the market in which few producers supply a commodity and can influence its price is known as a(n) _____.

4. The total amount or the sum of those things in a large group, such as consumer demands, is a(n) _____.

5. A(n) _____ is a list of duties that a government charges on imports and exports.

6. A policy designed to handle public finance issues is known as a(n) _____ policy.

7. A period of temporary business reduction less extreme than a depression and that influences the total economy is called a(n) _____.

8. A sudden increase in prices resulting from too great expansion in paper money or bank credit defines a(n) _____ period.

9. Something on the outside that is a result of economic activity is called a(n) _____.

10. The economic system within the United States is known as _____.

11. A(n) _____ is one who owns and manages his own business.

12. _____ is defined as the amount used up, such as in the use of a resource.

13. A source of income for the government such as through taxes is called _____.

14. Using up or paying out of money, time, or effort is a(n) _____.

15. A(n) _____ is a large group of business firms that agree to operate as a monopoly.

Answers to this pretest are in Appendix B.

Unless your instructor tells you to do otherwise, complete the exercises for each word that you missed on the pretest. The words, with their meanings and exercises, are in alphabetical order. The superscript numbers indicate where the words appeared in the reading selection so that you can refer to them when necessary. There are several types of exercises, but for each word you will be asked to write a sentence using context clues. (See Chapter 4 if you need information about how to create context clues.) You are also asked to perform some activity that will help you make your concept of the word personal. *Complete this activity thoughtfully, for creating a personalized concept of the word will help you remember it in the future.*

Answers to all the exercises are at the end of the exercise segment.

ECONOMICS EXERCISES

Aggregate[5]

ag|gre|gate (*n., adj.* ag′rə git, -gāt; *v.* ag′rə gāt), *n., adj., v.,* **-gat|ed, -gat|ing**. —*n.* **1** total amount; sum: *The aggregate of all the gifts was over $100.* **2** a mass of separate things joined together; combined mass; collection: *A lump of sugar is an aggregate of sugar crystals.* **3** any material, such as sand or gravel, that is mixed with water and cement to make concrete. **4** *Geology.* rock composed of several different mineral constituents capable of being separated by mechanical means: *Granite is a type of aggregate.* —*adj.* **1a** total. **b** gathered together in one mass or group. SYN: combined, collective. **2** *Botany.* consisting of many florets arranged in a dense mass: *an aggregate flower.* **3** *Geology.* composed of different mineral fragments united into one rock by heat, as granite.

—*v.t.* **1** to amount to; come to; total: *The money collected will aggregate $1,000.* **2** to gather together in a mass or whole; collect; unite: *Granite is made of small particles aggregated together.* SYN: mass.
—*v.i.* to come together in a mass; accumulate.
in the aggregate, taken together; considered as a whole; collectively: *The payments on our house amount in the aggregate to a big sum of money. Our judgment of a man's character is derived from observing a number of successive acts, forming in the aggregate his general course of conduct* (George C. Lewis).
[< Latin *aggregātus,* past participle of *aggregāre* add to, ultimately < *ad-* to + *grex, gregis* flock]
—**ag′gre|gate′ly,** *adv.* —**ag′gre|gate′ness,** *n.*
—**ag′gre|ga′tor,** *n.*

1. In which of the following sentences can *aggregate* be correctly placed in the blank?

    _____ a. An individual can purchase an _____ for his collection.

    _____ b. The _____ was lost when the company moved to another location.

    _____ c. Households can influence the level of _____ demand by the amount that they consume or use.

    _____ d. The _____ of all the donations to the charity for abused children was $1,000.

2. Select the synonym(s) of *aggregate.*

    _____ a. individual   _____ c. collective

    _____ b. total   _____ d. solitary

3. The etymology of *aggregate* shows that the word comes from Latin *aggregare* (to + flock). Use this information, and your background knowledge to match the following:

    _____ a. congregate   aa. to separate from others; set apart; isolate

    _____ b. egregious   bb. to come together into a crowd or mass; assemble

    _____ c. gregarious   cc. group or division in classification; class

    _____ d. segregate   dd. fond of being with others

    _____ e. category   ee. very great; outrageous; flagrant

4. One of the concerns of economists is the study of *aggregates,* or totals, in the entire nation. Some of these *aggregates* include total production, national income, and total employment. What might be some of the other *aggregates* you might study if you were an economist?

    _____

    _____

5. Write a sentence correctly using *aggregate.* (Be sure to include context clues to show you understand the meaning of the word.)

    _____

    _____

Capitalism[6]

cap|i|tal|ism (kap′ə tə liz′əm), *n.* **1** an economic system in which private individuals or groups of individuals own land, factories, and other means of production. They compete with one another, using the hired labor of other persons, to produce goods and services for profit: *The characteristic feature of modern capitalism is mass production of goods destined for consumption by the masses* (Newsweek). **2** the concentration of wealth with its power and influence in the hands of a few. **3** a system which favors the existence of capitalists or the concentration of wealth in the hands of a few.

1. In which of the following sentences is *capitalism* used correctly?

_____ a. Capitalism is an economic system in which the means of production are owned and operated by individual owners, or capitalists.

_____ b. Capitalism is a form of political dictatorship, since the state owns all production and property.

_____ c. The United States is an example of capitalism, since there is private ownership of capital and freedom of choice for people to buy what they please and to work where they wish.

_____ d. The first economic stage in modern civilization was capitalism in which the means of production were controlled by the landed aristocracy.

2. Complete the verbal analogy.

communism : Russia :: *capitalism* : _____

a. China   c. Yugoslavia

b. USA   d. Cuba

3. Select the characteristics of *capitalism*.

_____ a. government control

_____ b. private ownership

_____ c. production of goods and services for profit

_____ d. competition

4. Write a sentence correctly using *capitalism*. (Be sure to include context clues to show you understand the meaning of the word.)

_____

_____

5. We live in the economic system of *capitalism*. In your opinion, what are some of the positive aspects of *capitalism*? What are some of the negative aspects?

_____

_____

Cartel[4]

car|tel (kär tel´, kär´təl), *n.* **1** a large group of business firms that agree to operate as a monopoly, especially to regulate prices and production: *The methodical Swiss, who think that there is a place for everything, staunchly believe that the place for industry is in cartels* (Time). **SYN:** syndicate, combine. **2** a written agreement between countries at war for the exchange of prisoners or some other purpose. **3a** a written challenge to a duel. **b** a letter of defiance. **4** Also, **Cartel.** (in France and Belgium) a political group with a common cause or object; a bloc. **5** *Rare.* a paper or card bearing writing or printing. [< Middle French *cartel* < Italian *cartello* little card < *carta* card < Latin *charta*]

1. What is an example of an international *cartel* famous for influencing gasoline prices?

_____ a. Shell Oil   _____ c. ARCO

_____ b. Russian-American   _____ d. OPEC

2. What are some characteristics of a *cartel*?
_____ a. two or three businesses
_____ b. a large group of businesses
_____ c. an agreement
_____ d. regulation of prices and production

3. In which of the following sentences is *cartel* used correctly?
_____ a. The oil cartel regulated prices throughout the world.
_____ b. A cartel is illegal in the United States, since it does not allow for open competition.
_____ c. One cartel merged with another to form a duopoly.
_____ d. A cartel needs to advertise to help it compete with other companies.

4. How do *cartel* and monopoly relate to each other? Do we have recognized *cartels* in the United States?

_____

_____

5. Write a sentence correctly using *cartel*. (Be sure to include context clues to show you understand the meaning of the word.)

_____

_____

Consumption[13]

con|sump|tion (kən sump'shən), *n.* **1** the act of consuming; using up; use: *We took along some food for our consumption on the trip. The science of economics deals with the production, distribution and consumption of wealth.* **2** the amount used up: *Our consumption of fuel oil increases in cold weather.* **3** a disease that destroys part of the body, especially the lungs; tuberculosis. [< Latin *cōnsumptiō, -ōnis* < *cōnsūmere;* see etym. under **consume**]

from **consume:**

[< Latin *cōnsūmere* < *com-* (intensive) + *sūmere* take up]

1. Select the synonym(s) of *consumption*.
_____ a. fiscal   _____ c. expense
_____ b. inflation   _____ d. using up

2. Complete the verbal analogy.
capitalism : communism :: *consumption* : _____
a. saving   c. working
b. spending   d. exercising

3. The etymology of *aggregate* shows that the word comes from Latin *aggregare* (to + flock). Use this information, your imagination, and your background knowledge to match the following:
_____ a. resume   aa. to take for granted without proving; suppose
_____ b. sumptuous   bb. to begin again; go on

____	c. presume	cc. costly; magnificent; rich
____	d. subsume	dd. having to do with the spending of money; regulating expenses, especially to control extravagance or waste
____	e. sumptuary	ee. to bring (an idea, term, principle, proposition, or the like) under another

4. Write a sentence correctly using *consumption*. (Be sure to include context clues to show you understand the meaning of the word.)

_____

_____

5. Not all purchased goods are intended for *consumption*. What are some goods that you have purchased that you did not intend for *consumption*?

_____

_____

Entrepreneur[11]

en|tre|pre|neur (än'trə prə nèr'), *n.* a person who organizes and manages a business or industrial undertaking. An entrepreneur takes the risk of not making a profit and gets the profit when there is one: *In the uppermost executive echelons of TV, there is not one recognized major theatrical entrepreneur* (New York Times). [< Old French *entrepreneur* < *entreprendre* undertake; see etym. under **enterprise**]

from **enterprise:**

[< Old French *entreprise,* feminine past participle of *entreprendre* undertake < *entre-* between (< Latin *inter-*) + *prendre* take < Latin *prehendere*]

1. In which of the following sentences is *entrepreneur* used correctly?
   - ____ a. Henry Ford was a famous entrepreneur who started the Ford Motor Company.
   - ____ b. The entrepreneur went to work at the government office in the suburbs.
   - ____ c. An entrepreneur usually is not very independent and prefers to be a follower.
   - ____ d. There may be more than one entrepreneur in a company who is very creative and takes risks in developing new products.

2. Who of the following might likely be an *entrepreneur*?
   - ____ a. a government employee
   - ____ b. a city worker
   - ____ c. a man who owns a travel agency
   - ____ d. a woman in real estate sales

3. The etymology of *entrepreneur* shows that the word comes from the Old French *enterprendre* (to undertake). Use this information, your imagination, and your background knowledge to match the following.

_____	a. reprehend	aa.	open to attack; assailable; vulnerable
_____	b. comprise	bb.	to arrest; seize
_____	c. apprehend	cc.	to be made up of; consist of; include
_____	d. prehensile	dd.	to reprove or blame; rebuke
_____	e. pregnable	ee.	adapted for seizing, grasping, or holding on

4. Would you like to be an *entrepreneur?* Why or why not? What business would you operate or own as an *entrepreneur?*

_____

_____

5. Write a sentence correctly using *entrepreneur.* (Be sure to use context clues to show you understand the meaning of the word.)

_____

_____

Expenditure[15]

ex|pend|i|ture (ek spen′də chŭr, -chər), *n.* **1** the act or process of spending; a using up or paying out: *A large piece of work requires the expenditure of money, time, and effort.* **2** the amount of money, time, or effort, spent; expense: *Her expenditures for Christmas presents were $25 and several hours of work.*

1. Select the synonym(s) of *expenditure.*

   _____ a. savings   _____ c. payment
   _____ b. earnings   _____ d. outlay

2. Which of the following have *expenditures?*

   _____ a. consumers   _____ c. businesses
   _____ b. governments   _____ d. resources

3. In which of the following sentences is *expenditure* used correctly?

   _____ a. One expenditure within the large metropolitan city is that for welfare assistance.
   _____ b. The annual expenditure includes a new entrepreneur for the company.
   _____ c. The budget process tries to balance some revenue or income for each expenditure.
   _____ d. New taxes were needed because of the unexpected expenditure for emergency aid to the flood-stricken area of the state.

4. Write a sentence correctly using *expenditure.* (Be sure to include context clues to show you understand the meaning of the word.)

_____

_____

5. What is the biggest *expenditure* for you as a student? Why?

_____

_____

Externality[12]

ex|ter|nal|i|ty (eks′tér nal′ə tē), *n., pl.* **-ties. 1** the quality or condition of being external. **2** an external thing.
ex|ter|nal (ek stér′nəl), *adj., n.* —*adj.* **1** on the outside; outer: *An ear of corn has an external husk.* **syn:** outward, exterior. **2** entirely outside; coming from without: *the external air.* **3** to be used only on the outside of the body: *Liniment and rubbing alcohol are external remedies.* **4** having existence outside one's mind. **5** *Figurative.* easily seen but not essential; superficial: *Going to church is an external act of worship. His art criticism had external brilliance but no substance.* **6** having to do with international affairs; foreign: *War affects a nation's external trade.* **7** *Zoology,* *Anatomy.* situated toward or on the outer surface; remote from the median line or center. **8** *British.* (of a student) having studied elsewhere than in the university where he is examined: *Once a year he returned to London to sit for his exams as an external student after pirating the appropriate learning from half a dozen different universities* (Manchester Guardian).
—*n.* an outer surface or part; outside.
externals, clothing, manners, or other outward acts or appearances: *He judges people by mere externals rather than by their character.*
[< Latin *externus* outside (< *exterus* outside < *ex* out of) + English *-al*[1]] —**ex|ter′nal|ly,** *adv.*

1. What are some of the characteristics of an *externality*? (Review the reading selection if necessary.)
   _____ a. related to economic production
   _____ b. side effect
   _____ c. positive or negative
   _____ d. related to an entrepreneur

2. The etymology of *externality* (see *external*) shows that the word comes from the Latin *externus* (outside). Use this information, your imagination, and your background knowledge to match the following:
   _____ a. extremity   aa. an outer surface or part; outward appearance
   _____ b. exotic   bb. the very end; farthest possible place; last part or point
   _____ c. exodus   cc. a going out; departure
   _____ d. exorbitant   dd. from a foreign country; not native
   _____ e. exterior   ee. exceeding what is customary, proper, or reasonable; very expensive

3. What are some examples of negative *externalities* in the economy?
   _____ a. air pollution
   _____ b. water pollution
   _____ c. increase in employment
   _____ d. destruction of resources

4. *Externalities* are the side effects, both positive and negative, of economic production. The reading selection discusses some *negative externalities*. What do you think are some of the *positive externalities* of economic production?

_____

_____

5. Write a sentence correctly using *externality*. (Be sure to include context clues to show you understand the meaning of the word.)

_____

_____

Fiscal[9]

fis|cal (fis′kəl), *adj., n. —adj.* **1** = financial. **SYN:** See syn. under **financial**. **2** having to do with public finance: *Important changes were made in the government's fiscal policy.* —*n.* a public prosecutor in some countries: *cited before the fiscal of the empire* (Sarah Austin). [< Latin *fiscālis* < *fiscus* purse; see etym. under **fisc**] —**fis′cal|ly,** *adv.*

1. Select the synonym(s) of *fiscal*.
   _____ a. physical _____ c. monetary
   _____ b. aggregate _____ d. financial

2. Which of the numbered dictionary definitions of *fiscal* best fits the word's use in the reading selection? _____

3. In which of the following sentences can *fiscal* be correctly placed in the blank?
   _____ a. The _____ statements presented the plans for the holiday meeting.
   _____ b. The national _____ policy deals with military situations only.
   _____ c. The budget for _____ 1981 was based on receipts estimated to be $600 billion.
   _____ d. The government can choose to pursue a _____ policy to stimulate or reduce demand for goods and services.

4. Write a sentence correctly using *fiscal*. (Be sure to include context clues to show you understand the meaning of the word.)

_____

_____

_____

5. The government has a *fiscal* policy by which our leaders make decisions that will affect the economy related to spending money and raising taxes. Do you have your own personal *fiscal* policy? If so, what is it?

_____

_____

_____

Inflationary[8]

in|fla|tion|ar|y (in flā'shə ner'ē), *adj.* of or having to do with inflation; tending to inflate: *the inflationary effect of government spending.*

in|fla|tion (in flā'shən), *n.* **1** the act of swelling (as with air, gas, pride, or satisfaction). **2** a swollen state; too great expansion. **3** an increase of the currency of a country by issuing much paper money. **4** a sharp and sudden rise in prices resulting from a too great expansion in paper money or bank credit: *Inflation spirals inexorably on* (Atlantic).

1. Complete the verbal analogy.
   recessonary : decline :: *inflationary* : _____
   a. moderation   c. status quo
   b. increase   d. decline

2. What happens during an *inflationary* cycle?
   _____ a. a sharp and sudden increase in prices
   _____ b. a sharp and sudden decrease in prices
   _____ c. a reduction in money or credit
   _____ d. too great an expansion in money and credit

3. Select the synonym(s) of *inflationary.*
   _____ a. lessening   _____ c. decreasing
   _____ b. expanding   _____ d. swelling

4. Why should we be concerned about *inflationary* spirals or increases in our economy? How might *inflationary* spirals affect your earning and spending abilities?

   _____

   _____

   _____

5. Write a sentence correctly using *inflationary.* (Be sure to include context clues to show you understand the meaning of the word.)

   _____

   _____

Monopoly[2]

mo|nop|o|ly (mə nop'ə lē), *n., pl.* **-lies.** **1** the exclusive control of a commodity or service: *In most communities, the telephone company has a monopoly. You have, in this Kingdom, an advantage in lead, that amounts to a monopoly* (Edmund Burke). **2** such a control granted by a government: *An inventor has a monopoly on his invention for a certain number of years. Raleigh held a monopoly of cards, Essex a monopoly of sweet wines* (Macaulay). **3** control that is not exclusive but which enables the person or company to fix prices. **4** a commercial product or service that is exclusively controlled or nearly so. **5** a person or company that has a monopoly on some commodity or service: *The pilots' association was now the compactest monopoly in the world* (Mark Twain). **6** the exclusive possession or control of something intangible: *a monopoly of a person's time. No one person has a monopoly of virtue. Neither side has a monopoly of right or wrong* (Edward A. Freeman). [< Latin *monopōlium* < Greek *monopōlion* < *mónos* single + *pōleîn* to sell]

1. In which of the following sentences can *monopoly* be correctly placed in the blank?

_____ a. A _____ represents a division or segment of the population.

_____ b. Some of the shortcomings of a _____ include misallocation of resources and restriction of new technology.

_____ c. An example of a natural _____ is a public utility, such as a gas or electric company, that is regulated by the government.

_____ d. A _____ is the practice in international trade of setting lower prices in distant markets than in the home country.

2. Select the characteristics of a *monopoly*.

_____ a. a unique good or service

_____ b. many companies

_____ c. a single seller

_____ d. exclusive control

3. What are some possible problems with the structure of a *monopoly*?

_____ a. increased competition

_____ b. concentration of power

_____ c. reduction in prices

_____ d. price controls

4. Write a sentence correctly using *monopoly*. (Be sure to include context clues to show you understand the meaning of the word.)

_____

_____

5. How does the definition of *monopoly* relate to the board game Monopoly, which is divided into real estate segments? If you have not played the game, what type of *monopoly* (gas company, water company, etc.) affects your daily living or your community, and how?

_____

_____

Oligopoly[3]

ol|i|gop|o|ly (ol'ə gop'ə lē), *n., pl.* **-lies.** a condition in a market in which so few producers supply a commodity or service that each of them can influence its price, with or without an agreement between them: *Ultimately, it is the oligopolies and not the State that set the economic priorities of our society* (Manchester Guardian). [< *oligo-* + *-poly,* as in *monopoly*]

1. What would be an example of an *oligopoly*?

_____ a. the steel industry

_____ b. a local small liquor store

_____ c. an automobile company

_____ d. an independent garage owner

2. Select the characteristics of an *oligopoly*.

_____ a. many producers

_____ b. a condition in the market

_____ c. influences prices

_____ d. few producers

3. In which of the following sentences is *oligopoly* correctly used?

_____ a. An oligopoly carries out its production in a large scale and has a nationwide sales network.

_____ b. The local oligopoly is run by a small businessman who started the company by himself.

_____ c. An example of an oligopoly is the steel industry, since a few large firms control industry output.

_____ d. A telephone or a gas company is an example of an oligopoly.

4. How do monopoly and *oligopoly* relate to each other? Do they have any common characteristics?

_____

_____

5. Write a sentence correctly using *oligopoly*. (Be sure to include context clues to show you understand the meaning of the word.)

_____

_____

Recession[7]

re|ces|sion[1] (ri sesh'ən), *n.* **1** the action or fact of going backward; moving backward. **2** the action or fact of sloping backward. **3** withdrawal, as of the minister and choir after the service in some churches. **4** a period of temporary business reduction, shorter and less extreme than a depression: *When the country entered the 1949 recession, many analysts again warned business* *to batten down the hatches* (Newsweek). [< Latin *recessiō, -ōnis* < *recēdere;* see etym. under **recede**]

from **recede:**

[< Latin *recēdere* < *re-* back + *cēdere* to go]

1. Select the characteristics of *recession*.

_____ a. more extreme than a depression

_____ b. temporary business reduction

_____ c. less extreme than a depression

_____ d. long-term business reduction

2. Which of the numbered dictionary definitions of *recession* best fits the word's use in the reading selection? _____

3. The etymology of *recession* shows that the word comes from the Latin *recedere* (back + to go). Use this information, your imagination, and your background knowledge to match the following:

_____ a. secede

aa. to go before or in front of; precede in time or place

_____ b. abscess

bb. a granting, yielding

_____ c. predecessor

cc. collection of pus in the tissues of some part of the body

_____ d. antecede

dd. to withdraw formally from an organization

_____ e. concession

ee. a person holding a position of office before another

4. Write a sentence correctly using *recession*. (Be sure to include context clues to show you understand the meaning of the word.)

_____

_____

5. What do you think are some of the consequences of a *recession* for individual businesses? For the nation as a whole? Have you ever been affected by a *recession*?

_____

_____

Revenue[14]

rev|e|nue (rev′ə nü, -nyü), *n.* **1** money coming in; income: *The government got much revenue from taxes last year.* **2** a particular item of income. **3** a source of income. **4** the government department that collects taxes: *the Internal Revenue Service.* [< Middle French *revenue* < Old French, a return, feminine past participle of *revenir* come back < Latin *revenīre* < *re-* back + *venīre* come]

1. Select the synonym(s) of *revenue*.

_____ a. earnings   _____ c. income

_____ b. debit   _____ d. assets

2. The etymology of *revenue* shows that the word comes from the Latin *revenire* (back + to come). Use this information, your imagination, and your background knowledge to match the following:

_____ a. circumvent

aa. to come as something additional or interrupting

_____ b. parvenu

bb. meeting arranged for some particular purpose; gathering; assembly

_____ c. intervention

cc. person who has risen above his class, especially one who has risen through the acquisition of wealth or political power

_____ d. supervene

dd. to get the better of or defeat by trickery

_____ e. convention

ee. interfering in any affair so as to affect its course or issue

3. *Revenue* is the income that the government receives from a variety of sources. What are some of these sources?

_____ a. gasoline taxes _____ c. cartels

_____ b. tariffs _____ d. income taxes

4. What is the primary source of your *revenue*? Is the amount of *revenue* that you will receive an important criterion in a career decision? Why or why not?

_____

_____

_____

5. Write a sentence correctly using *revenue*. (Be sure to include context clues to show you understand the meaning of the word.)

_____

_____

Sector[1]

sec|tor (sek′tər), *n., v.* —*n.* **1** the part of a circle, ellipse, or the like, between two radii and the included arc. **2** a clearly defined military area which a given military unit protects or covers with fire; part of a front held by a unit. **3** any clearly defined section or division; segment: *the consumer-oriented sector of the economy* (Atlantic). *Direct mail is the fastest growing sector in the advertising industry* (London Times). SYN: zone, quarter. **4** an instrument consisting of two rulers connected by a joint, used in measuring or drawing angles. — *v.t.* to divide into sectors; provide with sectors. [< Late Latin *sector, -ōris* (in Latin, a cutter) < *secāre* to cut]

1. Select the synonym(s) of *sector*.

_____ a. division _____ c. entirety

_____ b. section _____ d. segment

2. Which of the numbered dictionary definitions of *sector* best fits the word's use in the reading selection? _____

3. The etymology of *sector* shows that the word comes from the Late Latin *secare* (to cut). Use this information and your background knowledge to match the following:

_____ a. sectile   aa. to cut apart (animal, plant, organ, or tissue) in order to examine or study the structure

_____ b. segment   bb. that can be cut smoothly by a knife but cannot withstand pulverization

_____ c. dissect   cc. cross-section of the vegetation of an area, usually that part growing along a long narrow strip

_____ d. intersect   dd. piece or part cut off, marked off, or broken off; division; section

_____ e. transect   ee. to cut or divide by passing through or crossing; cross

4. Write a sentence correctly using *sector*. (Be sure to include context clues to show you understand the meaning of the word.)

_____

_____

5. Which *sector* of the economy do you find more interesting, public or private? Why?

_____

_____

_____

Tariff[10]

tar|iff (tar′if), *n., v.* —*n.* **1** a list of duties or taxes that a government charges on imports or exports. **2** the system of duties or taxes on imports and exports. **3** any duty or tax in such a list or system: *There is a very high tariff on imported jewelry. Heavy revenue duties . . . have the same effect as protective tariffs in obstructing free trade* (Time). **4** the table of prices in a hotel, restaurant, or similar establishment: *The tariff at the Grant Hotel ranges from $10 to $25 a day for a* single room. **5** any scale of prices; book of rates; schedule: *a revised tariff for passenger travel.* **6** *Obsolete.* an arithmetical table, especially one used to save calculating discounts; ready reckoner. —*v.t.* **1** to put a tariff on. **2** to set a value or price for, according to a tariff. **3** to list the tariff or tariffs on. [< Italian *tariffa* schedule of customs rates < Arabic *ta′rīf* information, notification]

1. Which of the numbered dictionary definitions of *tariff* best fits the word's use in the reading selection? _____

2. Why would the government impose a *tariff*?
   _____ a. to generate additional money
   _____ b. to reduce government revenue
   _____ c. to encourage importation
   _____ d. to discourage importation of certain goods

3. Select the synonym(s) of *tariff*.
   _____ a. credit   _____ c. tax
   _____ b. duty   _____ d. cartel

4. What foreign items have you purchased that have included a *tariff* on them that you are aware of (car, jewelry, motorcycle, cigars, toys)?

_____

_____

5. Write a sentence correctly using *tariff*. (Be sure to include context clues to show you understand the meaning of the word.)

_____

_____

_____

ANSWERS TO CHAPTER 12 EXERCISES

Aggregate: **1.** c, d **2.** b, c **3.** bb, ee, dd, aa, cc
Capitalism: **1.** a, c **2.** b (example) **3.** b, c, d
Cartel: **1.** d **2.** b, c, d **3.** a, b
Consumption: **1.** d **2.** a (antonym) **3.** bb, cc, aa, ee, dd
Entrepreneur: **1.** a, d **2.** c, d **3.** dd, cc, bb, ee, aa
Expenditure: **1.** c, d **2.** a, b, c **3.** a, c, d
Externality: **1.** a, b, c **2.** bb, dd, cc, ee, aa **3.** a, b, d
Fiscal: **1.** c, d **2.** 2 **3.** c, d
Inflationary: **1.** b (characteristic) **2.** a, d **3.** b, d
Monopoly: **1.** b, c **2.** a, c, d **3.** b, d
Oligopoly: **1.** a, c **2.** b, c, d **3.** a, c
Recession: **1.** b, c **2.** 4 **3.** dd, cc, ee, aa, bb
Revenue: **1.** a, c **2.** dd, cc, ee, aa, bb **3.** a, b, d
Sector: **1.** a, b, d **2.** 3 **3.** bb, dd, aa, ee, cc
Tariff: **1.** *n.* 3 **2.** a, d **3.** b, c

If you missed any of the items in the exercises, return to the exercise and to the dictionary definition to see where you went wrong. Remember: If you get something right, you only affirm that you knew it. If you get something wrong and understand why, *you have learned something.*

ECONOMICS POSTTEST

Fill in the blanks with the words from this list.

aggregate	expenditure	oligopoly
capitalism	externality	recession
cartel	fiscal	revenue
consumption	inflationary	sector
entrepreneur	monopoly	tariff

1. A tax, or duty, on imports is a type of _____.

2. An expense is a(n) _____.

3. OPEC is an example of a(n) _____.

4. _____ is the side effect of economic production.

5. Competition among private individuals or groups is also known as _____.

6. *Use* is a synonym for _____ .

7. A synonym for _____ is *financial.*

8. Another word for *total amount* is _____ .

9. A market condition of few producers influencing the price of a commodity or service is called a(n) _____ .

10. A(n) _____ is a temporary business reduction.

11. Tending to increase or rise in prices describes a(n) _____ cycle.

12. An independent businessman could also be called a(n) _____ .

13. A(n) _____ is a segment or division.

14. *Income* is another word for _____ .

15. Exclusive control or exclusive possession is a characteristic of a(n) _____ .

Answers to this posttest are in the Instructor's Manual.

If you missed any of the words, you may need to return to the exercises and to the dictionary entries to see why your concepts for some words are incomplete.

CHAPTER THIRTEEN

SOCIAL SCIENCES: POLITICAL SCIENCE

◆

OVERVIEW

Political science studies the principles, organization, and conduct of citizens and their governments. This field of study is important because an educated person is also a citizen and must know about the nature of government and the political system in which he or she lives.

Political science has six subfields: American politics, public administration, political philosophy, public law, comparative government, and international relations.

Students who major in political science may be interested in careers in government service, public administration. U.S. foreign service agencies, or international corporations or organizations. They may pursue careers in law, public relations, journalism, or teaching and research.

Introductory textbooks in political science are usually expository, that is, they explain broad concepts or generalizations. There may be many examples and illustrations in the form of charts, diagrams, or tables. Some textbooks may be organized in a chronological framework around a historical context. Since political science is concerned with people and their governments throughout history, essential dates and names of people and places are also important to recognize.

The vocabulary in political science consists mainly of general vocabulary terms that can also have a specialized meaning within the context of political science. Examples of such words are regime, pluralism, legitimacy, *and so on.*

VOCABULARY SELF-EVALUATION

The following words will be introduced in this reading selection. Place a check mark (√) in front of any that you know thoroughly and use in your speech and writing. Place a question mark (?) in front of any that you recognize but do not use yourself.

_____ aristocracy	_____ elite	_____ methodology
_____ attenuate	_____ eradicate	_____ polity
_____ coup	_____ ideology	_____ regime
_____ democracy	_____ indictment	_____ republic
_____ despotism	_____ mandate	_____ scope

POLITICS, GOVERNMENT, AND ECONOMY

Throughout history the term *politics* has been associated with many concepts and meanings, and its study has been just as varied. Then in 1953, American political scientist David Easton helped to define the modern discipline of political science by identifying its scope,[1] methodology,[2] and subject matter. According to Easton, politics is concerned with "the authoritative allocation of values." That is, politics is involved when things considered to be of worth, such as wealth, freedom, equality, and justice, are granted or denied to people. Those who are affected by these decisions accept the authority of the political system and consider these allocations to be binding. Another political theorist, Harold Lasswell, has phrased this idea as "who gets what, when, and how."

The analysis of politics often centers on government, which is one entity that makes authoritative allocations for a territory. Government appears in many forms, but Americans are most familiar with the forms of government that include some control by the citizens. The idea of participatory government was proposed in the eighteenth century by French philosopher Jean-Jacques Rousseau, who conceived of the ideal polity[3] as a democracy.[4] This concept of government requires active and direct participation by all citizens to make decisions involving the authoritative allocation of values. But primarily due to large population size, most nations that call themselves democracies are actually republics[5] or representative democracies. In this form of government, citizens elect people to represent their interests in the governing of the territory. This process grants a great deal of power to those elected, yet they remain responsible to the citizens and to the regulations of the land. An elected official who breaks the law may face an indictment,[6] just like any other citizen of the territory.

In contrast to governments that have some citizen control are those that are administered by an individual (such as a monarchy or a despotism[7] or by an elite[8] group (such as an aristocracy[9] or an oligarchy*). In these authoritarian or totalitarian regimes[10] citizens are not allowed to question or challenge the leaders' authority. The individual ruler or ruling group assumes an unlimited mandate[11] and has no direct responsibility to the citizens. Totalitarian regimes differ from their authoritarian counterparts in one important respect: the government's control permeates every aspect of the people's lives, including economics, culture, religion, and morality. Control is so complete that citizens have no opportunity to replace the leadership without a coup[12] or a revolution.

Yet the political decisions of almost every form of government intrude on numerous aspects of the citizens' day-to-day lives. For example, political ideology[13] often is the basis of the type of economy carried out in the territory. In capitalist† systems, such as that of the United States, ownership and economic decisions are largely assumed by private individuals or corporations. In theory, there is minimal government intervention in the production, pricing, and distribution of goods and services. In reality, all of these factors are controlled in some way by governmental laws and regulations. One notable result of a capitalist system is the unequal distribution of wealth and status.

Communism, evolving from the theories of Karl Marx, sought to eradicate[14] the social problems generated by a capitalist economy. Communists are committed to creating economic and social equality among all citizens. Accordingly, they believe that government, on behalf of the people, should own all the property and labor used to produce goods and services.

The government also is to decide how much goods and services will be produced, at what level they will be priced, and to what extent they will be distributed to the citizenry. An investment made by a citizen in the production of goods and services is not directly related to the compensation received. Lack of a profit motive often results in low productivity and in the manufacture of shoddy products.

A third type of political economy, termed socialism, was devised to avoid the disadvantages of both capitalism and communism. In a socialist system, such as that of Sweden, government ownership and control of production is intermingled with private enterprise. A private-sector market provides the stimulus for efficiency and innovation, while the public sector bridges the gap between the wealthy and the poor by offering free public transportation, education, and health care.

Views on the extent of government responsibility typically serve as the basis for constructing these political economies. Those who hold the conservative view believe that government intervention must be minimal. There is great confidence in the capitalist market to provide economic incentives and to coordinate human action. On the other hand, the liberal view of the state authorizes more government intervention to offset the negative social effects of the free capitalist market. This entails the reallocation of wealth to attenuate[15] the gap between rich and poor, as well as the regulation of individual and group actions that might harm the public interest. Proponents of a radical view believe that the overthrow of capitalist governments is the only way to create political, social, and economic equality for all citizens.

The focus on government and its relationship to economics is only one area in the field of political science. Other areas

---

* *Oligarchy* is introduced in Chapter 15.
† *Capitalism* is introduced in Chapter 12.

include studies of the actual workings of government bodies and the documents of those bodies. Political scientists are also concerned with political parties and pressure groups, with public administration of government, and with international relations. Since politics affects individuals in all segments of their lives, an understanding of how values are allocated is important to the citizens of a territory as well as to those who study the field. ◆

POLITICAL SCIENCE PRETEST

Select words from this list and write them in the blanks to complete the sentences.

aristocracy	elite	methodology
attenuate	eradicate	polity
coup	ideology	regime
democracy	indictment	republic
despotism	mandate	scope

1. The common people rather than the privileged are a(n) _____.

2. To weaken in force is to _____.

3. The distance something can reach is called its _____.

4. To _____ means to remove all traces of something.

5. _____ is a term used for a system of methods and procedures.

6. A command or order is a(n) _____.

7. A nation in which citizens elect representatives in a(n) _____.

8. A synonym of _____ is *government*.

9. _____ may be defined as as absolute power or control.

10. A body of opinions that people have is a(n) _____.

11. An unexpected, clever move is a(n) _____.

12. A formal, written accusation is a(n) _____.

13. A government in which the upper class rules is called a(n) _____.

14. Any prevailing political system is a(n) _____.

15. Those thought of as the best people are the _____.

Answers to this pretest are in Appendix B.

Unless your instructor tells you to do otherwise, complete the exercises for each word you missed on the pretest. The words, with their meanings and exercises, are in alphabetical order. The superscript numbers indicate where the words appeared in the reading selection so that you can refer to them when necessary. There are several types of exercises, but for each word you will be asked to write a sentence using context clues. (See Chapter 4 if you need information about how to create context clues.) You are also asked to perform some activity that will help you make your concept of the word personal. *Complete this activity thoughtfully, for creating a personalized concept of the word will help you remember it in the future.*

Answers to all the exercises are at the end of the exercise segment.

POLITICAL SCIENCE EXERCISES

Aristocracy[9]

ar|is|toc|ra|cy (ar′ə stok′rə sē), *n., pl.* **-cies. 1** a class of people having a high position in society by birth, rank, or title; nobility. Earls, dukes, and princes belong to the aristocracy. **2** any class of people that is considered superior because of birth, intelligence, culture, or wealth; upper class. SYN: élite, gentry, patriciate. **3** government in which the nobles or a privileged upper class rules. SYN: oligarchy. **4** a country or state having such a government. **5** a government by the best citizens: ... *the attainment of a truer and truer aristocracy, or government again by the best* (Thomas Carlyle). [< Late Latin *aristocratia* < Greek *aristokratiā* rule of the best born < *áristos* best + *krátos* rule]

1. Check any synonym of *aristocracy.*

_____ a. gentry _____ c. elite _____ e. nobility
_____ b. commoner _____ d. upper class _____ f. oligarchy

2. Complete the verbal analogy.
   comedy : funny :: *aristocracy* : _____

   _____ a. people _____ c. superior
   _____ b. snobbish _____ d. appearance

3. Which of the numbered dictionary definitions of *aristocracy* best fits the word's use in the reading selection? _____

4. Write a sentence correctly using *aristocracy.* (Be sure to include context clues to show you understand the meaning of the word.)

_____

_____

5. The dictionary lists several groups that are labeled *aristocracy.* If you could belong to one of the groups listed, which would it be?

_____

_____

Attenuate[15]

at|ten|u|ate (*v.* ə ten′yù āt; *adj.* ə ten′yù it), *v.,* **-at|ed, -at|ing,** *adj.* —*v.t.* **1** to weaken in force, amount, or value; reduce: *The authority of kings has been attenuated in modern times.* **2** *Bacteriology.* to make (microorganisms or viruses) less virulent: *Former vaccines against anthrax, dating back to the time of Pasteur, were made from attenuated, or weakened, spores of the anthrax germs* (Science News Letter). **3** to make thin or slender: *He was attenuated by hunger.* **4** to make less dense; dilute.

—*v.i.* to become thin or slender: *An earthworm's body alternately attenuates and thickens as it crawls.*
—*adj.* **1** slender; thin. **2** thin in consistency. **3** *Botany.* gradually tapering. [< Latin *attenuāre* (with English *-ate*[1]) < *ad-* to + *tenuāre* make thin < *tenuis* thin] —**at|ten′u|a′tion,** *n.* —**at|ten′u|a′tor,** *n.*

1. In which of the following sentences can *attenuate* correctly be placed in the blank?

   _____ a. Our task in the laboratory is to _____ the acid solution.

   _____ b. Will you be able to _____ the party with me on Saturday?

   _____ c. There is a new medicine available that will_____ the effects of that virus.

   _____ d. The artist's work is known for its _____d design elements.

2. Check any term or phrase that describes *attenuate.*

   _____ a. to weaken   _____ d. diluted

   _____ b. made slender   _____ e. to reduce in value

   _____ c. to intensify   _____ f. to make firm

3. The etymology of *attenuate* shows that the word comes from a Latin word meaning "to stretch or extend." Use that information, your imagination, and your background knowledge to match the following:

   _____ a. extenuate   aa. stretched tight
   _____ b. tender   bb. narrow, slim; not thick
   _____ c. tense   cc. to excuse in part
   _____ d. tenuate   dd. delicate; not strong and hardy
   _____ e. thin   ee. having slight importance

4. If you had the power to *attenuate* any part of your body, what would it be? (Use definition number 3.)

   _____

   _____

5. Write a sentence correctly using *attenuate.* (Be sure to include context clues to show you understand the meaning of the word.)

   _____

   _____

Coup[12]

coup[1] (kü), *n., pl.* **coups** (küz). **1** a sudden, brilliant action; unexpected, clever move; master stroke. **2** = coup d'état. **3** the act or practice by some American Indians, especially Plains Indians, of touching a live opponent with a stick (coup stick) in battle and moving on without killing him, as a feat of bravery.
count coup, to be the first among Indian warriors to touch an enemy with a coup stick: *Warriors who counted coups wore eagle feathers as signs of their courage.*

[< Old French *coup* < Late Latin *colpus* < Latin *colaphus* < Greek *kólaphos* a blow, slap]

coup d'é|tat (kü′ dä tä′), *pl.* **coups d'é|tat** (kü′ dä tä′), **coup d'é|tats** (kü′ dä täz′). a sudden and decisive act in politics, usually bringing about a change of government unlawfully and by force: *It is nearly eight years since a coup d'état brought the present Government into power* (London Times). [< French *coup d'état* (literally) stroke of state; see etym. under **coup**[1]]

(Note: This word is not yet fully naturalized, and it retains its French pronunciation.)

1. Select any appropriate response to the following statement:
   "We were surprised that the *coup* was so successful."
   _____ a. You shouldn't be surprised; the coup is the fastest car on the road.
   _____ b. The group was well organized and had local support.
   _____ c. My mother has a recipe for coup that tastes even better.
   _____ d. Two years ago a coup failed. This one was planned more carefully.

2. Which of the numbered dictionary definitions of *coup* best fits its use in the reading selection? _____

3. In which of the following areas might a *coup* be employed?
   _____ a. politics   _____ c. gardening
   _____ b. business   _____ d. social affairs

4. What kind of government is likely to experience a *coup*?

   _____

   From your knowledge of world politics, in which country would you expect one to be attempted? _____

5. Write a sentence correctly using *coup*. (Be sure to use context clues to show you understand the meaning of the word.)

   _____

   _____

Democracy[4]

de|moc|ra|cy (di mok′rə sē), *n., pl.* **-cies. 1** a government that is run by the people who live under it. In a democracy, the people rule either directly through meetings that all may attend, such as the town meetings in New England, or indirectly through the election of certain representatives to attend to the business of running government: *Democracy means the community's governing through its representatives for its own benefit* (Thomas P. Thompson). *Puritanism . . . laid, without knowing it, the egg of democracy* (James Russell Lowell). **2** a country, state, or community in which the government is a democracy: *The United States is a democracy.* **3** the common people, distinguished from the privileged class, or their political power. **4** the treating of other people as one's equals: *The teacher's democracy made her popular among her pupils.* [< Middle French *démocratie*, learned borrowing from Medieval Latin *democratia* < Greek *dēmokratiā* < *dēmos* people + *krátos* rule, power]

1. Check any of the following that is a characteristic of a *democracy*.
_____ a. The head of state has unlimited power.
_____ b. The people have some say in government.
_____ c. Citizens may vote on representatives and laws.
_____ d. People are free to do as they please.

2. Complete the verbal analogy.
automobile : engine :: *democracy* : _____
_____ a. happiness   _____ c. bill of rights
_____ b. people   _____ d. loyalty

3. The etymology of *democracy* shows that it comes from the Greek *demos* (people). Use that information, your imagination, and your background knowledge to match the following:
_____ a. demagogue   aa. a disease affecting many people at the same time
_____ b. demos   bb. the populace; common people
_____ c. epidemic   cc. something spread over an entire country or area
_____ d. pandemic   dd. a popular leader who stirs up emotions and prejudices

4. Write a sentence correctly using *democracy*. (Be sure to use context clues to show you understand the meaning of the word.)

_____

_____

5. The United States is a representative *democracy,* which requires participation by citizens. What part have you played in maintaining this form of government?

_____

_____

Despotism[7]

des|pot|ism (des′pə tiz əm), *n.* **1** government by a monarch having unlimited power. **2** tyranny or oppression. **3** *Figurative.* absolute power or control: *Such is the despotism of the imagination over uncultivated minds* (Macaulay).
des|pot (des′pət, -pot), *n.* **1** a monarch having unlimited power; absolute ruler: *In ancient times many rulers were despots.* **2** a person who does just as he likes; one who exercises tyrannical power; tyrant or oppressor. **3** a title meaning "master" or "lord," used in Byzantine times to refer to an emperor, or a ruler of one of certain local Byzantine states. **4a** a bishop or patriarch in the Greek Church. **b** a noble, prince, or military leader in Italian cities in the 1300's and 1400's. [< Middle French *despot,* learned borrowing from Medieval Greek *despótēs* absolute ruler, master < Greek, master (of the household)]

1. Which of the following would be an example of *despotism?*
_____ a. a father who makes all the decisions in the family without considering wishes of the other family members
_____ b. a government headed by a president elected by the people
_____ c. a business manager who takes advice from his coworkers
_____ d. a government headed by a leader who has complete power

2. If the government of your country were a *despotism,* you might
_____ a. be able to change things with your vote.
_____ b. feel angry because you were controlled so completely.
_____ c. move away.
_____ d. persuade the ruler to give up some power.

3. Which of the following words describe(s) *despotism?*
_____ a. absolute   _____ d. strict
_____ b. tyrannical   _____ e. moderate
_____ c. oppressive   _____ f. unlimited

4. Have you ever had to deal with *despotism,* if not in a governmental situation, perhaps in a family or school situation, or in a relationship with another person?

_____

_____

5. Write a sentence correctly using *despotism.* (Be sure to include context clues to show you understand the meaning of the word.)

_____

_____

Elite[8]

e|lite or **é|lite** (i lēt′, ā-), *n., adj.* —*n.* **1** the choice or distinguished part; those thought of as the best people: *Only the elite of society attended the reception for the new governor. Scholars are an important part of the intellectual elite of this country* (Saturday Review). **2** a size of typewriter type, smaller than pica, equivalent to 10-point printing type. There are 12 elite characters to the inch. —*adj.* distinguished: *An elite group of scientists participated in the experiment.* [< French *élite,* feminine past participle of *élire* choose < Old French *eslire* < Vulgar Latin *exlegere,* for Latin *ēligere;* see etym. under **elect**]

(Note: Read the pronunciation carefully!)

1. In which of the following sentences can *elite* correctly be placed in the blank?
_____ a. The White House party was attended by the _____ of the political world.
_____ b. In an army, privates are the _____ .
_____ c. The _____ of Hollywood are usually seen at the Academy Awards ceremony.
_____ d. Members of that club think of themselves as _____ .

2. Check any adjective that describes *elite.*
_____ a. choice   _____ d. prominent
_____ b. distinguished   _____ e. celebrated
_____ c. common   _____ f. unknown

3. Check any appropriate response to the following statement: "Only the *elite* shop in that store."
_____ a. It must be a discount store.
_____ b. The owners carry only the finest goods.

SOCIAL SCIENCES: POLITICAL SCIENCE

_____ c. The prices probably are very high.

_____ d. I prefer to order things from a catalog.

4. Write a sentence correctly using *elite*. (Be sure to include context clues to show you understand the meaning of the word.)

_____

5. If you could be a member of any *elite* group (social, academic, financial, or other), what would it be?

_____

Eradicate[14]

e|rad|i|cate (i rad′ə kāt), *v.t.*, **-cat|ed, -cat|ing.**
1 to get rid of entirely; destroy completely; extirpate: *Yellow fever has been eradicated in the United States but it still exists in some countries.*
SYN: eliminate. **2** to pull out by the roots: *The gardener eradicated weeds from the garden.* [< Latin *ērādīcāre* (with English *-ate*¹) < *ex-* out + *rādīx, rādīcis* root]

1. In which of the following sentences can *attenuate* correctly be placed in the blank?

_____ a. The eruption of the volcano Mount St. Helens seemed to _____ all signs of life on the mountain.

_____ b. The city and volunteer groups are working together to _____ graffiti in this area.

_____ c. The police want to _____ the suspect to learn more about the crime.

_____ d. There is a new spray that will _____ all the weeds in your garden.

2. The etymology of *eradicate* shows that it comes from the Latin *ex* (out) and *radix* (root). Use that information, your imagination, and your background knowledge to match the following:

_____ a. radical   aa. root or point of origin

_____ b. radish   bb. to displace; dislocate

_____ c. radix   cc. carried to the farthest limit; extreme

_____ d. deracinate   dd. plant with a thickened, edible root

3. Match the following statement with one below that is most similar: "If you try to *eradicate* all thoughts of some occasion, you are likely to think of it more often."

_____ a. We forget things easily, even when we try to remember them.

_____ b. Concentration improves our mental abilities.

_____ c. Trying to forget things makes the memory stronger.

_____ d. We often fail to remember things but recall them when a friend reminds us of them.

4. Suppose you could *eradicate* one habit you have. What would it be?

_____

_____

5. Write a sentence correctly using *eradicate*. (Be sure to use context clues to show you understand the meaning of the word.)

_____

_____

Ideology[13]

i|de|ol|o|gy (ī′dē ol′ə jē, id′ē-), *n., pl.* **-gies. 1** a set of doctrines or body of opinions that people have: *The majority of teachers and professors do not teach any ideology* (Bulletin of Atomic Scientists). **2** the combined doctrines, assertions, and intentions of a social or political movement: *com-munist ideology.* **3** abstract speculation, especially theorizing or speculation of a visionary or impractical nature. **4** the science of the origin and nature of ideas. **5** a system of philosophy that derives all ideas exclusively from sensations.

1. Which of the following might be an *ideology?*
   _____ a. Private ownership of property makes a society more productive.
   _____ b. God has a plan for the universe.
   _____ c. Property should be owned by the state, not the individual.
   _____ d. The best governments are those that interfere least with the lives of citizens.

2. Which of the numbered dictionary definitions of *ideology* best fits the word's use in the reading selection? _____

3. In which of the following sentences can *ideology* (or *ideologies*) correctly be placed in the blank?
   _____ a. The national _____ of a democratic country differs a great deal from that of a communistic country.
   _____ b. Some languages, such as Chinese, are written using symbols called _____ .
   _____ c. The _____ of a hermit separates him from society.
   _____ d. Professions such as law and medicine have _____ that govern the thinking and actions of their members.

4. Write a sentence correctly using *ideology*. (Be sure to use context clues to show you understand the meaning of the word.)

_____

_____

5. Do you believe that the *ideology* of capitalism (individual investment of money and labor, and competition) makes a society more productive? _____ Would you work as hard as you do, or harder, if you were not in competition with others?

_____

_____

SOCIAL SCIENCES: POLITICAL SCIENCE

Indictment[6]

in|dict|ment (in dīt′mənt), *n.* **1** a formal written accusation, especially on the recommendation of a grand jury: *an indictment for murder. When an indictment does come down, the accused individuals will have an opportunity at trial to defend their innocence* (New York Times). *I do not know the method of drawing up an indictment against a whole people* (Edmund Burke). **2** an indicting or being indicted; accusation: *Mr. Bond has written . . . a perfectly stunning indictment of the welfare state* (New Yorker).

in|dict (in dīt′), *v.t.* **1** to charge with an offense or crime; accuse: *Let anyone who will, indict him on the charge of loving base gains* (Benjamin Jowett). **2** (of a grand jury) to find evidence against (an accused person) to be enough so that a trial is necessary: *The jury indicted all eleven men named by the FBI* (Newsweek). [alteration of Middle English *endyten* < Anglo-French *enditer* to charge, accuse, Old French, to indite, dictate < Latin *in-* in + *dictāre* declare, dictate, express in writing (frequentative) < *dīcere* say, speak]

(Note: In the pronunciation of this word, the "c" is silent, and the second "i" is long.)

1. Which of the following would be an *indictment?*
   - _____ a. a letter thanking a party hostess for a good time
   - _____ b. a form accusing someone of murder
   - _____ c. a note telling someone about plans for a trip
   - _____ d. a letter telling someone of the terrible things that person has done

2. Check any appropriate response to the following statement:
   "The politician's speech yesterday was an *indictment* of our current tax laws."
   - _____ a. I agree with him. They are the best we have ever had.
   - _____ b. He likes them because he helped pass the tax bill.
   - _____ c. He thinks they are terrible, doesn't he?
   - _____ d. He certainly is outspoken in his dislike of them.

3. Which of the numbered dictionary definitions of *indictment* best fits the word's use in the reading selection? _____

4. If you could issue an *indictment* against any one person or thing in your life, who or what would it be?_____

   _____

5. Write a sentence correctly using *indictment.* (Be sure to include context clues to show you understand the meaning of the word.)

   _____

   _____

Mandate[11]

man|date (*n.* man′dāt, -dit; *v.* man′dāt), *n., v.,* **-dat|ed, -dat|ing.** — *n.* **1** a command or order: *a royal mandate. The mandate of God to His creature man is: Work!* (Thomas Carlyle). **SYN:** edict, behest, injunction. **2** an order from a higher court or official to a lower one: *Towards the close of Adams's term, Georgia had bid defiance to the mandates of the Supreme Court* (Theodore Roosevelt). **3** a direction or authority given to a government by the votes of the people in an election: *After his election the governor said he had a mandate to increase taxes.* **4** a commission given to one nation by a group of nations to administer the government and affairs of a territory or colony. The system of mandates established after World War I was administered by the League of Nations. *The character of the Mandate must differ according to the stage of the development of the people* (League of Nations Covenant). **5** a mandated territory or colony. **6** an order issued by the Pope stating that a certain person should be given a benefice. **7** a contract in Roman and civil law, by which one person requests another to act for him gratuitously, agreeing to indemnify him against losses. **8** any contract of agency. **9** a command in ancient

Rome from the emperor, especially to the governor of a province.
— **v.t.** to put (a territory or colony) under the administration of another nation: *The result of the late war has been to eliminate Germany from the map, her territories being mandated to the British and other nations* (Times Literary Supplement). [< Latin *mandātum*, noun use of neuter past participle of *mandāre* to order]

1. In which of the following sentences can *mandate* correctly be placed in the blank?
   _____ a. When we are really hungry, we _____ a pizza from Joe's Pizza Parlor.
   _____ b. An elected official is considered to have the _____ of the people.
   _____ c. The police have a _____, under the law, to maintain law and order.
   _____ d. A politician may claim to have a _____ to pass certain legislation.

2. Which of the following describes a *mandate*?
   _____ a. a direction   _____ d. an order
   _____ b. a suggestion   _____ e. authority
   _____ c. a command   _____ f. injunction

3. The etymology of *mandate* shows that the word comes from the Latin *mandare* (to order). Use that information, your imagination, and your background knowledge to match the following:
   _____ a. command   aa. to send back
   _____ b. commend   bb. to have power over
   _____ c. demand   cc. to speak well of; praise
   _____ d. remand   dd. to ask for as a right

4. Write a sentence correctly using *mandate*. (Be sure to use context clues to show you understand the meaning of the word.)

   _____

   _____

5. What *mandate* would you like to give to the governor of your state?

   _____

   _____

Methodology[2]

meth|od|ol|o|gy (meth′ə dol′ə jē), *n., pl.* **-gies.**
1 the system of methods or procedures used in any field: *the methodology of the modern historian.* **2** a branch of logic dealing with the application of its principles in any field of knowledge. **3** the methods of teaching; the branch of education dealing with the means and ways of instruction. [< New Latin *methodologia* < Greek *méthodos* method + *-logīā* science, system, treatment < *légein* speak]

1. In which of the following sentences can *methodology* correctly be placed in the blank?

      a. In the academic world, each field has its own accepted _____ .

      b. Before John can get his teaching credential, he must take a course in _____ .

      c. Jane's _____ for weight loss includes diet and exercise.

      d. A branch of logic that analyzes principles that should guide inquiry is _____ .

2. Complete the verbal analogy.
   woman : women :: *methodology* : _____
   a. methodologys   c. methodologist
   b. noun   d. methodologies

3. Which of the numbered dictionary definitions of *methodology* best fits the word's use in the reading selection? _____

4. Write a sentence correctly using *methodology*. (Be sure to include context clues to show you understand the meaning of the word.)

   _____

   _____

5. What do you think some of the differences in *methodology* are between chemistry and political science?

   _____

   _____

Polity[3]

pol|i|ty (pol′ə tē), *n., pl.* **-ties. 1** = government. **2** a particular form or system of government: *that the true historical polity of the Netherlands was a representative, constitutional government* (John L. Motley). **3** a community with a government; state: *The Jewish polity was utterly destroyed, and the nation dispersed over the face of the earth* (Joseph Butler). **4** the condition of having a government or civil organization: *races without polity.* [< Middle French *politie,* learned borrowing from Late Latin *polītīa* government < Latin, citizenship < Greek *polīteiā* < *polītēs* citizen; of one's city < *pólis* city. See etym. of doublets **police, policy**[1].]

1. *Polity* is related to which of the following?
        a. city   d. citizenship
        b. citizen   e. police
        c. politeness   f. policy

2. In which of the following sentences can *polity* (or *polities*) correctly be placed in the blank?
        a. The ideas of communism are not based on United States _____ .

_____ b. We usually think our form of _____ is better than that of other countries.

_____ c. When I dialed 911, the _____ responded quickly.

_____ d. Some _____ are more supportive of the arts than others.

3. Complete the verbal analogy.

flower : rose :: *polity* : _____

_____ a. policy   _____ c. government
_____ b. people   _____ d. city

4. Write a sentence correctly using *polity*. (Be sure to use context clues to show you understand the meaning of the word.)

_____

_____

5. You are responsible to more than one *polity*. Among them are the federal government and the state (or territorial) government. What other *polities* determine what you can and cannot do?

_____

_____

Regime[10]

re|gime or **ré|gime** (ri zhēm′, rā-), *n.* **1** the system of government or rule; prevailing system: *Under the old regime women could not vote. The Russians may mean what they say when they describe their present régime as a transitory stage* (Bulletin of Atomic Scientists). **2** any prevailing political or social system. **3** the period or length of a regime. **4** *Informal.* a system of living; regimen: *The baby's regime includes two naps a day.* [< French *régime,* learned borrowing from Latin *regimen.* See etym. of doublet **regimen.**]

reg|i|men (rej′ə men, -men), *n.* **1** a set of rules or habits of diet, exercise, or manner of living intended to improve health, reduce weight, cultivate the mind, or otherwise make something better or achieve some goal. **2** the act of governing; government; rule. **3** *Grammar.* the influence of one word in determining the case or mood of another; government. [< Latin *regimen, -inis* < *regere* to rule, straighten. See etym. of doublet **regime.**]

(Note: Read the pronunciation guide carefully!)

1. In which of the following sentences can *regime* correctly be placed in the blank?

_____ a. I try to follow a healthful _____ of diet and exercise.

_____ b. If you _____ your life carefully, you can be happy and healthy.

_____ c. The purpose of the revolution is to overthrow the current _____.

_____ d. That author belongs to the old _____; no one reads him today.

SOCIAL SCIENCES: POLITICAL SCIENCE

2. Which of the following might be called a *regime?*

_____ a. a city government

_____ b. a textbook

_____ c. a group of friends

_____ d. an established system

_____ e. a school administration

_____ f. a national government

3. Which of the numbered dictionary definitions of *regime* best fits the word's use in the reading selection? _____

4. List four elements of a *regime* that may result in better grades for you.

_____

_____

5. Write a sentence correctly using *regime.* (Be sure to include context clues to show you understand the meaning of the word.)

_____

_____

_____

Republic[5]

re|pub|lic (ri pub'lik), *n.* **1** a nation or state in which the citizens elect representatives to manage the government, which is usually headed by a president rather than a monarch. The United States and Mexico are republics. **SYN:** commonwealth. **2** the form of government existing in suc a state. **3** any one of the major political divisions of the Soviet Union or of Yugoslavia: *the Latvian Republic, the Croatian Republic, the Republic of Turkmenistan.* **4** *Figurative.* any body of persons or things: *the republic of authors and scholars.* [< Middle French *république,* learned borrowing from Latin *rēs pūblica* public interest; the state; *rēs* affair, matter(s); things; *pūblica,* feminine adjective, public]

1. Check any characteristic of a *republic.*

_____ a. has a monarch   _____ d. government according to law

_____ b. people vote   _____ e. general equality

_____ c. lack of unity   _____ f. totalitarian

2. In which of the following sentences can *republic* correctly be placed in the blank?

_____ a. The _____ of the United States is a representative democracy.

_____ b. The United Kingdom (England) is a _____ .

_____ c. Participation of the citizens is an important part of a

_____ .

_____ d. I pledge allegiance to the flag of the United States of America and to the _____ for which it stands.

3. Which of the numbered dictionary definitions of *republic* best fits its use in the reading selection? _____

4. Write a sentence correctly using *republic*. (Be sure to include context clues to show you understand the meaning of the word.)

_____

_____

5. You may live in a country that is a *republic*, but you also may be part of at least one other *republic* (using definition 4). What group might that be?

_____

_____

Scope[1]

scope[1] (skōp), *n.* **1a** the distance the mind can reach; extent of view: *Very hard words are not within the scope of a child's understanding.* **SYN:** compass. See syn. under **range**. **b** the area over which any activity operates or is effective; range of application: *This subject is not within the scope of our investigation. Beyond the scope of all speculation* (Edmund Burke). **SYN:** compass. See syn. under **range**. **2** room to range; space; opportunity: *Football gives scope for courage and quick thinking. I gave full scope to my imagination* (Laurence Sterne). **3** the range or length of flight of an arrow or other missile. **4a** extent; length; sweep: *The yacht's gig was towing easily at the end of a long scope of line* (Joseph Conrad). **b** the length of cable at which a ship rides when at anchor. **5** *Archaic.* an aim; purpose; ultimate object. [< Italian *scopo,* learned borrowing from Late Latin *scopus* < Greek *skopós* aim, object < *skopeîn* behold, consider]

1. Check any appropriate response to the following statement:
   "The *scope* of Margaret Mead's interests led her beyond what had previously been thought of as the field of anthropology."
   _____ a. She should have investigated more things.
   _____ b. She made the field broader, didn't she?
   _____ c. So many things were of interest to her.
   _____ d. A narrow person in a narrow field.

2. Select the synonym(s) of *scope*.
   _____ a. range   _____ d. sweep
   _____ b. extent   _____ e. compass
   _____ c. length   _____ f. object

3. Which of the numbered and lettered dictionary definitions of *scope* best fits the word's use in the reading selection? _____

4. Write a sentence correctly using *scope*. (Be sure to include context clues to show you understand the meaning of the word.)

_____

_____

5. What is the *scope* of your interest in athletics? List the sports you care about. Is the *scope* of your interest broad or narrow?

_____

_____

ANSWERS TO CHAPTER 13 EXERCISES

Aristocracy: 1. a, c, d, e, f 2. c (definition) 3. 3
Attenuate: 1. a, c, d 2. a, b, d, e 3. cc, dd, aa, ee, bb
Coup: 1. b, d 2. 2 3. a, b, d
Democracy: 1. b, c 2. b (source of energy) 3. dd, bb, aa, cc
Despotism: 1. a, d 2. b, c 3. a, b, c, d, f
Elite: 1. a, c, d 2. a, b, d, e 3. b, c, d
Eradicate: 1. a, b, d 2. cc, dd, aa, bb 3. c
Ideology: 1. a, c, d 2. 2 3. a, c, d
Indictment: 1. b, d 2. c, d 3. 2
Mandate: 1. b, c, d 2. a, c, d, e, f 3. bb, cc, dd, aa
Methodology: 1. a, b, d 2. d (plural) 3. 1
Polity: 1. a, b, d, e, f 2. a, b, d 3. a (general-specific)
Regime: 1. a, c, d 2. a, d, e, f 3. 1
Republic: 1. b, d, e 2. a, c, d 3. 1
Scope: 1. b, c 2. a, b, c, d, e 3. 1b

If you missed any of the items in the exercises, return to the exercise and to the dictionary definition to see where you went wrong. Remember: If you get something right, you only affirm that you knew it. If you get something wrong and understand why, *you have learned something.*

POLITICAL SCIENCE POSTTEST

Fill in the blanks with the words from this list.

aristocracy	elite	methodology
attenuate	eradicate	polity
coup	ideology	regime
democracy	indictment	republic
despotism	mandate	scope

1. To make something less dense is to _____ it.
2. Twelve-point printing type is _____.
3. *Extirpate* is a synonym for _____.
4. Another word for oppression is _____.
5. A(n) _____ is an accusation.
6. *Regimen* is a synonym for _____.

7. _____ is the treating of people as one's equal.

8. _____ is from the Greek and means "rule of the best born."

9. *Commonwealth* is a synonym for _____.

10. _____ is a synonym for *length* and *extent*.

11. A community with a government is a _____.

12. _____ means "methods of teaching."

13. A(n) _____ is a masterstroke.

14. Abstract speculation can be called _____.

15. *Behest* is a synonym for _____.

Answers to this posttest are in the Instructor's Manual.

If you missed any of the words, you may need to return to the exercises and to the dictionary entries to see why your concepts for some words are incomplete.

CHAPTER FOURTEEN

SOCIAL SCIENCES: PSYCHOLOGY

◆

OVERVIEW

Psychology is the study of the nature of humans as they interact with their environment. It is useful in understanding ourselves and others, either in daily social and business contacts or in a vocational or career area.

There are many different subfields in psychology, each representing a different emphasis in its application to human beings. These subfields include experimental psychology, humanistic psychology, social psychology, developmental psychology, and applied professional psychology. Experimental psychology is concerned with the understanding of our general life processes and interactions, such as thinking processes, sensory perceptions, motivation, and so on. The subfield of humanistic psychology includes an emphasis on the human personality, the study of the family, and clinical studies. Developmental psychology focuses on the various phases of human development from childhood through adulthood, and social psychology relates the study of psychology to general societal issues, including theories of culture, application to law, and death and dying. Lastly, the applied professional study of psychology is concerned with the preparation of trained and licensed counselors for work in industry, mental hospitals, clinics, law enforcement, and social welfare.

Introductory textbooks in psychology are usually expository, that is, they explain broad concepts or generalizations. The ideas may also be presented to show relationships between theories or principles as well as cause-and-effect interactions of observed phenomena. The text may be adversative in that it will show opposing viewpoints on the same theory. Many texts also include historical references and may be organized according to a chronological sequence.

The vocabulary in psychology is a combination of technical and general vocabulary. The general words are those we might use every day but that can also have a specific meaning in the context of psychology. Examples of such words are intelligence, readiness, *and* learning. *Many of the technical words such as* neurosis *and* psychosis *are scientific in nature and have Latin or Greek etymology.*

Be sure to read any charts or graphs in psychology textbooks, as they may reinforce the vocabulary presented in other parts of the text. Additional sources of vocabulary in the field of psychology come from other activities in which you apply psychological concepts or ideas. These include lab experiments, audiovisual presentations, fieldwork experiences, and guest speakers or lecturers.

VOCABULARY SELF-EVALUATION

The following words will be introduced in this reading selection. Place a check mark (√) in front of any that you know thoroughly and use in your speech or writing. Place a question mark (?) in front of any that you recognize but do not use yourself.

_____ cognition	_____ hypothesis	_____ parsimony
_____ contiguity	_____ innate	_____ semantic
_____ eidetic	_____ mediate	_____ specificity
_____ episode	_____ mnemonic	_____ theory
_____ ethical	_____ paradigm	_____ validity

A PERSPECTIVE ON PSYCHOLOGY

Psychology is the study of behavior. It attempts to understand, to explain, to predict, and sometimes, to control behavior. The origins of psychology are in philosophy, so it seeks to resolve some age-old questions. For example, one continuing problem in the field of psychology is the relative contribution of inheritance and environment to the behavior of organisms. Psychologists investigate both innate[1] and learned factors in an effort to understand their influences on behavior. Individuals outside the field can also profit from the conclusions that these scientists reach after their careful studies.

Psychologists employ the scientific

method in their investigations. Studies begin with observations, from which hypotheses[2] are formed. In some areas of the field, where human subjects are involved, psychologists are careful about interfering with behaviors or attempting to alter them, since such actions might not be ethical.[3] Nevertheless, careful observations over long periods of time can result in useful hypotheses. (Long-term, careful observations where no attempt is made to manipulate the variables are called naturalistic observations; other sciences, such as astronomy, also use naturalistic observations.)

In other areas of psychology, such as experimental psychology, psychologists design and carry out experiments to test the validity[4] of each hypothesis. These experiments regularly include independent variables (factors that are set up and controlled by the experimentor) and dependent variables (factors that change depending on the situation presented by the independent variable). If the hypotheses being tested are found to be inaccurate, they are discarded, and others must be formulated. When a set of hypotheses that have not been disproved fit together to form a whole, they are said to be a theory.[5] (Note that the hypotheses are not *proved;* they are merely *not disproved.* Science is cautious about stating that it has found "the truth," since so many factors always remain unknown.) In determining the composition of a theory, psychologists follow the principle of parsimony.[6] That is, they look for a theory that is simple and that is consistent with theories already accepted. The theory then may serve as a paradigm[7] around which other psychologists can develop and investigate more hypotheses.

An important area of study for psychologists is that of learning. Many of the studies of learning behavior have been carried out using animals as subjects, but the results of the experiments frequently can be applied to humans. For example, researchers have found that rats can be trained to perform an act (such as pressing a lever) in order to receive a reward (such as food). That is, reinforcement can increase a behavior. Yet the reinforcement need not be continuous: in fact, variable reinforcements are more effective than regular ones. It is also important that the reward be given shortly after the act so that there is a clear relationship between them. In other words, there must be temporal contiguity[8] between the performance and its reinforcement. Gambling casinos recognize these factors when they set the payoff schedules and procedures for slot machines: People continue to put money into the machines for longer periods of time when the payoffs are variable and when the reward drops into the cup directly after the wheels stop spinning.

Learning that involves human intelligence is termed cognition;[9] it is more complicated than learning demonstrated by animals. Humans are more complicated in other ways also. For instance, past experiences influence behavior, and mental processes mediate[10] behavior. These factors can alter results, and experimenters must be alert to problems caused by variables that are not intended to be part of the experiment.

Studies of human memory continue to supply data about how individuals store information and past experience. The capacity to remember and the different types of memory appear to be innate. For instance, learners with eidetic[11] imagery have strong visual memories. Other types of memory are procedural, those that permit us to remember how to perform acquired acts; and factual, which are those that deal with information. Factual memory is of two types: Memory for information concerning episodes[12] is termed episodic, while memory for information concerning words and concepts is called semantic.[13]

Effective retrieval of information, particularly semantic information, requires learners to use specific types of rehearsal, to space or distribute practice, and to employ mnemonic[14] devices. Such memory devices can help organize seemingly meaningless or unrelated material into associations that can be recalled when needed. Yet another factor in remembering information is the relationship between where and how it is learned and where and how it must be recalled. For example, material learned in one environment can best be recalled in that same environment. This is called encoding specificity.[15]

Discoveries made by psychologists regarding learning and memory are of particular interest to students, since students are called on to learn and remember large amounts of information and to perform well under what can be demanding and stressful circumstances. Thus, finding out how psychologists study behavior and understanding what they have learned about it can be truly beneficial to the serious student. ◆

PSYCHOLOGY PRETEST

Select words from this list and write them in the blanks to complete the sentences.

cognition	hypothesis	parsimony
contiguity	innate	semantic
eidetic	mediate	specificity
episode	mnemonic	theory
ethical	paradigm	validity

1. An inborn ability is a(n) _____ characteristic.

2. Something assumed because it seems likely to be a true explanation is a(n) _____ .

3. An explanation that has been tested and confirmed as a general principle is a(n) _____ .

4. To use extreme economy is to practice _____ .

5. A(n) _____ is an assist to the memory.

6. Information dealing with words and concepts is _____ .

7. Another word for *pattern* is _____ .

8. _____ is the quality of being characteristic of or peculiar to something.

9. Items that are close to each other have _____ .

10. _____ is an intellectual process by which knowledge is gained.

11. Another word for *event* is _____ .

12. To occupy an intermediate place or position is to _____ .

13. _____ matters have to do with moral considerations.

14. Something _____ is a true representation.

15. Testing for the truth of an idea is testing for its _____.

Answers to this pretest are in Appendix B.

Unless your instructor tells you to do otherwise, complete the exercises for each word you missed on the pretest. The words, with their meanings and exercises, are in alphabetical order. The superscript numbers indicate where the words appeared in the reading selection so that you can refer to them when necessary. There are several types of exercises, and more than one answer may be correct. For each word you will be asked to write a sentence using context clues. (See Chapter 4 if you need information about how to create context clues.) You are also asked to perform some activity that will help you make your concept of the word personal. *Complete this activity thoughtfully, for creating a personalized concept of the word will help you remember it in the future.*

Answers to all the exercises are at the end of the exercise segment.

PSYCHOLOGY EXERCISES

Cognition[9]

cog|ni|tion (kog nish′ən), *n.* **1** the act of knowing; perception; awareness. **SYN:** sensation. **2** a thing known, perceived, or recognized. **3** (in Scottish law) official notice; cognizance: *The Council appointed a Committee to take cognition of the matter* (James Grant). **4** *Obsolete.* the act or faculty of coming to know; knowledge. [< Latin *cognitiō, -ōnis* < *cognōscere* recognize < *co-* (intensive) + *gnōscere* know]

1. In which of the following sentences can *cognition* correctly be placed in the blank?
   ____ a. Through _____ we can gain knowledge and can reason about that knowledge.
   ____ b. Psychologists who study _____ conduct experiments using rats.
   ____ c. Problem solving is an act of _____.
   ____ d. Remembering, reasoning, and analyzing are included in _____.

2. Which of the following would be an example of *cognition*?
   ____ a. swimming   ____ c. studying for an exam
   ____ b. reading a book   ____ d. driving a car

3. The etymology of *cognition* shows that the word comes from the Latin

gnoscere (to know). Use this information, your imagination, and your background knowledge to match the following:

_____ a. recognize aa. to let know
_____ b. connoisseur bb. to know again
_____ c. notify cc. one who knows things well: an expert
_____ d. diagnosis dd. well known because of something bad
_____ e. notorious ee. the process of finding out about a disease

4. What act of *cognition* do you enjoy most? Studying alone? Reading in the library? Researching a paper? Other?

_____

_____

5. Write a sentence correctly using *cognition*. (Be sure to include context clues to show you understand the meaning of the word.)

_____

_____

Contiguity[8]

con|ti|gu|i|ty (kon′tə gyü′ə tē), *n., pl.* **-ties. 1** a being very close together; nearness: *The contiguity of the house and garage was a convenience in bad weather.* **SYN:** proximity, adjacency. **2** contact: *The candidate's contiguity with the common people served him well.* **3** a continuous mass; unbroken stretch: *a contiguity of mountain scenery.*

1. In which of the following sentences can *contiguity* correctly be placed in the blank?

_____ a. The _____ of fences left us no pathway between the houses.
_____ b. The _____ of buildings in the shopping center made shopping convenient.
_____ c. The agreement between the two nations was a _____ of a previous treaty.
_____ d. The _____ of the United States and Canada makes travel from one to the other easy.

2. Check any synonym of *contiguity*.

_____ a. contact _____ d. nearness
_____ b. similarity _____ e. closeness
_____ c. proximity _____ f. adjacency

3. Complete the verbal analogy.

happiness : sadness :: *contiguity* : _____
a. abundance c. branching
b. proximity d. distance

4. Write a sentence correctly using *contiguity*. (Be sure to include context clues to show you understand the meaning of the word.)

_____

_____

5. As you sit filling out these pages, with what object do you have *contiguity*?

_____

_____

Eidetic[11]

ei|det|ic (T det′ik), *adj.* of or having to do with extremely clear images of previous optical impressions: *eidetic imagery.* [< German *eidetisch* < Greek *eidētikós* < *eidos* form] —**ei|det′i|cal|ly,** *adv.*

eidetic image, an image (experienced especially by children) which revives a previous optical impression with the clearness of hallucination.

1. Check any appropriate response to the following statement: "Suzie's *eidetic* imagery faded as she grew older."

     _____ a. Leaving things out in the sun makes them fade.
     _____ b. She should take better care of her things.
     _____ c. Adults seldom have the strong visual memory that children have.
     _____ d. It's too bad she no longer sees the clear images she used to see.

2. In which of the following sentences can *eidetic* correctly be placed in the blank?

     _____ a. Angela is able to predict the future; she is an

       _____.

     _____ b. Tom seldom forgets what he hears. He has

       _____ hearing.

     _____ c. Carmen seems to remember, word for word, the books she reads, so we think she has _____ imagery.

     _____ d. An _____ image can be a very clear and sharp memory.

3. The etymology of *eidetic* shows that the word comes from the Greek *eidos* (form). Use that information, your imagination, and your background knowledge to match the following:

     _____ a. idol   aa. a series of changing phases or events
     _____ b. idyll   bb. an image used as an object of worship
     _____ c. ideogram   cc. resembling a human being in appearance

_____ d. humanoid   dd. a short poem describing a scene of rural life

_____ e. kaleidoscope   ee. a graphic symbol representing an idea or thing

4. What scene do you remember very clearly from your childhood? _____

_____

_____

Does this seem to be an *eidetic* image? _____

_____

5. Write a sentence correctly using *eidetic*. (Be sure to include context clues to show you understand the meaning of the word.)

_____

_____

Episode[12]

ep|i|sode (ep′ə sōd), *n.* **1** an incident or experience that stands out from others: *Being named the best athlete of the year was an important episode in the baseball player's life. His meeting with Matisse was an important episode in the artist's year in France.* **2a** a set of events or actions separate from the main plot of a novel, story, or other literary work. **b** *Music.* a passage separated from and in contrast to the principal themes, especially in a sonata or fugue. **3** the part in a Greek tragedy between two choric songs. [< Greek *epeisódion* addition, neuter of *epeisódios* coming in besides < *epi-* in addition + *eis* into + *hodós* way]

1. In which of the following sentences can *episode* correctly be placed in the blank?

_____ a. The Greek chorus performed before and after the _____ .

_____ b. The statue had an _____ engraved on its base.

_____ c. The _____ that occurred at the party stands out in my mind.

_____ d. A long poem that tells of heroic events is an _____ .

2. The etymology of *episode* shows that the word comes from the Greek *hodos* (way, in the sense of "journey"). Use that information, your imagination, and your background knowledge to match the following:

_____ a. exodus   aa. an interval of time

_____ b. odometer   bb. a procedure and technique used in a discipline

_____ c. period   cc. a council or assembly of churches

_____ d. method   dd. a departure, usually by a large number of people

_____ e. synod   ee. an instrument that indicates distance traveled

3. Which of the numbered and lettered definitions in the dictionary entry for *episode* best fits its use in the reading selection? _____

4. Write a sentence correctly using *episode*. (Be sure to include context clues to show you understand the meaning of the word.)

_____

_____

5. Imagine that you are given the ability to relive any *episode* in your life. What will you choose?

_____

Ethical[3]

eth|i|cal (eth′ə kəl), *adj., n.* —*adj.* **1** having to do with standards of right and wrong; of ethics or morals: *ethical standards.* SYN: See syn. under **moral. 2** morally right: *ethical conduct.* **3** in accordance with formal or professional rules of right and wrong: *It is not considered ethical for a doctor to repeat a patient's confidences.* **4** of or having to do with ethical drugs: *ethical products, an ethical consultant firm.*
—*n.* Usually, **ethicals.** a drug that cannot be obtained without a doctor's prescription; ethical drug: *The proprietary industry is not growing as fast as the ethicals* (Wall Street Journal).
—**eth′i|cal|ly,** *adv.* —**eth′i|cal|ness,** *n.*

from **moral:**

— *Syn. adj.* **1 Moral, ethical** mean in agreement with a standard of what is right and good in character or conduct. **Moral** implies conformity to the customary rules and accepted standards of society: *He leads a moral life.* **Ethical** implies conformity to the principles of right conduct expressed in a formal system or code, such as that of a profession or business: *It is not considered ethical for doctors to advertise.*

1. Which of the following behaviors would be *ethical*?
   _____ a. A priest refuses to tell the police that someone has confessed a robbery.
   _____ b. A parent will not spank a child.
   _____ c. A child does not steal candy from a store.
   _____ d. A psychologist uses human subjects only in studies where there will be no physical or psychological aftereffects.

2. Check any appropriate response to the following statement:
   "Dr. Gonzalez abides by the *ethical* standards of the medical society."
   _____ a. Good doctors are responsible for behaving ethically.
   _____ b. Lawyers follow the same standards.
   _____ c. Everyone in our society is bound by those rules.
   _____ d. Doctors agree to do that when they take their oath.

3. Which of the numbered definitions in the dictionary for *ethical* best fits its use in the reading selection? _____

4. Write a sentence correctly using *ethical*. (Be sure to include context clues to show you understand the meaning of the word.)

_____

_____

5. You may not be aware of the fact, but as a student you are expected to abide by a set of *ethical* standards. Write down one thing you must

do (or not do) in order to remain a member of the student body of your school.

_____

_____

Hypothesis[2]

hy|poth|e|sis (hī poth′ə sis, hi-), *n., pl.* **-ses.**
1 something assumed because it seems likely to be a true explanation; theory: *Let us act on the hypothesis that he is honest.* **syn**: See syn. under **theory. 2** a proposition assumed as a basis for reasoning; supposition. A theorem in geometry is made up of a hypothesis and a conclusion. **3** a mere assumption; guess: *Your reasoning ... seems plausible, but still it is only hypothesis* (Scott). [< New Latin *hypothesis* < Greek *hypóthesis* < *hypo-* under + *thésis* a placing < *tithénai* to place]

from **theory:**

— *Syn.* **1a, b. Theory, hypothesis** as terms in science mean a generalization reached by infer-ence from observed particulars and proposed as an explanation of their cause, relations, or the like. **Theory** implies a larger body of tested evidence and a greater degree of probability: *The red shift in the spectra of galaxies supports the theory that the universe is continuously expanding.* **Hypothesis** designates a merely tentative explanation of the data, advanced or adopted provisionally, often as the basis of a theory or as a guide to further observation or experiment: *Archeological discoveries strengthened the hypothesis that Troy existed.*

1. In which of the following sentences can *hypothesis* correctly be placed in the blank?
   _____ a. In this case, our _____ is that *a* is the cause of *b*.
   _____ b. Something proved is _____.
   _____ c. Your reasoning is good, but it is only _____.
   _____ d. The _____ you have suggested can be worked out in our experiment.

2. Complete this verbal analogy.
   explain : tell :: *hypothesis* : _____
   a. imagination   c. conclusion
   b. supposition   d. condition

3. Which of the following might be said of *hypothesis?*
   _____ a. It requires further testing.
   _____ b. It may explain a few observations.
   _____ c. It attempts to explain.
   _____ d. It is known to be true.

4. Write a sentence correctly using *hypothesis.* (Be sure to include context clues to show you understand the meaning of the word.)

_____

_____

5. Do you have a *hypothesis* about what makes you happy? (You must experiment to find out if it is true; since it doesn't apply generally, it isn't a theory.)

_____

_____

Innate[1]

in|nate (i nāt′, in′āt), *adj.* **1** born in a person; natural: *A good artist has an innate talent for drawing. A good comedian has an innate wit.* **SYN:** native, inborn, inbred. **2** existing naturally in anything; inherent. **3** *Philosophy.* (of ideas or principles) present in the mind or soul as originally constituted or created; not learned or otherwise acquired. [< Latin *innātus* < *in-* in + *nāscī* be born] — **in|nate′ly**, *adv.* — **in|nate′ness**, *n.*

1. In which of the following sentences is *innate* used correctly?

    _____ a. John has innate musical ability. Someday he will be famous.

    _____ b. Mother says my stubbornness is innate.

    _____ c. A hospital is an innate place to have a baby.

    _____ d. Mary's innate energy has resulted in many accomplishments.

2. The etymology of *innate* shows that the word comes from the Latin *nasci* (to be born). Use this information, your background knowledge, and your imagination to match the following:

    _____ a. natal   aa. a people occupying the same country

    _____ b. native   bb. like a child

    _____ c. nation   cc. born in a certain place or country

    _____ d. naive   dd. having to do with or dating from one's birth

    _____ e. renaissance ee. a revival; new birth

3. Place an "s" before any synonym and an "a" before any antonym of *innate*.

    _____ a. inherent   _____ d. natural

    _____ b. inbred   _____ e. native

    _____ c. learned   _____ f. inborn

4. Write down at least two of your own *innate* characteristics.

    _____

    _____

5. Write a sentence correctly using *innate*. (Be sure to include context clues to show you understand the meaning of the word.)

    _____

    _____

Mediate[10]

me|di|ate (*v.* mē′dē āt; *adj.* mē′dē it), *v.,* **-at|ed, -at|ing,** *adj.* —*v.i.* **1** to come in to help settle a dispute; be a go-between; act in order to bring about an agreement between persons or sides: *Mother mediated in the quarrel between the two boys. The mayor tried to mediate between the bus company and its employees.* **2** to occupy an intermediate place or position.
—*v.t.* **1** to effect by intervening; settle by intervening: *to mediate an agreement, to mediate a strike.* **2** to be a connecting link between. **3** to be the medium for effecting (a result), for conveying (a gift), or for communicating (knowledge).
—*adj.* **1** connected, but not directly; connected through some other person or thing: *A vassal's relation with his king was mediate through the lord on whose estate he lived.* **2** intermediate: *After many mediate preferments . . . at last he became Archbishop of Canterbury* (Thomas Fuller). [< Late Latin *mediārī* (with English *-ate*[1]) to be in the middle, intervene < Latin *medius* middle] — **me′di|ate|ly**, *adv.* — **me′di|ate|ness**, *n.*

1. In which of the following sentences can *mediate* correctly be placed in the blank?

    _____ a. My mother often must _____ an argument between my brother and my sister.

    _____ b. The _____ grade on the test was 65 points.

    _____ c. His job with the union was to _____ between management and labor.

    _____ d. Tom is so consistent. He always orders his steaks _____ rare.

2. Which of the numbered definitions in the dictionary entry for *mediate* best fits its use in the reading selection? _____

3. The etymology of *mediate* shows that the word comes from the Latin *medius* (middle). Use that information, your imagination, and your background knowledge to match the following:

    _____ a. mean   aa. pertaining to the Middle Ages

    _____ b. moiety   bb. a vertical strip dividing the panes of a window

    _____ c. mullion   cc. the middle point between two extremes

    _____ d. medieval   dd. a great circle passing through both of earth's geographical poles

    _____ e. meridian   ee. a half

4. If you had the power to *mediate* a dispute in any area of the world, where would you use your power?

    _____

5. Write a sentence correctly using *mediate*. (Be sure to include context clues to show you understand the meaning of the word.)

    _____

    _____

Mnemonic[14]

mne|mon|ic (ni mon′ik), *adj., n.* —*adj.* **1** aiding the memory. **2** intended to aid the memory: *The strongly mnemonic nature of the catchword system certainly supports the idea that the writing grew out of a memory-aid device* (Scientific American). **3** of or having to do with the memory. —*n.* **1** a mnemonic device. **2** = mnemonics. [< Greek *mnēmonikós* < *mnâsthai* remember] —**mne|mon′i|cal|ly,** *adv.*

1. Which of the following might serve as a *mnemonic* device?

    _____ a. a string tied around your finger

    _____ b. a sentence in which each word begins with the letter of something you want to remember

    _____ c. a word whose letters stand for material to be remembered

    _____ d. a rhyme that contains information you want to recall

2. Select any appropriate reply to the following statement:
"To remember things you might want to use *mnemonic* devices."

_____ a. Yes, but you have to use the special set in that book.

_____ b. They work best for me when I make them up for myself.

_____ c. There are some standard devices, but self-made ones work too.

_____ d. They are just a joke; they never work.

3. The following is a *mnemonic* device to help spell what school subject?
"George Elder's oldest grandmother rode a pig home yesterday."

_____

4. Write a sentence correctly using *mnemonic*. (Be sure to include context clues to show you understand the meaning of the word.)

_____

_____

5. Do you know a *mnemonic* for the names of the five Great Lakes? If not, create one. The lakes are Erie, Superior, Ontario, Huron, and Michigan.

_____

_____

_____

Paradigm[7]

par|a|digm (par′ə dim, -dīm), *n.* **1** a pattern; example: *Sir John is impeccable, a paradigm of the gentleman soldier* (Harper's). **2** *Grammar.* **a** an example, such as of a noun, verb, or pronoun, in all its inflections. **b** the set of inflectional forms for a word or class of words: *The final step in morphology is the establishment of paradigms, which can be viewed as sets of grammatical suffixes* (Harold B. Allen). [< Latin *paradigma* < Greek *parádeigma, -matos* pattern, ultimately < *para-* side by side + *deiknýnai* to show, point out]

1. In which of the following sentences is *paradigm* used correctly?

_____ a. Sam found a paradigm on the sidewalk.

_____ b. Captain James is the paradigm of the gentleman officer.

_____ c. Some people regard science as the paradigm of knowledge.

_____ d. The student's task was to write out the paradigm of an irregular verb.

2. Select the synonym(s) of *paradigm*.

_____ a. example   _____ d. model

_____ b. description   _____ e. pattern

_____ c. perfection   _____ f. reprint

3. If you create a *paradigm*,
   _____ a. others are likely to copy it.
   _____ b. you are certain to win the lottery.
   _____ c. you may be recognized as an expert in your field.
   _____ d. it may set out all the forms of a noun or verb.

4. Write a sentence correctly using *paradigm*. (Be sure to use context clues to show you understand the meaning of the word.)

   _____

   _____

5. Who, in your opinion, is an outstanding *paradigm* of a professional athlete?

   _____

   _____

Parsimony[6]

par|si|mo|ny (pär′sə mō′nē), *n.* **1** extreme economy; stinginess: *There is no need to dwell on the other limitations of his character, his jealousy, his parsimony* (Atlantic). **SYN**: niggardliness. **2** sparingness in the use or expenditure of means: (*Figurative.*) *This is the grand overriding law of the parsimony of nature: every action within a system is executed with the least possible expenditure of energy* (Scientific American). [< Latin *parsimōnia,* ultimately < *parcere* spare]

1. In which of the following sentences can *parsimony* correctly be placed in the blank?
   _____ a. He is rich and can afford to be generous but still practices _____.
   _____ b. A childhood spent in poverty might cause one to live a life of _____.
   _____ c. Mr. Smith's _____ led him to give much money to charity.
   _____ d. _____ in early life can result in a comfortable retirement.

2. Place an "s" in front of any synonym and an "a" in front of any antonym of *parsimony*.
   _____ a. miserliness   _____ d. frugality
   _____ b. stinginess   _____ e. liberalness
   _____ c. charity   _____ f. generosity

3. If you practice *parsimony*, you might
   _____ a. have lots of money in the bank.
   _____ b. do so because you are poor.
   _____ c. annoy your friends.
   _____ d. spend too much money.

4. Write a sentence correctly using *parsimony*. (Be sure to include context clues to show you understand the meaning of the word.)

_____

_____

5. In what area of your life would you be *least* likely to practice *parsimony*?

_____

_____

Semantic[13]

se|man|tic (sə man′tik), *adj*. **1** having to do with meanings of words and other linguistic forms and expressions: *There is a semantic difference between bear* (*animal*) *and bear* (*carry*), *though the two words are identical in sound and spelling.* **2** having to do with semantics. — **se|man′ti|cal|ly**, *adv*.

se|man|tics (sə man′tiks), *n*. **1** the scientific study of the meanings, and the development of meanings, of words. **2** the scientific study of symbols as denotative units, of their relationship to each other, and of their impact on society. **3** any explanation of meaning or use of interpretation: *We are getting so technical with your semantics it is impossible for us to understand* (William J. Fulbright). [< Late Latin *sēmanticus* < Greek *sēmantikós* significant < *sēmainein* signify, show < *sêma*, *-atos* sign]

1. Match the following statement with a similar statement below: "College students need a good *semantic* memory in order to do well in school."

   _____ a. Clear memories of events are necessary to getting good grades.

   _____ b. Remembering how to carry out procedures can help a student get an A.

   _____ c. Understanding concepts and the terms that identify them is of prime importance to a college student.

   _____ d. The greatest need of a good student is an extensive factual memory.

2. The etymology of *semantic* indicates that the word comes from the Greek *sema* (to show). Use that information, your imagination, and your background knowledge to match the following:

   _____ a. semaphore   aa. a person who studies semantics

   _____ b. sematic   bb. a system for flag signaling using arm positions

   _____ c. semanticist   cc. the science dealing with signs or sign language

   _____ d. seminology   dd. serving as a sign or warning of danger

3. In which of the following sentences can *semantic* correctly be placed in the blank?

   _____ a. If there are no pictures in the text there will be no _____ meanings.

   _____ b. The study of word meanings is the study of _____(s).

_____ c. A _____ memory is one that stores words and their meanings.

_____ d. The Navy trains sailors to send messages using _____ flags.

4. Write a sentence correctly using *semantic*. (Be sure to include context clues to show you understand the meaning of the word.)

_____

_____

5. *Semantic* meanings deal with words and the concepts attached to them (their meanings). Write down four words that list the concepts you have attached to the word "friend."

_____

_____

Specificity[15]

spec|if|ic|i|ty (spes′ə fis′ə tē), *n.* specific quality: **a** the quality of having specific character or relation: *There has always been a certain lack of specificity about these fears; people have been bothered . . . without being able to say precisely why* (New Yorker). **b** the quality of being specific in operation or effect: *It is also known that the protein coat determines the specificity of the virus, i.e., whether or not it will attack a certain bacterium* (Scientific American).

spe|cif|ic (spi sif′ik), *adj., n.* —*adj.* **1** definite; pre- cise; particular: *a specific command or request, a specific sum of money. There was no specific reason for the quarrel. When you describe something, be specific.* SYN: explicit. **2** specially belonging to a thing or group of things; characteristic (of); peculiar (to): *A scaly skin is a specific feature of snakes. Feathers are a feature specific to birds.* SYN: distinctive. **3a** preventing or curing a particular disease: *a specific remedy.* **b** produced by a special cause or infection: *a specific disease.* **4** of, having to do with, or characteristic of a species: *the specific name of a plant.*

1. Which of the following would be an example of encoding *specificity*?

_____ a. A student hears information in a classroom lecture and later recalls it on a test given in the same classroom.

_____ b. An athlete learns to play soccer and competes in a tennis tournament.

_____ c. A student studies material by playing an audiotape while driving, then takes a test while sitting in a classroom.

_____ d. Students view a presentation in an outdoor theater. Later they take a test on the presentation while sitting in the same theater.

2. Which of the lettered dictionary definitions of *specificity* best fits its use in the reading selection? _____

3. Check any appropriate response to the following statement: "The *specificity* of my description helped the police locate the thief."

_____ a. You really should be more observant.

_____ b. I admire someone who is a good citizen.

_____ c. You remind me of Sherlock Holmes.

_____ d. Your attention to special details brought results.

4. Write a sentence correctly using *specificity*. (Be sure to include context clues to show you understand the meaning of the word.)

_____

_____

_____

5. In a few words, describe your best friend with a degree of *specificity* that would enable me to identify him or her in a group of people.

_____

_____

_____

Theory[5]

the|o|ry (thē′ər ē, thir′ē), *n., pl.* **-ries. 1a** an explanation; explanation based on thought; explanation based on observation and reasoning, especially one that has been tested and confirmed as a general principle explaining a large number of related facts: *the theory of evolution. Einstein's theory of relativity explains the motion of moving objects. According to one scientific theory of life, the more complicated animals developed from the simpler ones.* **b** a hypothesis proposed as an explanation; conjecture: *Whether I am right in the theory or not . . . the fact is as I state it* (Edmund Burke). **2** the principles or methods of a science or art rather than its practice: *the theory of music, the theory of modern warfare.* **3a** an idea or opinion about something: *I think the fire was started by a careless smoker. What is your theory?* **b** thought or fancy as opposed to fact or practice: *He is right only as to theory, because the facts contradict him.* **4** *Mathematics.* a set of theorems which constitute a connected, systematic view of some branch of mathematics: *the theory of probabilities.* **5** *Obsolete.* mental view; contemplation.

in theory, according to theory; theoretically: *In theory the plan should have worked.*

[< Late Latin *theōria* < Greek *theōriā* a looking at, thing looked at < *theōreîn* to consider, look at < *theōrós* spectator < *théā* a sight + *horán* see]

— **Syn. 1a, b. Theory, hypothesis** as terms in science mean a generalization reached by inference from observed particulars and proposed as an explanation of their cause, relations, or the like. **Theory** implies a larger body of tested evidence and a greater degree of probability: *The red shift in the spectra of galaxies supports the theory that the universe is continuously expanding.* **Hypothesis** designates a merely tentative explanation of the data, advanced or adopted provisionally, often as the basis of a theory or as a guide to further observation or experiment: *Archeological discoveries strengthened the hypothesis that Troy existed.*

1. In which of the following sentences is *theory* used correctly?
   _____ a. Einstein was famous for his theory of relativity.
   _____ b. Mary used the theory of fudge making to cook that candy.
   _____ c. Freshman students at the music school must study music theory.
   _____ d. Harry had a theory about how the fire started.

2. Which of the following might correctly be called a *theory*?
   _____ a. the theory of gravity
   _____ b. the theory of probabilities
   _____ c. the theory of relativity
   _____ d. the theory of heights

3. Which of the numbered dictionary definitions of *theory* best fits the word's use in the reading selection? _____

4. Have you ever discussed *theories* of life and love with a friend? Who was the friend? Did you reach any conclusions?

_____

_____

_____

5. Write a sentence correctly using *theory*. (Be sure to include context clues to show you understand the meaning of the word.)

_____

_____

Validity[4]

va|lid|i|ty (və lid′ə tē), *n., pl.* **-ties. 1** truth or soundness: *the validity of an argument, the validity of an excuse.* **SYN:** authenticity. **2** legal soundness or force; being legally binding: *the validity of a contract.* **SYN:** legality. **3** effectiveness: *He had ... too high an opinion of the validity of regular troops* (Benjamin Franklin). **SYN:** efficacy.

from **valid:**

[< Latin *validus* strong < *valēre* be strong]

(Note: *Specifically, validity* refers to the extent to which the results of an evaluation procedure serve the particular uses for which they were intended. That is, if the purpose of a test is to measure computation skill, the valid test will do that with some degree of success.)

1. In which of the following sentences is *validity* used correctly?
   _____ a. I admire John's validity; he is an honest man.
   _____ b. I believe your argument; it has validity.
   _____ c. The court has given validity to common-law marriages.
   _____ d. Our test produces the desired effect, so we say it has validity.

2. Select the synonym(s) of *validity*.
   _____ a. ineffectiveness _____ d. effectiveness
   _____ b. authenticity   _____ e. illegality
   _____ c. legality   _____ f. efficacy

3. Which of the numbered dictionary definitions of *validity* best fits the word's use in the reading selection? _____

4. Write a sentence correctly using *validity*. (Be sure to include context clues to show you understand the meaning of the word.)

_____

_____

_____

5. Think of the last time you were late for an appointment. Did your excuse have *validity?*

_____

_____

ANSWERS TO CHAPTER 14 EXERCISES

Cognition: **1.** a, c, d **2.** b, c **3.** bb, cc, aa, ee, dd
Contiguity: **1.** a, b, d **2.** a, c, d, e, f **3.** d (antonym)
Eidetic: **1.** c, d **2.** c, d **3.** bb, dd, ee, cc, aa
Episode: **1.** a, c **2.** dd, ee, aa, bb, cc **3.** 1
Ethical: **1.** a, d **2.** a, d **3.** 3
Hypothesis: **1.** a, c, d **2.** b (synonym) **3.** a, b, c
Innate: **1.** a, b, d **2.** dd, cc, aa, bb, ee **3.** s, s, a, s, s, s
Mediate: **1.** a, c **2.** v.t. 3 **3.** cc, ee, bb, aa, dd
Mnemonic: **1.** a, b, c, d **2.** b, c **3.** geography
Paradigm: **1.** b, c, d **2.** a, d, e **3.** a, c, d
Parsimony: **1.** a, b, d **2.** s, s, a, s, a, a **3.** a, b, c
Semantic: **1.** c **2.** bb, dd, aa, cc **3.** b, c
Specificity: **1.** a, d **2.** b **3.** b, c, d
Theory: **1.** a, c, d **2.** a, b, c **3.** 1a
Validity: **1.** b, c, d **2.** b, c, d, f **3.** 1

If you missed any of the items in the exercises, return to the exercise and to the dictionary definition to see where you went wrong. Remember: If you get something right, you only affirm that you knew it. If you get something wrong and understand why, *you have learned something.*

PSYCHOLOGY POSTTEST

Fill in the blanks with the words from this list.

cognition	hypothesis	parsimony
contiguity	innate	semantic
eidetic	mediate	specificity
episode	mnemonic	theory
ethical	paradigm	validity

1. If we _____, we effect by intervening.

2. Things _____ refer to meanings of words.

3. A noun or verb set out in all its inflectional forms is a(n) _____.

4. The truth or soundness of something is its _____.

5. _____ refers to adjacency.

6. An assertion that must be tested to find out if it is true is a(n) _____.

7. *Niggardliness* is a synonym for _____.

8. Standards of right and wrong are _____ standards.

9. Einstein is responsible for the _____ of relativity.

10. Extremely clear mental pictures of past events are _____ images.

11. A memory aid is a(n) _____.

12. _____ refers to a definite and precise quality.

13. A musical passage, in contrast to a principle theme, is a(n) _____.

14. Something not learned but natural is _____.

15. _____ is the act of knowing.

Answers to this posttest are in the Instructor's Manual.

If you missed any of the words, you may need to return to the exercises and to the dictionary entries to see why your concepts for some words are incomplete.

C H A P T E R   F I F T E E N

SOCIAL SCIENCES: SOCIOLOGY

◆

OVERVIEW

Sociology is the study of social life and the social causes and consequences of human behavior. Sociology is concerned with the nature and structure of groups, institutions, and societies. Training in sociology provides a special perspective on human development and social life, which is an especially important part of a liberal education.

There is a wide variety of areas of study in sociology, including understanding the social functions and processes of the family, races, cultures, social classes, and age groups (child, adolescent, adult, older adult). Sociology considers issues of conformity as well as deviance and also looks at the place of work, sport, and leisure in our society.

Career opportunities for those who study sociology include social work, politics, public administration, urban and environmental planning, public relations, personnel, criminal justice, mental health counseling, and other service professions. Work in applied sociology can also prepare students for careers in applied social research and in evaluation research and program evaluation at various levels in government, industry, and education. A degree in sociology can also serve as preparation for advanced work in sociology, social welfare, environmental studies, education, evaluation research, public health, and urban planning.

The introductory textbooks in the field usually are expository, presenting theoretical concepts and historical perspectives. Many textbooks also include extended presentations of personal case histories. Other visual reinforcement is also present in the form

226

of the use of photographs and illustrations that are linked to the concepts and issues in the textbook.

Most of the vocabulary in sociology consists of general terms, such as subsistence, deviant, *and* status, *that can also have a specialized meaning within the context of sociology. There are also specialized vocabulary terms to identify social structures, such as* oligarchy *and* caste, *as well as combinations of terms to identify theories or hypotheses, such as* power elite, multiple nuclei, *and* concentric zone.

VOCABULARY SELF-EVALUATION

The following words will be introduced in this reading selection. Place a check mark (√) in front of any that you know thoroughly and use in your speech or writing. Place a question mark (?) in front of any that you recognize but do not use yourself.

_____ alienation	_____ hallmark	_____ precarious
_____ arable	_____ hierarchy	_____ propagation
_____ cohesive	_____ horde	_____ sanction
_____ deviant	_____ oligarchy	_____ status
_____ ethnicity	_____ peer	_____ subsistence

THE STUDY OF SOCIETIES AND GROUPS

Sociology is the scientific study of human society and the social interactions among people. It is interested in groups rather than individuals. It studies the various types of societies, the kinds of groups that people form, and the organization of the social structure. Sociologists work at two levels to understand human behavior. When they focus on interactions of individuals in groups they work at the microsociological level. When they focus on social structures such as societies, institutions, and communities, they work at the macrosociological level. Of these larger structures, the largest is a society.

TYPES OF SOCIETIES

Members of the earliest human societies survived by searching for plants and animals to eat. They belonged to hunting and food-gathering societies, and their subsistence[1] depended on whatever was at hand. Eventually, changes in climate produced conditions too precarious[2] for living by hunting and food-gathering. In order to survive, certain groups, called horticultural societies, stayed in one place and cultivated plants to ensure themselves of a food supply. Yet another type of society, the pastoral society, was mobile and usually small. It relied on herding and the propagation[3] of animals for food and clothing. Occasionally throughout history, pastoral societies became large, well organized, and aggressive. Such pastoral societies were called hordes.[4]

In contrast to the mobile, pastoral societies, agricultural societies settled permanently in fertile areas. The arable[5] soil attracted many settlers; in time, cities evolved. For the first time, societies were not organized on the basis of kinship, or family relationships, and life became more complicated.

Life became even more complicated when machines and chemical processes were developed and industrial societies formed. An industrial society requires not only mechanical means of production but a highly skilled and specialized labor force. Because many members of the labor force must be able to read and write, an educational system is the hallmark[6] of an industrial society. Today, we are moving beyond that society, and sociologists are looking at what is called postindustrial society. Its hallmarks are knowledge and information.

TYPES OF GROUPS

Social groups may be primary, with face-to-face associations, or secondary, with less intimacy among members. The position that a person occupies in a group (or in a society) is his or her status.[7] Common statuses have to do with religion, education, ethnicity,[8] and occupation. A person usually occupies more than one status at a time. Members of a group are expected to conform to accepted norms* of behavior; if they do not, sanctions[9] may be imposed. Primary groups usually are more tolerant of deviant[10] behavior than are secondary groups, who see such behavior as a threat and may expel the offending member.

Groups are also classified according to size. In a small group, such as a family group, a peer[11] group, or a work group, members will know one another. The smallest groups are dyads (two members) and triads (three members). The success of a small group in meeting its goals and satisfying its members depends on how cohesive[12] it is. For example, a cohesive military group will have higher morale and, subsequently, greater success.

Much of the activity in modern society is carried on in large groups called associations. Associations have a formal structure, which consists of rules and regulations, and an informal structure, through which activities are carried out by members who "bend the rules" and thus help one another. One such association is bureaucracy. Almost every society today has several bureaucracies to carry out its work. Both business and government employ the hierarchy[13] that characterizes bureaucracy. Bureaucracies are also characterized by written rules, employment based on qualifications, a division of labor, and impartiality. While bureaucracies offer a means of accomplishing many of the goals of a society, they also present problems. Because they tend to be so large, they often become oligarchies[14] and are controlled by those who hold positions of power. Individuals who are surrounded by organizations that base their procedures on impartiality and sets of rules may feel a deep sense of alienation[15] from their society.

The sociologist's investigation of societies, of groups, and of social interactions

---

* *Norms* are standards of behavior that are accepted by a group.

can help us understand how our society works. Such an understanding can create better lives for individuals and may lead to social change that would make the society, as a whole, more productive and content. ◆

SOCIOLOGY PRETEST

Select words from this list and write them in the blanks to complete the sentences.

alienation	hallmark	precarious
arable	hierarchy	propagation
cohesive	horde	sanction
deviant	oligarchy	status
ethnicity	peer	subsistence

1. Something fit for plowing is _____.
2. _____ has to do with cultural background.
3. The fact of keeping alive is _____.
4. A(n) _____ is an organization of things arranged in grades.
5. Something _____ is not safe.
6. An organization where few rule is a(n) _____.
7. A turning away in feeling is _____.
8. Something differing from the norm is _____.
9. A person of the same rank is a(n) _____.
10. A binding force is a(n) _____.
11. Something _____ tends to hold together.
12. A distinguishing characteristic is a(n) _____.
13. The process of breeding plants or animals is called _____.
14. A wandering tribe is a(n) _____.
15. Social or professional standing is _____.

Answers to this pretest are in Appendix B.

Unless your instructor tells you to do otherwise, complete the exercises for each word you missed on the pretest. The words, with their exercises, are in alphabetical order. The superscript numbers indicate where the words appeared in the reading selection so that you can refer to them when necessary. There are several types of exercises, but for each word you will be asked to write a sentence using context clues. (See Chapter 4 if you need information about how to create context clues.) You are also asked to perform some activity that will help you make your concept of the word personal. *Complete this activity thoughtfully, for creating a personalized concept of the word will help you remember it in the future.*

Answers to all the exercises are at the end of the exercise segment.

SOCIOLOGY EXERCISES

Alienation[15]

alien|a|tion (āl′yǝ nā′shǝn ā′lē ǝ-), *n.* **1** a turning away in feeling or affection: **a** the act of alienating; making unfriendly. **SYN:** estrangement. **b** the state of being alienated; not feeling interested in or involved with one's family, associates, or society: *The condition that sociologists call "alienation," the mass society in which the old securities vanish and the individual feels adrift in an alien world, are secular facts about which party programs do nothing* (Harper's). **2** the transfer of the ownership of property to another. **3** mental disease; insanity.

1. Which of the following might experience *alienation?*

   ——— a. an employee ——— d. a married person

   ——— b. a child ——— e. a mental patient

   ——— c. an attorney ——— f. a doctor

2. In which of the following sentences can *alienation* correctly be placed in the blank?

   ——— a. Mark meets tomorrow with his attorney for the ——————— of the apartment building.

   ——— b. Sometimes one parent will bring about the ——————— of a child's affection for the other parent.

   ——— c. Karl Marx believed that ——————— was a common occurrence in a capitalist society.

   ——— d. Experiencing ——————— is a good way to feel at home in a society.

3. Which of the numbered and lettered dictionary definitions of *alienation* best fits its use in the reading selection? ———————

4. Write a sentence correctly using *alienation.* (Be sure to include context clues to show you understand the meaning of the word.)

   ————————————————————————————

   ————————————————————————————

5. Under what conditions might you experience a feeling of *alienation?* What could you do about it?

   ————————————————————————————

   ————————————————————————————

Arable[5]

ar|a|ble (ar'ə bəl), *adj., n.* —*adj.* fit for plowing; suitable for producing crops which require plowing and tillage: *There is not much arable land on the side of a rocky mountain.*
—*n.* arable land, now especially such land actually in use.
[< Latin *arābilis* < *arāre* to plow]

1. Which of the following might be *arable?*
   _____ a. a hillside   _____ d. a plateau
   _____ b. an ocean   _____ e. a sandy desert
   _____ c. a forest   _____ f. pastureland

2. If a farmer has *arable* land,
   _____ a. he should own a plow.
   _____ b. he may have good crops.
   _____ c. he may go broke.
   _____ d. he is unlucky.

3. In which of the following sentences is *arable* used correctly?
   _____ a. The United States has much arable soil.
   _____ b. Arable soil can produce good crops.
   _____ c. Ocean farming depends on arable conditions.
   _____ d. Arable comes from a Latin verb meaning "to plow."

4. Write a sentence correctly using *arable*. (Be sure to include context clues to show you understand the meaning of the word.)

   _____

   _____

5. What would you do if you were given five acres of *arable* soil?

   _____

   _____

Cohesive[12]

co|he|sive (kō hē'siv), *adj.* 1 sticking together; tending to hold together: *Magnetized iron filings form a cohesive mass.* (Figurative.) *The members of a family are a cohesive unit in our society.* (Figurative.) *What is important in determining the work output of an industrial group is whether the group is tight-knit and cohesive enough to be properly called a group* (Science News Letter). 2 causing cohesion: *When a substance is heated, the heat energy causes its molecules to move faster. Eventually, the molecules will move so rapidly that their cohesive forces cannot hold them together* (Louis Marick). —**co|he'sive|ly,** *adv.* —**co|he'sive|ness,** *n.*

1. Check any appropriate response to the following statement:
   "Our college choir is a *cohesive* group."
   _____ a. If you only got along better, singing would be more fun.
   _____ b. I understand you work together well.
   _____ c. That means you sing a wide variety of songs.
   _____ d. Your morale must be high.

SOCIAL SCIENCES: SOCIOLOGY

2. Which of the following might be *cohesive?*
   _____ a. ice cubes   _____ d. a fraternity
   _____ b. a family   _____ e. boiling water
   _____ c. a workforce   _____ f. cold water

3. In which of the following sentences is *cohesive* used correctly?
   _____ a. King Arthur's Knights of the Round Table formed a cohesive group.
   _____ b. In cohesive writing, sentences work together to support the author's thesis.
   _____ c. Peanut butter is cohesive.
   _____ d. Jane's new dress was created by a cohesive designer.

4. Write a sentence correctly using *cohesive.* (Be sure to include context clues to show you understand the meaning of the word.)

   _____

   _____

5. You probably belong to several groups. Which one of them is the most *cohesive?* Speculate as to why.

   _____

   _____

Deviant[10]

de|vi|ant (dē'vē ənt), n., adj. —n. 1 = deviate. 2 anything that deviates from the norm: [He] sees no reason why chemists cannot produce deviants from other medically important alkaloids such as quinine (New Scientist). —adj. that deviates; deviating: ... the persecution of deviant shades of opinion (Time).
de|vi|ate (v. dē'vē āt; n., adj. also dē'vē it), v., -at|ed, -at|ing, n., adj. —v.i. to turn aside (from a way, course, rule, truth, standard, or the like): The principal deviated from her custom and did not attend the school's annual pet show. His statements sometimes deviated slightly from the truth. SYN: See syn. under **diverge.** —v.t. to cause to turn aside; deflect: Light rays entering the earth's atmosphere from the sun or the stars are continuously deviated so as to follow a curved path (Sears and Zemansky). —n. 1 an individual who shows a marked deviation from the norm: He wasn't a recluse or a deviate, but for some reason there was no family, no responsibility (Atlantic). 2 Statistics. the value of a variable measured from some standard point, usually the mean. —adj. 1 characterized by a marked deviation from the standard or norm. 2 that deviates; deviant.
[< Late Latin dēviāre (with English -ate¹) < dēvius devious < dē- aside + via way]

1. *Deviant* behavior might be
   _____ a. acceptable to society.   _____ c. intellectual.
   _____ b. sexual.   _____ d. a social maladjustment.

2. Complete the verbal analogy.
   water : wet :: *deviant* : _____
   a. person   c. different
   b. social   d. actions

3. Check any appropriate response to the following statement:
   "Do you think Joe's behavior is really *deviant?*"
   _____ a. Yes. He does not conform to society's norms.
   _____ b. Yes. We all approve of the way he acts.

———— c. No. He's a bit strange, that's all.

———— d. No. He's just responding to society's demands.

4. Write a sentence correctly using *deviant*. (Be sure to include context clues to show you understand the meaning of the word.)

_____

_____

5. Name someone who displays *deviant* behavior. (Some public figures do, so it does not have to be someone you know personally.)

_____

Ethnicity[8]

eth|nic|i|ty (eth nis′ə tē), *n.* ethnic status, quality, or character: *There are vast differences among American families, differences related to ... ethnicity and social class, to region and religion* (American Scholar).

eth|nic (eth′nik), *adj., n.* —*adj.* **1** having to do with the various racial and cultural groups of people and the characteristics, language, and customs of each; of, having to do with, or peculiar to a people: *The diverse ethnic and economic interests that make up the political machines frequently clash* (Harper's). **2** of or having to do with people of foreign birth or descent: *There are many ethnic groups in our large cities.* **3** having to do with nations not Christian or Jewish; heathen; pagan: *These are ancient ethnic revels, Of a faith long since forsaken* (Longfellow). **4** of or for ethnics: *Ethnic [Christmas]cards with black, brown or yellow Santas testify to the fact that American melting pot is still bubbling, despite gloomy assertions to the contrary* (Time). —*n.* a member of a racial, cultural, or national minority; a member of an ethnic group: *All sports are now saturated with ethnics* (Harper's). *"If the ethnic pulled himself up with the help of the rope,"* wrote Dahl, *"he could often gain a toehold in the system"* (Time). [< Latin *ethnicus* < Greek *ethnikós* < *éthnos* nation] —**eth′ni|cal|ly**, *adv.*

1. Which of the following would be an example of *ethnicity*?

———— a. Norwegians in the United States celebrating the 17th of May.

———— b. Americans in the United States celebrating the 4th of July.

———— c. Mexicans in the United States celebrating Cinco de Mayo.

———— d. Germans in the United States celebrating Octoberfest.

2. *Ethnicity* has to do with

———— a. race. ———— d. language.

———— b. religion. ———— e. customs.

———— c. culture. ———— f. personality.

3. A person might show his or her *ethnicity* by

———— a. his or her scores on an intelligence test.

———— b. the type of clothing worn.

———— c. the food he or she cooks and eats.

———— d. the holidays celebrated.

4. Write a sentence correctly using *ethnicity*. (Be sure to include context clues to show you understand the meaning of the word.)

_____

_____

5. What are some of the ways you might display your *ethnicity*? (Whether or not you or your family have been in the United States for a long

time, you still have at least one ethnic background, perhaps a number of them.)

_____

_____

Hallmark[6]

hall|mark (hôl′märk′), *n., v.* —*n.* **1** an official mark indicating standard of purity, put on gold or silver articles. **2** such a mark on any manufactured article. **3** *Figurative.* any mark or sign of genuineness or good quality: *Courtesy and self-control are hallmarks of a gentleman.* **4** any distinctive mark or characteristic: *The bowler was their hallmark and they used it as their main prop* (New York Times). *When measles virus attacks tissues such as the lungs, it leaves "hallmarks"* (Science News Letter). —*v.t.* to put a hallmark on. [< Goldsmiths' *Hall* in London, the seat of the Goldsmiths' Company, by whom the stamping was legally regulated + *mark*[1]]

1. In which of the following sentences can *hallmark* correctly be placed in the blank?
   _____ a. Perry's essay has all the _____s of good writing.
   _____ b. The antique dealer inspected the _____ on the back of the silver spoon.
   _____ c. We knew where to go because the building _____ said "Union Members Only."
   _____ d. The _____s of an angel are a halo and wings.

2. Complete the verbal analogy.
   tears : sadness :: *hallmark* : _____
   a. sign   c. happiness
   b. official   d. purity

3. Which of the numbered dictionary definitions of *hallmark* best fits its use in the reading selection? _____

4. Write a sentence correctly using *hallmark*. (Be sure to include context clues to show you understand the meaning of the word.)

_____

_____

5. What do you believe to be the *hallmarks* of a good education? Manner of speaking and vocabulary? Style of dress? Variety of interests? Others?

_____

_____

Hierarchy[13]

hi|er|ar|chy (hī′ə rär′kē), *n., pl.* **-chies.** **1** an organization of persons or things arranged into higher and lower ranks, classes, or grades: *O latest born ... Of all Olympus' faded hierarchy* (Keats). **2** government by priests or church officials. **3** a group of church officials of different ranks. The church hierarchy is composed of archbishops, bishops, priests, and deacons. **4** *Theology.* **a** one of the divisions of the angels, each made up of three orders, and each ranked according to its duties and nearness to God. **b** the angels. [< Medieval Latin *hierarchia* < Greek *hierarchiā* < *hierarchíein* be high priest < *hierárchēs;* see etym. under **hierarch**]

from **hierarch:**
[< Medieval Latin *hierarcha* < Greek *hierárchēs* leader of sacred rites < *hierós* sacred + *árchein* to lead]

1. In which of the following is there an established *hierarchy?*
   - _____ a. a family   _____ d. a large business
   - _____ b. the army   _____ e. a group of friends
   - _____ c. the government   _____ f. a university

2. In which of the following sentences can *hierarchy* correctly be placed in the blank?
   - _____ a. In the Roman Catholic _____ the Pope ranks highest.
   - _____ b. If you divide the candy bar into four equal parts, each child can have one _____ .
   - _____ c. There is a _____ in our sorority, and the pledges have the lowest rank.
   - _____ d. Most schools are arranged in a _____ .

3. Which of the numbered and lettered dictionary definitions of *hierarchy* best fits its use in the reading selection? _____

4. Write a sentence correctly using *hierarchy.* (Be sure to include context clues to show you understand the meaning of the word.)

   _____

   _____

5. Are you part of any *hierarchy?* Is it social, political, educational, or occupational? What rank do you hold?

   _____

   _____

Horde[4]

horde (hôrd, hōrd), *n., v.,* **hord|ed, hord|ing.** —*n.*
1 a crowd; swarm; multitude: *hordes of grasshoppers. Society is now one polished horde, Formed of two mighty tribes, the Bores and Bored* (Byron). **SYN:** troop, gang, crew. **2** a wandering tribe or troop: *Hordes of Mongols and Turks invaded Europe in the Middle Ages.*
—*v.i.* to gather in a horde; live in a horde: *My fathers' house shall never be a cave For wolves to horde and howl in* (Byron).
[probably < French *horde* < German *Horde,* earlier *Horda,* perhaps < Polish *horda* < Turkic (compare Tatar *urda* horde). Compare etym. under **Urdu.**]

1. Which of the following might come in a *horde?*
   - _____ a. apples   _____ d. tourists
   - _____ b. gypsies   _____ e. laborers
   - _____ c. locusts   _____ f. elephants

2. Place an "s" by any synonym of *horde.*
   - _____ a. swarm   _____ d. trio
   - _____ b. bore   _____ e. multitude
   - _____ c. gang   _____ f. troupe

3. Which of the numbered dictionary definitions of *horde* best fits its use in the reading selection? _____

4. Write a sentence correctly using *horde*. (Be sure to include context clues to show you understand the meaning of the word.)

_____

_____

5. Have you ever been in a *horde* of people? Where were you? (Perhaps gift shopping the day before Christmas.)

_____

_____

_____

Oligarchy[14]

ol|i|gar|chy (ol′ə gär′kē), *n., pl.* **-chies. 1** a form of government in which a few people have the ruling power: *The Pilgrims at Plymouth Colony were governed by a Puritan oligarchy.* **2** a country or state having such a government: *Most ancient Greek city-states were classic examples of oligarchies* (William Ebenstein). **3** the ruling few. **4** any organization, such as a business or a church, having an administration controlled by a few people. [< Greek *oligarchíā*, ultimately < *olígos* few + *árchein* to rule < *archós* leader]

1. In which of the following sentences can *oligarchy* correctly be placed in the blank?
   - _____ a. If a king is absolute ruler, he has an _____.
   - _____ b. An _____ might be an efficient government.
   - _____ c. In a democracy, the people are supposed to rule; but if the country is large, the democracy may become an _____.
   - _____ d. A business or club might be an _____.

2. Complete the verbal analogy.
   tribe : many :: *oligarchy* : _____
   a. rule   c. others
   b. few   d. government

3. Which of the numbered dictionary definitions of *oligarchy* best fits its use in the reading selection? _____

4. Write a sentence correctly using *oligarchy*. (Be sure to include context clues to show you understand the meaning of the word.)

_____

_____

5. You surely are involved in at least one group that is an *oligarchy*. What is it? If there are several, name them. Do you hope to be part of the ruling few some day?

_____

_____

_____

Peer[11]

peer[1] (pir), *n., v. —n.* **1a** a person of the same rank, ability, or qualities as another; equal: *a jury of one's peers. He is so fine a man that it would be hard to find his peer. And drunk delight of battle with my peers* (Tennyson). **b** anything equal to something else in quality: *a book without a peer.* **2** a man who has a title; man who is high and great by birth or rank. A duke, marquis, earl, count, viscount, or baron is a peer.
—v.t. **1** to rank with; equal. **2** *Informal.* to raise to the peerage; ennoble.
[< Old French *per* < Latin *pār, paris* equal. See etym. of doublet **par**.]

1. If you are someone's *peer*, you
   _____ a. are his or her equal.
   _____ b. are of the same rank.
   _____ c. are like him or her in many ways.
   _____ d. may serve on a jury to judge him or her.

2. In which of the following sentences is *peer(s)* used correctly?
   _____ a. Mary prefers to associate only with her peers.
   _____ b. George Washington was a man without peer.
   _____ c. I wish I had been born a peer of the British Empire.
   _____ d. I wanted to buy a Mercedes, but instead I bought a peer car, for less money.

3. Which of the numbered and lettered dictionary definitions of *peer* best fits its use in the reading selection? _____

4. Write a sentence correctly using *peer*. (Be sure to include context clues to show you understand the meaning of the word.)

_____

_____

5. When you are in a *peer* group, what are those people like?

_____

_____

_____

Precarious[2]

pre|car|i|ous (prɪ kar′ē əs), *adj.* **1** not safe or secure; uncertain; dangerous; risky: *Soldiers on the battlefield lead a precarious life. His poor hold on the branch was precarious. His power was more precarious than ... he was willing to admit* (Scott). **SYN:** perilous, hazardous. **2** dependent on chance or circumstance. **3** poorly founded; doubtful; assumed: *a precarious opinion or conclusion.* [< Latin *precārius* (with English *-ous*) obtainable by entreaty; dependent on another's will, uncertain < *prex, precis* prayer] — **pre|car′i|ous|ly,** *adv.* — **pre|car′i|ous|ness,** *n.*

1. Place an "s" by any synonym and an "a" by any antonym of *precarious.*

   _____ a. safe   _____ e. doubtful

   _____ b. risky   _____ f. uncertain

   _____ c. perilous   _____ g. hazardous

   _____ d. certain   _____ h. dangerous

2. If you have a *precarious* occupation,

   _____ a. you may wear a hard hat.

   _____ b. you may have trouble getting insurance.

   _____ c. your work is easy and worry-free.

   _____ d. your wages may be high as compensation.

3. Which of the numbered dictionary definitions of *precarious* best fits its use in the reading selection? _____

4. Write a sentence correctly using *precarious.* (Be sure to include context clues to show you understand the meaning of the word.)

   _____

   _____

5. What was the most *precarious* situation you have ever been in? (Did you get out of it alive, or was that the last anyone ever saw of you?)

   _____

   _____

Propagation[3]

prop|a|ga|tion (prop′ə gā′shən), *n.* **1** the act or process of breeding plants or animals: *The propagation of poppies is by seed and of roses by cuttings.* **2** the act or process of making more widely known; getting more widely believed; spreading: *the propagation of the principles of science.* **3** the act or fact of passing on; sending further; spreading or extending: *the propagation of the shock of an earthquake, the propagation of a family trait from father to son.* **4** the travel of electromagnetic or sound waves through a medium such as air or water.

prop|a|gate (prop′ə gāt), *v.,* **-gat|ed, -gat|ing.** — *v.i.* to produce offspring; reproduce: *Pigeons propagate at a fast rate.* — *v.t.* **1** to increase in number or intensity: *Trees propagate themselves by seeds.* **SYN:** multiply. **2** to cause to increase in number by the production of young: *Cows and sheep are propagated on farms.* **3** to spread (news or knowledge): *Don't propagate unkind reports.* **SYN:** extend, diffuse. **4** to pass on; send further: *Sound is propagated by vibrations.* [< Latin *prōpāgāre* (with English *-ate*[1]) to multiply plants by slips or layers < *prō-* forth + *pag-*, root of *pangere* make fast, pin down]

1. In which of the following sentences can *propagation* correctly be placed in the blank?

_____ a. I have ordered a _____ set of coins from the
U.S. Mint.

_____ b. His primary goal as a minister was _____ of the
gospel.

_____ c. Johnny Appleseed was responsible for _____ of
several varieties of apple.

_____ d. _____ of sound is almost five times faster in
water than in air.

2. Complete the verbal analogy.
proper : correct :: *propagation* : _____
a. spreading   c. excelling
b. plants   d. rate

3. Which of the numbered dictionary definitions of *propagation* best fits its
use in the reading selection? _____

4. Write a sentence correctly using *propagation*. (Be sure to include context
clues to show you understand the meaning of the word.)

_____

_____

5. How are you involved in the *propagation* of information? Do you write
letters? Use the telephone? Speak in person?

_____

_____

Sanction[9]

sanc|tion (sangk'shen), *n., v. — n.* **1a** permission with authority; support; approval: *We have the sanction of the recreation department to play ball in this park. Plans are also being prepared for the building of nine others, for which all necessary sanctions from various interested authorities have been obtained* (London Times). **SYN:** approbation. **b** *Figurative.* encouragement given to an opinion or practice, as by an influential person or by custom or public opinion: *Religion gave her sanction to that intense and unquenchable animosity* (Macaulay). **2** the act of making legally authoritative or binding; solemn ratification or confirmation: *The day on which the royal sanction was ... solemnly given to this great Act* (Macaulay). **3a** a provision of a law stating a penalty for disobedience to it or a reward for obedi-ence. **b** the penalty or reward. **4** an action by several nations toward another nation, such as a blockade, restrictions on trade, or withholding loans, intended to force it to obey international law: *to apply economic sanctions, rather than to threaten with military ones.* **5** a consideration that leads one to obey a rule of conduct. **6** binding force: *This word [honor] is often made the sanction of an oath* (Jonathan Swift).
— *v.t.* **1** to approve; allow: *Her conscience does not sanction stealing. The use of a site in Hyde Park, selected by the Prince, was sanctioned by the Government* (Lytton Strachey). **SYN:** authorize. See syn. under **approve.** **2** to make valid or binding; confirm.
[< Latin *sānctiō, -ōnis* < *sānctus* holy; see etym. under **saint**] — **sanc'tion|er,** *n.*

1. Check any appropriate response to the following statement:
"Should Congress *sanction* the treaty with Mexico?"
_____ a. Yes. They should cancel it.
_____ b. Yes. They should approve it.
_____ c. No. If they approve it, there may be trouble.
_____ d. No. I favor a treaty with Mexico.

2. A *sanction* may be

_____ a. support.	_____ d. permission.
_____ b. approbation.	_____ e. confirmation.
_____ c. a penalty.	_____ f. a reward.

3. Which of the numbered and lettered dictionary definitions of *sanction* best fits its use in the reading selection? _____

4. Write a sentence correctly using *sanction*. (Be sure to include context clues to show you understand the meaning of the word.)

_____

_____

5. For what activity would you like to receive *sanction* from some authority?

_____

_____

Status[7]

sta|tus (stā′təs, stat′əs), *n.* **1a** social or professional standing; position; rank: *the status of a doctor. What is her status in the government? Making way for no one under the status of a priest* (Rudyard Kipling). *Mr. Polly's status was that of a guest pure and simple* (H. G. Wells). SYN: footing, station. **b** standing, position, or rank considered to be desirable: *to seek status, to lose status.* **2** condition; state: *Diplomats are interested in the status of world affairs. The status of the world in 1970 was discouraging to lovers of peace.* **3** legal position of a person as determined by his membership in some class of persons with certain rights or limitations: *the status of the foreign-born in America.* SYN: classification. [< Latin *status, -ūs* < *stāre* to stand. See etym. of doublets **estate, state.**]

1. In which of the following sentences is *status* used correctly?

_____ a. Bill's status as bachelor makes him a popular dinner guest.

_____ b. Tim's status as new father has made him very happy.

_____ c. Mr. Olson has finally achieved the status of full professor at the college.

_____ d. What is the status of the peace talks between the superpowers?

2. If you record (write down) your *status*, you might

_____ a. state your age (whether or not you are a minor).

_____ b. tell whether you are married or unmarried.

_____ c. list your religion.

_____ d. give your position at your place of employment.

3. The etymology of *status* shows that the word comes from the Latin verb *stare* (to stand). Use this information, your imagination, and your background knowledge to match the following:

_____ a. station   aa. an image of a person or animal produced by modeling, sculpting, or casting

_____ b. stator   bb. the height of a person or thing

_____ c. statue   cc. a stationary portion enclosing rotating parts in a machine

_____ d. stature   dd. a regular stopping place in a transportation route

4. Write a sentence correctly using *status*. (Be sure to include context clues to show you understand the meaning of the word.)

_____

_____

5. What *status* do you hold in society? (There will be more than one, so write down several of them.)

_____

_____

_____

Subsistence[1]

sub|sist|ence (səb sis′təns), *n.* **1** the condition or fact of keeping alive; living: *Selling papers was the poor old man's only means of subsistence.* **2** a means of keeping alive; livelihood: *The sea provides a subsistence for fishermen.* **3** continued existence; continuance. **4** *Philosophy.* **a** the individualizing of substance, especially as a particular rational (human) being standing apart from all others but possessing certain rights, powers, and functions in common with all others of the same type. **b** the condition of subsisting. **5** *Obsolete.* the condition or quality of inhering or residing (in something). [< Late Latin *subsistentia* < Latin *subsistēns, -entis,* present participle of *subsistere;* see etym. under **subsist**]

sub|sist (səb sist′), *v.i.* **1** to keep alive; live: *People in the far north subsist chiefly on fish and meat.* **2** to continue to be; exist: *Many superstitions still subsist. A club cannot subsist without members.* **3** *Philosophy.* **a** to stand as fact or truth; hold true. **b** to be logically necessary, probable, or conceivable. **4** *Obsolete.* to continue in a condition or position; remain as such. — *v.t.* to provide for; feed; support. [< Latin *subsistere* stand firm; support < *sub-* up to + *sistere* to stand < *stāre* to stand]

1. If the money you earn provides a *subsistence,*
   _____ a. you are comfortable and saving for retirement.
   _____ b. you need to get a better, or a second, job.
   _____ c. money is tight.
   _____ d. you might need to borrow money.

2. Complete the verbal analogy.
   wealth : luxuries :: *subsistence* : _____
   a. subsidies   c. money
   b. living   d. necessities

3. Which of the numbered and lettered dictionary definitions of *subsistence* best fits its use in the reading selection? _____

4. Write a sentence correctly using *subsistence*. (Be sure to include context clues to show you understand the meaning of the word.)

_____

_____

5. If you found yourself living at *subsistence* level, what would you do to change the situation?

_____

_____

ANSWERS TO CHAPTER 15 EXERCISES

Alienation: 1. a, b, c, d, e, f 2. a, b, c 3. 1b
Arable: 1. a, d, f 2. a, b, c 3. a, b, d
Cohesive: 1. b, d 2. a, b, c, d, f 3. a, b, c
Deviant: 1. b, c, d 2. c (characteristic) 3. a, c
Ethnicity: 1. a, c, d 2. a, c, d, e 3. b, c, d
Hallmark: 1. a, b, d 2. d (symbol/quality) 3. 4
Hierarchy: 1. b, c, d, f 2. a, c, d 3. 1
Horde: 1. b, c, d, e 2. a, c, e, f 3. 2
Oligarchy: 1. b, c, d 2. b (quantity) 3. 4
Peer: 1. a, b, c, d 2. a, b, c 3. *n.* 1a
Precarious: 1. a, s, s, a, s, s, s, s 2. a, b, d 3. 1
Propagation: 1. b, c, d 2. a (synonym) 3. 1
Sanction: 1. b, c 2. a, b, c, d, e, f 3. *n.* 3b
Status: 1. a, b, c, d 2. a, b, d 3. dd, cc, aa, bb
Subsistence: 1. b, c, d 2. d (cause-effect) 3. 3

If you missed any of the items in the exercises, return to the exercise and to the dictionary definition to see where you went wrong. Remember: If you get something right, you only affirm that you knew it. If you get something wrong and understand why, *you have learned something.*

SOCIOLOGY POSTTEST

Fill in the blanks with the words from this list.

alienation	hallmark	precarious
arable	hierarchy	propagation
cohesive	horde	sanction
deviant	oligarchy	status
ethnicity	peer	subsistence

1. The act of making legally binding is a(n) _____.

2. _____ means "estrangement."

3. Cultural practices may reveal _____.

4. The angels form a(n) _____.

5. _____ means "livelihood."

6. Something turned aside is _____.

7. A(n) _____ indicates an official standard of purity.

8. _____ means "sticking together."

9. A(n) _____ is an equal.

10. _____ is the act of sending further.

11. A(n) _____ is a multitude.

12. _____ has to do with plowing.

13. If few rule, a(n) _____ exists.

14. _____ means "doubtful."

15. *Rank* is a synonym for _____ .

Answers to this posttest are in the Instructor's Manual.

If you missed any of the words, you may need to return to the exercises and to the dictionary entries to see why your concepts for some words are incomplete.

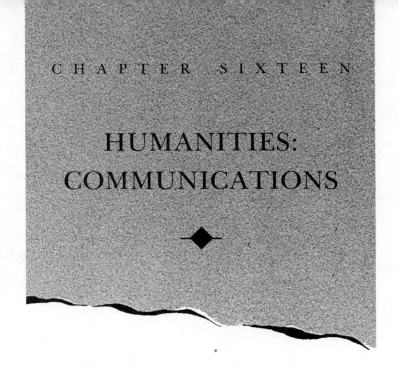

C H A P T E R   S I X T E E N

HUMANITIES: COMMUNICATIONS

◆

OVERVIEW

Communication studies are concerned with the nature of human communication, the symbol systems by which it functions, the context or environment in which it occurs, its media, its ethics, and its effects. The field offers training in skills generally believed to be necessary for success in public or private life.

Communications curriculum can include coursework in mass communication, interpersonal communication, intercultural communication, organizational communication, and oral communication. Some programs include opportunities for participation in intercollegiate forensics as well as practical experience with on-campus production labs for film, audio, graphics, journalism (school newspaper), and television.

Career opportunities for those with communications backgrounds include advertising, journalism, news, photocommunications, public relations, radio, television, and film. Because of the importance of effective communications in all aspects of our society, other career opportunities include work in management, personnel training, sales, education, and law.

Introductory communications textbooks are usually expository and descriptive in that they explain broad principles, concepts, or generalizations as well as statements of ideas, problems, or situations. There may be charts, diagrams, and photographs to visually represent concepts or exercises, games, case problems, and speeches as practical applications of concepts and theories presented in the text. Some textbooks are instructional and present step-by-step information related to the production aspects of the various specializations or fields within communication.

The majority of vocabulary for this field consists of general terms, such as stimuli *and* persuasion, *that also have specialized meanings in the context of communications. There are also technical terms related to the production aspects of media, including* masthead *and* by-line, *or to oral communication, including* oculesics *and* hypernasality. *Those programs offering forensics within the communication program (if they do not have a separate speech communications department) would use specific terminology related to argument analysis with* generalizations *and* fallacies *of various types.*

VOCABULARY SELF-EVALUATION

The following words will be introduced in this reading selection. Place a check mark (√) in front of any that you know thoroughly and use in your speech or writing. Place a question mark (?) in front of any that you recognize but do not use yourself.

_____ admonitory   _____ diversified   _____ pragmatic

_____ augment   _____ diversion   _____ prodigality

_____ covert   _____ libel   _____ slander

_____ defamation   _____ ostensibly   _____ vast

_____ demographic   _____ overt   _____ vicarious

THE BUSINESS OF MASS COMMUNICATION

The old saying that "love makes the world go round" is romantic but inaccurate. Actually, communication makes the world go round, for if it were not for the giving and receiving of messages, the world would likely be in confusion. These messages can be carried out on the interpersonal level (you and a friend, for example) or on the machine-assisted interpersonal level (you and your friend using the telephone or you and the automatic bank teller) or by means of mass communications (you playing a tape or listening to the radio, going to a movie, reading a magazine, and so forth). Most of us have enough experience with the first two types of communication to understand the processes involved, but the field of mass communication is complex and requires some explanation.

The business of mass communication is vast[1] and in some ways diversified.[2] It includes the forms of communication called "sight media" (newspapers and magazines), those called "sound media" (radio and sound recording), and those called "sight and sound media" (films and television). But in many ways these different media are alike. Each employs one or more machines in order to transmit public messages to a large, scattered, heterogeneous audience. Each is in fact a business, which is controlled by a complex, formal organization in which control of expenditures, management of employees, and coordination of activities are all overseen by various levels of authority. Each business is, in fact, a bureaucracy.

Another way the media businesses are alike is that each is guarded by many gatekeepers* who have control over what material eventually reaches the public. Anyone who wants to have his material published or produced will find that there is overt[3] rejection all along the line: from clerks who return unsolicited material, from editors who declare it unfit, and from receptionists who refuse to admit the author to the inner office, to name but a few of the gatekeepers!

Two other ways the different media businesses are alike have to do with money. All media businesses require a great deal of money to operate, and they exist to make a profit. Millions of dollars may be needed to publish a weekly news magazine, and, although business managers are sometimes accused of prodigality,[4] it is generally agreed that spending large amounts is necessary. Radio and television stations require many thousands of dollars to operate, while producing a film may cost many millions. The pragmatic[5] manager prepares for this expense by recruiting backers to supply funds, and in many cases the manager must augment[6] those funds by selling advertising. (The cost of the advertising, of course, is passed on to the consumer of the product being advertised.) Unless the business has enough money to cover all its costs and can generate enough to have a profit, it will not last long. To produce that money, publications and productions must appeal to readers and viewers so that direct sales (purchase of materials and tickets for attendance) and advertising revenues keep coming in. Demographic[7] data can provide information about intended audiences and are often consulted, for competition is keen in the business of mass communications.

THE FUNCTIONS OF MASS COMMUNICATORS

The different mass communicators function alike in several ways. First, they provide information. Correspondents working for newspapers, news magazines, and radio and television stations gather and turn in information from around the globe. Their employers then report the information to their audiences. Mass communicators also serve an admonitory[8] function. Warnings may vary from facts about weather fronts approaching an area, to programs on contagious diseases, to page spreads on the dangers of smoking.

A second function is that of interpretation of information. Frequently, this is straightforward and is labeled "opinion." But covert[9] views of the management may appear in the news reports, and even an ostensibly[10] factual report may be full of interpretation and opinion. For example, a public figure supported by the communication medium (singular of *media*) may be given favored treatment: Only appro-

---

* A *gatekeeper* is any person or group who has control over what material will reach the public.

priate statements will be made public; only appealing pictures will be shown. On the other hand, for a candidate the medium does not support, management may report segments of statements so that a negative impression is given, or unflattering photos or film shots will be shown. However, care will always be taken that no defamation[11] of character takes place. Printing or speaking material that is openly false and unjust is illegal. Our laws protect all of us, including public figures, against libel[12] and slander.[13]

A third function served by mass communicators is the transmission of social values. For instance, photos, films, and stories of happy, helpful mothers serve to remind us of the value of motherhood in our society. Currently, whether it should be so or not, we are reminded of the importance of being thin. This function is usually carried out intentionally, but sometimes the work produced by reporters, writers, photographers, and filmmakers is influenced by acculturation.*

A final function provided by mass communicators is that of entertainment. For many of us, newspapers, magazines, radio, television, and films provide the only diversions[14] we have in our lives. We do not play games or musical instruments or enjoy lengthy conversations. We do not participate in life but observe it through the actions of others, and we thus obtain vicarious[15] pleasure through the media.

And so we see that mass communicators give us information, tell us what to think of it, tell us what social values to embrace and what practices to avoid, and provide us with amusement for our spare time. Communications surround us and do, indeed, make our world go round. ◆

---

* *Acculturation,* in this case, is the tendency of media professionals to accept the ideas, attitudes, and opinions of the group that they cover or with whom they have a great deal of contact.

COMMUNICATIONS PRETEST

Select words from this list and write them in the blanks to complete the sentences.

admonitory	diversified	pragmatic
augment	diversion	prodigality
covert	libel	slander
defamation	ostensibly	vast
demographic	overt	vicarious

1. Something kept from sight is _____.

2. _____ information gives statistics of populations.

3. Something _____ warns against a fault or oversight.

4. _____ means "of immense extent."

5. A rich abundance is a(n) _____.

6. Something apparent is _____.

7. To make greater in size is to _____.

8. Relief from work or care is _____.

9. _____ means "concerned with practical results."

10. A written, damaging statement is _____.

11. Work done for others is _____ work.

12. _____ means "as openly stated or shown."

13. An attack on the good name of someone is _____.

14. Something _____ is in various forms.

15. To speak falsely is to _____.

Answers to this pretest are in Appendix B.

Unless your instructor tells you to do otherwise, complete the exercises for each word you missed on the pretest. The words, with their meanings and exercises, are in alphabetical order. The superscript numbers indicate where the words appeared in the reading selection so that you can refer to them when necessary. There are several types of exercises, but for each word you will be asked to write a sentence using context clues. (See Chapter 4 if you need information about how to create context clues.) You are also asked to perform some activity that will help you make your concept of the word personal. *Complete this activity thoughtfully, for creating a personalized concept of the word will help you remember it in the future.*

Answers to all the exercises are at the end of the exercise segment.

COMMUNICATIONS EXERCISES

Admonitory[8]

ad|mon|i|to|ry (ad mon′ə tôr′ē, -tōr′-), *adj.* containing admonition; admonishing; warning: *The librarian raised an admonitory finger for silence.*
ad|mo|ni|tion (ad′mə nish′ən), *n.* **1** an admonishing; gentle reproof or warning: *He received an admonition from his teacher for not doing his homework. Now all these things … are written for our admonition* (I Corinthians 10:11). **2** counsel; recommendation: *The doctor's admonition was to work out a stiff knee.* [< Old French *amonition*, learned borrowing from Latin *admonitiō, -ōnis* < *admonēre* advise < *ad-* to + *monēre* advise, warn]

1. Something *admonitory* is intended to be
   - _____ a. good advice.
   - _____ b. a promise.
   - _____ c. cautioning.
   - _____ d. a reproof.
   - _____ e. a direct order.
   - _____ f. helpful.
2. Which of the following might serve an *admonitory* function?
   - _____ a. a counselor
   - _____ b. a parent
   - _____ c. a child
   - _____ d. a teacher

_____ e. a book   _____ h. an employer
_____ f. a film   _____ i. an advertisement
_____ g. a TV program

3. In which of the following sentences is *admonitory* used correctly?

_____ a. John's parents sent him an admonitory letter.

_____ b. At the Academy Awards, each winner gave an admonitory speech.

_____ c. Have you seen the admonitory videotape on smoking produced by the American Cancer Society?

_____ d. A computer spelling-checker serves an admonitory function.

4. Write a sentence correctly using *admonitory*. (Be sure to include context clues to show you understand the meaning of the word.)

_____

_____

5. What is the most recent *admonitory* information you have received?

_____

_____

Augment[6]

aug|ment (*v.* ôg ment′; *n.* ôg′ment), *v., n.* —*v.t.*
1 to make greater in size, number, amount, or degree; enlarge: *The king augmented his power by taking over rights that had belonged to the nobles.* **SYN:** amplify, swell. See syn. under **increase. 2** to add an augment to. —*v.i.* to become greater; increase; grow; swell: *The sound of traffic augments during the morning rush hour.*
—*n.* **1** a prefix or lengthened vowel marking the past tenses of verbs in Greek and Sanskrit.
2 *Obsolete.* increase; augmentation.
[< Late Latin *augmentāre* < Latin *augmentum* an increase < *augēre* to increase] —**aug|ment′a-ble,** *adj.* —**aug|ment′er, aug|men′tor,** *n.*

1. In which of the following sentences can *augment* correctly be placed in the blank?

_____ a. Authorities fear the rain will _____ the river and cause a flood.

_____ b. If they permit jets to land at this airport, the noise level will _____ greatly.

_____ c. The gambler planned to _____ his bank roll by going to Las Vegas.

_____ d. A few hours spent at the shopping mall will probably _____ your bank account.

2. Select the synonym(s) of *augment*.

_____ a. enlarge   _____ d. amplify
_____ b. lessen   _____ e. increase
_____ c. expand   _____ f. decrease

3. Complete the verbal analogy.
   happy : sad :: *augment* : _____
   a. enlarge   d. extend
   b. intense   e. more
   c. diminish

4. What have you done recently to *augment* your bank account?

   _____

   _____

5. Write a sentence correctly using *augment*. (Be sure to include context clues to show you understand the meaning of the word.)

   _____

   _____

Covert[9]

co|vert (*adj.* 1, *n.* 3 kō′vərt, kuv′ərt; *adj.* 2,3; *n.* 1, 2 kuv′ərt, kō′vərt), *adj., n.* —*adj.* **1** kept from sight; secret; hidden; disguised: *The children cast covert glances at the box of candy they were told not to touch.* SYN: concealed. See syn. under **secret. 2** *Law.* married and under the authority or protection of her husband. **3** *Rare.* covered; sheltered.
—*n.* **1a** a hiding place; shelter. **b** a thicket in which wild animals or birds hide. **2** a covering. **3** = covert cloth.
coverts, the smaller and weaker feathers of a bird that cover the bases of the larger feathers of the wing and tail; tectrices: *The coverts of the wings are of a deep blackish green* (Goldsmith). [< Old French *covert,* past participle of *covrir;* see etym. under **cover**] —**co′vert|ly,** *adv.* —**co′vert|ness,** *n.*

from **secret:**
— *Syn. adj.* **1 Secret, covert, clandestine** mean done, made, or carried on without the knowledge of others. **Secret** is the general word and applies to concealment of any kind and for any purpose: *They have a secret business agreement.* **Covert,** a more formal word, suggests partial concealment, and applies to anything kept under cover, disguised, or not openly revealed: *A hint is a covert suggestion.* **Clandestine,** also formal, suggests concealment for an unlawful or improper purpose: *He feared someone would learn of his clandestine trips.*

1. Place an "s" by any synonym and an "a" by any antonym of *covert*.
   _____ a. secret   _____ d. concealed
   _____ b. obvious   _____ e. disguised
   _____ c. hidden   _____ f. overt

2. Check any appropriate response to the following statement: "John made *covert* remarks to Bill about Mary's behavior."
   _____ a. John always speaks right up.
   _____ b. Why is he being so secretive?
   _____ c. John is a gossip, I think.
   _____ d. At least he is open about it.

3. Which of the numbered and lettered dictionary definitions of *covert* best fits the word's use in the reading selection? _____

4. Write a sentence correctly using *covert*. (Be sure to include context clues to show you understand the meaning of the word.)

   _____

   _____

5. Have you ever participated in any *covert* activity? (Something you did not want your friends or parents to know about, perhaps.) What was it?

_____

_____

_____

Defamation[11]

def|a|ma|tion (def′ə mā′shən, dē′fə-), *n.* the act of defaming or condition of being defamed; slander or libel: *It contrives to mention accusingly or suspiciously a far larger number of scholars and public figures than any earlier exercise in defamation* (Harper's).
de|fame (di fām′), *v.t.,* **-famed, -fam|ing. 1** to attack the good name of; harm the reputation of; speak evil of; slander or libel: *Men in public life* are sometimes defamed by opponents. Other ventures have tried to defame respectable people by use of the ... principle of guilt by association (Harper's). **SYN:** calumniate, vilify, malign. **2** *Archaic.* to disgrace. **3** *Obsolete.* to accuse. [< Old French *diffamer,* and Medieval Latin *defamare,* both < Latin *diffāmāre* damage by rumor, spread rumor < *dis-* abroad + *fāma* rumor]

1. *Defamation* of one's character might
   _____ a. be carried out by a friend.
   _____ b. be the act of an opponent.
   _____ c. lead to a lawsuit.
   _____ d. make one happy.

2. Complete the verbal analogy.
   demonstration : demonstrate :: *defamation* : _____
   a. defame   c. defamate
   b. defamatory   d. defamer

3. Check any appropriate response to the following statement:
   "Alice's *defamation* of Sue was heard by many people at the party."
   _____ a. That may damage Sue's reputation.
   _____ b. Alice and Sue are such good friends.
   _____ c. What an unkind thing to do!
   _____ d. Oh, that doesn't matter.

4. If it is true that "sticks and stones may break my bones, but names will never hurt me," what is so bad about *defamation?*

_____

_____

_____

5. Write a sentence correctly using *defamation.* (Be sure to include context clues to show you understand the meaning of the word.)

_____

_____

Demographic[7]

dem|o|graph|ic (dem′ə graf′ik), *adj.* of or having to do with demography: *Migration offers little by way of a solution of the world's demographic problem* (Wall Street Journal). —**dem′o|graph′i-cal|ly**, *adv.*

de|mog|ra|phy (di mog′rə fē), *n.* the science dealing with statistics of human populations, in-cluding size, distribution, diseases, births and deaths: *The analysis of fluctuations of animal populations has importance for human demogra-phy* (F. S. Bodenheimer). [< Greek *dêmos* peo-ple + English *-graphy*]

1. In which of the following sentences can *demographic* correctly be placed in the blank?

     _____ a. The latest _____ data tell the size of the U.S. population.

     _____ b. If you want to know how many people had measles last year, you can consult the _____ tables.

     _____ c. _____ data show the number of live births in each state.

     _____ d. You can find out which state has the most people by read-ing _____ information.

2. Which of the following is a characteristic of *demographic* data?

     _____ a. scientific   _____ d. useful

     _____ b. guesswork   _____ e. factual

     _____ c. careful   _____ f. careless

3. Complete the verbal analogy.

   submarine : under :: *demographic* : _____

     a. data   d. people
     b. over   e. facts
     c. science

4. Write a sentence correctly using *demographic*. (Be sure to include context clues to show you understand the meaning of the word.)

     _____

     _____

5. What kind of *demographic* data might you use in an attempt to get a job?

     _____

     _____

Diversified[2]

di|ver|si|fied (də vėr′sə fīd, dī-), *adj.* in various forms; varied; diverse: *diversified producers, diversified investments.*

di|verse (də vėrs′, dī-), *adj.* **1** different; com-pletely unlike: *A great many diverse opinions were expressed at the meeting. But O the truth,* the truth! the many eyes That look on it! the di-verse things they see (George Meredith). **2** var-ied: *A person of diverse interests can talk on many subjects.* syn: multiform, diversified. [variant of *divers;* the *-e* added on analogy of *converse, reverse*] — **di|verse′ly**, *adv.* — **di|verse′ness**, *n.*

1. In which of the following sentences is *diversified* used correctly?

_____ a. The diversified scenery of California ranges from mountains to desert to seacoast.

_____ b. Music by Beethoven and Elton John formed the diversified program.

_____ c. My stock broker recommends a diversified investment portfolio.

_____ d. John wore a diversified suit to the interview.

2. Which of the following might be *diversified*?

_____ a. the crops a farmer raised

_____ b. the parts played by an actor during his career

_____ c. the courses one must take in college

_____ d. the books in a library

3. Complete the verbal analogy.

eat : verb :: *diversified* : _____

a. noun   c. adjective

b. adverb   d. conjunction

4. What *diversified* activities do you carry out at home? At your job? At school?

_____

_____

5. Write a sentence correctly using *diversified*. (Be sure to include context clues to show you understand the meaning of the word.)

_____

_____

Diversion[14]

di|ver|sion (də vėr′zhən, dī-), *n.* **1** the act or process of diverting; turning aside: *A magician's talk creates a diversion of attention so that people do not see how he does his tricks. High tariffs often cause a diversion of trade from one country to another.* **SYN:** deviation. **2** a relief from work or care; amusement; entertainment; pastime: *Watching television is a popular diversion. Golf is my father's favorite diversion.* **SYN:** sport, recreation. **3** an attack or feint intended to distract an opponent's attention from the point of main attack. **SYN:** distraction. [< Late Latin *dīversiō, -ōnis* < Latin *dīvertere;* see etym. under **divert**]

di|vert (də vėrt′, dī-), *v.t.* **1** to turn aside: *A ditch diverted water from the stream into the fields.*

2 to amuse; entertain: *We were diverted by the clown's tricks. Listening to music diverted him after a hard day's work. I diverted myself with talking to my parrot (Daniel Defoe).* **3** to distract: *A juggler or magician diverts attention from one hand by making feints with the other. The siren of the fire engine diverted the audience's attention from the play.* **4** *Figurative.* to embezzle; steal: *The dishonest treasurer diverted funds from the club's treasury.* — *v.i.* to turn aside from a course: *They ordered the pilot of the routine domestic flight to divert to North Korea (Manchester Guardian Weekly).* [< Old French *divertir,* learned borrowing from Latin *dīvertere* < *dis-* aside, apart + *vertere* turn]

1. In which of the following sentences can *diversion* correctly be placed in the blank?

_____ a. Harold created a _____ while Maude stole the diamond ring.

_____ b. Jimmy knows the multiplication tables but still has trouble with long _____.

    c. The military plan calls for the _____ to be carried out by Sergeant Miller's platoon.

    d. My favorite _____ is bowling.

2. Check any appropriate response to the following statement:
   "The treasurer has been charged with *diversion* of club funds."

   _____ a. Now we won't be able to pay our bills.

   _____ b. I'm glad we voted him into office.

   _____ c. Do we have insurance to cover that?

   _____ d. Will we have a party to celebrate?

3. Which of the numbered dictionary definitions of *diversion* best fits the word's use in the reading selection? _____

4. Write a sentence correctly using *diversion*. (Be sure to include context clues to show you understand the meaning of the word.)

   _____

   _____

5. What is your favorite *diversion?* (Definition 2.)

   _____

   _____

Libel[12]

li|bel (lī′bəl), *n., v.,* **-beled, -bel|ing** or (*especially British*) **-belled, -bel|ling**. —*n.* **1** a written or published statement, picture, etc., that is likely to harm the reputation of the person about whom it is made; false or damaging statement. syn: calumny. **2** the act or crime of writing or publishing such a statement, picture, etc. **3** any false or damaging statement or implication about a person: *His conversation is a perpetual libel on all his acquaintance* (Richard Brinsley Sheridan). syn: slander, vilification. **4** (in admiralty, ecclesiastical, and Scottish law) a formal written declaration of the allegations of a plaintiff and the grounds for his suit.
—*v.t.* **1** to write or publish a libel about, such as a statement or picture. **2** to make false or damaging statements about. syn: malign. **3** to institute suit against by means of a libel, as in an admiralty court.
[Middle English *libel* a formal written statement, little book < Old French *libel,* or *libelle,* learned borrowing from Latin *libellus* (diminutive) < *liber* book]
▶See **slander** for usage note.

from **slander:**

▶ **Slander** and **libel** are sharply distinguished from each other in modern United States law. *Slander* applies only to what is spoken; *libel* applies only to what is written or printed.

1. Check any appropriate response to the following statement:
   "I understand that Jim's disagreement with Bill has become *libel.*"

   _____ a. A friendly argument won't hurt anything.

   _____ b. Another instance where the lawyers will make some money!

   _____ c. I'm sorry it has gone so far.

   _____ d. Which one put it in writing, Jim or Bill?

2. Complete the verbal analogy.
   clown : funny :: *libel* : _____

     a. slander   c. unhappy

     b. small   d. false

3. Which of the numbered dictionary definitions of *libel* best fits the word's use in the reading selection? _____

4. The next time you read a news story about a crime, read carefully and note the care taken by the reporting service (newspaper or magazine) to keep from committing *libel*. List two recent crime news stories where the term *allege,* which means "to state as a fact without proof," is used. Why is the term used?

_____

_____

5. Write a sentence correctly using *libel*. (Be sure to include context clues to show you understand the meaning of the word.)

_____

_____

Ostensibly[10]

os|ten|si|bly (os ten′sə blē), *adv.* on the face of it; as openly stated or shown; apparently: *Though ostensibly studying his history, he was really drawing pictures behind the big book.*
os|ten|si|ble (os ten′sə bəl), *adj.* according to appearances; declared as genuine; apparent; pretended; professed: *Her ostensible purpose was to borrow sugar, but she really wanted to see her neighbor's new furniture.* **SYN:** seeming. [< French *ostensible* < Latin *ostēnsus,* past participle of *ostendere* to show < *ob-* toward + *tendere* stretch]

1. In which of the following sentences can *ostensibly* correctly be placed in the blank?
   _____ a. Mark was dismissed from his job, _____ for reasons of economy.
   _____ b. Jim flies to Mexico in his private plane every month _____ to bring back Mexican works of art.
   _____ c. Ruth works at the mission two days a week and _____ helps the poor.
   _____ d. Every day Peggy visits the store where John works, _____ to see if any new items are in stock.

2. If you do something *ostensibly,*
   _____ a. you are honest and open.
   _____ b. you are hiding something.
   _____ c. you may have good reason to do so.
   _____ d. someone may catch you at it.

3. Complete the verbal analogy.
   ghostly : adjective :: *ostensibly* : _____
   a. adjective   d. adverb
   b. verb   e. conjunction
   c. noun

4. Write a sentence correctly using *ostensibly*. (Be sure to include context clues to show you understand the meaning of the word.)

_____

_____

5. Have you ever carried out an activity *ostensibly* for one reason but actually for another reason? What was it?

_____

_____

Overt[3]

o|vert (ō′vėrt, ō vėrt′), *adj.* **1** open or public; evident; not hidden: *Hitting someone is an overt act. I know only his overt reasons for refusing; he may have others.* **syn**: plain, manifest, apparent. **2** *Heraldry,* (of a bearing) having an open figure; outspread, as the wings of a bird in flight. [< Old French *overt* < Vulgar Latin *ōpertus,* alteration of Latin *apertus,* past participle of *aperīre* open] — **o′vert|ly,** *adv.* — **o′vert|ness,** *n.*

1. In which of the following sentences is *overt* used correctly?
   _____ a. Robbing a bank is an overt act against society.
   _____ b. Peter says he is happy, but his overt behavior makes us wonder.
   _____ c. A swap meet or flea market is held in an overt place.
   _____ d. "Body language" is overt.

2. Place an "s" by any synonym and an "a" by any antonym of *overt*.
   _____ a. open   _____ d. hidden
   _____ b. public   _____ e. evident
   _____ c. manifest   _____ f. apparent

3. Complete the verbal analogy.
   weary : tired :: *overt* : _____
   a. plane   c. show
   b. plain   d. secret

4. In what *overt* way do you like to celebrate your birthday?

_____

_____

_____

5. Write a sentence correctly using *overt*. (Be sure to include context clues to show you understand the meaning of the word.)

_____

_____

Pragmatic[5]

prag|mat|ic (prag mat′ik), *adj., n.* —*adj.* **1** concerned with practical results or values; viewing things in a matter-of-fact way. **2** of or having to do with pragmatism: *a pragmatic philosophy.* **3** having to do with the affairs of a state or community. **4** busy; active. **5** meddlesome; interfering. **SYN:** officious. **6** conceited; opinionated. **7** matter-of-fact: *Their pragmatic ... approach increasingly fits the apolitical mood of the workers* (Economist). **8** treating the facts of history systemati-cally, with special reference to their causes and effects.
—*n.* **1** = pragmatic sanction. **2** = busybody. **3** a conceited person.
[< Latin *prāgmaticus* < Greek *prāgmatikós* efficient, one skilled in business or civil affairs < *prâgma, -atos* civil business; deed, act < *prâssein* to do, act. Compare etym. under **practical.**]
— **prag|mat′i|cal|ly,** *adv.* — **prag|mat′i|cal|ness,** *n.*

1. In which of the following sentences can *pragmatic* correctly be placed in the blank?
   _____ a. I'm not interested in philosophy; I'm far too _____.
   _____ b. John's _____ approach to the problem helped him find a solution.
   _____ c. However, Betty finds his _____ outlook on life very annoying.
   _____ d. My dog's death was a _____ experience for me.

2. If a person is *pragmatic,*
   _____ a. he deals with facts.
   _____ b. she is practical and active.
   _____ c. he is contemplative and deeply thoughtful.
   _____ d. she is a meddlesome busybody.

3. Which of the numbered dictionary definitions of *pragmatic* best fits the word's use in the reading selection? _____

4. In what areas of life are you most *pragmatic* (definition *adj.* 1)? Housework? Schoolwork? Your job? Love life?

   _____

   _____

5. Write a sentence correctly using *pragmatic.* (Be sure to include context clues to show you understand the meaning of the word.)

   _____

   _____

Prodigality[4]

prod|i|gal|i|ty (prod′ə gal′ə tē), *n., pl.* **-ties.**
1 wasteful or reckless extravagance: *It is often surprising how men begin to curb their prodigality when convinced they must pay for it* (Wall Street Journal). **2** rich abundance; profuseness: *the prodigality of jungle growth.* **SYN:** profusion.
[< Late Latin *prōdigālitās* < Latin *prōdigus* wasteful < *prōdigere* to squander, (literally) drive forth < *prōd-,* variant of *prō-* forth + *agere* to drive]

1. In which of the following sentences can *prodigality* correctly be placed in the blank?

_____ a. John's _____ led to the failure of the business.

_____ b. _____ can control inflation in the economy.

_____ c. The _____ of the newlyweds soon had them deep in debt.

_____ d. If a company has _____, it is considered a success.

2. Which of the following might be described as *prodigality?*

_____ a. spending beyond one's income

_____ b. a greatly overgrown garden

_____ c. extensively using earth's resources

_____ d. planting a vegetable garden

3. The etymology of *prodigality* shows that the word comes from the Latin *agere* (to drive). Use this information, your imagination, and your background knowledge to match the following:

_____ a. agile   aa. to engage in a lawsuit

_____ b. agitate   bb. to sail, manage, or steer (a ship)

_____ c. fumigage   cc. to expose to fumes

_____ d. litigate   dd. moving quickly or easily

_____ e. navigate   ee. to move or shake vigorously

4. Who in your family might be accused of *prodigality?* _____

5. Write a sentence correctly using *prodigality.* (Be sure to include context clues to show you understand the meaning of the word.)

_____

_____

Slander[13]

slan|der (slan′dər, slän′-), *n., v.* — *n.* **1a** a false report meant to do harm to the good name and reputation of another: *Do not listen to slander.* SYN: defamation, calumny. **b** *Law.* a spoken statement tending to damage a person's reputation. **2** the spreading of false reports about persons: *The mayor sued the television station for slander when it accused him of dishonest use of city funds. The worthiest people are the most injured by slander* (Jonathan Swift). — *v.t.* to talk falsely about. SYN: defame, calumniate. — *v.i.* to speak or spread slander. [< Anglo-French *esclandre* scandal, adapted from Latin *scandalum.* See etym. of doublet **scandal.**] — **slan′der|er,** *n.*
▶ **Slander** and **libel** are sharply distinguished from each other in modern United States law. *Slander* applies only to what is spoken; *libel* applies only to what is written or printed.

1. Which of the following describes *slander?*

_____ a. false   _____ d. damaging

_____ b. defaming   _____ e. harmful

_____ c. violent   _____ f. spoken

2. Check any appropriate response to the following statement: "John's *slander* of Mr. Williams took place on July 4th."

_____ a. That's a pleasant way to spend a holiday.

_____ b. Those who heard it were surprised and shocked.

_____ c. Yes, I know; I read it.

_____ d. I suppose this means a lawsuit.

3. Which of the numbered and lettered dictionary definitions of *slander* best fits the word's use in the reading selection? _____

4. Write a sentence correctly using *slander*. (Be sure to include context clues to show you understand the meaning of the word.)

_____

_____

5. What comment could you make about a political figure that would be *slander?*

_____

_____

Vast¹

vast (vast, väst), *adj., n. —adj.* **1** of great area; of immense extent; extensive: *Texas and Alaska cover vast territories.* syn: immense, tremendous, colossal. **2** of large dimensions; of very great size; huge; massive: *vast forms that move fantastically* (Edgar Allan Poe). syn: immense, tremendous, colossal. **3** very great in amount, quantity, or number: *A billion dollars is a vast amount of money. It is a building with a vast collection of chambers and galleries.* syn: immense, tremendous, colossal. **4** *Figurative.* unusually large or comprehensive in grasp or aims: *the vast and various affairs of government.* —*n.* **1** an immense space: *her return to the unconscious vast* (Eden Philpotts). **2** *Dialect.* a very great number or amount: *They had heard a vast of words* (Robert Louis Stevenson). [< Latin *vastus* immense, empty] —**vast'ness,** *n.*

1. Place an "s" by any synonym and an "a" by any antonym of *vast*.
   _____ a. tremendous   _____ d. limited
   _____ b. colossal   _____ e. miniature
   _____ c. immense   _____ f. extensive

2. In which of the following sentences can *vast* correctly be placed in the blank?
   _____ a. Jack has a _____ knowledge of botany.
   _____ b. Siberia has _____ areas where no people live.
   _____ c. The Eiffel Tower in Paris is a _____ monument to engineering skill.
   _____ d. The trout is a _____ fish.

3. Which of the numbered dictionary definitions of *vast* best fits the word's use in the reading selection? _____

4. Have you ever been in a structure that could be described as *vast?* Where were you?

_____

_____

5. Write a sentence correctly using *vast*. (Be sure to include context clues to show you understand the meaning of the word.)

_____

_____

Vicarious[15]

vi|car|i|ous (vī kãr′ē əs, vi-), *adj.* **1** done or suffered for others: *vicarious work, vicarious punishment.* **2** felt by sharing in the experience of another: *The invalid received vicarious pleasure from reading travel stories.* **3** taking the place of another; doing the work of another: *a vicarious agent.* **4** delegated: *vicarious authority.* **5** based upon the substitution of one person for another: this vicarious structure of society, based upon what others do for us. **6** *Physiology.* denoting the performance by or through one organ of functions normally discharged by another, as for example in vicarious menstruation. [< Latin *vicārius* (with English *-ous*) substituted < *vicis* a turn, change, substitution. See etym. of doublet **vicar.**] —**vi|car′i|ous|ly,** *adv.* —**vi|car′i|ous|ness,** *n.*

(Note: In several of its definitions, *vicarious* has to do with substitute activity where one person or thing acts in place of another. But in one definition (number 2 in the entry here) *vicarious* activity is carried out as a substitution. That is, the person who has the *vicarious* experience is not acting at all but is living through the actions of another person.)

1. In which of the following sentences is *vicarious* used correctly?

   _____ a. In earlier times a rich man who was supposed to serve in the military might pay someone to be his vicarious agent.

   _____ b. I can't attend the board meeting; please attend for me in a vicarious capacity.

   _____ c. Christians believe that Christ's vicarious sacrifice removes the sin of those who are His followers.

   _____ d. Mr. Smith was not able to go to medical school, but he receives vicarious satisfaction from the fact that his son is a doctor.

2. Check any appropriate response to the following statement: "I had a *vicarious* experience when I watched your color slides of Alaska yesterday."

   _____ a. I'm sorry they didn't mean anything to you.

   _____ b. Why don't you take the trip next year?

   _____ c. It was fun to share my trip with you.

   _____ d. It's the next best thing to actually traveling, isn't it?

3. Which of the numbered dictionary definitions of *vicarious* best fits the word's use in the reading selection? _____

4. Write a sentence correctly using *vicarious*. (Be sure to include context clues to show you understand the meaning of the word.)

   _____

   _____

5. What *vicarious* (definition 2) experiences do you enjoy most? Watching sports events? Romantic movies? Adventure films?

   _____

   _____

ANSWERS TO CHAPTER 16 EXERCISES

Admonitory: **1.** a, c, d, f **2.** a, b, c, d, e, f, g, h, i **3.** a, c, d
Augment: **1.** a, b, c **2.** a, c, d, e **3.** c (antonym)
Covert: **1.** s, a, s, s, s, a **2.** b, c **3.** *adj.* 1
Defamation: **1.** b, c **2.** a (noun/verb) **3.** a, c
Demographic: **1.** a, b, c, d **2.** a, c, d, e **3.** d (root meaning)
Diversified: **1.** a, b, c **2.** a, b, c, d **3.** c (part of speech)
Diversion: **1.** a, c, d **2.** a, c **3.** 2
Libel: **1.** b, c, d **2.** d (characteristic) **3.** 1
Ostensibly: **1.** a, b, d **2.** b, c, d **3.** d (part of speech)
Overt: **1.** a, b, d **2.** s, s, s, a, s, s **3.** b (synonym)
Pragmatic: **1.** a, b, c **2.** a, b, d **3.** *adj.* 1
Prodigality: **1.** a, c **2.** a, b, c **3.** dd, ee, cc, aa, bb
Slander: **1.** a, b, d, e, f **2.** b, d **3.** 1a
Vast: **1.** s, s, s, a, a, s **2.** a, b, c **3.** *adj.* 2
Vicarious: **1.** a, b, c, d **2.** b, c, d **3.** 2

If you missed any of the items in the exercises, return to the exercise and to
the dictionary definition to see where you went wrong. Remember: If you get
something right, you only affirm that you knew it. If you get something wrong
and understand why, *you have learned something.*

COMMUNICATIONS POSTTEST

Fill in the blanks with the words from this list.

admonitory	diversified	pragmatic
augment	diversion	prodigality
covert	libel	slander
defamation	ostensibly	vast
demographic	overt	vicarious

1. Printed vilification is _____.

2. _____ means "manifest."

3. *Colossal* is a synonym for _____.

4. _____ means "delegated."

5. Number of births would come from _____ data.

6. _____ is harming someone's reputation.

7. _____ means "warning."

8. Something _____ is concealed.

9. To enlarge is to _____ .

10. _____ means "varied."

11. *Profusion* is another word for _____ .

12. _____ means "matter-of-fact."

13. Spoken calumny is _____ .

14. A word meaning "turning aside" is _____ .

15. *Apparently* is a synonym for _____ .

Answers to this posttest are in the Instructor's Manual.

If you missed any of the words, you may need to return to the exercises and to the dictionary entries to see why your concepts for some words are incomplete.

HUMANITIES: ENGLISH

◆

OVERVIEW

English is a broadly based field that studies composition, language, and literature. It is versatile, helping develop lifelong skills related to writing, reading, and thinking. English has a broad application for a variety of careers, including business, communications, media, theater, teaching, law, and data processing, as well as providing a foundation for advanced graduate and professional study.

Composition courses help strengthen a student's ability to express ideas and feelings effectively in writing. They also help students understand the significance and complexity of the writing process. Courses are offered in such areas as basic writing, creative writing, functional composition for the vocationally oriented student, research methods and term paper writing, and technical writing related to the technical language of science and industry.

Language or linguistics courses taught in the English department focus on the study of the nature of language, its comparison with other symbol systems, and of language in the context of culture.

The study of literature ranges from the various types and periods (historical), to specific authors (biographical), to special groups in society. There are courses in the nature of literature and its forms (poem, play, novel, short story, film, biography) and how literature works to portray fundamental human concerns. World literature courses can range from antiquity to the modern era. British and American authors such as Shakespeare and Hemingway are studied, as well as the literature of specific groups in society, including women, children, Afro-Americans, Hispanic Americans, and so forth.

Introductory texts in English usually are expository; that is, they explain broad concepts or generalizations. Some provide narration or a story with a plot, characters, and settings. Many texts include historical references and present information in chronological sequence or time order. Some texts include anthologies with many articles or essays written by different authors.

The vocabulary in English is a combination of general and technical terms. The general words are those we might use every day but that can also have a specific meaning in the context of English, such as symbol, conflict, and critique. Many of the technical words, such as sonnet and fiction, have Latin, and Old or Middle English etymology.

VOCABULARY SELF-EVALUATION

The following words will be introduced in this reading selection. Place a check mark (√) in front of any that you know thoroughly and use in your speech or writing. Place a question mark (?) in front of any that you recognize but do not use yourself.

_____ delineate	_____ epitome	_____ patron
_____ denouement	_____ ligature	_____ personify
_____ deus ex machina	_____ montage	_____ profound
_____ eloquent	_____ motif	_____ repartee
_____ epithet	_____ narrative	_____ soliloquy

SHAKESPEARE AND HIS WRITING

William Shakespeare is regarded by many critics as the greatest writer in the history of the English language. His numerous tragedies and comedies contain such a wide variety of themes that they create a montage[1] of life. In his comedies he used improbable devices like mistaken identities and the transformation of humans into animals, yet he produced delightful works that pleased his audiences then and still please us today. He used the device of the fool as a ligature[2] between acts, as a transition between subplots, and in the denouement[3] of the play. *Twelfth Night* is typical of his use of the buffoon in this manner. Although the fool's appearance is somewhat a deus ex machina,[4] his final repartee[5] creates a convincing example of the wise fool* motif.[6]

Unlike many of the seventeenth-century dramatists who came after him, Shakespeare was able to delineate[7] believable characters. These characters were so forcefully portrayed that they became famous for the qualities they displayed, and their names are now inseparable from those qualities. Romeo, for example, represents the epitome[8] of male lovers. Shylock is the symbol of a moneygrubber, and Puck personifies[9] a mischievous spirit.

Shakespeare's eloquent[10] use of the English language produced elaborate dialogues between his characters, and his famous soliloquies[11] are among the most outstanding examples of English language use. This splendid use of the language is displayed not only in his plays but also in his narrative[12] poems and in his sonnets.† His narrative poems, dedicated to a noble patron,[13] were extremely popular, and as a result of their publication, Shakespeare prospered financially.

Although Shakespeare used traditional verse forms in his sonnets, his extraordinary use of the language produced glowing songs devoted to love, such as Sonnet 18, which begins "Shall I compare thee to a summer's day?" and profound[14] refrains depicting troubled man, as seen in Sonnet 55: "Like as the waves make towards the pebbled shore / So do our minutes hasten to their end."

While the works of many writers are unappreciated until after their creators are dead, William Shakespeare's works were received enthusiastically during his lifetime. He borrowed openly from works well known at that time and from English history, so he was not an original storyteller, but his talent and skill with the language have made modern readers give him the epithet,[15] "Shakespeare the Genius." ◆

---

* "Wise fool" is a figure of speech called an *oxymoron*. It contradicts itself. Other examples are John Milton's "visible darkness" and Byron's "when love is 'kindly cruel.'" (Also consider "rolling stop," "poor little rich girl," and "pretty ugly.")

† A sonnet is a fourteen-line poem usually grouped as eight lines (an octave) and six lines (a sestet).

ENGLISH PRETEST

Select words from this list and write them in the blanks to complete the sentences.

delineate	epitome	patron
denouement	ligature	personify
deus ex machina	montage	profound
eloquent	motif	repartee
epithet	narrative	soliloquy

1. Something that comes just in time to solve a problem is a(n) _____ .

2. If we represent a thing as a person, we _____ it.

3. An idea repeated in a work of art or literature is called a(n) _____ .

4. Anything used to tie or bind can be called a(n) _____.

5. One who supports something is its _____.

6. The solution of a plot is a(n) _____.

7. To _____ means "to trace the outline of something."

8. A fluent speaker uses _____ expression.

9. Witty replies are called _____.

10. A combination of images is a(n) _____.

11. A(n) _____ tells a story.

12. Something going far deeper than understood is _____.

13. Talking to oneself is called a(n) _____.

14. A person who is typical of something can be called a(n) _____.

15. A word or phrase used in place of a person's name is a(n) _____.

Answers to this pretest are in Appendix B.

Unless your instructor tells you to do otherwise, complete the exercises for each word you missed on the pretest. The words, with their meanings and exercises, are in alphabetical order. The superscript numbers indicate where the words appeared in the essay so that you can refer to them when necessary. There are several types of exercises, but for each word you will be asked to write a sentence using context clues. (See Chapter 4 if you need information about how to create context clues.) You are also asked to perform some activity that will help you make your concept of the word personal. *Complete this activity thoughtfully, for creating a personalized concept of the word will help you remember it in the future.*

Answers to all the exercises are at the end of the exercise segment.

ENGLISH EXERCISES

Delineate[7]

de|lin|e|ate (di lin′ē āt), *v.t.*, **-at|ed, -at|ing. 1** to trace the outline of: *The map delineated clearly the boundary between Mexico and Texas.* **2** to draw; sketch. **3** *Figurative.* to describe in words; portray: *He delineated his plan in a thorough report.* **SYN**: depict, picture. [< Latin *dēlīneāre* (with English *-ate¹*) < *dē-* + *līnea* line]

1. In which of the following sentences is *delineate* used correctly?
   - _____ a. Sometimes Sue is not able to delineate between right and wrong.
   - _____ b. In this test the student must delineate each of the states and name each capital.

_____ c. The artist was able to delineate the suspect's face as the witness described it.

_____ d. It is the writer's ability to delineate characters that makes her novels sell so well.

2. If you *delineate* something, you might

_____ a. sing it.   _____ d. throw it.

_____ b. write it.   _____ e. play it.

_____ c. draw it.   _____ f. sketch it.

3. Which of the numbered dictionary definitions of *delineate* best fits the word's use in the reading selection? _____

4. Write a sentence correctly using *delineate*. (Be sure to include context clues to show you understand the meaning of the word.)

_____

_____

5. *Delineate* the figure of a person here.

Denouement³

de|noue|ment or **dé|noue|ment** (dā′nü män′), *n.* **1a** the solution of a plot in a story, play, situation, or the like: *The particulars of the dénouement you shall know in due season* (Tobias Smollett). *It's all fairly conventional and unsubtle, with an anticlimactic dénouement; but the Cornish setting is attractive* (New York Times). **b** the passage in the story, play, or other literary work, in which this takes place. **2** outcome; end: *He also, no doubt, wanted to go himself as a fitting denouement to his career* (Atlantic). [< French *dénouement* < *dénouer* untie < *dé-* (< Latin *dis-*) out + *nouer* < Latin *nōdāre* to tie < *nōdus* knot]

(Note: Watch out for the pronunciation of this word. It is still very French. Do you see that it literally says, "to tie out (untie) the knot"?)

1. If you understand the *denouement* of a movie,

_____ a. you can't figure out what happened.

_____ b. you understand the plot.

_____ c. you are puzzled about what the story means.

_____ d. the director's development of the plot is clear.

2. Select the synonym(s) of *denouement*.

_____ a. puzzle   _____ c. outcome

_____ b. clarification   _____ d. solution

3. The *denouement* of a play would come

_____ a. in the first act.   _____ c. in the second act.

_____ b. in the last act.   _____ d. in every act.

4. Which movie or TV program that you have seen recently had a plot with a satisfying *denouement?* How about one with an unsatisfying *denouement?*

_____

_____

5. Write a sentence correctly using the word *denouement.* (Be sure to include context clues to show you understand the meaning of the word.)

_____

_____

Deus ex machina[4]

de|us ex ma|chi|na (dē′əs eks mak′ə nə), *Latin.* **1** a person, god, or event that comes just in time to solve a difficulty in a story, play, or other literary or dramatic work, especially when the coming is contrived or artificial: *There is ... Ferral, a French representative of big business, whom Malraux uses as the novel's deus ex machina* (New Yorker). (*Figurative.*) *Mr. Galbraith re-* jects the notion that somewhere in Wall Street *there was a deus ex machina who somehow engineered the boom and bust* (New York Times). **2** (literally) a god from a machine (referring to a mechanical device used in the ancient Greek and Roman theater by which actors who played the parts of gods were lowered from above the stage to end or resolve the dramatic action).

(Note: Read the pronunciation of this phrase very carefully!)

1. Which of the following is an example of *deus ex machina?*
   - _____ a. A poor man solves his problems by suddenly inheriting one million dollars.
   - _____ b. A poor man gets a job, works hard, and is a success.
   - _____ c. The enemy drops dead of a heart attack just before he can shoot the hero.
   - _____ d. Prince Charming arrives in time to take a dateless girl to the prom.

2. If a modern playwright uses a *deus ex machina,* he is likely to
   - _____ a. get bad reviews from the critics.
   - _____ b. get good reviews from the critics.
   - _____ c. be called unrealistic.
   - _____ d. be called realistic.

3. Complete this verbal analogy.
   happiness : rare :: *deus ex machina* : _____
   a. realistic   c. sadness
   b. unnatural   d. natural

4. Write a sentence correctly using *deus ex machina.* (Be sure to include context clues to show you understand the meaning of the word.)

_____

_____

5. Create and describe a *deus ex machina* for your present life situation.

_____

_____

_____

Eloquent[10]

el|o|quent (el′e kwent), *adj.* **1** having the power of expressing one's feeling or thoughts with grace and force; having eloquence: *an eloquent speaker. The curse of this country is eloquent men* (Ralph Waldo Emerson). **SYN:** voluble, fluent, glib. **2** very expressive: (*Figurative.*) *eloquent eyes.* [< Latin *ēloquēns, -entis*, present participle of *ēloquī* < *ex-* out + *loquī* speak] — **el′o-quent|ly,** *adv.*

1. Which professionals might find it necessary to be *eloquent?*
   - _____ a. a scientist
   - _____ b. an artist
   - _____ c. a minister
   - _____ d. a politician
   - _____ e. a lawyer
   - _____ f. a teacher

2. In which of the following sentences can *eloquent* correctly be placed in the blank?
   - _____ a. John's talk was so _____, we were moved to tears.
   - _____ b. The speaker who confuses his audience probably is _____ .
   - _____ c. An actress who is _____ will likely be offered many parts.
   - _____ d. I believe he is guilty, but his lawyer's _____ speech saved him.

3. Select the synonym(s) of *eloquent.*
   - _____ a. expressive
   - _____ b. informative
   - _____ c. forceful
   - _____ d. meaningful
   - _____ e. fluent
   - _____ f. factual

4. Identify someone who is *eloquent.* Is it a minister? An actor or actress? A politician?

_____

_____

5. Write a sentence correctly using *eloquent.* (Be sure to include context clues to show you understand the meaning of the word.)

_____

_____

Epithet[15]

ep|i|thet (ep′ə thet), *n.* **1** a descriptive expression; a word or phrase expressing some quality or attribute. In "crafty Ulysses," "Richard the Lion-Hearted," and "Honest Abe," the epithets are "crafty," "Lion-Hearted," and "Honest." *Such epithets like pepper, Give zest to what you write* (Lewis Carroll). **2** a word or phrase (sometimes insulting or contemptuous) used in place of a person's name. **3** that part of the scientific name of an animal or plant which denotes a species, variety, or other division of a genus. *Example:* In *Canis familiaris* (the dog), *familiaris* is the specific epithet. In *Prunus persica* (the peach), *persica* is the specific epithet. **4** *Obsolete.* a phrase or expression. [< Latin *epitheton* < Greek *epítheton* < *epi-* on, in addition + *tithénai* to place]

1. Which of the following sentences use(s) an *epithet?*
   _____ a. He won't be Clark Kent anymore, but instead will be *Dirty Harry.*
   _____ b. Good grief! She dresses like a *bag lady!*
   _____ c. A crowd of *three thousand* attended the concert.
   _____ d. Winston Churchill coined the term *iron curtain* in 1946.

2. If someone created an *epithet* for you, you might
   _____ a. punch him in the nose.
   _____ b. try to sell it at the swap meet.
   _____ c. be pleased to be thought of in such a manner.
   _____ d. give one back to him.

3. Which of the numbered dictionary definitions of *epithet* best fits the word's use in the reading selection? _____

4. Write a sentence correctly using *epithet.* (Be sure to include context clues to show you understand the meaning of the word.)
   _____
   _____

5. Think of an *epithet* for your best friend that reflects his or her best quality. Write it here.
   _____
   _____

Epitome[8]

e|pit|o|me (i pit′ə mē), *n.* **1** a condensed account; summary. An epitome contains only the most important points of a book, essay, article, or other literary work. *In general nothing is less attractive than an epitome* (Macaulay). **SYN:** compendium. **2** *Figurative.* a person or thing that is typical or representative of something: *Solomon is often spoken of as the epitome of wisdom.* [She] is *rated the epitome of fashion elegance* (Eugenia Sheppard). *The rubber plant and the antimacassar were the epitome of good taste* (New York Times Magazine). **SYN:** embodiment.
in epitome, in a diminutive form; in miniature: *The characteristics and pursuits of various ages and races of men are always existing in epitome in every neighborhood* (Thoreau).

[< Latin *epitomē* < Greek *epitomḗ* < *epitémnein* cut short < *epi-* into + *témnein* cut]
e|pit|o|mize (i pit′ə mīz), *v.t.,* **-mized, -miz|ing. 1** to make a summary of: *to epitomize a long report.* **SYN:** abridge, condense. **2** *Figurative.* to be typical or representative of: *Galahad and Lancelot epitomize the knighthood of ancient Britain. Helen Keller epitomizes the human ability to overcome handicaps. John Finley epitomized the sensible attitude for oldsters to take by his witty motto, "Nothing succeeds like successors"* (Harper's). **3** to contain in a brief form: *His problems epitomize the problems of the entire neighborhood.* **SYN:** concentrate. — **e|pit′o|miz′er,** *n.*

(Note: This word doesn't follow the usual pronunciation rules.)

1. Which of the following is a characteristic of an *epitome?*
   _____ a. It is one example of something.
   _____ b. It is a typical representative.
   _____ c. It contains unimportant details.
   _____ d. It is a summary.

2. Check any appropriate response to the following statement:
   "I think Elizabeth Taylor is the *epitome* of a fashionably dressed movie star."
   _____ a. I don't agree, but you have a right to think so.
   _____ b. Yes, she is awful, isn't she?
   _____ c. Yes, she is. It must cost a fortune.
   _____ d. Mr. Blackwell has put her on the permanent "best dressed" list.

3. Which of the numbered dictionary definitions of *epitome* best fits the word's use in the reading selection? _____

4. What song do you believe *epitomizes* modern rock music?

   _____

   _____

5. Write a sentence correctly using *epitome*. (Be sure to include context clues to show you understand the meaning of the word.)

   _____

   _____

Ligature²

*lig|a|ture (lig'ə chùr, -chər), n., v., -tured, -tur|ing.
— *n.* 1 anything used to bind or tie up, such as a band, bandage, or cord; tie. 2 a thread, wire, or string, used by surgeons to tie up a bleeding artery or vein or to remove a tumor by strangulation, etc. 3 the act of binding or tying up. 4 *Music.* a a slur or a group of notes connected by a slur, showing a succession of notes sung to one syllable or in one breath, or played with one stroke of the bow. b = tie. c (in some medieval music) one of various compound note forms designed to indicate groups of two or more tones which were to be sung to a single syllable.

5a two or three letters joined in printing to form one character. b a mark connecting two letters. — *v.t.* to bind, tie up, or connect with a ligature. [< Late Latin *ligātūra* < Latin *ligāre* bind]

*ligature
definitions 4a, 5a

ff ffi ffl fi fl
printing

music

1. In which of the following sentences can *ligature* correctly be placed in the blank?
   _____ a. The _____ was old and worn, so we replaced it with a plastic tie.
   _____ b. Between mother and child, the _____ is strong.
   _____ c. In first-aid class, we were taught how to make a _____ out of cloth.
   _____ d. If you don't want to invest in the stock market, I suggest that you buy _____s.

2. Which of the following is an example of a *ligature?*
_____ a. a group of notes to be played as a slur
_____ b. a series of pictures shown together
_____ c. type combining two or more letters
_____ d. a cord used to tie off a blood vessel

3. Which of the numbered and lettered dictionary definitions of *ligature* best fits the word's use in the reading selection? _____

4. Write a sentence correctly using *ligature.* (Be sure to include context clues to show you understand the meaning of the word.)

_____

_____

5. Do you ever wear a *ligature?* On what part of your body?

_____

_____

Montage[1]

mon|tage (mon täzh′), *n., v.,* **-taged, -tag|ing.**
—*n.* **1** the combination of several distinct pictures to make a composite picture. Montage is frequently used in photography. **2** a composite picture so made: *These dramatic photographs . . . were only montages* (Newsweek). **3** in motion pictures and television: **a** the use of a rapid succession of pictures, especially to suggest a train of thought. **b** the use of a combination of images on the screen at once, often revolving or otherwise moving around or toward a focal point. **c** a part of a motion picture using either of these devices. **4** *Radio.* a rapid sequence of separate or blended voices and sound effects which suggest varying states of mind. **5** any combining or blending of different elements: *His latest novel is a montage of biography, history, and fiction.*
—*v.t.* to make (pictures, scenes, voices, or other images, sounds, or elements) into a montage: *to montage a theatrical set.*
[< French *montage* a mounting < Old French *monter* to mount[1]]

(Note: Be careful about pronouncing this word. It still shows its French background.)

1. Which of the following could be called a *montage?*
_____ a. one large picture made up of several smaller pictures
_____ b. a rapid presentation of short scenes, all on the same theme
_____ c. a picture of a house painted on a wall
_____ d. several framed paintings hanging on a wall

2. If you create a *montage,*
_____ a. you may combine many sounds.
_____ b. it may be made up of many pictures.
_____ c. it may be made up of many designs.
_____ d. you must use a movie camera.

3. Which of the numbered and lettered dictionary definitions of *montage* best fits the word's use in the reading selection? _____

4. Imagine a *montage* representing your present life. What pictures would be included?

_____

_____

5. Write a sentence correctly using *montage*. (Be sure to include context clues to show you understand the meaning of the word.)

_____

_____

Motif[6]

mo|tif (mō tēf′), *n.* **1** a subject for development or treatment in art, literature, or music; principal idea or feature; motive; theme: *This opera contains a love motif.* **2** a distinctive figure in a design, painting, or decoration. **3** *Music.* motive. [< French *motif* < Middle French, adjective < Late Latin *mōtīvus* moving. See etym. of doublet **motive**.]

1. A *motif* might appear in the work of which of the following?
_____ a. a playwright   _____ d. a writer
_____ b. an architect   _____ e. a designer
_____ c. a composer   _____ f. a poet

2. A *motif* in a play would probably be
_____ a. apparent to the audience.
_____ b. hidden from view.
_____ c. important to the playwright.
_____ d. something repeated.

3. Which of the numbered dictionary definitions of *motif* best fits the word's use in the reading selection? _____

4. Write a sentence correctly using *motif*. (Be sure to include context clues to show you understand the meaning of the word.)

_____

_____

5. What is the *motif* of your favorite song? Of your favorite type of music?

_____

_____

Narrative[12]

nar|ra|tive (nar′ə tiv), *n., adj.* —*n.* **1** a story or account; tale: *pages of narrative broken by occasional descriptive passages. His trip through Asia made an interesting narrative.* SYN: anecdote. **2** the practice or act of telling stories; narration: *The path of narrative with care pursue, Still making probability your clue* (William Cowper). —*adj.* **1** that narrates or recounts: *"Hiawatha" and "Evangeline" are narrative poems.* **2** of or having the character of narration: *narrative conversation.* —**nar′ra|tive|ly,** *adv.* SYN: *n.* **1** Narrative, narration mean something told as a story or account. **Narrative** applies chiefly to what is told, emphasizing the events or experiences told like a story: *His experiences in the Near East made an interesting narrative.* **Narration** applies chiefly to the act of telling or to the way in which the story or account is put together and presented: *His narration of his trip was interesting.*

nar|rate (na rāt′, nar′āt), *v.,* **-rat|ed, -rat|ing.** —*v.t.* to tell the story of; relate: *In narrating interesting facts, his comments ... often fatigue by their plenitude* (Anna Seward). SYN: repeat, recount. See syn. under **describe.** —*v.i.* to tell events or stories: *Most men ... speak only to narrate* (Thomas Carlyle). [< Latin *nārrāre* relate (with English *-ate¹*)]

1. Which of the following might be a *narrative?*
   _____ a. a story   _____ d. fiction
   _____ b. poetry   _____ e. a dance
   _____ c. a history   _____ f. a painting

2. Check any appropriate response to the following statement:
   "I've been asked to speak the *narrative* for a film on Alaska."
   _____ a. Will you tell a story about the land or the people?
   _____ b. They want you to say just a few words.
   _____ c. So you will play the background music.
   _____ d. That should be an interesting tale.

3. Complete the verbal analogy.
   summary : short :: *narrative* : _____
   a. story   c. long
   b. short   d. tells

4. What was the subject of a recent *narrative* you gave? Was it about a trip you took? A movie you saw? A party you attended?

   _____

   _____

5. Write a sentence correctly using *narrative*. (Be sure to include context clues to show you understand the meaning of the word.)

   _____

   _____

Patron[13]

pa|tron[1] (pā′trən), *n., adj.* —*n.* **1** a person who buys regularly at a given store or goes regularly to a certain hotel or restaurant: *The enormous demand for military boots was rendering it ... difficult for him to give to old patrons that ... attention which he would desire to give* (Arnold Bennett). **2** a person who gives his approval and support to some person, art, cause, or undertaking: *a patron of artists; a renowned patron of learning* (Jonathan Swift). *Books ... ought to have no patrons but truth and reason* (Francis Bacon). SYN: sponsor, benefactor. **3** a guardian saint; patron saint: *St. Crispin, the patron of shoemakers.* **4** (in ancient Rome) an influential man who took certain persons under his protection, or a master who had freed a slave but retained some claims upon him. **5** a person who holds the right to present a clergyman to a benefice. **6** *Obsolete.* a founder of a religious order. —*adj.* guarding; protecting: *a patron saint.* [< Old French *patroun,* learned borrowing from Latin *patrōnus* patron advocate, protector; person to be respected < *pater, patris* father. See etym. of doublets **padrone, patroon**[1], **pattern**.]

1. Which of the following acts would show that a person was a *patron?*
   _____ a. visiting the same store frequently
   _____ b. sending $1,000 to the new performing arts center
   _____ c. attending a free movie
   _____ d. providing housing for a young artist

2. The etymology of *patron* shows that the word comes from the Latin *pater* (father). Use this information, your background knowledge, and your imagination to match the following:

_____	a. patriarch	aa. father; used as a title of address for a priest in some countries; also, a military chaplain
_____	b. patriot	bb. pertaining to the characteristics of a father; fatherly
_____	c. patrimony	cc. the paternal leader of a family or tribe
_____	d. padre	dd. a person who loves, supports, and defends his homeland
_____	e. paternal	ee. an inheritance from a father or other ancestor
_____	f. expatriate	ff. to leave one's homeland to reside in another country

3. Which of the numbered and lettered dictionary definitions of *patron* best fits the word's use in the reading selection? _____

4. Write a sentence correctly using *patron*. (Be sure to include context clues to show you understand the meaning of the word.)

_____

_____

5. If you were very wealthy, for what causes would you be a *patron?*

_____

_____

Personify[9]

per|son|i|fy (pər son′ə fī), *v.t.,* **-fied, -fy|ing. 1** to be a type of; embody: *Satan personifies evil.* SYN: exemplify. **2** to regard or represent as a person. We often personify the sun and moon, referring to the sun as *he* and the moon as *she.* We personify time and nature when we refer to *Father Time* and *Mother Nature. Greek philosophy has a tendency to personify ideas* (Benjamin Jowett). [probably patterned on French *personnifier < personne* person + *-fier* -fy] —**per|son′i|fi′er,** *n.*

1. In which of the following sentences is *personify* used correctly?
   - _____ a. Sam saved a man from drowning; I think he personifies bravery.
   - _____ b. We personify justice as a blindfolded woman to show it is impartial.
   - _____ c. Mary personified her date as "a real dog."
   - _____ d. Harry, on the other hand, personified Mary as "some tomato."

2. If we *personify* something, we
   - _____ a. make an unnecessary reference.
   - _____ b. give it the qualities of a person.
   - _____ c. refer to a person as a general example.
   - _____ d. must be aware of special qualities.

3. Complete the verbal analogy.
   personification : noun :: *personify* : _____
   a. adjective   d. adverb
   b. noun   e. conjunction
   c. verb

4. Complete this sentence: My best friend *personifies* the characteristic of

   _____

   _____

5. Write a sentence correctly using *personify*. (Be sure to include context
   clues to show you understand the meaning of the word.)

   _____

   _____

Profound[14]

pro|found (pre found′), *adj., n. —adj.* **1** very deep: *a profound sigh, a profound sleep.* **2** felt strongly; very great: *profound despair; profound sympathy.* **3** going far deeper than what is easily understood; having or showing great knowledge or understanding: *a profound book, a profound thinker, a profound thought. Could this conflict of attachments be resolved by a profounder understanding of the principle of loyalty?* (Atlantic). **SYN**: abstruse, recondite. **4** carried far down; going far down; low: *a profound bow.*
— *n.* **1** the deep; the sea; the ocean. **2** an immeasurable abyss, as of space or time. [Middle English *profound* < Old French *parfond,* and *profond,* learned borrowing from Latin *profundus* < *prō-* forth + *fundus* bottom] — **profound′ly,** *adv.* — **pro|found′ness,** *n.*

1. In which of the following sentences can *profound* correctly be placed in
   the blank?
   _____ a. After hearing of her grandfather's death, Mary gave
           a _____ sigh.
   _____ b. Martin's _____ knowledge of astronomy led him
           to the discovery of a new star.
   _____ c. His _____ comments made us realize he didn't
           know what he was talking about.
   _____ d. Instead, we think his ignorance is _____.

2. Place an "s" beside any synonym and an "a" beside any antonym of
   profound.
   _____ a. deep   _____ c. far reaching   _____ e. shallow
   _____ b. complete   _____ d. not understood   _____ f. superficial

3. Which of the numbered dictionary definitions of *profound* best fits the
   word's use in the reading selection? _____

4. Write a sentence correctly using *profound.* (Be sure to include context
   clues to show you understand the meaning of the word.)

   _____

   _____

5. Is there anyone for whom you have *profound* respect? Who is it?

   _____

   _____

Repartee[5]

rep|ar|tee (rep′ər tē′), *n.* **1** a witty reply or re-plies: *Droll allusions, good stories, and smart repartees ... fell thick as hail* (Charles J. Lever). **SYN:** sally, retort. **2** talk characterized by clever and witty replies: *accomplished in repartee.* **3** cleverness and wit in making replies: *framing comments ... that would be sure to sting and yet leave no opening for repartee* (H. G. Wells). [< French *repartie* < *repartir* to reply, set out again, ultimately < Latin *re-* back, again + *pars, partis* a part, portion, share]

(Note: This word does not follow the usual pronunciation rules.)

1. A person who is skilled in *repartee*
   _____ a. can think of a quick reply.
   _____ b. usually is thought of as clever.
   _____ c. probably dislikes talking.
   _____ d. likes an exchange of words.

2. Check any appropriate response to the following statement:
   "I love to listen to Jim's *repartee.*"
   _____ a. I do, too, It puts me right to sleep.
   _____ b. He is as clever as Bob Hope.
   _____ c. I think he should be host on the "Tonight" show.
   _____ d. It helps me understand the history lesson.

3. Which of the following adjectives describes *repartee?*
   _____ a. quick   _____ c. clever
   _____ b. witty   _____ d. intelligent

4. Name a television personality who is known for his or her *repartee.*

   _____

   _____

5. Write a sentence correctly using *repartee.* (Be sure to include context clues to show you understand the meaning of the word.)

   _____

   _____

Soliloquy[11]

so|lil|o|quy (sə lil′ə kwē), *n., pl.* **-quies. 1** a talking to oneself. **2** a speech made by an actor to himself, especially when alone on the stage. It reveals his thoughts and feelings to the audience, but not to the other characters in the play. **3** a similar speech by a character in a book, poem, or other literary work. [< Late Latin *sō-liloquium* (introduced by Saint Augustine) < Latin *sōlus* alone + *loquī* speak]

1. Which of the following could correctly be called a *soliloquy?*
   _____ a. a dramatist revealing a character's feelings to the audience
   _____ b. the president's state-of-the-union address
   _____ c. Lincoln's Gettysburg Address
   _____ d. talking to your reflection in the mirror

2. In which of the following sentences can *soliloquy* correctly be placed in the blank?

_____ a. A poem in which a person speaks his ideas could be called a _____.

_____ b. In the quiet room, the only thing to be heard was Susan's _____.

_____ c. Listening carefully, John could hear the _____ between Jim and Mary.

_____ d. Shakespeare uses Hamlet's _____ to set out the character's thoughts.

3. Which of the numbered dictionary definitions of *soliloquy* best fits the word's use in the reading selection? _____

4. Write a sentence correctly using *soliloquy*. (Be sure to include context clues to show you understand the meaning of the word.)

_____

_____

5. In what situation might you *hear* a *soliloquy*? When might you *give* one?

_____

_____

ANSWERS TO CHAPTER 17 EXERCISES

Delineate: 1. b, c, d 2. b, c, f 3. 3
Denouement: 1. b, d 2. b, c, d 3. b
Deus ex machina: 1. a, c, d 2. a, c 3. b (characteristic)
Eloquent: 1. c, d, e, f 2. a, c, d 3. a, c, e
Epithet: 1. a, b, d 2. a, c, d 3. 1
Epitome: 1. b, d 2. a, c, d 3. 2
Ligature: 1. a, c 2. a, c, d 3. 1
Montage: 1. a, b 2. a, b, c 3. 5
Motif: 1. a, b, c, d, e, f 2. a, c, d 3. 1
Narrative: 1. a, b, c, d 2. a, d 3. c (characteristic)
Patron: 1. a, b, d 2. cc, dd, ee, aa, bb, ff 3. 2
Personify: 1. a, b 2. b, d 3. c (part of speech)
Profound: 1. a, b, d 2. s, s, s, s, a, a 3. 2
Repartee: 1. a, b, d 2. b, c 3. a, b, c
Soliloquy: 1. a, d 2. a, b, d 3. 2

If you missed any of the items in the exercises, return to the exercise and to the dictionary definition to see where you went wrong. Remember: If you get something right, you only affirm that you knew it. If you get something wrong and understand why, *you have learned something*.

ENGLISH POSTTEST

Fill in the blanks with the words from this list.

delineate	epitome	patron
denouement	ligature	personify
deus ex machina	montage	profound
eloquent	motif	repartee
epithet	narrative	soliloquy

1. A(n) _____ is a contrived solution.

2. To embody is to _____.

3. A(n) _____ is a distinctive feature in a design.

4. A bandage is an example of a(n) _____.

5. A(n) _____ is a benefactor.

6. *Outcome* is a synonym for _____.

7. To draw is to _____.

8. To be very expressive is to be _____.

9. _____ is clever talk.

10. Another word for _____ is *composite*.

11. An anecdote is a(n) _____.

12. _____ means "very deep."

13. A special type of actor's speech is a(n) _____.

14. A(n) _____ represents a general class.

15. "Jack-the-giant-killer" is John's _____.

Answers to this posttest are in the Instructor's Manual.

If you missed any of the words, you may need to return to the exercises and to the dictionary entries to see why your concepts for some words are incomplete.

HUMANITIES: HISTORY

◆

OVERVIEW

History is the study of the past of our society and how it impacts the present. It is concerned with trends, movements, and the growth of ideas. The study of history can enhance the quality of life for an individual through analysis of the history of other civilizations and cultures.

Major fields of study, or subdisciplines, within history include ancient and medieval history, the history of Europe, Africa, Near East, India and Southeast Asia, East Asia, Latin America, the United States, and Western and world civilization. There are also special fields of study, such as the history of science, history of religion, Russian history, and so forth.

Training in history prepares students for a wide range of career opportunities, including work in business, public relations, advertising, journalism, law, government, police and police-related agencies, and teaching of either history or social science.

Introductory textbooks in history can be structured in a variety of formats, including expository, descriptive, chronological, narrative, or cause and effect. Various time periods and political and social events provide the framework for many textbooks. Others approach the study of history through the cause-and-effect structure, with detailed analysis of events and their consequences.

The vocabulary in the field of history consists primarily of general vocabulary terms that can also have a specialized meaning within the context of history. Examples of such words are agrarian, precedent, *and* schism. *There are also many terms that have come from individuals (eponyms) and become synonymous with an era, event, or practice of government.* Machiavellian, Napoleonic, *and* Hamiltonian, *are such terms. Finally, specialized vocabulary is coined to represent the unique character-istics of certain eras, or time periods, such as* enlightenment, progressivism, *and* reformation.

VOCABULARY SELF-EVALUATION

The following words will be introduced in this reading selection. Place a check mark (√) in front of any that you know thoroughly and use in your speech and writing. Place a question mark (?) in front of any that you recognize but do not use yourself.

_____ agrarian	_____ dissension	_____ nonpareil
_____ analogous	_____ draconian	_____ phenomenon
_____ antipathy	_____ facet	_____ polemic
_____ arbiter	_____ inherent	_____ quintessential
_____ cursory	_____ nascent	_____ schism

HOW HISTORIANS DIFFER:
LOOKING AT COLUMBUS

Two problems face students of history who expect to study the field and learn "the truth" about the past. One problem is that reports of the same event oftentimes differ. The second problem is that varying interpretations of an event may be presented in different history texts. But neither of these problems is a phenomenon[1] necessarily limited to historical events. You may have had a comparable experience when you and several friends took part in the same event and, discussing it later, discovered that you each had a different memory of the event and a different view of what the activities meant. Understanding how this kind of disagreement can come about is the first step in evaluating the polemics[2] that are inherent[3] to the field of history.

One outstanding example of this type of controversy concerns the voyages of Christopher Columbus. Complete information about events that took place so long ago is, of course, not available. In addition, many of the persons and societies affected kept limited records. Nevertheless, the accepted facts include the lengthy sea voyage that was made into largely uncharted waters, the territory on which the voyagers landed, and the overall effect of connecting the continent of Europe with the continents of North and South America. Interpretations of the events differ, however.

Four factors have aroused antipathy[4] in those who look at the available data and attempt to interpret them. A cursory[5] examination of the information seems to reveal that, as many historians have claimed, Columbus discovered America. Yet other historians disagree with this claim. Some argue with the term *discover*, saying that existing lands do not need to be found and that only the Europeans' ignorance of the territory led them to claim such a "discovery." Another disagreement has to do with the area where Columbus and his men landed. Some historians argue that credit for discovery of America should not be given to an explorer who landed on neither of the large continents that came to be called North and South America. They reason that this is analogous[6] to saying that England could be discovered by someone who landed in Ireland.

A third factor creating dissension[7] has to do with Columbus the man. One group views him as the quintessential[8] explorer, brave and resourceful. How else could he have set out on uncharted waters and located unknown lands? The opposing group, however, cites the voyages of other explorers, such as Magellan, Vasco da Gama, and Cortez, as equally daring and successful.

The final point of dissension, heatedly argued, has to do with the purposes and results of the "discovery." The schism[9] is primarily between historians with the Old World (western European) view and those with the New World (native American) view. Many who have the Old World view see the goals of Columbus as worthy and

the results as beneficial. They note that he introduced great numbers of people to Christianity and transformed a largely agrarian[10] society into one that would benefit both the Old World, in the form of resources, and the New World, in the form of progress. But other historians see the goals of Columbus as immoral and the results as a disaster nonpareil.[11] They point to Old World greed as the driving force behind the voyages, to the diseases introduced by the Europeans that destroyed thousands of natives, and to the draconian[12] measures that killed thousands more. The large number of deaths led to whole tribes of local natives being wiped out within one hundred years of the first voyage of Columbus.

The numerous disagreements concerning this one historical event demonstrate the difficulty facing the serious reader. As a nascent[13] student of history you must learn to evaluate the reliability of reporting sources to determine which of the presented information is likely to be accurate. In addition, you must try to determine if one of the opposing viewpoints is more accurate than another or if the alternate viewpoints are correct in some ways and incorrect in others. To do this you must examine the facets[14] of the past that are presented, link them to what you know of human nature and behavior, and reach your own conclusions. Extensive reading and discussion will help. In a free society there is no appointed arbiter[15] to make a final decision about what is "right" and what is "wrong" in the records and evaluations of history. ◆

HISTORY PRETEST

Select words from this list and write them in the blanks to complete the sentences.

agrarian   arbiter   draconian
analogous   cursory   facet
antipathy   dissension   inherent

nascent   phenomenon   quintessential
nonpareil   polemic   schism

1. Things comparable are _____.

2. Something superficial is _____.

3. _____ means "just beginning to develop."

4. Someone with the power to decide is a(n) _____.

5. A circumstance that can be observed is a(n) _____.

6. _____ means "agricultural."

7. A breach is a(n) _____.

8. _____ is another word for *disagreement.*

9. _____ means "without equal."

10. A(n) _____ is a feeling against something.

11. *Harsh* is a synonym for _____.

12. _____ refers to controversy.

13. Something born within us is _____.

14. _____ means "of the purest kind."

15. A distinct part of something is a(n) _____.

Answers to this pretest are in Appendix B.

Unless your instructor tells you to do otherwise, complete the exercises for each word you missed on the pretest. The words, with their meanings and exercises, are in alphabetical order. The superscript numbers indicate where the words appeared in the reading selection so that you can refer to them when necessary. There are several types of exercises, but for each word you will be asked to write a sentence using context clues. (See Chapter 4 if you need information about how to create context clues.) You are also asked to perform some activity that will help you make your concept of the word personal. *Complete this activity thoughtfully, for creating a personalized concept of the word will help you remember it in the future.*

Answers to all the exercises are at the end of the exercise segment.

HISTORY EXERCISES

Agrarian[10]

a|grar|i|an (ə grãr′ē ən), *adj., n. —adj.* **1a** having to do with farming land, its use, or its ownership. **b** for the support and advancement of farmers and farming: *an agrarian movement.* **2** agricultural. **3** growing wild in the fields, as certain plants. —*n.* a person who favors a new or more equitable division of rural land. [< Latin *agrārius* (< *ager, agrī* field)]

1. In which of the following sentences can *agrarian* correctly be placed in the blank?

    _____ a. My friend Tom farms sixty acres, so I call him an _____ .

    _____ b. Government _____ policies have harmed many farmers.

    _____ c. Certain _____ plants cause damage to those plants intentionally grown.

    _____ d. _____ practices in colonial America, particularly the continuous planting of cotton and tobacco, greatly depleted the soil.

2. If you are interested in things *agrarian,* you might

    _____ a. go to medical schoool.

    _____ b. raise hundreds of acres of wheat.

    _____ c. join with other farmers to influence government policy.

    _____ d. sell your farm to a land developer.

3. Which of the numbered and lettered dictionary definitions of *agrarian* best fits the word's use in the reading selection? _____

4. Write a sentence correctly using *agrarian.* (Be sure to include context clues to show you understand the meaning of the word.)

    _____

    _____

5. Can any country survive without a successful *agrarian* population? Do we have such a population in this country?

    _____

    _____

Analogous[6]

a|nal|o|gous (ə nal′ə gəs), *adj.* **1** alike in some way; similar in the quality or feature that is being thought of, or in circumstances or uses; comparable (to): *The human heart is analogous to a pump. Who can say that the anatomy of modern despotism is significantly analogous to the anatomy of despotism in the declining Roman Empire?* (Bulletin of Atomic Scientists). **SYN:** corresponding, like. **2** *Biology.* corresponding in function, but not in structure and origin: *The wing of a fly is analogous to the wing of a bird.* [< Latin *analogus* (with English *-ous*) < Greek *análogos* proportionate < *aná lógon* according to due ratio] — a|nal′o|gous|ly, *adv.* — a|nal′o|gous-ness, *n.*

1. Match the following statement with a similar statement below: "The historiographer showed that Hitler and Napoleon were *analogous.*"

    _____ a. The historian made a study of invading armies.

    _____ b. The writer saw differences between Germany and France.

    _____ c. Some historians are interested in powerful rulers.

    _____ d. The writer set out similarities between the German and the French leaders.

2. Select any adjective that describes something *analogous*.

　　_____ a. corresponding 　　_____ d. dissimilar

　　_____ b. inconsistent 　　_____ e. resembling

　　_____ c. comparable 　　_____ f. similar

3. Which of the following might be *analogous*, and how are they alike?

　　_____ a. a bird's wing and an airplane's wing

　　　　　　　　　　　　　Alike in _____.

　　_____ b. a window and a light bulb

　　　　　　　　　　　　　Alike in _____.

　　_____ c. love and hate

　　　　　　　　　　　　　Alike in _____.

　　_____ d. television and live theater

　　　　　　　　　　　　　Alike in _____.

4. If you could make your life *analogous* to the life of any public figure, whom would you choose?

　　_____

5. Write a sentence correctly using *analogous*. (Be sure to include context clues to show you understand the meaning of the word.)

　　_____

　　_____

Antipathy[4]

an|tip|a|thy (an tip'ə thē), *n., pl.* **-thies. 1** a strong or fixed dislike; a feeling against; aversion: *She felt an antipathy to snakes.* **SYN:** repugnance, abhorrence, disgust. **2** something or someone that arouses such a feeling; an object of aversion or dislike: *The Scots and nonconformists were antipathies of Dr. Johnson.* **3** *Obsolete.* contrariety of feeling, disposition, or nature. [< Latin *antipathīa* < Greek *antipátheia* < *anti-* against + *páthos* feeling]

1. Check any appropriate response to the following statement:

　　"George is developing an *antipathy* to his country's form of government."

　　_____ a. It must mean he is a happy citizen.

　　_____ b. He should try to move away.

　　_____ c. Oh, everyone has family problems.

　　_____ d. If enough others feel that way, there may be a change.

2. Place an "s" by any synonym and an "a" by any antonym of *antipathy*.

　　_____ a. repugnance 　　_____ d. disgust

　　_____ b. affection 　　_____ e. aversion

　　_____ c. fondness 　　_____ f. abhorrence

3. Which of the numbered dictionary definitions of *antipathy* best fits the word's use in the reading selection? _____

4. Write a sentence correctly using *antipathy*. (Be sure to include context clues to show you understand the meaning of the word.)

_____

_____

5. For what or whom do you have an *antipathy?*

_____

_____

Arbiter[15]

ar|bi|ter (är′bə tər), *n.* **1** a person with full power to judge or decide: *Dress designers are arbiters of ladies' fashion.* **2** a person chosen to decide or settle a dispute; arbitrator. SYN: umpire, judge. [< Latin *arbiter* (originally) one who approaches (two disputants) < *ad-* up to + *baetere* go]

1. In which of the following sentences can *arbiter* correctly be placed in the blank?
   _____ a. Irene thinks she is the _____ of correct dress, and she always finds fault with my clothing.
   _____ b. A movie critic may give an opinion about a film, but the movie-going public is the final _____.
   _____ c. An _____ has been chosen to settle the dispute between the two business owners.
   _____ d. My job is to find out which books people read most often so I can be an _____.

2. Check any characteristic of an *arbiter.*
   _____ a. expresses an opinion
   _____ b. makes a judgment
   _____ c. acts as an umpire
   _____ d. accepted by some as authority

3. Complete the verbal analogy.
   sun : warmth :: *arbiter* : _____
   a. approach   c. person
   b. leader   d. power

4. Your friends disagree on whether to serve "American" hamburgers or an ethnic food such as Mexican tacos or German sausages at an upcoming party. You are chosen to be *arbiter*. Which do you decide should be served? _____ Does an *arbiter* need good reasons for his or her choices? _____

5. Write a sentence correctly using *arbiter*. (Be sure to include context clues to show you understand the meaning of the word.)

_____

_____

CHAPTER EIGHTEEN

Cursory[5]

cur|so|ry (kėr′sər ē), *adj.* without attention to details; hasty and superficial: *He gave the lesson a cursory glance, expecting to study it later. Even a cursory reading of the letter showed many errors.* SYN: rapid, hurried. [< Latin *cursŏrius* of a race < *currere* run] —**cur′so|ri|ly,** *adv.* —**cur′so|ri|ness,** *n.*

1. Place an "s" by any synonym and an "a" by any antonym of *cursory*.

   _____ a. careful   _____ d. superficial
   _____ b. thorough   _____ e. hurried
   _____ c. painstaking   _____ f. swearing

2. In which of the following sentences is *cursory* used correctly?

   _____ a. This is too important to be treated in a cursory manner.
   _____ b. He gave her a cursory look and went on down the street.
   _____ c. Her cursory attitude made her continually late.
   _____ d. Although his studies were cursory, he still passed the examination.

3. The etymology of *cursory* shows that it comes from the Latin *currere* (to run). Use this information, your background knowledge, and your imagination to match the following:

   _____ a. concur   aa. to have or express the same opinion
   _____ b. current   bb. a steady and smooth movement, as of water
   _____ c. cursive   cc. covering a wide field of subjects; rambling
   _____ d. cursor   dd. to happen again repeatedly
   _____ e. discursive   ee. a flashing moving pointer on a computer screen
   _____ f. recur   ff. written with flowing strokes

4. What is the most recent thing you read in a *cursory* fashion?

   _____

   _____

5. Write a sentence correctly using *cursory*. (Be sure to include context clues to show you understand the meaning of the word.)

   _____

   _____

Dissension[7]

dis|sen|sion (di sen′shən), *n.* a disputing; a quarreling; hard feeling caused by a difference in opinion: *The club broke up because of dissension among its members.* SYN: discord, disagreement, contention. Also, **dissention.** [< Old French *dissension,* learned borrowing from Latin *dissensiō, -ōnis* < *dissentīre;* see etym. under **dissent**]

from **dissent:**

[< Latin *dissentīre* < *dis-* apart, differently + *sentīre* think, feel]

HUMANITIES: HISTORY

1. Select any appropriate response(s) to the following statement:
"There is *dissension* in the political science department of this university."
   _____ a. Understanding and cooperation are the causes.
   _____ b. It probably occurs because the faculty members come from such different backgrounds.
   _____ c. A situation like that makes the university a better school.
   _____ d. Sometimes the more we know the less we can agree.

2. Check any characteristic of *dissension*.
   _____ a. disagreeing   _____ d. at odds
   _____ b. harmonious   _____ e. unanimous
   _____ c. quarrelsome   _____ f. discordant

3. The etymology of *dissension* shows that it comes from the Latin *dis* (apart) and *sentire* (to feel). Use that information, your imagination, and your background knowledge to match the following:
   _____ a. assent   aa. to feel angry
   _____ b. consent   bb. to give permission
   _____ c. resent   cc. a mixture of thought and feeling
   _____ d. sense   dd. to express agreement
   _____ e. sentiment   ee. judgment; intelligence

4. If you wanted to cause *dissension* in a group, what is one thing you might do?

   _____

   _____

5. Write a sentence correctly using *dissension*. (Be sure to include context clues to show you understand the meaning of the word.)

   _____

   _____

Draconian[12]

Dra|co|ni|an (drə kō′nē ən), *adj.* **1** of or having to do with Draco, a legislator of Athens in the 600's B.C., or his severe code of laws. **2** severe; cruel; harsh.

(Note: There is not yet agreement whether this word is completely naturalized. Some writers and dictionaries use a capital D, while others do not. A capital letter indicates that the word still refers primarily to the person or place that inspired it (in this case, the Athenian legislator), while a lowercase letter indicates the word has been used widely enough to have taken on a more general meaning, in this instance the meanings "severe," "cruel," and "harsh.")

1. Match the following statement with a similar statement below:
   "Some believe war preferable to a *draconian* peace."
   _____ a. Peace promotes a happy society.
   _____ b. Only the strong can endure a harsh peace.
   _____ c. Wars are fought by those who believe might makes right.
   _____ d. Some prefer to fight in open battle rather than live in a peaceful but cruel society.

2. Place an "s" by any synonym and an "a" by any antonym of *draconian*.
   _____ a. lenient   _____ d. stringent
   _____ b. stern   _____ e. mild
   _____ c. rigid   _____ f. merciful

3. Complete the verbal analogy.
   open : closed :: *draconian* : _____
   a. indulgent   c. intemperate
   b. inflexible   d. impartial

4. Write a sentence correctly using *draconian*. (Be sure to include context clues to show you understand the meaning of the word.)

   _____

   _____

5. Do you believe the death penalty is a *draconian* law?

   _____

   _____

Facet[14]

✳**fac|et** (fas′it), *n., v.,* -et|ed, -et|ing or (*especially British*) -et|ted, -et|ting. —*n.* 1 any one of the small, polished, flat surfaces of a cut gem. 2 anything like the facet of a gem. See the picture above on the following page. 3 *Figurative.* any one of several sides or views; a distinct part; phase; aspect: *a facet of the mind, a facet of a problem. Selfishness was a facet of his character that we seldom saw.* 4 *Zoology.* one of the individual external visual units of a compound eye: *The eyes of certain insects have facets.* 5 *Architecture.* the vertical band or strip between the flutes of a column. 6 *Anatomy.* a small, smooth, flat surface, especially on a bone.

—*v.t.* 1 to cut facets on: *Next, we visited the rooms in which the diamonds were faceted* (New Yorker). 2 *Geology.* to grind off flat surfaces on (ridges, stones, or the like).
—*v.i. Geology.* to be ground off by glacial action, winds, or water.
[< French *facette* (diminutive) < Old French *face;* see etym. under **face**]

facets

✳**facet**
definition 1

1. In which of the following sentences is *facet(s)* used correctly?
   _____ a. The facet of Tony's personality I like best is his honesty.
   _____ b. In biology, we are studying the facets of a fly's eye.
   _____ c. My job is to facet stones for jewelry.
   _____ d. Bob damaged the facet of his ulna when he broke his arm.

2. Check any appropriate response to the following statement:
"That *facet* of the problem is easily understood."
_____ a. We will have to work hard to figure this out.
_____ b. That is an easy phase.
_____ c. But some other aspects are difficult.
_____ d. Each distinct part should be considered carefully.

3. Which of the numbered dictionary definitions of *facet* best fits the word's use in the reading selection? _____

4. What *facet* of your education is the most interesting?

_____

_____

5. Write a sentence correctly using *facet*. (Be sure to include context clues to show you understand the meaning of the word.)

_____

_____

Inherent[3]

in|her|ent (in hir′ənt, -her′-), *adj.* belonging to a person or thing as a quality or attribute; essential: *inherent honesty. In spite of flattery, the pretty girl kept her inherent modesty. There is an inherent tendency in opinion to feed upon rumors excited by our own wishes and fears* (Atlantic). **SYN:** innate, inborn, inbred, intrinsic. [< Latin *inhaerēns, -entis*, present participle of *inhaerēre* inhere] — **in|her′ent|ly**, *adv.*

1. Place an "s" in front of any synonym of *inherent*.
_____ a. innate   _____ d. inbred
_____ b. inborn   _____ e. immaterial
_____ c. intrinsic   _____ f. acquired

2. In which of the following sentences can *inherent* correctly be placed in the blank?
_____ a. There is often a difference between our _____ feelings and our outward expression of them.
_____ b. Mary's character is notable for its _____ laziness.
_____ c. The constitution of the United States is based on a belief in _____ human rights.
_____ d. Juan was lucky enough to _____ a large amount of money from his grandfather.

3. Complete the verbal analogy.
talkative : mute :: *inherent* : _____
a. alien   c. orderly
b. necessary   d. component

4. What characteristic do you have that is like that of another family member (brother, sister, father, mother, aunt, uncle, etc.)? _____ Do you believe this characteristic is *inherent*, or is it acquired? _____

5. Write a sentence correctly using *inherent*. (Be sure to include context clues to show you understand the meaning of the word.)

_____

_____

Nascent[13]

nas|cent (nas′ənt, nā′sənt), *adj.* **1** in the process of coming into existence; just beginning to exist, grow, or develop: *a nascent sense of right and wrong.* SYN: incipient, inchoate. **2** *Chemistry.* **a** having to do with the state or condition of an element at the instant it is set free from a combination. **b** (of an element) being in a free or uncombined state. [< Latin *nāscēns, -entis,* present participle of *nāscī* be born] —**nas′cent|ly,** *adv.*

1. Match the following statement with a similar statement below:
   "A study of the population revealed *nascent* revolutionary tendencies."
   _____ a. A study of the people showed history was repeating itself.
   _____ b. Information gathered offered evidence of the beginnings of a revolution.
   _____ c. Facts demonstrated a revolution had occurred.
   _____ d. A study has been made of the beginnings of the nation.

2. The etymology of *nascent* shows that the word comes from the Latin *nasci* (to be born). Use this information, your imagination, and your background knowledge to match the following:
   _____ a. cognate   aa. a song pertaining to the birthday of Christ
   _____ b. natal   bb. a newborn child
   _____ c. neonate   cc. having a common ancestor; related by blood
   _____ d. noël   dd. pertaining to the time or place of one's birth

3. Which of the following describes something *nascent?*
   _____ a. beginning   _____ d. incipient
   _____ b. completed   _____ e. initial
   _____ c. ultimate   _____ f. commencing

4. What segment of your knowledge base is *nascent?* Traveling abroad? Making investments? Learning a profession?

_____

_____

5. Write a sentence correctly using *nascent*. (Be sure to include context clues to show you understand the meaning of the word.)

_____

_____

Nonpareil[11]

non|pa|reil (non′pe rel′), *adj., n.* — *adj.* having no equal; peerless: *The literary salons have had a major part in making Paris the city nonpareil, for centuries the undisputed cultural centre of the world* (Canadian Forum).
— *n.* **1** a person or thing having no equal: *Though you were crown'd The nonpareil of beauty* (Shakespeare). **2** a beautifully colored finch of the southern United States; painted bunting. **3** a kind of apple. **4** *Printing.* **a** a size of type; 6-point. **b** a slug 6 points high used between lines. **5** a small chocolate drop covered with tiny white pellets of sugar.
[< Middle French *nonpareil* < *non-* not (< Latin) + *pareil* equal < Vulgar Latin *pāriculus* (diminutive) < Latin *pār, paris* equal]

1. In which of the following sentences can *nonpareil* correctly be placed in the blank?
   _____ a. My sister Ann is a _____ housekeeper and cook.
   _____ b. The art critic praised the _____ beauty of the Mona Lisa.
   _____ c. The violinist Itzhak Perlman is a virtuoso and a _____ .
   _____ d. The candidate does not belong to any political party, so he is said to be _____ .

2. Complete the verbal analogy.
   clean : spotless :: *nonpareil* : _____
   a. careless   c. restless
   b. helpless   d. matchless

3. The etymology of *nonpareil* indicates the word comes from the Latin *par, paris* (equal). Use this information, your imagination, and your background knowledge to match the following:
   _____ a. compare   aa. equality, as in amount or value
   _____ b. pair   bb. to bet an original wager and its winnings on a subsequent event
   _____ c. parity   cc. a person who has equal standing with another
   _____ d. parlay   dd. two equal or similar items
   _____ e. peer   ee. to represent as similar or equal

4. Write a sentence correctly using *nonpareil*. (Be sure to include context clues to show you understand the meaning of the word.)

_____

_____

5. Who do you think is the female singer *nonpareil* today?

_____

_____

Phenomenon[1]

phe|nom|e|non (fə nom′ə non), *n., pl.* **-na** or (*especially for def. 4*) **-nons. 1** a fact, event, or circumstance that can be observed: *Lightning is an electrical phenomenon.* **2** any sign, symptom, or manifestation: *Fever and inflammation are phenomena of disease.* **3** any exceptional fact or occurrence: *historical phenomena.* **4** something or someone extraordinary or remarkable: *The Grand Canyon is a phenomenon of nature. The fond grandparents think their daughter's little son is a phenomenon.* **5** *Philosophy.* something that the senses or the mind directly takes note of; an immediate object of perception, as distinguished from a thing-in-itself. [< Late Latin *phaenomenon* appearance < Greek *phainómenon,* ultimately < *phaínein* show forth]

1. In which of the following sentences can *phenomenon* correctly be placed in the blank?

   _____ a. A total eclipse of the sun is a _____ that occurs rarely.

   _____ b. In some societies, an unexplained _____ is thought to be a form of magic.

   _____ c. The _____ of an organism is its physical appearance.

   _____ d. A man seven feet tall could be considered a _____ .

2. The etymology of *phenomenon* shows that the word comes from the Greek *phainein* (show forth). Use that information, your imagination, and your background knowledge to match the following:

   _____ a. diaphanous   aa. a sudden insight into something

   _____ b. epiphany   bb. a shadowy appearance; ghost

   _____ c. phantom   cc. transparent; translucent

   _____ d. phosphine   dd. a colorless, poisonous gas with an odor like garlic

3. Which of the numbered dictionary definitions of *phenomenon* best fits the word's use in the reading selection? _____

4. Write a sentence correctly using *phenomenon.* (Be sure to include context clues to show you understand the meaning of the word.)

   _____

   _____

5. What person in the sports or entertainment world would you identify as a *phenomenon* (definition 4)?

   _____

   _____

Polemic[2]

pol|lem|ic (pə lem′ik), *n., adj.* —*n.* **1** a disputing discussion; argument; controversy: *Writing polemics against a czar in a candlelit cellar could be dangerous* (Newsweek). **2** a person who takes part in a controversy or argument.
—*adj.* of controversy or disagreement; of dispute: *My father's little library consisted chiefly of books in polemic divinity* (Benjamin Franklin). **SYN:** controversial.
[< Greek *polemikós* belligerent < *pólemos* war]
—**pol|lem′i|cal|ly,** *adv.*

1. A *polemic* is likely to be
   _____ a. harmonious.   _____ d. peaceable.
   _____ b. an argument.   _____ e. neutral.
   _____ c. a debate.   _____ f. a disagreement.

2. In which of the following sentences can *polemic* correctly be placed in the blank?
   _____ a. I don't find the book interesting; it is too full of _____s.
   _____ b. Olson's writing is _____ and not always fair to his opponents.
   _____ c. Their discussion was calm, and neither resorted to _____s.
   _____ d. If you practice _____s in the United States, you will be sent to jail.

3. Complete the verbal analogy.
   happy : sad :: *polemic* : _____
   a. argumentative   c. belligerent
   b. amiable   d. interminable

4. In what area of your life are you likely to engage in a *polemic?* Why do you feel so strongly?

   _____

   _____

5. Write a sentence correctly using *polemic.* (Be sure to include context clues to show you understand the meaning of the word.)

   _____

   _____

Quintessential[8]

quin|tes|sen|tial (kwin'tə sen'shəl), *adj.* having the nature of a quintessence; of the purest or most perfect kind: *Costain has created what amounts to a quintessential recapture of the English novel, from Smollett to Dickens* (Wall Street Journal). *They don't pay sufficient attention to the quintessential requirement: that it be easy for the reader to find what he is looking for* (Atlantic).
quin|tes|sence (kwin tes'əns), *n.* **1** the purest form of some quality; pure essence. **SYN:** pith. **2** the most perfect example of something: *Her costume was the quintessence of good taste and style.* **3** (in medieval philosophy) the ether of Aristotle, a fifth element (added to earth, water, fire, and air) permeating all things and forming the substance of the heavenly bodies. [< Middle French *quinte essence,* learned borrowing from Medieval Latin *quinta essentia* fifth essence, translation of Greek *pémptē ousíā* Aristotle's "fifth substance"]

1. In which of the following sentences can *quintessential* correctly be placed in the blank?
   _____ a. Sam is the _____ bore, as far as I am concerned.
   _____ b. Many believe Paris to be the _____ city of the world.
   _____ c. When I travel, I take only the _____s.
   _____ d. According to my teacher, the _____ characteristic of music is melody.

2. If John is the *quintessential* stage actor,

_____ a. he performs best in the movies.

_____ b. he probably has won many awards.

_____ c. he has yet to be discovered.

_____ d. others study his acting methods.

3. Complete the verbal analogy.

ease : without discomfort :: *quintessential* : _____

a. an example   c. only example

b. best example   d. natural example

4. Write a sentence correctly using *quintessential*. (Be sure to include context clues to show you understand the meaning of the word.)

_____

_____

5. In your opinion, who is the *quintessential* male singer today?

_____

_____

Schism[9]

schism (siz′əm, skiz′-), *n.* **1** a division into hostile groups: ... *the possibility of a serious schism in the ranks of one of the two big British parties* (Wall Street Journal). **2** a discord or breach between persons or things. **3a** the division, either of the whole Church or of some portion of it, into separate and hostile organizations, because of some difference of opinion about religion. **b** the offense of causing or trying to cause such a schism. **c** a sect or group formed by a schism within a church. [< Latin *schisma* < Greek *schisma, -atos* < *schizein* to split]

1. In which of the following sentences is *schism* correctly used?

_____ a. A schism in the earth causes an earthquake.

_____ b. There is a difference of opinion in the church, but we hope it will not produce a schism.

_____ c. Any schism in a political party weakens it.

_____ d. There seems to be a widening schism between the rich and the poor in many countries.

2. Place an "s" by any synonym and an "a" by any antonym of *schism*.

_____ a. division   _____ d. healing

_____ b. union   _____ e. unanimity

_____ c. rupture   _____ f. split

3. Which of the numbered and lettered dictionary definitions of *schism* best fits the word's use in the reading selection? _____

4. What might cause a *schism* in a family?

_____

_____

5. Write a sentence correctly using *schism*. (Be sure to include context clues to show you understand the meaning of the word.)

_____

_____

ANSWERS TO CHAPTER 18 EXERCISES

Agrarian: **1.** b, c, d **2.** b, c **3.** 2
Analogous: **1.** d **2.** a, c, e, f **3.** a (function), b (function and composition), c (intense emotion), d (function or purpose)
Antipathy: **1.** b, d **2.** s, a, a, s, s, s **3.** 1
Arbiter: **1.** a, b, c **2.** a, b, c, d **3.** d (characteristic)
Cursory: **1.** a, a, a, s, s,— **2.** a, b, d **3.** aa, bb, ff, ee, cc, dd
Dissension: **1.** b, d **2.** a, c, d, f **3.** dd, bb, aa, ee, cc
Draconian: **1.** d **2.** a, s, s, s, a, a **3.** a (antonym)
Facet: **1.** a, b, c, d **2.** b, c, d **3.** *n.* 3
Inherent: **1.** a, b, c, d **2.** a, b, c **3.** a (opposite)
Nascent: **1.** b **2.** cc, dd, bb, aa **3.** a, d, e, f
Nonpareil: **1.** a, b, c **2.** d (synonym) **3.** ee, dd, aa, bb, cc
Phenomenon: **1.** a, b, d **2.** cc, aa, bb, dd **3.** 1
Polemic: **1.** b, c, f **2.** a, b, c **3.** b (antonym)
Quintessential: **1.** a, b, d **2.** b, d **3.** b (definition)
Schism: **1.** b, c, d **2.** s, a, s, a, a, s **3.** 2

If you missed any of the items in the exercises, return to the exercise and to the dictionary definition to see where you went wrong. Remember: If you get something right, you only affirm that you knew it. If you get something wrong and understand why, *you have learned something.*

HISTORY POSTTEST

Fill in the blanks with the words from this list.

agrarian   dissension   nonpareil
analogous   draconian   phenomenon
antipathy   facet   polemic
arbiter   inherent   quintessential
cursory   nascent   schism

1. A(n) ＿＿＿＿＿＿＿ is a small, polished flat surface.

2. A synonym of ＿＿＿＿＿＿＿ is *incipient.*

3. A small chocolate drop with white sugar pellets is a(n) ＿＿＿＿＿＿＿.

4. ＿＿＿＿＿＿＿ means "aversion."

5. A disputing discussion is a(n) ＿＿＿＿＿＿＿.

6. *Umpire* is a synonym of ＿＿＿＿＿＿＿.

7. The perfect example of something is ＿＿＿＿＿＿＿.

8. A(n) ＿＿＿＿＿＿＿ is a division into hostile groups.

9. One who favors equitable division of rural land is a(n) ＿＿＿＿＿＿＿.

10. Something that is similar is ＿＿＿＿＿＿＿.

11. ＿＿＿＿＿＿＿ refers to a severe code of laws.

12. *Hasty* is a synonym of ＿＿＿＿＿＿＿.

13. A(n) ＿＿＿＿＿＿＿ is a sign or symptom.

14. *Contention* is another word for ＿＿＿＿＿＿＿.

15. Something that is ＿＿＿＿＿＿＿ is an essential attribute.

Answers to this posttest are in the Instructor's Manual.

If you missed any of the words, you may need to return to the exercises and to the dictionary entries to see why your concepts for some words are incomplete.

CHAPTER NINETEEN

HUMANITIES:
MUSIC

◆

OVERVIEW

Music is the art of making sounds that are beautiful and putting them together into pleasing or interesting arrangements. The study of music deals with the principles of melody, harmony, rhythm, tempo, and timbre. Through the study of music one can acquire a deeper understanding of the many ways that music permeates our cultures, affects our feelings, and influences our lives.

Concentrations within music include coursework in composition and theory, history and literature, musicology, performance (solo instruments, voice, opera, conducting), and music education.

A degree in music provides preparation for teaching and advanced studies in theory, literature, musicology, musical acoustics, library science in music, and music in industry and recreation. Another emphasis within music programs prepares students in composition, instrumental performance (violin, flute, etc.), keyboard performance (piano, organ, etc.), vocal performance, accompanying, and conducting.

Introductory textbooks in music combine expository, instructional, and historical formats. They provide information on broad concepts or generalizations, present a historical perspective with time lines of individual works and composers, and include instructional procedures very often linked to an auditory reproduction of music. Many texts include examples of musical scores or movements from pages of music notation.

The vocabulary in music is a combination of the general and the specialized. Some words have a general meaning outside of the context of music but a specific meaning

298

within its context, such as tone, theme, *and* phrase. *There are also specialized vocabulary terms unique to the study of music, such as* opera, sonata, *and* monophony.

VOCABULARY SELF-EVALUATION

The following words will be introduced in this reading selection. Place a check mark (√) in front of any that you know thoroughly and use in your speech and writing. Place a question mark (?) in front of any that you recognize but do not use yourself.

_____ adagio	_____ counterpoint	_____ secular
_____ allegro	_____ dynamics	_____ sonata
_____ andante	_____ homophony	_____ timbre
_____ cantata	_____ oratorio	_____ tone
_____ concerto	_____ polyphony	_____ virtuosity

THE ORIGINS OF MUSIC PERFORMANCE

The history of music can be traced back to ancient times. Vocal music was one of the earliest types of music, being an important part of religious ceremonies. Slowly, instruments, particularly wind instruments, began to evolve and to be used to accompany the vocal part. Each instrument provided its own distinctive timbre[1] that enhanced the vocal performance. Eventually, keyboard instruments such as the clavichord, harpsichord, and organ were invented. These instruments enabled composers to add more depth of tone[2] and virtuosity[3] to the pieces of the time. Today, there are three major classifications of musical performance—vocal, instrumental, and keyboard—with each having its own beauty and uniqueness. Vocal music's beauty is in the production of tone and phrasing. Instrumental music has its beauty not only in the production of tone but also in the various instruments' distinctive timbres. Finally, keyboard music acquires its beauty from delicate phrasing, greater depth of tone, and fiery virtuosity.

The earliest vocal music, known as monophony, was melody without harmony or counterpoint.[4] The elements of notation, with a system of symbols for musical sounds as we know them today, did not exist at that time. There were neither time signatures nor key signatures. Gradually, composers began juxtapositioning two or more melodies against each other, thereby creating polyphony.[5] Even later, chordal instrumental music was added to the solo vocal melody. When all the parts moved in the same, or nearly the same, rhythm, this became known as homophony.[6] The development of time signatures and key signatures helped instrumentalists and vocalists to agree on how the piece was to be performed.

Three major forms in vocal music are opera, cantata,[7] and oratorio.[8] An opera is a play, mostly sung, with costumes, scenery, acting, and music. Well-known examples are Georges Bizet's *Carmen* and Giuseppe Verdi's *La Traviata*. Both the cantata and the oratorio, however, are performed without action, costumes, or scenery. The cantata is a dramatic narrative, about ten to fifteen minutes in length, and is similar to a scene from an opera. Both operas and cantatas may be based on secular[9] themes. Noted cantata composers are Giacomo Carissimi, Luigi Rossi, and Marc Antonio Cesti. The oratorio, on the other hand, usually is based on a religious theme and is written for solo voices and orchestra. George Frideric Handel and Franz Joseph Haydn are noted composers of the oratorio.

Both instrumental and keyboard music began as accompaniments for vocal music. Later, as instruments began to be considered specialties in their own right, composers began writing instrumental solo pieces. As keyboard instruments evolved, the pieces became more complex and were written to incorporate different tempos, such as adagio,[10] andante,[11] and allegro,[12] to indicate whether the piece should be played slowly, moderately, or quickly, respectively. These designations indicated the spirit of the music as well as the speed at which it should be played. Keyboard instruments began to use dynamics[13] that controlled force and volume.

Both instrumental and keyboard music experienced the transition from monophony to polyphony in their development. Two major forms of instrumental and keyboard music are the sonata[14] and the concerto.[15] The sonata is a form written for one or two instruments, with three or four movements in different keys and contrasting rhythms; the concerto is written for an orchestra and one or more solo instruments, such as the violin or piano, and typically consists of three movements. The different movements divide a long selection into separate units, distinguished from each other by tempo and by melodic and rhythmic structure. The concerto became the most important type of orchestral music after 1700.

Over time, vocal, instrumental, and keyboard forms of music have evolved new features, and performers of each type have developed new performing styles. Early music, in original form, played on classical instruments, may be heard today only in special performances. Nevertheless, information about the historical development of music can add quality to our appreciation of it as a performing art. ◆

MUSIC PRETEST

Select words from this list and write them in the blanks to complete the sentences.

adagio	cantata	dynamics
allegro	concerto	homophony
andante	counterpoint	oratorio

polyphony   sonata   tone
secular   timbre   virtuosity

1. Having skill or cultivated appreciation in the techniques of an art, such as in playing a musical instrument, is called _____.

2. The difference in pitch between two notes or a sound of definite pitch and character is known as _____.

3. Something played quickly and lively is being played _____.

4. A piece of music to be played by one or more principal instruments, such as violin or piano, with orchestral accompaniment is a(n) _____.

5. Music having two or more voices or parts, each with an independent but harmonizing melody, is called _____.

6. Any offsetting point or contrast might be called _____.

7. Things not religious or sacred are _____.

8. The quality in sounds, regardless of their pitch or volume, by which a voice or an instrument can be distinguished from another voice or instrument is known as _____.

9. _____ describes a moderately slow movement of music.

10. A(n) _____ is an instrumental composition with three or four movements in contrasted rhythms or keys.

11. Variation in force or loudness, such as decrease or increase in volume, is known as _____.

12. _____ refers to a musical composition, usually based on a religious theme, for solo voices, chorus, and orchestra.

13. Music that is played slowly is described as _____.

14. A(n) _____ is a musical composition consisting of a story or play that is sung by a chorus and soloists but not acted.

15. _____ is the musical texture in which the voice parts move in the same, or nearly the same, rhythm.

Answers to this pretest are in Appendix B.
　　Unless your instructor tells you to do otherwise, complete the exercises for each word you missed on the pretest. The words, with their meanings and exercises, are in alphabetical order. The superscript numbers indicate where the words appeared in the reading selection so that you can refer to them when necessary. There are several types of exercises, and more than one answer may be correct. For each word you will be asked to write a sentence using context clues. (See Chapter 4 if you need information about how to create context clues.) You are also asked to perform some activity that will help you make your concept of the word personal. *Complete this*

activity thoughtfully, for creating a personalized concept of the word will help you remember it in the future.

Answers to all the exercises are at the end of the exercise segment.

MUSIC EXERCISES

Adagio[10]

a|da|gio (ə dä′jō, -zhē ō, -zhō), *adv., adj., n., pl.* **-gios.** —*adv. Music.* somewhat slowly; more slowly than andante (used as a direction). —*adj. Music.* somewhat slow; leisurely. —*n.* **1** *Music.* a slow part. **2** in ballet: **a** a slow dance in which the female partner performs difficult feats of balancing. **b** the movements practiced in a ballet lesson for development of balance, line, and grace. [< Italian *adagio* < *ad agio* at ease]

1. In which of the following sentences can *adagio* correctly be placed in the blank?

   _____ a. The _____ movement of the concerto was played rather quickly.

   _____ b. Our ballet lesson today includes _____ movements.

   _____ c. Music faster than andante is _____.

   _____ d. To indicate leisurely feelings, the composer noted that the music should be played _____.

2. Select any synonym of *adagio*.

   _____ a. at ease   _____ c. moderately

   _____ b. leisurely   _____ d. slowly

3. In a movie that has mood music, which of the following emotions would be most likely to be accompanied by music played *adagio*?

   _____ a. happiness   _____ c. loneliness

   _____ b. sadness   _____ d. excitement

4. Write a sentence correctly using *adagio*. (Be sure to use context clues to show you understand the meaning of the word.)

   _____

   _____

5. What contemporary song or songs that you like are written or performed *adagio*?

   _____

   _____

Allegro[12]

al|le|gro (ə lā′grō, -leg′rō), *adj., adv., n., pl.* **-gros.** *Music.* —*adj.* quick and lively, but not so quick as *presto*. —*adv.* in quick time; briskly. —*n.* a quick, lively part in a piece of music. [< Italian *allegro* < Latin *alicer, alecris,* unrecorded variant of *alacer, -cris* brisk]

1. Select any synonym of *allegro*.
   _____ a. leisurely   _____ c. quick and lively
   _____ b. moderately slow   _____ d. briskly

2. In which of the following sentences can *allegro* correctly be placed in the blank?
   _____ a. The _____ movement was played swiftly to the end of the music.
   _____ b. Labeled _____ , the music was played faster than presto.
   _____ c. Please play the _____ segment. I like slow music.
   _____ d. He is quick and lively, so we say he is an _____.

3. Complete the verbal analogy.
   adagio : slow :: *allegro* : _____
   a. moderate   c. leisurely
   b. at ease   d. rapid

4. Write a sentence correctly using *allegro*. (Be sure to use context clues to show you understand the meaning of the word.)

   _____

   _____

5. In Henry Wadsworth Longfellow's poem "The Children's Hour," he refers to one of his daughters as "Laughing Allegra." What characteristics do you imagine she had to be given this name?

   _____

   _____

Andante[11]

an|dan|te (än dän′tā, an dan′tē), *adv., adj., n.*
Music. —*adv., adj.* moderately slow: *The move-ment was played andante* (adv.). *an andante movement* (adj.).
—*n.* a moderately slow movement; piece of mu-sic in this time.
[< Italian *andante* < *andare* walk]

1. In which of the following sentences is *andante* used correctly?
   _____ a. The sonata was performed andante.
   _____ b. He walked andante across the street; he was in a hurry to get home.
   _____ c. The andante movement preceded the adagio movement.
   _____ d. The andante sound could be heard in all parts of the audi-torium.

2. Select the characteristics of music labeled andante.
   _____ a. faster than adagio   _____ c. moderately fast
   _____ b. leisurely   _____ d. moderately slow

3. Complete the verbal analogy.
   adagio : slow :: *andante* : _____
   a. fast   c. moderate
   b. brisk   d. rapid

4. Write a sentence correctly using *andante*. (Be sure to use context clues to show you understand the meaning of the word.)

   _____

   _____

5. Imagine yourself walking across your school campus (or perhaps from your car to your place of work), in rhythm with the *andante* tempo of a song. What tune are you imagining?

   _____

   _____

Cantata[7]

can|ta|ta (kən tä′tə), *n.* **1** a musical composition consisting of a story or play which is sung by a chorus and soloists, but not acted. **2** (originally) a narrative in verse set to recitative or alternate recitative and air, for a single voice accompanied by one or more instruments. [< Italian *cantata* < *cantare* sing < Latin *cantāre*]

1. Check any appropriate response to the following statement:
   "I have been practicing for weeks to perform in the school *cantata*."
   _____ a. I know you can sing very well.
   _____ b. It must be hard to sing and dance at the same time.
   _____ c. For how long did you take acting lessons?
   _____ d. Are you singing, or playing an instrument?

2. The etymology of *cantata* shows that the word comes from the Latin *cantare* (to sing). Use that information, your background knowledge, and your imagination to match the following:
   _____ a. cantor   aa. to take back formally or publicly; withdraw or renounce
   _____ b. chant   bb. a motive; stimulus
   _____ c. enchant   cc. a short, simple melody
   _____ d. incentive   dd. to use magic on; bewitch
   _____ e. recant   ee. a person who sings the liturgy in a synagogue

3. Check any characteristic of *cantata*.
   _____ a. story or play   _____ c. acted
   _____ b. instrumental accompaniment _____ d. chorus and soloists

4. Write a sentence correctly using *cantata*. (Be sure to use context clues to show you understand the meaning of the word.)

_____

_____

5. How are an opera and a *cantata* different? (Consult the reading selection if necessary.) An opera is _____ and

includes _____. A *cantata*

is _____

and includes _____.

Concerto[15]

con|cer|to (kən cher′tō), *n., pl.* **-tos, -ti** (-tē). a piece of music to be played by one or more principal instruments, such as a violin or piano, with the accompaniment of an orchestra. It usually has three movements. Also, **concert**. [< Italian *concerto*. See etym. of doublet **concert**.]

from **concert:**

[< French *concert* < Italian *concerto* < Latin *concertāre* strive with < *con-* with + *certāre* strive. See etym. of doublet **concerto**.]

1. Match the following statement with one below.
   "Last night at the concert hall we heard Rachmaninoff's piano *concerto*."
   _____ a. The concert last night featured a famous piano solo work.
   _____ b. The main performance at last night's concert was a violin-piano duet.
   _____ c. The orchestra performance last night featured piano as the principal instrument.
   _____ d. An arrangement for chorus and orchestra was the first number on last night's program.

2. Which of the following might you hear if you listened to a *concerto?*
   _____ a. violin or piano
   _____ b. vocalists
   _____ c. orchestral accompaniment
   _____ d. five movements

3. The etymology of *concerto* shows that the word comes from the Latin *con* (with) and *certare* (to strive). Use that information, your background knowledge, and your imagination to match the following:
   _____ a. concern   aa. small, hexagonal accordian with bellows and buttons for keys
   _____ b. concerted   bb. to see clearly, make a distinction; discriminate
   _____ c. concertina cc. to have to do with; to belong to
   _____ d. discern   dd. planned or accomplished together

4. Imagine that you are writing a *concerto* that does not feature the piano or violin. What other instrument might you select as principal instrument?

_____

_____

5. Write a sentence correctly using *concerto*. (Be sure to use context clues to show you understand the meaning of the word.)

_____

_____

Counterpoint[4]

coun|ter|point[1] (koun′ter point′), *n., v.* —*n.* **1** a melody added to another as an accompaniment. **2** the art of adding melodies to a given melody according to fixed rules. **3** the style of musical composition resulting from the way in which more or less individual melodies are combined according to fixed rules. **4** = polyphony. **5** a style of literary or dramatic composition which uses a number of themes running counter to one another, usually at different levels and from shifting points of view. **6** *Figurative.* any offsetting point or element; contrast: *Their white robes ... were a counterpoint to the predominant black of diplomats* (New York Times). —*v.t.* to stress by the use of counterpoint or contrasts. [< Middle French *contrepoint*]

coun|ter|point[2] (koun′ter point′), *n. Obsolete.* a coverlet for a bed; a counterpane. [< Old French *contrepointe,* earlier *cuiltepointe* a quilt stitched through < Latin *culcita puncta*]

1. Match the following statement with one below:
   "In the music we are about to hear, *counterpoint* is carried by the brass section."

   _____ a. The vocal music we will hear is a solo without accompaniment.

   _____ b. This music was written as a duet for two voices singing in unison.

   _____ c. The next piece of music on the program has trumpets playing a countermelody.

   _____ d. Now we will hear violins play a four-part harmony.

2. Check any characteristic of *counterpoint.*

   _____ a. follows fixed rules

   _____ b. synonym is *polyphony*

   _____ c. harmonious chords

   _____ d. themes run counter to one another

3. Which of the numbered dictionary definitions of *counterpoint* best fits the word's use in the reading selection? _____

4. Many of us wish that our lives had some *counterpoint* (definition 6) to the working and studying that we do. What would you like to have as a contrast in your life?

   _____

   _____

5. Write a sentence correctly using *counterpoint*. (Be sure to use context clues to show you understand the meaning of the word.)

_____

_____

Dynamics[13]

dy|nam|ics (dī nam′iks), *n.* **1** *sing. in use.* the branch of physics dealing with the motion of bodies and the action of forces on bodies either in motion or at rest. Dynamics includes kinematics, kinetics, and statics. **2** *sing. in use.* the science of force acting in any field. **3** *pl. in use.* the forces, physical or moral, at work in any field: *the dynamics of education.* **4** *pl. in use.* the variation and contrast of force or loudness in the production of musical sounds.

from **dynamic:**
[< Greek *dynamikós* < *dýnamis* power < *dýnasthai* be powerful]

1. In which of the following sentences can *dynamics* correctly be placed in the blank?
   _____ a. A family with power is called a _____.
   _____ b. Next semester I plan to take a physics course called "_____."
   _____ c. The _____ of climatic change depend on the sun.
   _____ d. Knowledge of cultural _____ makes us more sensitive to individual needs.

2. Which of the numbered dictionary definitions of *dynamics* best fits the word's use in the reading selection? _____

3. The etymology of *dynamics* shows that the word comes from the Greek *dynasthai* (be powerful). Use that information, your background knowledge, and your imagination to match the following:
   _____ a. aerodyne   aa. a powerful explosive used in blasting
   _____ b. dynamite   bb. a motor that turns electrical energy into mechanical energy
   _____ c. dynamo   cc. an apparatus for measuring the force of power
   _____ d. dynamometer   dd. a line or succession of individuals who attain fame or distinction related as a family or by other ties
   _____ e. dynasty   ee. any heavier-than-air aircraft

4. Write a sentence correctly using *dynamics*. (Be sure to use context clues to show you understand the meaning of the word.)

_____

_____

5. Write the name of at least one song you know in which there is a range in *dynamics,* that is, in which the music often increases and decreases in volume.

_____

_____

Homophony[6]

ho|moph|o|ny (hō mof′ə nē, hom′ə fō′-), *n.*
1 sameness of sound. **2** homophonic music.

hom|o|phon|ic (hom′ə fon′ik, hō′mə-), *adj.* **1** having the same sound. **2** *Music.* **a** in unison. **b** having one part or melody predominating.

from **homophone:**
[< Greek *homóphōnos*
< *homós* same + *phonē* sound]

1. Match the following statement with the most similar sentence below:
   "The early religious chant was an example of *homophony*"
   _____ a. The musical accompaniment was presented as counterpoint.
   _____ b. The contrasting melodies provided harmony.
   _____ c. All the voices sang the same melody.
   _____ d. There were many voices singing in different rhythms.

2. Select any characteristic of *homophony.*
   _____ a. same sound   _____ d. contrasting melodies
   _____ b. very loud   _____ e. in unison
   _____ c. instrumental accompaniment

3. Complete the verbal analogy.
   polyphony : many :: *homophony* : _____
   _____ a. varied   _____ c. harmony
   _____ b. sound   _____ d. same

4. Write a sentence correctly using *homophony.* (Be sure to use context clues to show you understand the meaning of the word.)

   _____

   _____

5. What contemporary kind of songs could be described as *homophony?*

   _____

   _____

   Would you call "rap" *homophony?* _____

Oratorio[8]

or|a|to|ri|o (ôr′ə tôr′ē ō, -tôr′-; or′-), *n., pl.* **-ri|os.**
a musical composition, usually based on a reli-
gious theme, for solo voices, chorus, and orchestra. It is dramatic in character, but performed
without action, costumes, or scenery. [< Italian
oratorio (originally) place of prayer < Late Latin
ōrātōrium. See etym. of doublet **oratory²**]

from **oratory:**

[< Late
Latin *ōrātōrium,* noun use of adjective < Latin
ōrāre pray, recite formally. See etym. of doublet
oratorio.]

1. In which of the following sentences can *oratorio* correctly be placed in
   the blank?
   _____ a. The text of the _____ was based on the biblical
   book of Joshua.
   _____ b. The _____ was performed in the cathedral in
   Rome.
   _____ c. His dramatic _____ before the senate won votes
   for his political party's legislation.
   _____ d. After her excellent performance the audience gave her a
   standing _____ .

2. Check any characteristic of an *oratorio.*
   _____ a. action   _____ d. orchestra
   _____ b. chorus   _____ e. religious theme
   _____ c. solo voices   _____ f. costumes

3. The etymology of *oratorio* shows that the word comes from the Latin
   orare (to pray or recite formally). Use that information, your background
   knowledge, and your imagination to match the following:
   _____ a. adore   aa. a person who can speak well
   _____ b. oracle   bb. a formal public speech
   _____ c. oration   cc. to admire greatly; idolize
   _____ d. orator   dd. a priest who relates God's answer to a
                           question

4. Write a sentence correctly using *oratorio.* (Be sure to use context clues
   to show you understand the meaning of the word.)

   _____

   _____

5. What are the differences between a cantata and an *oratorio?* (Check the
   definitions, if necessary.)

   _____

   _____

Polyphony[5]

pol|lyph|o|ny (pə lif′ə nē), *n.* **1** *Music.* polyphonic composition; counterpoint. **2** a multiplicity of sounds. **3** *Phonetics.* the representation of more than one sound by the same letter or symbol. [< Greek *polyphōniā* < *polýphōnos* having many sounds or voices < *polýs* many + *phōnē̂* sound]

pol|y|phon|ic (pol′ē fon′ik), *adj.* **1** *Music.* having two or more voices or parts, each with an independent melody but all harmonizing; contrapuntal. **2** that can produce more than one tone at a time, as a piano or harp can. **3** producing many sounds; many-voiced. **4** *Phonetics.* representing more than one sound. English *oo* in *food, good* is polyphonic. — **pol′y|phon′i|cal|ly,** *adv.*

1. Select any characteristic of *polyphony*.

    _____ a. single sound   _____ c. many sounds

    _____ b. counterpoint   _____ d. harmonious

2. In which of the following sentences can *polyphony* correctly be placed in the blank?

    _____ a. One example of _____ is an echo where many sounds are heard.

    _____ b. When each voice sings the same melody at the same time, _____ is produced.

    _____ c. A musical piece that has many harmonious sounds represents _____ .

    _____ d. Harmonizing melodies, moving independently, produce _____ .

3. Which of the numbered dictionary definitions of *polyphony* best fits the word's use in the reading selection? _____

4. Think of several pieces of music that you enjoy. Which of them are examples of *polyphony*?

    _____

    _____

    _____

5. Write a sentence correctly using *polyphony*. (Be sure to use context clues to show you understand the meaning of the word.)

    _____

    _____

Secular[9]

sec|u|lar (sek′yə lər), *adj., n.* — *adj.* **1** connected with the world and its affairs; of things not religious or sacred; worldly: *secular music, a secular education. Bishops now were great secular magistrates, and ... were involved in secular occupations* (Cardinal Newman). **2** living in the world; not belonging to a religious order: *a secular clergy, a secular priest.* **3** occurring once in an age or century: *When Augustus celebrated the secular year, which was kept but once in a century ...* (Joseph Addison). **4** lasting through long ages; going on from age to age: *the secular cooling or refrigeration of the globe.*
— *n.* **1** a secular priest; clergyman living among the laity and not in a monastery: *While the Danish wars had been fatal to the monks—the "regular clergy" as they were called—they had also dealt heavy blows at the seculars, or parish priests* (J. R. Green). **2** = layman.
[< Latin *saeculāris* < *saeculum* age, span of time; later, the present age or world, the world]

1. Check any word or phrase that describes *secular*.
   - _____ a. worldly
   - _____ b. religious
   - _____ c. living outside a monastery
   - _____ d. once a century
   - _____ e. sacred
   - _____ f. layman

2. In which of the following sentences can *secular* correctly be placed in the blank?
   - _____ a. In the United States, _____ schools do not provide religious training.
   - _____ b. Father John was a _____ priest, and he lived in a monastery.
   - _____ c. My _____ education took place in the public schools.
   - _____ d. He is not a priest but a layman, a _____.

3. Which of the numbered dictionary definitions of *secular* best fits the word's use in the reading selection? _____

4. Write a sentence correctly using *secular*. (Be sure to include context clues to show you understand the meaning of the word.)

   _____

   _____

5. Consider your own formal education. Has it been religious _____, *secular* _____, or both _____?

Sonata[14]

so|na|ta (sə nä′tə), *n.* **1** a piece of music, for one or two instruments, having three or four movements in contrasted rhythms and keys. **2** (originally) any instrumental composition, as contrasted with a vocal composition or cantata. [< Italian *sonata* (literally) sounded (played on an instrument, contrasted with singing) < Latin *sonāre* to sound]

1. Check any characteristic of a *sonata*.
   - _____ a. vocal composition
   - _____ b. contrasted rhythms
   - _____ c. two movements
   - _____ d. contrasted keys
   - _____ e. religious theme
   - _____ f. costumed players

2. In which of the following sentences can *sonata* correctly be placed in the blank?
   - _____ a. The _____ flowed gracefully through three movements.
   - _____ b. Mary sang a _____ in last night's program.
   - _____ c. The school orchestra is practicing a _____ to be played by members of the violin section.
   - _____ d. The young composer wrote a _____ for four voices, all in the key of C.

3. The etymology of *sonata* shows that the word comes from the Latin *sonare* (to sound). Use that information, your background knowledge, and your imagination to match the following:

    _____ a. consonant   aa. to give back sound; echo

    _____ b. dissonant   bb. in agreement; in accord; harmonious

    _____ c. resound   cc. giving out or having a deep, loud sound

    _____ d. sonorous   dd. harsh in tone or sound; not harmonious

4. Write a sentence correctly using *sonata*. (Be sure to use context clues to show you understand the meaning of the word.)

    _____

    _____

5. Have you heard a piece of music that you recognized as a *sonata*? _____ What was its title?

    _____

    What instrument(s) would you prefer to hear playing a *sonata*?

    _____

Timbre[1]

tim|bre (tim′bər, tam′-), *n.* **1** *Music.* the quality in sounds, regardless of their pitch or volume, by which a certain voice, instrument, or condition can be distinguished from other voices, instruments, or conditions. Because of differences in timbre, identical notes played on a violin, an oboe, and a trumpet can be distinguished from one another. **2** *Phonetics.* the quality in the resonance of a sound, distinct from loudness and pitch, that gives it its identity. [< Old French *timbre* hemispherical bell without a clapper; heraldic crest, seal or stamp; (originally) a drum, timbrel, ultimately < Greek *týmpanon* kettledrum. See etym. of doublets **timpani, tympan, tympanum.**]

1. In which of the following sentences can *timbre* correctly be placed in the blank?

    _____ a. The companies that produce lumber cut _____ in the forests.

    _____ b. The _____ of an oboe helps bring texture to a musical composition.

    _____ c. One factor that helps us identify the voice of someone speaking is _____.

    _____ d. The _____ of the tone produced by a clarinet makes it easy to distinguish in an orchestra.

2. Which of the following professionals might be interested in the *timbre* of sound?

    _____ a. dialect coach   _____ c. music teacher

    _____ b. orchestra conductor   _____ d. singing coach

3. Complete the verbal analogy.
   volume : loudness :: *timbre* : _____
   a. rhythm   c. harmony
   b. quality   d. pitch

4. Are you able to distinguish the type of instrument being played by the *timbre* of its sound? _____ What is your favorite instrument? _____

5. Write a sentence correctly using *timbre*. (Be sure to use context clues to show you understand the meaning of the word.)

   _____

   _____

Tone[2]

tone (tōn), *n., v.,* **toned, ton|ing.** —*n.* **1** any sound considered with reference to its quality, pitch, strength, or source: *angry tones, gentle tones, the deep tone of an organ.* **2** quality of sound: *Her voice was silvery in tone.* **3** *Music.* **a** a sound of definite pitch and character. **b** the difference in pitch between two notes; whole step. *C and D are one tone apart.* **c** any one of the nine melodies or tunes in Gregorian music, used in singing the Psalms; Gregorian tone. **4** *Figurative.* a manner of speaking or writing: *a moral tone. We disliked the haughty tone of her letter.* **5** *Figurative.* **a** spirit; character; style: *A tone of quiet elegance prevails in her home.* **b** mental or emotional state; mood; disposition: *These hardy exercises produce also a healthful tone of mind and spirits* (Washington Irving). **6** normal healthy condition; vigor: *He exercised regularly to keep his body in tone.* **7** the degree of firmness or tension normal to the organs or tissue when healthy. **8** a proper responsiveness to stimulation. **9** the effect of color and of light and shade in a picture: *a painting with a soft green tone.* **10a** the quality given to one color by another color: *blue with a greenish tone.* **b** a shade of color: *The room is furnished in tones of brown.* **11** *Linguistics.* **a** the pitch of the voice as it is high or low, or as it rises and falls, regarded as a distinctive feature of a language. **b** any one of the tonal levels distinctive in a language: *Mandarin Chinese has four phonemic tones.* **c** the pronunciation characteristic of a particular person, group of people, or area; accent. **12** *Phonetics.* **a** the sound produced by the vibration of the vocal cords; voice. **b** the stress or emphasis on a syllable.
— *v.i.* to harmonize: *This rug tones in well with the wallpaper and furniture.*
— *v.t.* **1** to change the tone of: **a** to soften or change the color or value contrasts in (a painting or photograph). **b** *Photography.* to alter the color of (a print), especially from gray to some other color. **2** to give a tone to; give the proper or desired tone to (a musical instrument); tune. **3** to utter with a musical or other tone; intone. **tone down,** to soften; moderate: *to tone down one's voice, tone down the colors in a painting.* **tone up,** to give more sound, color, or vigor to; strengthen: *Bright curtains would tone up this dull room.* [< Latin *tonus* < Greek *tónos* vocal pitch, raising of voice; (originally) a stretching, taut string, related to *teinein* to stretch. See etym. of doublets **tune, ton².**]

1. In which of the following sentences can *tone* correctly be placed in the blank?
   _____ a. Gregorian _____ was used often in early church services.
   _____ b. Maria sings with a clear, full _____.
   _____ c. Our _____ frequently carries as much meaning as our words.
   _____ d. In some languages, _____ is an important part of pronunciation and meaning.

2. Which of the numbered and lettered dictionary definitions of *tone* best fits the word's use in the reading selection? _____

3. The etymology of *tone* shows that the word comes from the Greek *teinein*

(to stretch). Use that information, your background knowledge, and your imagination to match the following:

_____ a. attenuate aa. narrow, slim; not thick
_____ b. extenuate bb. a cord of tissue
_____ c. tendon cc. having slight importance; not substantial
_____ d. tenuous dd. to make less dense; dilute
_____ e. thin ee. to make the serious seem less so

4. Consider the *tone* you use with a child. Compare it with the *tone* you use with a teacher or an employer. Which is softer? _____

   Is the difference in *tone* important to the impression you want to give? _____

5. Write a sentence correctly using *tone*. (Be sure to include context clues to show you understand the meaning of the word.)

   _____

   _____

Virtuosity[3]

vir|tu|os|i|ty (vėr'chů os'ə tē), *n., pl.* **-ties. 1** the character or skill of a virtuoso. **2a** interest or taste in the fine arts, especially of a trifling, dilettante nature. **b** excessive attention to technique, or to the production of special effects, especially in music. **3** lovers of the fine arts.
vir|tu|o|so (vėr'chů ō'sō), *n., pl.* **-sos, -si** (-sē), *adj.* —*n.* **1** a person skilled in the techniques of an art, especially in playing a musical instrument. **2** a person who has a cultivated appreciation of artistic excellence; connoisseur. **3** a student or collector, as of objects of art, curios, or antiquities. **4** *Obsolete.* a person who pursues special investigations or has a general interest in the arts or sciences; learned person; scientist or scholar. —*adj.* showing the artistic qualities and skills of a virtuoso; virtuosic: *virtuoso singing. The play is built around Sir Alec's virtuoso performance as Dylan* (Maclean's). [< Italian *virtuoso* learned person; of exceptional worth < Late Latin *virtuōsus;* see etym. under **virtuous**]

1. Check any characteristic(s) of someone having *virtuosity*.

   _____ a. special interest   _____ d. extensive knowledge
   _____ b. love of art   _____ e. appreciation
   _____ c. outstanding ability   _____ f. attention to detail

2. Which of the numbered and lettered dictionary definitions of *virtuosity* best fits the word's use in the reading selection? _____

3. Who of the following might be known as a virtuoso, that is, for *virtuosity?*

   _____ a. a collector of rare clocks
   _____ b. a prize-winning scientist
   _____ c. an appreciator of fine paintings
   _____ d. a classical violinist

4. If you could demonstrate *virtuosity* in some area of performing music, what would it be? _____ What instrument would you play? _____

5. Write a sentence correctly using *virtuosity*. (Be sure to use context clues to show you understand the meaning of the word.)

_____

_____

ANSWERS TO CHAPTER 19 EXERCISES

Adagio: **1.** b, d **2.** b, d **3.** b, c
Allegro: **1.** c, d **2.** a, b **3.** d (description)
Andante: **1.** a, b **2.** a, d **3.** c (description)
Cantata: **1.** a, d **2.** ee, cc, dd, bb, aa **3.** a, b, d
Concerto: **1.** c **2.** a, c **3,** cc, dd, aa, bb
Counterpoint: **1.** c **2.** a, b, d **3.** 3
Dynamics: **1.** b, c, d **2.** 4 **3.** ee, aa, bb, cc, dd
Homophony: **1.** c **2.** a, e **3.** d (root meaning)
Oratorio: **1.** a, b **2.** b, c, d, e **3.** cc, dd, bb, aa
Polyphony: **1.** b, c, d **2.** a, c, d **3.** 1
Secular: **1.** a, c, d, f **2.** a, c, d **3.** *adj.* 1
Sonata: **1.** b, d **2.** a, c **3.** bb, dd, aa, cc
Timbre: **1.** b, c, d **2.** a, b, c, d **3.** b (definition)
Tone: **1.** a, b, c, d **2.** 3a **3.** dd, ee, bb, cc, aa
Virtuosity: **1.** a, b, c, d, e, f **2.** 2b **3.** a, c, d

If you missed any of the items in the exercises, return to the exercise and to the dictionary definition to see where you went wrong. Remember: If you get something right, you only affirm that you knew it. If you get something wrong and understand why, *you have learned something.*

MUSIC POSTTEST

Fill in the blanks with the words from this list.

adagio	counterpoint	secular
allegro	dynamics	sonata
andante	homophony	timbre
cantata	oratorio	tone
concerto	polyphony	virtuosity

1. A musical composition of three movements for piano and orchestra is an example of a(n) _____.

2. Music with themes that run counter to each other is _____.

3. _____ is the distinctive quality of a sound.

4. A piece of music for one or two instruments and having three or four movements, as contrasted with a vocal composition, is a(n) _____.

5. Quick and lively is characteristic of music written _____.

6. A(n) _____ is sound of definite pitch and character.

7. A multiplicity of musical sounds is called _____.

8. _____ refers to the increase or decrease in volume or in the production of sound.

9. A vocal composition sung by a chorus and soloists is a(n) _____.

10. A religious theme in a musical composition is characteristic of a(n) _____.

11. Music performed in the same, or nearly the same, rhythm by all the voice parts is known as _____.

12. _____ is skill in the techniques of an art.

13. A synonym of _____ is *worldly*.

14. _____ means "leisurely or somewhat slow."

15. Moderately slow refers to music written or performed _____.

Answers to this posttest are in the Instructor's Manual.

If you missed any of the words, you may need to return to the exercises and to the dictionary entries to see why your concepts for some words are incomplete.

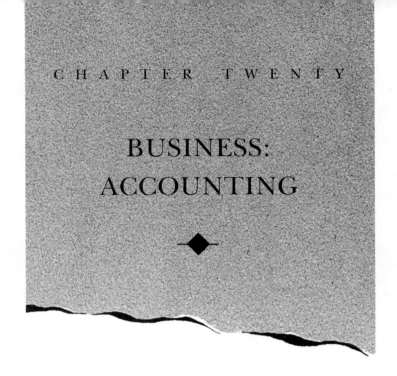

CHAPTER TWENTY

BUSINESS:
ACCOUNTING

◆

OVERVIEW

Accounting is the art, practice, or system of keeping, analyzing, and interpreting business accounts. Accounting enables companies and governmental agencies to summarize and report in an understandable fashion a large number of transactions.

Accounting is usually an option or concentration within the business administration degree program. An Associate of Arts or Associate in Science degree can also be earned in accounting. Courses in accounting include financial and managerial accounting, income taxation, cost accounting, auditing, governmental and not-for-profit accounting, and controllership.

Career options for students with accounting degrees include professional employment in public, private, or governmental accounting. Specific employment opportunities include work as a certified public accountant (CPA), tax specialist, auditor, or controller.

The introductory textbooks in the field are a combination of expository and process analysis in format. They explain broad concepts or generalizations as well as statements of situations, ideas, or problems with explanations or examples. They also include step-by-step processes for completing accounting tasks. Charts, graphs, and tables help to visually represent concepts.

The vocabulary in accounting consists mainly of general vocabulary terms that also have a specialized meaning within the context of accounting, such as cost, audit, credit, *and* earnings.

VOCABULARY SELF-EVALUATION

The following words will be introduced in this reading selection. Place a check mark (√) in front of any that you know thoroughly and use in your speech and writing. Place a question mark (?) in front of any that you recognize but do not use yourself.

_____ amortize	_____ depreciation	_____ ledger
_____ assets	_____ disclosure	_____ liabilities
_____ audit	_____ dividends	_____ requisition
_____ credit	_____ equity	_____ transaction
_____ debit	_____ intangible	_____ voucher

AN ACCOUNTING SYSTEM
FOR A NEW BUSINESS

Starting a new business requires developing an accounting system to keep track of the financial activities for both management and tax purposes.

The basic unit of an accounting system is the ledger[1] account. A ledger account should be kept for every aspect of the business. It is a double-entry two-sided system. The left side is the debit[2] side and the right side is the credit[3] side, and these can be abbreviated as dr. and cr.

The various aspects of the business will fall into one of three major categories: assets,[4] liabilities,[5] and owner's equity.[6] Assets are resources owned by the business that are expected to benefit future operations. Cash on hand, machinery, and accounts receivable are examples of asset accounts. Liabilities are the company's debts. These are the obligations that the business must pay in money or services at some time in the future. These can include accounts payable to creditors, short-term notes payable for money borrowed, and salaries owed employees. Asset accounts normally have debit balances, and liability accounts have credit balances.

The last category is owner's equity, which is the value of cash or other assets invested by the owner in the company as well as proceeds from the profitable operation of the company. The owner's equity includes revenue and expenses and is equal to assets minus liabilities. An owner's equity account normally has a credit balance. For publicly held corporations, this category is called "stockholder's equity." The owner of a privately held company may withdraw his equity from the company at any time. On the other hand, the owners of a public company, the stockholders, remove a portion of their equity in the company through the distribution of dividends,[7] or shares of the profit of the company.

If a company borrows money to buy machinery, this transaction[8] will require that two ledger account entries be made. A ledger account for the asset of plant equipment would be increased by placing the amount paid for the machinery in the left, or debit, side of the account. This would be offset by an entry on the right, or credit, side of the ledger account for notes payable (liability). This double-entry system allows the accounts to always be in balance.

Assets such as machinery decline in economic potential due to wear, age, and deterioration over time. Depreciation[9] is the spreading of the cost of such a tangible asset over its useful life. The cost of intangible[10] assets such as trademarks may also be spread over their lifetime, or amortized.[11] Amortization is the conversion of an intangible asset to an expense. The reason for spreading the cost of these assets over their lifetimes is because they help generate revenue, or income, for that entire period. To assign all the cost of the asset to one accounting period overstates expenses for that period and then understates them for the rest of the asset's life.

Of all the accounts, the cash account (paper money, coins, checks, money orders, and banks deposits) is one of the most difficult to adequately control. One cash-control procedure is the voucher[12] system, which requires written authorizations, records, and other procedures. For example, when a member of a company or business needs supplies, he or she completes a requisition[13] form that lists the supplies and their costs. This will result in both a purchase order (PO) being generated by the purchasing department and an invoice by the outside firm supplying the goods. The purpose of the voucher is to ensure that the purchase is authorized and that both the purchase order and invoice have the same amount listed before a check is written in payment for the goods or supplies.

Once an accounting system has been established, a certified public accountant (CPA) should periodically audit[14] the records to ensure that generally accepted accounting principles and procedures are being followed and that no fraud has occurred. Public corporations are required to make a public disclosure[15] of their financial statements to aid potential investors, stockholders, creditors, financial analysts, and others interested in the company.

Finally, accounting is basically an information system. Procedures for systematically recording and evaluating daily business activities help manage the financial information of a company. ◆

ACCOUNTING PRETEST

Select words from this list and write them in the blanks to complete the sentences.

amortize	depreciation	ledger
assets	disclosure	liabilities
audit	dividends	requisition
credit	equity	transaction
debit	intangible	voucher

1. A complete record of all assets, liabilities, and proprietorship items are kept in a(n) _____.

2. A(n) _____ is the left-hand side of an account.

3. The amount that a business or property is worth beyond what is owed is called its _____.

4. The _____ are entries on a balance sheet that express the value of the resources of a person, business, or organization.

5. A(n) _____ is money earned as a profit by a company and divided among the owners or stockholders.

6. A business with more _____, or debts, than assets has a good chance of failing.

7. A piece of business or the carrying on of any kind of business is called a(n) _____.

8. The right-hand side of an account in the ledger account is called a(n) _____.

9. A(n) _____ is a lessening, or lowering, in price, value, or estimation and can be spread over time.

10. A(n) _____ asset is something that cannot be touched or felt, such as honesty or goodwill.

11. Choosing to make monthly payments on a house shows that you have decided to _____ your debt.

12. Written evidence of payment, such as a cancelled check, is called a(n) _____.

13. A demand made for something, especially a formal written demand, is called a(n) _____.

14. The company policy requires an annual _____, or systematic examination, of business accounts.

15. A written statement of the company's financial position is an act of public _____.

Answers to this pretest are in Appendix B.

Unless your instructor tells you to do otherwise, complete the exercises for each word that you missed on the pretest. The words, with their meanings and exercises, are in alphabetical order. The superscript numbers indicate where the words appeared in the reading selection so that you can refer to them when necessary. There are several types of exercises, but for each word you will be asked to write a sentence using context clues. (See Chapter 4 if you need information about how to create context clues.) You are also asked to perform some activity that will help you make your concept of the word personal. *Complete this activity thoughtfully, for creating a personalized concept of the word will help you remember it in the future.*

Answers to all the exercises are at the end of the exercise segment.

ACCOUNTING EXERCISES

Amortize[11]

am|or|tize (am′ər tīz, ə môr′-), *v.t.,* **-tized, -tiz|ing.**
1 to set money aside regularly in a special fund
to accumulate at interest, for future paying or
settling of (a debt or other liability). **2** *Law.* to
convey (property) to a body, especially an ec-
clesiastical body, which does not have the right
to sell or give it away, as in mortmain. [< Old
French *amortiss-,* stem of *amortir* deaden < *a-* to
+ *mort* death < Latin *mors, mortis*] **— am′or|tiz′a-
ble,** *adj.* **— am′or|ti|za′tion,** *n.* **— a|mor′tize-
ment,** *n.*

1. When you *amortize* a debt, you
   _____ a. pay it all at once.
   _____ b. continue to add to it.
   _____ c. write it off through payments over a certain period of time.
   _____ d. make payments every ten years.

2. The etymology of *amortize* shows that the word comes from the Old
   French *amortiss* (to + death). Use this information, your imagination,
   and your background knowledge to match the following:

   _____ a. mortify   aa. building or room where dead bodies
                                             are kept until burial or cremation

   _____ b. mortgage   bb. after death

   _____ c. mortal   cc. to give a lender a claim to one's prop-
                                             erty in case a debt is not paid when due

   _____ d. postmortem   dd. sure to die sometime

   _____ e. mortuary   ee. to wound (a person's feelings); to make
                                             a person feel humbled and ashamed;
                                             humiliate

3. Complete the verbal analogy.
   depreciate: value :: *amortize* : _____
   a. asset   c. credit
   b. debt   d. debit

4. Have you ever *amortized* a debt (credit cards, car loan, house mortgage,
   and so forth)? How did such a process affect your monthly budget?

   _____

   _____

5. Write a sentence correctly using *amortize.* (Be sure to include context
   clues to show you understand the meaning of the word.)

   _____

   _____

Assets[4]

as|sets (as′ets), *n.pl.* **1** things of value; all items of value owned by a person or business and constituting the resources of the person or business. Real estate, cash, securities, inventories, patents, and good will are assets. *His assets include a house, a car, stocks, bonds, and jewelry.* (Figurative.) *Honesty is one of the judge's most valuable assets.* **2** property that can be used to pay debts. **3** *Accounting.* the entries on a balance sheet that express in terms of money the value of the tangible things or intangible rights which constitute the resources of a person, business, or organization, as of a given date. [< Old French *asez* enough < Latin *ad satis* sufficiently (misunderstood as a plural noun "sufficient things")]

1. Complete the verbal analogy.
   debit : owed :: *assets* : _____
   a. produced   c. owned
   b. claimed   d. loaned

2. In which of the following sentences can *assets* be correctly placed in the blank?
   _____ a. _____ are the economic resources of a business, such as land, buildings, and equipment.
   _____ b. Businesses can have "liquid" _____, which include cash, receivables, and supplies.
   _____ c. He had many _____ and therefore had to amortize a debt.
   _____ d. The businesswoman needed to locate her _____, which were left on the answering machine.

3. The etymology of *assets* shows that the word comes from the Latin *ad satis* (sufficiently). Use this information, your imagination, and your background knowledge to match the following:
   _____ a. satiety   aa. to feed fully; satisfy fully
   _____ b. saturate   bb. to give enough to (a person); meet or fulfill (as desires, hopes, or demands)
   _____ c. satire   cc. to soak thoroughly; fill up
   _____ d. satiate   dd. the use of mockery, irony, or wit to attack or ridicule something
   _____ e. satisfy   ee. the feeling of having had too much; disgust or weariness caused by excess

4. Write a sentence correctly using *assets*. (Be sure to include context clues to show you understand the meaning of the word.)

   _____

   _____

5. What tangible *assets* (money, clothes, motorcycle, car, house, and so forth) do you have? What intangible *assets* (honesty, fairness) do you possess?

   _____

   _____

Audit[14]

au|dit (ô′dit), *v., n.* —*v.t.* **1** to examine and check (business accounts) systematically and officially. **2** to attend (a class or course) as a listener without receiving academic credit. **3** make an energy audit of: *"Honeywell," he says, "would audit a building, identify conservation possibilities, install the equipment, and monitor its operation* (Christian Science Monitor). —*v.i.* to examine the correctness of a business account: *Auditing is the Government's chief tax enforcement weapon* (Wall Street Journal). [< noun]

—*n.* **1** a systematic and official examination and check of business accounts. **2** a statement of an account that has been examined and checked officially. **3** = energy audit: *Audits to determine the needs of various offices are being initiated* (Tuscaloosa News). **4** *Archaic.* **a** a hearing. **b** a judicial hearing of complaints.
[< Latin *audītus* a hearing < *audīre* hear]

1. Select the synonym(s) of *audit*.
   _____ a. transaction   _____ c. acceptance
   _____ b. examination   _____ d. inspection

2. Complete the verbal analogy.
   amortize : debt :: *audit* : _____
   a. ledger   c. assets
   b. dividends   d. financial records

3. The etymology of *audit* shows that the word comes from the Latin *audire* (to hear). Use this information, your background knowledge, and your imagination to match the following:
   _____ a. audiovisual   aa. a hearing to test the ability or suitability of a musician, actor, or other performer
   _____ b. audible   bb. attentive listening to speech sounds and patterns, as opposed to simple hearing
   _____ c. auding   cc. an instrument for measuring keenness and range of hearing
   _____ d. audiometer   dd. having to do with or involving the transmission or reception of both sounds and images.
   _____ e. audition   ee. can be heard; loud enough to be heard

4. Why do you think it is important to conduct an *audit* of a company or business?

   _____

   _____

5. Write a sentence correctly using *audit*. (Be sure to include context clues to show you understand the meaning of the word.)

   _____

   _____

Credit[3]

cred|it (kred′it), *n., v.* —*n.* **1a** belief in the truth of something; faith; trust: *I know he is sure of his facts and put credit in what he says.* **b** personal influence or authority based on the confidence of others or on one's own reputation: *Buckingham ... resolved to employ all his credit to prevent*

the marriage (David Hume). **c** credibility; trustworthiness: *His revelations destroy their credit by running into detail* (Emerson). **2a** trust in a person's ability and intention to pay: *This store will extend credit to you by opening a charge account in your name.* **b** one's reputation in money matters: *If you pay your bills on time, your credit will be good.* **3a** money in a person's bank account: *When I deposit this check, I will have a credit of fifty dollars in my savings account.* **b** the balance in a person's favor in an account: *His bookseller's statement shows a credit of $5.* **4** *Bookkeeping.* **a** the entry of money paid on account. **b** the right-hand side of an account where such entries are made. **c** the sum entered, or the total shown, on this side. **5** delayed payment; time allowed for delayed payment: *The store allowed us six months' credit on our purchase.* **6** favorable reputation; good name: *The mayor was a man of credit in the community.* **SYN:** repute, standing, honor. **7** praise, honor, recognition: *The person who does the work should get the credit. He claims no credit for the scheme.* **SYN:** commendation, esteem, appreciation. **8** a person or thing that brings honor or praise: *Benjamin Franklin's great scientific achievements were a credit to his young country. You are a credit to the school* (Dickens). **9a** an entry on a student's record showing that he has passed a course of study: *You must pass the examination to get credit for the course.* **b** a unit of work entered in this way: *He needs three credits to graduate.* **c** *British.* a mark between a mere pass and distinction, awarded in examinations. **10** Usually, **credits. a** an acknowledgment of the authorship or source of material used in a publication, work done on a dramatic show, radio or television program, or other artistic production: *The credits are often listed at the beginning of a motion picture.* **b** a listing of the producers, directors, actors, technicians, and others who have given their skills to a motion picture, radio or television show, or a play. *Abbr.* cr.
— *v.t.* **1** to have faith in; believe; trust: *I can credit all that you are telling me because I had a similar experience. I ... am content to credit my senses* (Samuel Johnson). **2a** to enter on the credit side of an account: *The bank credited fifty*

dollars to his savings account. **b** to assign to as a credit: *The grocer was credited with the value of two hundred deposit bottles.* **3** to give credit in a bank account or other statement of account. **4** to put an entry on the record of (a student) showing that he has passed a course of study. **5** *Archaic.* to bring honor to. **6** *Obsolete.* to supply with goods on credit.

credit to, to ascribe to; attribute to: *The shortage of wheat was credited to lack of rain. Some excellent remarks were ... borrowed from and credited to Plato* (Oliver Wendell Holmes).

credit with, to think that one has; give recognition to: *You will have to credit him with some sense for not panicking during the fire.*

do credit to, to bring honor or praise to: *The winning team did credit to the school's reputation.*

give credit for, a to think that one has: *Give me credit for some brains.* **b** to give recognition to: *Give him credit for the idea.* [*They*] *give her credit for sincerity* (J. Wilson).

give credit to, to have faith in; believe; trust: *He gives no credit to kings or emperors* (James Mozley).

on credit, on a promise to pay later. When you buy anything and promise to pay for it later, you are getting it on credit. *He bought a new car on credit since he could not afford to make such a large purchase in cash.*

to one's credit, to bring honor to; be to the honor or praise of; worthy of approval: *It is to the students' credit that they hate war and social injustice* (Fred M. Hechinger).

[< Middle French *crédit* < Italian *credito,* learned borrowing from Latin *creditum* a loan < *crēdere* trust, entrust, lend (money)] — **cred'it|less,** *adj.*

▶ **Credit with, accredit with** mean to believe someone or something responsible for saying, doing, feeling, or causing something. **Credit** emphasizes the idea of believing, not always with enough reason or evidence: *You credit me with doing things I never thought of.* **Accredit** emphasizes the idea of accepting because of some proof: *We accredit Peary with having discovered the North Pole.*

1. The etymology of *credit* shows that the word comes from the Latin *credere* (to trust, entrust, or lend, as in money). Use this information, your imagination, and your background knowledge to match the following:

_____ a. credo   aa. a base or wicked person; villain

_____ b. credulous   bb. worthy of belief; believable; reliable

_____ c. miscreant   cc. statement of belief; creed

_____ d. credible   dd. too ready to believe; easily deceived

_____ e. credence   ee. belief or credit; faith; trust

2. Select the synonym(s) of *credit.*

_____ a. assets   _____ c. cash

_____ b. abilities   _____ d. confidence

3. Which of the numbered and lettered dictionary definitions of *credit* best fits the word's use in the reading selection? _____

4. Write a sentence correctly using *credit*. (Be sure to include context clues to show you understand the meaning of the word.)

_____

_____

5. Have you ever applied for or received *credit*? For what? Do you have a *credit* card? What do you think of the large number of *credit* cards in our society today?

_____

_____

Debit²

deb|it (deb'it), *n., v. Bookkeeping.* —*n.* **1** an entry of something owed in an account. **2** the left-hand side of an account, where such entries are made. **3** the sum or total shown on this side. *Abbr:* dr.
—*v.t.* **1** to charge with or as a debt: *The bank debited his account $500.* **2** to enter on the debit side of an account.
[alteration of earlier *debte;* spelling influenced by Latin *dēbitum.* Compare etym. under **debt.**]

from **debt:**
[< Old French *dete,* or *debte* < Latin *dēbitum* (thing) owed, neuter past participle of *dēbēre* to owe; (originally) keep (something) from someone < *dē-* away + *habēre* have. Compare etym. under **debit.**]

1. Where is the location of a *debit* in an accounting system?
   _____ a. bottom   _____ c. left
   _____ b. right   _____ d. middle

2. The etymology of *debit* shows that the word comes from the Latin *debere* (to owe). Use this information, your background knowledge, and your imagination to match the following:
   _____ a. duty   aa. an act of civility or respect
   _____ b. debenture   bb. a person's right; what is owed to a person
   _____ c. endeavor   cc. a written acknowledgment of a debt
   _____ d. devoir(s)   dd. a thing that is right to do; what a person ought to do; obligation
   _____ e. due   ee. to try hard; make an effort; strive

3. Select the synonym(s) of *debit*.
   _____ a. notation   _____ c. asset
   _____ b. account   _____ d. entry

4. What is a recent *debit* that you had in either your savings or checking account?

_____

_____

5. Write a sentence correctly using *debit*. (Be sure to include context clues to show you understand the meaning of the word.)

_____

_____

Depreciation[9]

de|pre|ci|a|tion (di prē'shē ā'shən), *n.* **1a** a lessening or lowering in price, value, or estimation: *The depreciation of a car is greatest during its first year.* **b** such a loss figured as part of the cost of doing business: *Depreciation, of course, is a bookkeeping charge which reduces reported earnings but does not involve the expenditure of cash* (Wall Street Journal). **2** a reduction in the value of money: *Foreign currency depreciation is a result of economic depression in the country* concerned. **3** *Figurative.* a speaking slightly (of); belittling; disparagement.
de|pre|ci|ate (di prē'shē āt), *v.,* -at|ed, -at|ing. — *v.t.* **1** to lessen the value or price of: *The government has the power to depreciate currency.* **2** *Figurative.* to speak slightingly of; belittle: *That lazy boy is always depreciating the value of exercise.* **SYN:** underrate, disparage. — *v.i.* to lessen in value: *The longer an automobile is driven the more it depreciates.*

1. Which of the following would qualify for *depreciation?*
   _____ a. a computer   _____ c. a food supply
   _____ b. a water bill   _____ d. a car

2. The etymology of *depreciation* (see *depreciate*) shows that the word comes from the Latin *depretiare* (down + price). Use this information, your imagination, and your background knowledge to match the following:
   _____ a. premium   aa. to think highly of; recognize the worth or quality of
   _____ b. precious   bb. a reward, especially given as an incentive to buy; prize
   _____ c. appraise   cc. a nearly correct amount; close estimate
   _____ d. approximation   dd. to estimate the value, amount, quality, or merit of; judge
   _____ e. appreciate   ee. having great value; worth much; valuable; of great importance

3. Select the synonym(s) of *depreciation*.
   _____ a. accelerate   _____ c. lessen
   _____ b. decrease   _____ d. increase

4. Write a sentence correctly using *depreciation*. (Be sure to include context clues to show you understand the meaning of the word.)

_____

_____

5. How does *depreciation* affect a person's equity? What do you own that you could consider for *depreciation?*

_____

_____

Disclosure[15]

dis|clo|sure (dis klō′zhər), *n.* **1** the act of disclosing: *disclosure of a secret. His reluctant disclosure of his whereabouts led to many misunderstandings.* **2** a thing disclosed; revelation: *The newspaper's disclosures shocked the public.*

dis|close (dis klōz′), *v.,* **-closed, -clos|ing,** *n.*
—*v.t.* **1** to open to view; uncover: *The lifting of the curtain disclosed a beautiful painting.* **2** to make known; reveal: *This letter discloses a secret.* **SYN:** See syn. under **reveal. 3** *Obsolete.* to unfold; unfasten. —*n. Obsolete.* disclosure.

1. Select the synonym(s) of *disclosure.*
   _____ a. transaction   _____ c. acknowledgment
   _____ b. requisition   _____ d. revelation

2. In which of the following sentences can *disclosure* be correctly placed in the blank?
   _____ a. The student needed to obtain a _____ before she could register.
   _____ b. A summary of accounting principles a company follows should be part of its _____.
   _____ c. The secretary needed a _____ from the president before he could order new supplies.
   _____ d. The annual report of a company, which includes its financial status, is a form of _____.

3. Why do companies make public *disclosures?*
   _____ a. to discuss recent audits
   _____ b. to present employee job descriptions
   _____ c. to acknowledge new board members
   _____ d. to inform stockholders and others of the company's financial status

4. Have you ever read an annual report of a company that is the public *disclosure* of its financial status? How might this information affect you if you were a stockholder in the company?

   _____

   _____

5. Write a sentence correctly using *disclosure.* (Be sure to include context clues to show you understand the meaning of the word.)

   _____

   _____

Dividends[7]

div|i|dend (div′ə dend), *n.* **1** a number or quantity to be divided by another: *In 8 ÷ 2, 8 is the dividend.* **2** money earned as profit by a company and divided among the owners or stockholders of the company. **3** a share of such money. **4** a refund of part of the premiums paid to an insurance company, given to a person holding a participating insurance policy out of the company's surplus earnings: *With our policy-holder dividends your total savings can be really surpris-*

ing (Newsweek). **5** *Law.* a sum of money divided among the creditors of a bankrupt estate. **6** *Especially British.* a bonus: *Soldiers are citizens of death's grey land, Drawing no dividend from time's tomorrows* (Siegfried Sassoon). [< Latin *dīvidendum* (thing) to be divided; neuter gerundive of *dīvidere;* see etym. under **divide**]

1. In which of the following sentences is *dividends* used correctly?

   _____ a. The insurance company filed its dividends of the insurance policy.

   _____ b. After the board of directors had given its approval, shareholders were sent their year-end dividends.

   _____ c. Sometimes shares of stock are given to stockholders in addition to cash dividends.

   _____ d. The dividends were considered a liability by the policyholder.

2. Who might receive *dividends?*

   _____ a. a stockholder   _____ c. a policyholder

   _____ b. a mortgage lender   _____ d. a company owner

3. Which of the numbered dictionary definitions of *dividend* best fits the word's use in the reading selection? _____

4. Write a sentence correctly using *dividends.* (Be sure to include context clues to show you understand the meaning of the word.)

   _____

   _____

5. Is it a good idea to put *dividends* that you might receive into a savings account? Why or why not?

   _____

   _____

Equity[6]

eq|ui|ty (ek'wə tē), *n., pl.* **-ties.** **1** fairness; justice: *The judge was noted for the equity of his decisions.* **SYN:** impartiality. **2** what is fair and just: *In all equity, he should pay for the damage he did.* **SYN:** justice, right. **3a** a system of rules and principles as to what is fair or just. Equity supplements common law and statute law in the United States and the Commonwealth by covering cases in which fairness and justice require a settlement not covered by the common law. In the United States, law and equity are usually administered by the same court. **b** a claim or right according to equity. **c** fairness in the adjustment of conflicting interests. **d** = equity of redemption. **4a** the amount that a property is worth beyond what is owed on it. **b** a share in the ownership of a business; stock: *Leading industrial equities were fairly firm on selective demand today, although the best prices were not always maintained* (New York Times). [< Old French *equite,* learned borrowing from Latin *aequitās* < *aequus* even, just]

1. Select the synonym(s) of *equity.*

   _____ a. liabilities   _____ c. debit

   _____ b. impartiality   _____ d. stock

2. Which of the numbered dictionary definitions of *equity* best fits the word's use in the reading selection? _____

3. In which of the following sentences can *equity* be correctly placed in the blank?

___ a. The owner's _____ needed to be entered in the ledger account.

___ b. The firm needed to calculate its debits, or _____ .

___ c. The difference between the assets and the liabilities of a company is called its _____ .

___ d. The company had a large _____ , which included money invested in the company and its net earnings that had not been withdrawn by the owner.

4. Do you have *equity* in any tangible property such as a car, house, boat, or other item? If not, what would you like to have some *equity* in and why?

_____

_____

5. Write a sentence correctly using *equity*. (Be sure to include context clues to show you understand the meaning of the word.)

_____

_____

Intangible[10]

in|tan|gi|ble (in tan′jə bəl), *adj., n.* —*adj.* **1** not capable of being touched or felt: *Sound and light are intangible.* SYN: insubstantial, impalpable. **2** *Figurative.* not easily grasped by the mind; vague: *She had that intangible something called charm.* —*n.* something intangible, such as good will. —**in|tan′gi|ble|ness,** *n.* —**in|tan′gi|bly,** *adv.*

1. Complete the verbal analogy.
   tangible : physical :: *intangible* : _____
   a. palpable   c. substantial
   b. nonmaterial   d. touchable

2. Select the synonym(s) of *intangible*.
   ___ a. flexible   ___ c. insubstantial
   ___ b. intellectual   ___ d. impalpable

3. Is the following sentence a literal or figurative (symbolic) use of *intangible?* (See the dictionary entry.)
   "He had an *intangible* understanding of the nature of the problem."
   ___ a. literal
   ___ b. figurative

4. Write a sentence correctly using *intangible*. (Be sure to include context clues to show you understand the meaning of the word.)

_____

_____

5. What do you value that is *intangible* in your life (health, friendship, intelligence, and so forth)?

_____

_____

_____

Ledger[1]

ledg|er (lej′ər), *n., v.* — *n.* **1a** a book of accounts in which a business keeps a record of all money transactions. **b** the book of final entry in book-keeping and accounting, where a complete record of all assets, liabilities, and proprietorship items are kept. It shows the changes that occur in these items during the month as a result of business operations carried on, by means of debits and credits. **2** a flat stone slab covering a grave. **3** a horizontal member of a scaffold, attached to the uprights and supporting the putlogs. **4a** Also, **leger.** = ledger bait. **b** = ledger tackle.
— *v.i.* to fish with a ledger.
[probably Middle English *leggen* lay[1]. Compare Dutch *ligger, legger* ledger.]

1. In which of the following sentences is *ledger* used correctly?
   _____ a. The small company entered all the charges to and payments from customers in a single-entry ledger account.
   _____ b. The secretary left a phone message in the ledger.
   _____ c. The accounting cycle includes making debit and credit entries in a general ledger.
   _____ d. The business manager used the ledger to write a business letter.

2. A *ledger* is a record book of financial matters for a business. What are other types of record books?
   _____ a. an address book   _____ c. a phone book
   _____ b. a calendar   _____ d. a journal

3. Who would probably need to see a *ledger* for a company?
   _____ a. a customer   _____ c. a bookkeeper
   _____ b. an accountant   _____ d. a company president

4. Have you ever kept a *ledger* for your personal money transactions? Could you compare a ledger to a checkbook? Why or why not?

_____

_____

5. Write a sentence correctly using *ledger*. (Be sure to include context clues to show you understand the meaning of the word.)

_____

_____

Liabilities[5]

li|a|bil|i|ty (lī′ə bil′ə tē), *n., pl.* **-ties. 1** the state of being susceptible: *liability to disease.* **SYN:** susceptibility. **2** the state of being under obligation: *liability for a debt.* **3** something that is to one's disadvantage: *His poor handwriting is a liability in getting a job as a clerk.* **SYN:** handicap, impediment.
liabilities, the debts or other financial obligations of a business, for money, goods, or services received: *A business with more liabilities than assets is bound to fail.*

1. In which of the following sentences is *liabilities* used correctly?
   _____ a. The company's liabilities were larger than their assets, and they were in financial trouble.
   _____ b. His liabilities included his charming personality and his trustworthiness.
   _____ c. The company car, office building, and machinery that had been paid for composed the company's liabilities.
   _____ d. A company can have short-term and long-term liabilities that they must pay.

2. Select the synonym(s) of *liabilities.*
   _____ a. obligation   _____ c. selection
   _____ b. permission   _____ d. indebtedness

3. Which of the following are part of a company's *liabilities?*
   _____ a. credits   _____ c. assets
   _____ b. debts   _____ d. financial obligations

4. Write a sentence correctly using *liabilities.* (Be sure to include context clues to show you understand the meaning of the word.)

   _____

   _____

5. Do you have any large *liabilities,* or financial obligations? If not, what do you think are the most common *liabilities* for adults today?

   _____

   _____

Requisition[13]

req|ui|si|tion (rek′wə zish′ən), *n., v. — n.* **1** the act of requiring: *His requisition of the car prevented others from using it.* **2** a demand made, especially a formal written demand: *The requisition of supplies for troops included new shoes, uniforms, and blankets.* **3** the condition of being required for use or called into service: *The car was in constant requisition for errands.* **4** an essential condition; requirement.
— v.t. **1** to demand or take by authority: *to requisition supplies, horses, or labor.* **SYN:** commandeer. **2** to make demands upon: *The hospital requisitioned the city for more funds.*

1. In which of the following sentences is *requisition* used correctly?
   - _____ a. The requisition was included in the message on the phone machine.
   - _____ b. A requisition was signed by the president before the office equipment could be ordered.
   - _____ c. The requisition for the additional software was lost in the mail.
   - _____ d. The company needed a requisition from the stockholders.

2. Which of the numbered dictionary definitions of *requisition* best fits the word's use in the reading selection? _____

3. Select the synonym(s) of *requisition*.
   - _____ a. transaction   _____ c. debit
   - _____ b. demand   _____ d. request

4. What types of items do you think a company would include on a *requisition* for office supplies?

   _____

   _____

5. Write a sentence correctly using *requisition*. (Be sure to include context clues to show you understand the meaning of the word.)

   _____

   _____

Transaction[8]

trans|ac|tion (tran zak'shən, -sak'-), *n.* **1** the carrying on of any kind of business: *The store manager attends to the transaction of important matters himself.* **2** a piece of business: *A record is kept of every transaction of the firm.* **SYN:** proceeding, deal, matter, affair. **3** *Psychology.* any event or situation that is determined by a person's perception or participation rather than by external factors. **transactions**, a record of what was done at the meetings of a society, club, or other group: *What the club says has an audience far beyond Manchester, because its transactions are sent to li-* braries in this country and to American libraries, including Harvard, the Library of Congress, and the main library in New York (Manchester Guardian). *Abbr:* trans. [< Latin *trānsāctiō, -ōnis* < *trānsigere;* see etym. under **transact**].

from **transact:**

[< Latin *trānsāctus,* past participle of *trānsigere* accomplish < *trāns-* through + *agere* to drive]

1. In which of the following sentences can *transaction* be correctly placed in the blank?
   - _____ a. Each business _____ is entered on the balance sheet.
   - _____ b. The ledger provides a financial record of each _____ of the company.
   - _____ c. The student needed a _____ to complete the assignment.
   - _____ d. The _____ allowed the engine to run more efficiently.

2. Which of the numbered dictionary definitions of *transaction* best fits the word's use in the reading selection? _____

3. The etymology of *transaction* (see *transact*) shows that the word comes from the Latin *agere* (to drive). Use this information, your imagination, and your background knowledge to match the following:

_____ a. antagonize   aa. a person who takes a leading part; active supporter; champion

_____ b. stratagem   bb. a teacher of children; schoolmaster

_____ c. demagogue   cc. to make an enemy of; arouse dislike in

_____ d. protagonist   dd. a popular leader who stirs up the people by appealing to their emotions and prejudices

_____ e. pedagogue   ee. a scheme or trick for deceiving an enemy

4. Write a sentence correctly using *transaction*. (Be sure to include context clues to show you understand the meaning of the word.)

_____

_____

5. What method do you use to record your financial *transactions* (checkbook, savings account passbook, personal journal or diary)? If you do not now have some sort of recording system, what might you use in the future and why?

_____

_____

Voucher[12]

vouch|er[1] (vou′chər), *n.* **1** a person or thing that vouches for something. **2** a written evidence of payment; receipt. Canceled checks returned to a person from his bank are vouchers.
vouch (vouch), *v., n. —v.i.* **1** to be responsible; give a guarantee (for): *I can vouch for the truth of the story. The principal vouched for the boy's honesty.* **2** to give evidence or assurance of a fact (for): *The success of the campaign vouches for the candidate's popularity.*
—v.t. **1** to guarantee (as a statement or document) to be true or accurate; confirm; bear witness to; attest. **2** to support or uphold with evidence; back with proof. **3** to support or substantiate (as a claim or title) by vouchers. **4** to cite, quote, or appeal to (as authority, example, or a passage in a book) in support or justification as of a view. **5** *Law.* to call into court to give warranty of title. **6** to sponsor or recommend (a person or thing); support; back. **7** *Archaic.* to call to witness.
—n. Obsolete. an assertion, declaration, or attestation of truth or fact.
[Middle English *vouchen* < Anglo-French *voucher*, Old French *vochier* < Latin *vocāre* call]

1. What is an example of a *voucher*?

_____ a. a receipt   _____ c. a money order

_____ b. a bill   _____ d. a cancelled check

2. The etymology of *voucher* (see *vouch*) shows that the word comes from the Latin *vocare* (to call). Use this information, your background knowledge, and your imagination to match the following:

_____ a. evoke   aa. to make angry; vex

_____ b. vocation   bb. to take back; repeal; cancel; withdraw

_____ c. revoke   cc. a particular occupation, business, profession, or trade

_____ d. advocate   dd. to call forth; bring out

_____ e. provoke   ee. to speak or write in favor of; recommend publicly; support

3. Which of the numbered dictionary definitions of *voucher* best fits the word's use in the reading selection? _____

4. What is the most common type of *voucher* that you receive each month as a record of payments that you have made for purchases?

_____

_____

5. Write a sentence correctly using *voucher*. (Be sure to include context clues to show you understand the meaning of the word.)

_____

_____

ANSWERS TO CHAPTER 20 EXERCISES

Amortize   **1.** c   **2.** ee, cc, dd, bb, aa   **3.** b (example)

Assets: **1.** c (definition)   **2.** a, b   **3.** ee, cc, dd, aa, bb

Audit: **1.** b, d   **2.** d (example)   **3.** dd, ee, bb, cc, aa

Credit: **1.** cc, dd, aa, bb, ee   **2.** a, c, d   **3.** 4abc

Debit: **1.** c   **2.** dd, cc, ee, aa, bb   **3.** a, d

Depreciation: **1.** a, d   **2.** bb, ee, dd, cc, aa   **3.** b, c

Disclosure: **1.** c, d   **2.** b, d   **3.** d

Dividends: **1.** b, c   **2.** a, c, d   **3.** 2

Equity: **1.** b, d   **2.** 4a   **3.** a, c, d

Intangible: **1.** b (definition)   **2.** c, d   **3.** b

Ledger: **1.** a, c   **2.** a, b, d   **3.** b, c, d

Liabilities: **1.** a, d   **2.** a, d   **3.** b, d

Requisition: **1.** b, c   **2.** *n.* 2   **3.** b, d

Transaction: **1.** a, b   **2.** 2   **3.** cc, ee, dd, aa, bb

Voucher: **1.** a, d   **2.** dd, cc, bb, ee, aa   **3.** 2

If you missed any of the items in the exercises, return to the exercise and to the dictionary definitions to see where you went wrong. Remember: If you get something right, you only affirm that you knew it. If you get something wrong and understand why, *you have learned something.*

ACCOUNTING POSTTEST

Fill in the blanks with the words from this list.

amortize	depreciation	ledger
assets	disclosure	liabilities
audit	dividends	requisition
credit	equity	transaction
debit	intangible	voucher

1. _____ is another word for debts or other financial obligations.

2. *Proceeding, deal, matter,* or *affair* are synonyms of _____.

3. A loss figured as part of the cost of doing business is called a(n) _____.

4. A(n) _____ is a book of business transactions and can be structured as single entry or double entry.

5. The amount that a property is worth beyond what is owed on it is called the _____.

6. _____ refers to money earned as profit by a company and divided among the owners or stockholders.

7. *Insubstantial* is a synonym of _____.

8. A receipt is a type of _____.

9. _____ means "to set money aside regularly for future payment or settlement of a debt or other liability."

10. An act of uncovering, revelation, or opening to public view is a(n) _____.

11. Money paid on an account or a delayed payment is known as a(n) _____.

12. A(n) _____ is a demand or requirement, often written.

13. Resources that are owned and paid for are _____.

14. An entry of an amount owed, or the left-hand side of an account where such entries are made, is called a(n) _____.

15. An examination and check of business accounts is a(n) _____.

Answers to this posttest are in the Instructor's Manual.

If you missed any of the words, you may need to return to the exercises and to the dictionary entries to see why your concepts for some words are incomplete.

BUSINESS: BUSINESS ADMINISTRATION

◆

OVERVIEW

The field of business administration is concerned with the social, economic, and behavioral environment in which we live and which underlies the effective administration of contemporary businesses at both the national and international levels. Coursework in business helps prepare students to be professional managers of today's and tomorrow's business organizations and for lifelong careers in commerce, finance, and industry in both the public and not-for-profit sectors.

There are numerous areas within business administration, including accounting, finance, general business, computer accounting, resource administration, international business, management, marketing, production and operations management, real estate, and small business and entrepreneurship.

Employment opportunities for business administration majors include careers in a variety of organizations, including public accounting firms, banks, savings and loans, and other financial institutions. Additional employment opportunities are with commercial and high-technology industries, aerospace, transportation, communications, computer information systems, and the foreign trade sector. Finally, those entrepreneurs who want to own their own businesses will benefit from a degree in business administration.

Introductory textbooks in business administration are usually expository and descriptive in nature. They present broad concepts and generalizations as well as statements of situations, ideas, or problems. Many texts also include case studies and career and business profiles as realistic examples of the concepts and ideas of business administration.

The vocabulary in business administration is a combination of general and specialized terminology. There are general terms, such as incentive *and* pecuniary, *that also have a specialized meaning within the context of business administration. Specialized vocabulary in the form of compound nouns* (business cycle, gross national product, venture capital) *have also been developed to represent unique concepts or theoretical constructs.*

VOCABULARY SELF-EVALUATION

The following words will be introduced in this reading selection. Place a check mark (√) in front of any that you know thoroughly and use in your speech or writing. Place a question mark (?) in front of any that you recognize but do not use yourself.

_____ adversary	_____ fiat	_____ pecuniary
_____ axiom	_____ incentive	_____ proliferation
_____ contingency	_____ innovative	_____ ramification
_____ ensconced	_____ lucrative	_____ redress
_____ entitlement	_____ minutiae	_____ remuneration

MANAGEMENT STYLE
AND ITS EVOLUTION

The oldest method of management theory is the autocratic* system. This system was not invented by industry; it was a natural continuation of age-old relationships. Those in power ruled by fiat;[1] they gave orders, and their subjects obeyed or suffered the consequences. With the advent of the Industrial Age, the ruled became the factory workers, and a new class of ruler emerged: the factory owner-manager. Ensconced[2] in his position as owner, the manager decided what should be produced, how it should be produced, and what the worker would be paid. Few objected. It was not necessarily an efficient method of getting things done, but in those days competition was weak, raw materials were cheap and plentiful, and labor

---

* Autocratic means "having absolute power or authority; ruling without checks or limitations."

worked for what the owner was willing to pay. The accepted axiom[3] was "the boss knows what is best for business."

With the passage of time, both employers and employees recognized the inefficiency of the factory system. In 1912 Frederick Winslow Taylor developed what came to be called "scientific management." Taylor's time and motion studies measured the minutiae[4] of the workplace in order to increase the efficiency of both men and machines. Unfortunately, efficiency seemed to call for fitting the worker to the needs of the machine. Employee opinions were not sought because it did not occur to the employer that the employee might know a better, more efficient way to get the job done. The employer believed that the harder the employee worked, the more lucrative[5] the business would be. Changes were made for the sake of "efficiency" and only incidentally for the convenience of the worker. The employee could not yet expect attention to his problems or the right to seek redress[6] for wrongs.

About twenty-five years later, Elton Mayo's work at the Western Electric plant in Chicago produced further information about the worker's place in efficient production. Mayo's investigation showed the workplace to be essentially a social situation. The worker's view of work and willingness to be productive were closely linked to the worker's interactions with coworkers and supervisors and to perceptions of the company's attention to his or her welfare. When coworkers and supervisors did "a fair day's work," the worker performed better. When the company "cared about" the worker, he or she was more efficient. One ramification[7] of Mayo's study was the realization that the worker's *total* life affected job performance.

In the late 1940s Peter Drucker, sometimes called "the father of corporate society," reinforced the idea that the job should be designed to fit the worker psychologically as well as physically. Yet it was not until the 1970s that major companies started using incentives,[8] job enrichment programs, and other humanistic approaches to increase productivity through worker satisfaction. Researchers continued to expound the theory that workers are motivated by psychological rewards as well as the usually acknowledged pecuniary[9] rewards.

By 1970 competition was keen between highly developed countries. *Quality* and *cost* were now key words. The United States was finding out that some countries were outproducing us and that the quality of their goods and services was superior to ours.

At the end of World War II, Japanese industry was in ruins. Before the war, Japan had been known as the producer of cheap trinkets. Its new government made a decision to drop the emphasis on cheap products and concentrate on high-quality goods. But how was the desired level of quality to be achieved?

Japan turned to the United States for help. They wanted to know how we were able to produce goods with superior quality. Our response was that we had quality control inspectors on every assembly line. Every defective part of a product was removed from the line and added to the scrap pile. The Japanese, however, could not afford this system; they could not afford to throw away expensive raw materials.

To overcome this problem, the Japanese initiated an innovative[10] system called the "quality circle": Quality will automatically be built into all products when workers understand exactly what they are to do and why they are to do it and when they are able to control many of their own activities on the job. Compensation for a job well done would extend beyond the usual remuneration.[11] Salary might not be particularly high, but the feeling that the workplace was much like a family would give the worker a sense of being necessary and appreciated. Entitlements[12] might include payment of rent and utilities, meals while on the job, and group vacations. Management's attitude was "Let's listen carefully to what the workers have to say. After all, the person closest to the job usually knows the most about it." Such a notion could never have been imagined in the early days of business management!

Quality circles were formed in all areas of business and industry, manufacturing, banking, and even education. Now more than nine million Japanese workers are members of circles, each contributing to the quality of the product and the quality of working life. Not all circles are effective, but the quality of Japanese products has prompted U.S. businessmen to look at Japan's styles of management in order to adapt them to the American working environment.

Today, American management does not consider one particular management style to be best. Rather, managers look at each situation and modify their styles accordingly. This contingency[13] approach pays particular attention to the educational level of workers, to the task involved, and to the relationship of the supervisor-manager to the employee. Many testing instruments have been devised and administered to both employees and employers to find the preferred and most productive style of management. Such an approach keeps management and labor from being adversaries.[14] The newer approach is to work together as partners toward a common goal.

The success of Japanese business and industry has led to a proliferation[15] of the quality circle idea. Many leading American companies have adapted and integrated it into their organizational structure. Hewlett-Packard, Monsanto, Gaines Dog Food, and other companies are now strong advocates of a more participative system. And the commitment of some Japanese companies is very strong: When Honda, Nissan, and Toyota develop new plants in their worldwide markets, they spend as much money on the training of their workers as they do on equipping their plants. ◆

BUSINESS ADMINISTRATION PRETEST

Select words from this list and write them in the blanks to complete the sentences.

adversary	fiat	pecuniary
axiom	incentive	proliferation
contingency	innovative	ramification
ensconced	lucrative	redress
entitlement	minutiae	remuneration

1. Something one has a right to is a(n) _____.
2. Doing things a new way is _____.
3. _____ means "sheltered safely."
4. A spreading into parts is a(n) _____.
5. Something yielding gain is _____.
6. A person or group opposing is a(n) _____.

7. Something in the form of money is _____.

8. An authoritative order is a(n) _____.

9. Something incidental to something else is a(n) _____.

10. To set right is to _____.

11. A cause of action or effort is a(n) _____.

12. Reproduction, as by cell division, is _____.

13. A self-evident truth is a(n) _____.

14. Another term for *payment* is _____.

15. Trifling details are _____.

    Answers to this pretest are in Appendix B.

    Unless your instructor tells you to do otherwise, complete the exercises for each word you missed on the pretest. The words, with their exercises, are in alphabetical order. The superscript numbers indicate where the words appeared in the reading selection so that you can refer to them when necessary. There are several types of exercises, but for each word you will be asked to write a sentence using context clues. (See Chapter 4 if you need information about how to create context clues.) You are also asked to perform some activity that will help you make your concept of the word personal. *Complete this activity thoughtfully, for creating a personalized concept of the word will help you remember it in the future.*

    Answers to all the exercises are at the end of the exercise segment.

BUSINESS ADMINISTRATION EXERCISES

Adversary[14]

ad|ver|sar|y (ad′vər ser′ē), *n., pl.* **-sar|ies,** *adj.*
— *n.* **1** a person or group opposing or hostile to another person or group; enemy; antagonist: *The United States and Japan were adversaries in World War II.* **SYN**: foe. **2** a person or group on the other side in a contest; opponent: *Which school is our adversary in this week's football game?* **SYN**: rival, contestant.
— *adj.* antagonistic; adverse: *"The hearings,"* Senator Watkins said on the opening day, *"are not to be adversary in character"* (New Yorker).

the Adversary, Satan, as the enemy of mankind; the Devil: *Or shall the Adversary thus obtain his end?* (Milton).

from **adverse:**
[< Latin *adversārius* < *adversus;* see etym. under **adverse**]

(Note: The term *adversarial* is sometimes used as the adjective form, instead of *adversary.*)

1. If you are an *adversary,* you
    _____ a. may cooperate with everyone.
    _____ b. may be angry.
    _____ c. may plan to get even.
    _____ d. are working against someone or something.

2. In which of the following sentences can *adversary* correctly be placed in the blank?

    _____ a. An _____ relationship may involve a lawsuit.

    _____ b. Another term for *best friend* is _____.

    _____ c. Don't think of your teacher as an _____ but rather as an ally.

    _____ d. A good football coach will know the plays used by each _____.

3. Place an "s" before any synonym and an "a" before any antonym of *adversary*.

    _____ a. opponent   _____ f. supporter

    _____ b. backer   _____ g. ally

    _____ c. rival   _____ h. competitor

    _____ d. foe   _____ i. opposer

    _____ e. comrade

4. Write a sentence correctly using *adversary*. (Be sure to include context clues to show you understand the meaning of the word.)

_____

_____

5. Is there someone who is your *adversary*? How do you handle the situation? If you have no *adversary*, how do you maintain this situation?

_____

_____

Axiom[3]

ax|i|om (ak′sē əm), *n.* **1** a statement taken to be true without proof; self-evident truth: *It is an axiom that a whole is greater than any one of its parts. It is an axiom that if equals are added to equals the results will be equal.* **2** a well-established principle, rule, or law: *It is an axiom that medicine should be kept out of the reach of young children.* [< Latin *axiōma* < Greek *axiōma* < *áxios* worthy]

1. Check any appropriate response to the following statement: "A good parent guides a child by *axiom* and by example."

    _____ a. The rules of behavior have to be set out clearly.

    _____ b. I agree that punishment is what works best.

    _____ c. Tell them what you expect and then show them.

    _____ d. Children learn by hearing and by seeing.

2. Select the synonym(s) of *axiom*.

    _____ a. statement   _____ d. proof

    _____ b. law   _____ e. evidence

    _____ c. principle   _____ f. rule

3. Which of the numbered dictionary definitions of *axiom* best fits the word's use in the reading selection? _____

4. Write down an *axiom* you heard when you were growing up. For example: "Beauty is skin deep," "Pretty is as pretty does," "If at first you don't succeed, try, try again."

_____

_____

5. Write a sentence correctly using *axiom*. (Be sure to include context clues to show you understand the meaning of the word.)

_____

_____

Contingency[13]

con|tin|gen|cy (kən tin′jən sē), *n., pl.* **-cies.** **1** a happening or event depending on something that is uncertain; possibility: *The explorer carried supplies for every contingency.* **2** an accidental happening; uncertain event; chance: *Football players seldom think of injury as a contingency while they are playing.* **3** uncertainty of occurrence; dependence on chance. **4** *Philosophy.* **a** the mode of existence, or of coming to pass, which does not involve necessity. **b** a happening by chance or free will. **5** something incidental to something else.

1. Check any appropriate response to the following statement: "Johanna is a good manager and plans for every *contingency*."
   _____ a. She is in charge of every social gathering.
   _____ b. Her business is likely to succeed.
   _____ c. She tries to prepare for the unexpected.
   _____ d. Life can be full of surprises.

2. Complete the verbal analogy.
   delight : please :: *contingency* : _____
   a. plans   c. event
   b. dependent   d. possibility

3. Which of the numbered and lettered dictionary definitions of *contingency* best fits the word's use in the reading selection? _____

4. Write a sentence correctly using *contingency*. (Be sure to include context clues to show you understand the meaning of the word.)

_____

_____

5. What *contingencies* have you considered in planning your formal school-

ing? A change in the job market? An increase in costs and fees? A change of interests?

_____

_____

Ensconced[2]

en|sconce (en skons´), *v.t.*, **-sconced, -sconc-ing.** **1** to shelter safely; hide: *The soldiers were ensconced in strongly fortified trenches. We were ensconced in the cellar during the tornado.* **2** to settle comfortably and firmly: *The cat ensconced itself in the armchair.* [< *en-*[1] + *sconce*[3] fortification, probably < Dutch *schans*]

1. Which of the following might be *ensconced?*
   _____ a. a large stand of trees
   _____ b. the president of a company
   _____ c. a flock of birds
   _____ d. several children

2. If you were *ensconced,* you might be
   _____ a. situated.   _____ d. placed.
   _____ b. established.   _____ e. settled.
   _____ c. stationed.   _____ f. installed.

3. Which of the numbered dictionary definitions of *ensconced* best fits the word's use in the reading selection? _____

4. Who is *ensconced* as the boss of your family? Of your love relationship?

   _____

   _____

5. Write a sentence correctly using *ensconced.* (Be sure to include context clues to show you understand the meaning of the word.)

   _____

   _____

Entitlement[12]

en|ti|tle|ment (en tī´təl mənt), *n.* something to which one is entitled; a privilege: *A careful campaign ... must be developed to enable older people fully to understand their entitlements under the new law* (New York Times).
en|ti|tle (en tī´təl), *v.t.*, **-tled, -tling.** **1** to give a claim or right (to); provide with a reason to ask or get something: *The one who wins is entitled to first prize. A ticket will entitle you to admission.*
SYN: empower, qualify, enable. **2** to give the title of; name: *The author entitled his book "Treasure Island." The Queen of England is also entitled "Defender of the Faith."* **SYN:** denominate, designate. **3** to give or call by an honorary title. Also, **intitle.** [< Old French *entituler,* learned borrowing from Late Latin *intitulāre* < Latin *in-* in + *titulus* title, inscription, claim]

1. Check any appropriate response to the following statement:
"My new job has no *entitlements*."
_____ a. I would purchase some health insurance, if I were you.
_____ b. It sounds like the ideal job!
_____ c. That's probably okay if they pay you enough.
_____ d. That may be all right for you, but I prefer a few extras.

2. An *entitlement* is
_____ a. something you buy.
_____ b. something you earn.
_____ c. something you give to your employer.
_____ d. something in addition to regular pay.

3. Complete the verbal analogy:
entitle : v.t. :: *entitlement* : _____
a. claim   d. v.i.
b. n.   e. adj.
c. privilege

4. If you owned a business, what *entitlements* would you offer your employees? What would be your purpose in offering those *entitlements*?

_____

_____

5. Write a sentence correctly using *entitlement*. (Be sure to include context clues to show you understand the meaning of the word.)

_____

_____

Fiat[1]

fi|at (fī′ət, -at), *n., v.* —*n.* **1** an authoritative order or command; decree: *to determine by the fiat of the king alone the course of national policy* (William Stubbs). **2** an authoritative sanction; authorization.
—*v.t.* **1** to attach a fiat to; sanction. **2** to declare by a fiat.
[< Latin *fīat* let it be done < *fierī*, passive of *facere* do]

1. Which of the following might issue a *fiat*?
_____ a. the president of a democracy
_____ b. a president-for-life
_____ c. the owner of a business
_____ d. a medical doctor

2. Check any appropriate response to the following statement:
"My father rules our family by *fiat*."
_____ a. That seems fair enough.
_____ b. I wouldn't like that at all!

_____ c. It's nice when everyone has a say in family policy.

_____ d. How soon do you plan to move out?

3. Which of the numbered dictionary definitions of *fiat* best fits the word's use in the reading selection? _____

4. Write a sentence correctly using *fiat*. (Be sure to include context clues to show you understand the meaning of the word.)

_____

_____

5. If you could issue a *fiat* that would be obeyed in your family or in your school, what would it be?

_____

_____

Incentive[8]

in|cen|tive (in sen′tiv), *n., adj.* — *n.* a thing that urges a person on; a cause of action or effort; motive; stimulus: *The fun of playing the game was a greater incentive than the prize. This accentuated the world shortage, and added incentive to soaring prices for the metal* (Wall Street Journal). SYN: spur, incitement, provocation. See syn. under **motive**.
— *adj.* arousing to feeling or action; inciting; encouraging. SYN: exciting, provocative.
[< Latin *incēntīvum,* noun use of neuter adjective (in Late Latin, inciting) < *incinere* strike up; blow into (a flute) < *in-* in, into + *canere* to sing]

1. In which of the following sentences can *incentive* correctly be placed in the blank?

_____ a. His father's promise of a bicycle was the _____ Joe needed to work harder in school.

_____ b. Our company has a system of _____ pay.

_____ c. It is a good idea to _____ a child for good behavior.

_____ d. The _____ offered was a cookie now, nothing later.

2. Which of the following might be an *incentive?*

_____ a. extra pay   _____ d. vacation time

_____ b. a candy bar   _____ e. a half-price sale

_____ c. an A in a class   _____ f. failing a class

3. Select the synonym(s) of *incentive.*

_____ a. spur   _____ d. incitement

_____ b. payment   _____ e. exciting

_____ c. provocation   _____ f. provocative

4. School is hard work. What is the major *incentive* that keeps you attending classes?

_____

_____

5. Write a sentence correctly using *incentive*. (Be sure to include context clues to show you understand the meaning of the word.)

_____

_____

Innovative[10]

in|no|va|tive (in′ə vā′tiv), *adj.* tending to innovate; characterized by innovation: *Inventors are innovative people.* — **in′no|va′tive|ness**, *n.*
in|no|vate (in′ə vāt), *v.,* **-vat|ed, -vat|ing.** — *v.i.* to make changes; bring in something new or new ways of doing things: *It is difficult to innovate when people prefer the old, familiar way of doing things. It were good ... that men in their innovations would follow the example of time itself, which indeed innovateth greatly, but quietly* (Francis Bacon).
— *v.t.* to introduce (something); bring in for the first time: *The scientist innovated new ways of research. Every moment alters what is done, And innovates some act till then unknown* (John Dryden).
[< Latin *innovāre* (with English *-ate*[1]) < *in-* (intensive) + *novus* new] — **in′no|va′tor**, *n.*
in|no|va|tion (in′ə vā′shən), *n.* **1** a change made in the established way of doing things: *The new principal made many innovations. The scheme of a Colony revenue by British authority appeared therefore to the Americans in the light of a great innovation* (Edmund Burke). SYN: novelty. **2** the act of making changes; bringing in new things or new ways of doing things: *Many people are opposed to innovation. Innovation is for showoffs and pioneers alike* (New Yorker).

1. Check any appropriate response to the following statement:
   "I think Kim is a truly *innovative* person."
   _____ a. Yes, I agree. Same old thing all the time: boring, boring.
   _____ b. She thinks of new and different ways to do things.
   _____ c. I like the changes she makes.
   _____ d. Kim and I prefer the old, familiar way of doing things.

2. Something *innovative* may be
   _____ a. a change.   _____ d. familiar.
   _____ b. a novelty.   _____ e. opposed.
   _____ c. different.   _____ f. new.

3. Complete the verbal analogy.
   national : nation :: *innovative* : _____
   a. innovativeness   c. innovating
   b. innovated   d. innovational

4. Write a sentence correctly using *innovative*. (Be sure to include context clues to show you understand the meaning of the word.)

_____

_____

5. What popular musician do you think is *innovative*?

_____

_____

Lucrative[5]

lu|cra|tive (lü′krə tiv), *adj.* bringing in money; yielding gain or profit; profitable: *a lucrative profession, a lucrative investment.* SYN: gainful, remunerative. [< Latin *lucrātīvus* < *lūcrārī* to gain < *lucrum* gain] —**lu′cra|tive|ly**, *adv.* —**lu′ cra|tive|ness**, *n.*

1. If you had a *lucrative* business, you might
   _____ a. plan carefully and work hard.
   _____ b. be able to retire at an early age.
   _____ c. have to sell at a loss.
   _____ d. find it easy to get investors.

2. If something is *lucrative,* it
   _____ a. is remunerative.   _____ d. is gainful.
   _____ b. produces wealth.   _____ e. is profitable.
   _____ c. is expensive.   _____ f. pays well.

3. Complete the verbal analogy.
   lucrative : lucrativeness :: _____ : _____
   a. noun : verb   c. adjective : adverb
   b. adjective : noun   d. noun : adjective

4. What do you think is the most *lucrative* business in the world? Does it have any disadvantages?

   _____

   _____

5. Write a sentence correctly using *lucrative.* (Be sure to include context clues to show you understand the meaning of the word.)

   _____

   _____

Minutiae[4]

mi|nu|ti|ae (mi nü′shē ē, -nyü′-), *n.pl.* very small matters; trifling details: *scientific minutiae. They waited ... for the exchange of pass-words, the delivery of keys, and all the slow minutiae attendant upon the movements of a garrison in a well-guarded fortress* (Scott). [< Latin *minūtiae* trifles, plural of *minūtia* smallness < *minūtus;* see etym. under **minute**[2]]

mi|nu|ti|a (mi nu′shē ə, -nyü′-), *n.* singular of **minutiae**.

from **minute:**[2]

[< Latin *minūtus* made small, past participle of *minuere* diminish < *minus* less; see etym. under **minus**. See etym. of doublet **menu**.]

(Note: Read the pronunciation of this word carefully. It is usually used in the plural.)

1. Match the following statement with a similar statement below:
   "The editor was overconcerned with *minutiae.*"
   _____ a. She watched the passage of time very closely.
   _____ b. She made very sure that no one earned a bonus.
   _____ c. She worried about minor details too much.
   _____ d. She fired anyone who was a clock watcher.

2. Complete the verbal analogy.

facts : fact :: *minutiae* : _____

a. minute   c. minutiae

b. minutia   d. minutus

5. Check any appropriate response to the following statement:
"Martin is concerned with the *minutiae* of life."

_____ a. Why does he focus on trifling matters?

_____ b. He is wise to take a broad view of life, I think.

_____ c. Small details drive me crazy.

_____ d. He would probably make a good scientist.

4. Write a sentence correctly using *minutiae*. (Be sure to include context clues to show you understand the meaning of the word.)

_____

_____

5. Is there a part of your life in which *minutiae* are important? The upkeep of your car? Your wardrobe? Your hair? Your love life?

_____

_____

Pecuniary[9]

pe|cu|ni|ar|y (pi kyü′nē er′ē), *adj.* **1** of or having to do with money: *I pass my whole life, miss, in turning an immense pecuniary mangle* (Dickens). **2** in the form of money: *pecuniary assistance, a pecuniary gift.* [< Latin *pecūniārius* < *pecūnia* money < *pecū* money; cattle] — **pe|cu′ni|ar′i|ly,** *adv.*

(Note: The etymology is interesting. Why would the Latin word *pecu* mean both "money" and "cattle"?)

1. In which of the following sentences is *pecuniary* correctly used?

_____ a. Last year's pecuniary loss caused the company to lower its dividend.

_____ b. Bill took the job for pecuniary motives only.

_____ c. He shouldn't be surprised then, if his only reward is pecuniary.

_____ d. Mary's haircut is really pecuniary; it makes her look like a turkey.

2. Check any appropriate response to the following statement:
"Sara has little interest in *pecuniary* gain."

_____ a. She is more interested in spiritual matters.

_____ b. She gives her time and effort for little pay.

_____ c. Do you suppose she inherited money from her family?

_____ d. The world doesn't need people like that!

3. Complete the verbal analogy.
   customary : adjective :: *pecuniary* : _____
   a. noun   c. adverb
   b. verb   d. adjective

4. With what project would you like *pecuniary* assistance? A new car? A better wardrobe? School expenses?

   _____

   _____

5. Write a sentence correctly using *pecuniary*. (Be sure to include context clues to show you understand the meaning of the word.)

   _____

   _____

Proliferation[15]

pro|lif|er|a|tion (prō lif′ə rā′shən), *n.* **1** reproduction, as by budding or cell division. **2** a spreading; propagation: *The draft of the test ban treaty contained an expression of desire to prevent the proliferation of nuclear weapons* (Seymour Topping). [< French *prolifération* < *prolifère* < Medieval Latin *prolifer;* see etym. under **proliferous**]
pro|lif|er|ate (prō lif′ə rāt), *v.i., v.t.,* **-at|ed, -at|ing.** **1** to grow or produce by multiplication of parts, as in budding or cell division. **2** to multiply; spread; propagate: *These conferences proliferate like measles spots* (Harper's). [back formation < *proliferation*]

from **proliferous:**

[< Medieval Latin *prolifer* < Latin *prōlēs* offspring (see etym. under **proletarian**) + *-fer* bearing + English *-ous*]

1. Check any appropriate response to the following statement:
   "In the past twenty years, there has been a great *proliferation* of fast-food outlets."
   _____ a. There are so many different kinds of them now.
   _____ b. I wish I had invested in them several years ago.
   _____ c. It's too bad they haven't caught on.
   _____ d. You can find them everywhere, it seems.

2. *Proliferation* might occur in which of the following areas?
   _____ a. in a disease
   _____ b. in a plant
   _____ c. in business practices
   _____ d. in television programming

3. Complete the verbal analogy.
   separation : division :: *proliferation* : _____
   a. multiplication   c. subtraction
   b. addition   d. growth

4. Write a sentence correctly using *proliferation*. (Be sure to include context clues to show you understand the meaning of the word.)

   _____

   _____

BUSINESS: BUSINESS ADMINISTRATION

5. If you could prevent the *proliferation* of one thing, what would it be?

_____

_____

Ramification[7]

ram|i|fi|ca|tion (ram′ə fə kā′shən), *n.* **1** a dividing or spreading out into branches or parts. **2** the manner or result of branching; offshoot; branch; part; subdivision; consequence.
ram|i|fy (ram′ə fī), *v.*, **-fied, -fy|ing.** — *v.i.* to divide or spread out into parts resembling branches: *Quartz veins ramify through the rock in all directions* (F. Kingdon-Ward).
— *v.t.* to cause to branch out.
[< French, Old French *ramifier* < Medieval Latin *ramificari* < Latin *rāmus* branch + *facere* make]

1. In which of the following sentences can *ramification* correctly be placed in the blank?
   _____ a. Kim has no interest at all in any _____ of party politics.
   _____ b. When we read the etymology of a word, we can explore the fine shades of meaning and all their _____s.
   _____ c. The _____s of the cypress tree create an unusual silhouette.
   _____ d. After the _____, all the parts are unified into one whole.

2. A *ramification* is
   _____ a. a dividing.   _____ d. a subdivision.
   _____ b. a branch.   _____ e. a part.
   _____ c. an offshoot.   _____ f. a consequence.

3. Complete the verbal analogy.
   <u>nonsense</u> : no :: *ramification* : _____
   a. tree   c. make
   b. branch   d. part

4. What *ramifications* do you hope for as a result of attending college?

_____

_____

5. Write a sentence correctly using *ramification*. (Be sure to include context clues to show you understand the meaning of the word.)

_____

_____

Redress[6]

re|dress (*v.* ri dres′; *n.* rē′dres, ri dres′), *v., n.*
— *v.t.* **1** to set right; repair; remedy: *King Arthur tried to redress wrongs in his kingdom.* **2** to adjust evenly again: *I called the New World into existence to redress the balance of the Old* (George Canning).
— *n.* **1** the act or process of setting right; relief; reparation: *Anyone who has been injured unfairly deserves redress. My griefs ... finding no redress, ferment and rage* (Milton). **SYN:** restitution. **2** the means of a remedy: *There was no redress against the lawless violence to which they were perpetually exposed* (John L. Motley).
[< Middle French *redresser* < *re-* again + Old French *dresser* to straighten, arrange. Compare etym. under **dress**, verb.] — **re|dress′er, re|dres′sor,** *n.*

(Note: *Redress* involves righting a wrong, usually without goodwill resulting.)

1. In which of the following sentences can *redress* correctly be placed in the blank?

   _____ a. Fired from his job, Mr. Martinez is seeking _____ in the courts.

   _____ b. Can we _____ social wrongs through legislation?

   _____ c. The Constitution says we can petition the government for _____ of grievances.

   _____ d. You can _____ for a month, but it won't help.

2. Check any appropriate response to the following statement: "The company says it intends to *redress* our grievances."

   _____ a. I'll believe it when I see it.

   _____ b. They are trying to make things better.

   _____ c. They must be doing that because all the workers are happy.

   _____ d. That survey must have made worker dissatisfaction clear to management.

3. Which of the numbered dictionary definitions of *redress* best fits the word's use in the reading selection? _____

4. Write a sentence correctly using *redress*. (Be sure to include context clues to show you understand the meaning of the word.)

   _____

   _____

5. Have you ever had to *redress* a wrong? What did it involve? Your family? A friend? Your job? Have you had to seek *redress* for yourself?

   _____

   _____

Remuneration[11]

re|mu|ner|a|tion (ri myü′nə rā′shən), *n.* reward; pay; payment: *Remuneration to employes for the quarter was down $3 million* (Wall Street Journal).
re|mu|ner|ate (ri myü′nə rāt), *v.t.,* -at|ed, -at|ing. to pay, as for work, services, or trouble; reward: *The boy who returned the lost jewels was remunerated. The harvest will remunerate the laborers for their toil.* **syn**: recompense. See syn. under **pay**. [< Latin *remūnerāre* (with English -ate¹) < re- back + *mūnerāre* to give < *mūnus, -eris* gift]

1. Check any appropriate response to the following statement: "My *remuneration* for this job is very small."

   _____ a. I'm glad it's no trouble.

   _____ b. Do you do it because you think it is a contribution to society?

   _____ c. You might as well be a volunteer.

   _____ d. You don't need a station wagon; a small car will do.

2. You might receive *remuneration* for which of the following?

_____ a. working as a regular employee
_____ b. serving as a consultant
_____ c. winning a lottery
_____ d. selling a business

3. Complete the verbal analogy.
remuneration : remunerate :: _____ : _____
a. v.t. : n.   c. adj. : n.
b. n. : v.t.   d. adj. : adv.

4. Some say a young person should not receive *remuneration* for jobs done around the home. Do you agree? Did/do you receive such *remuneration*?

_____

_____

5. Write a sentence correctly using *remuneration*. (Be sure to include context clues to show you understand the meaning of the word.)

_____

_____

ANSWERS TO CHAPTER 21 EXERCISES

Adversary: **1.** b, c, d **2.** a, c, d **3.** s, a, s, s, a, a, a, s, s
Axiom: **1.** a, c, d **2.** b, c, f **3.** 1
Contingency: **1.** b, c, d **2.** d (synonym) **3.** 5
Ensconced: **1.** b, d **2.** a, b, c, d, e, f **3.** 2
Entitlement: **1.** a, c, d **2.** b, d **3.** b (part of speech, abbrev.)
Fiat: **1.** b, c, d **2.** b, d **3.** *n.* 1
Incentive: **1.** a, b, d **2.** a, b, c, d, e, f **3.** a, c, d, e, f
Innovative: **1.** b, c **2.** a, b, c, e, f **3.** a (adjective : noun)
Lucrative: **1.** a, b, d **2.** a, b, d, e, f **3.** b (parts of speech)
Minutiae: **1.** c **2.** b (singular) **3.** a, c, d
Pecuniary: **1.** a, b, c **2.** a, b, c **3.** d (part of speech)
Proliferation: **1.** a, b, d **2.** a, b, c, d **3.** a (synonym)
Ramification: **1.** a, b, c **2.** a, b, c, d, e, f **3.** b (meaning of comb. form)
Redress: **1.** a, b, c **2.** a, b, d **3.** *n.* 1
Remuneration: **1.** b, c **2.** a, b **3.** b (parts of speech, abbrevs.)

If you missed any of the items in the exercises, return to the exercise and to the dictionary definition to see where you went wrong. Remember: If you get something right, you only affirm that you knew it. If you get something wrong and understand why, *you have learned something*.

BUSINESS ADMINISTRATION POSTTEST

Fill in the blanks with the words from this list.

adversary	fiat	pecuniary
axiom	incentive	proliferation
contingency	innovative	ramification
ensconced	lucrative	redress
entitlement	minutiae	remuneration

1. A(n) _____ is a decree.

2. _____ are very small matters.

3. An uncertain event is a(n) _____.

4. A(n) _____ is an enemy.

5. _____ means "gainful."

6. Something _____ is sheltered safely.

7. A(n) _____ is a motive or stimulus.

8. _____ means "having to do with money."

9. A consequence is also called a(n) _____.

10. _____ means "payment."

11. A(n) _____ is a well-established rule.

12. Something characterized by change is _____.

13. _____ means "propagation."

14. *Restitution* is a synonym for _____.

15. A(n) _____ is a privilege.

Answers to this posttest are in the Instructor's Manual.

If you missed any of the words, you may need to return to the exercises and to the dictionary entries to see why your concepts for some words are incomplete.

CHAPTER TWENTY-TWO

BUSINESS: COMPUTER SCIENCE

◆

OVERVIEW

Computer science is the study of computers, including their design, programming, and operation. This rapidly expanding field is concerned with the interaction of man and machine and with the application of computers in contemporary society.

Computer science programs usually include coursework and related research in mathematics (geometry and calculus), statistics, computer languages, information structures, computer logic design, and specialized areas such as artificial intelligence.

Students who receive degrees in computer science are prepared for a variety of careers in business, industry, and government. This includes work in the areas of systems analysis, systems programming, applications programming, data engineering, data communications, and software engineering.

The introductory textbooks in computer science are a combination of expository and instructional, or process analysis, in format. They present concepts and generalizations along with instructions and the analysis of a process, particularly in the areas of programming and computer languages.

The vocabulary in computer science is an interesting mixture of general and specialized terms and acronyms. General terms that have a specialized meaning in computer science include boot, chip, disk, *and* memory. *Specialized terminology includes such words as* on-line, debug, *and* software. *There are many acronyms (words formed from the initial letters of a series of words) as terminology for operations, equipment, and procedures. These include RAM (random access memory), CPU (central processing unit), and BASIC (Beginners All-Purpose Symbolic Instruction Code).*

VOCABULARY SELF-EVALUATION

The following words will be introduced in this reading selection. Place a check mark (√) in front of any that you know thoroughly and use in your speech or writing. Place a question mark (?) in front of any that you recognize but do not use yourself.

_____ algorithm	_____ digital	_____ morphemics
_____ ambiguity	_____ heuristics	_____ network
_____ analog	_____ interactive	_____ neuron
_____ binary	_____ matrix	_____ robotics
_____ cybernetics	_____ modeling	_____ syntax

ARTIFICIAL INTELLIGENCE

BACKGROUND

One of the most interesting and often-controversial areas of study and research within the field of computer science is artificial intelligence (AI). Artificial intelligence is the ability of a computer to perform a task or function that is normally associated with human intelligence. This multifaceted field is characterized by rapid successes, many failures, and ongoing specialization. Some of the goals of AI include the development of theories of human intelligence, in the form of simulation models, and new programming languages and computer systems. In order to accomplish these goals, researchers have had to understand the highly complex nature of learning, language, and sensory perception. The ultimate test of any AI system is for it to pass the so-called "Turing test of machine intelligence." This was first proposed in the early 1950s by British scientist Alan Turing, who defined an "intelligent computer" as one that could deceive a human into believing that it was also human.

Early AI researchers employed electronic digital[1] computers. These operate on a numerical code based on the binary[2] number system, which makes use of 1s and 0s (1 means that the electric current is on and 0 means that the current is off). Most of this early research was done at MIT (Massachusetts Institute of Technology), where the researchers wanted to move beyond the digitals and to program computers with algorithms[3] so the computers could "think" like humans when solving problems. Some early applications of their work included computers that could play games (such as chess), solve brain teasers, and answer calculus problems. These programs utilized heuristics,[4] (rules of thumb), intuition, or good judgment based on experience and discovery that humans use to narrow the search for a solution to a problem. These early pioneers considered the mind, as the symbolic processing entity, to be separate from the brain. This approach came to be known as top-down through the development of complex programming patterned on human thought processes.

Norbert Wiener, also at MIT, extended AI research with his notion that feedback was a necessary component of intelligence. He coined the term cybernetics,[5] based on the theory that intelligent beings utilize feedback from their surroundings in accomplishing goals and adapting to their environments. This approach came to be known as neural-modeling,[6] because it tried to model, or simulate, a pattern of the brain based on the neurons,[7] the fundamental, active cells in all animal nervous systems. This approach was also called bottom-up, because it focuses on a mechanical analysis of the brain's decision-making process. This was accomplished through designing simple analogs[8] that represent directly the neurons of the brain of simple creatures containing a few neurons, and then working toward the human brain with its feedback process. A product of this type of AI research of the late 1950s was the perceptron, an electronic pattern-recognition machine (such as speech recognition) modeled on the human nervous system. Another application of cybernetics has been in the field of robotics,[9] with robots equipped with tactile receptors and able to perceive visual stimuli. Some of the current uses of robotics are in space exploration, hospitals, and hazardous-waste movement.

LANGUAGE PROCESSING

Another step in AI research involved nonnumerical applications, with an emphasis on using language convincingly. Some imperfect attempts in this direction included the use of computers in translating Russian into English and the development of an interactive[10] therapy program called ELIZA. ELIZA, developed in the mid-1960s by Joseph Weizenbaum, requires that a human respond to the questions that ELIZA asks as a type of psychiatric interviewer about one's family and problems. ELIZA also "reacts" to the responses typed in by the human.

One of the most obvious problems with the attempt to replicate language processing is the inability of current programs to understand the complexity of human language. In addition to knowing syntax[11] (rules of grammar) and sentence formation, a computer needs to know semantics, that is, the study of the meaning of words. But there is much ambiguity[12] in language because of additional variables such as context, tone, prior background and knowledge, and critical thinking and reasoning skills that a human uses when communicating and comprehending. A very simple example would be an interpretation of the following sentence: "Tom saw a bike in the store and he wanted it." What was the *it,* the bike or the store? What is meant by *want?* A computer would also need to be aware of morphemics,[13] which is the study of meaningful linguistic units and the rules describing how words are changed to form variations such as plurals and verb conjugations. In the sentence "When Tom accidentally ran into the tree, this was an act of carelessness on his part," *carelessness* has three morphemes—*care, less,* and *ness*—which must be properly interpreted and interrelated and reasoned about for understanding.

Another step in machine language was the development of a language program called SHRDLU, by Terry Winograd in the late 1960s. This was an integration of syntax, semantics, and reasoning. It next led to an interest in knowledge representation, whereby AI scientists tried to develop a system of human knowledge organized into a data structure that can include rules, facts, and common sense. M. Ross Quillian coined the term semantic network[14] to describe a hierarchical system of linking webs or lines that indicate relationships between objects and concepts, which he termed nodes. This semantic network is a storage technique within the computer's memory that can be activated rapidly during the computer's decision-making process. An example of a semantic network would be nodes linking terms such as ANIMAL–DOG–TERRIER–HOUND. Even though eventually abandoned, this approach inspired other conceptualizations of knowledge representation. In the mid-1970s, Marvin Minsky (also of MIT) developed the idea of frames and subframes, that is, a data structure that portrays an object or concept using descriptive information. An example of a BOY frame would be: PERSON; SEX—MALE; AGE—BELOW 12 YEARS; PLACE—SCHOOL. There have been other, often-conflicting, approaches to knowledge representation that continue to the present.

SPECIALIZATION AND THE FUTURE

The mid-1960s saw a move toward marketable specialization with AI research. Programs called expert systems were developed by Edward Feigenbaum at Stanford in such specialized areas as medicine and geology. They could make linked decisions guided by "if–then" rules and a knowledge base with which it was provided. A typical expert system is composed of two systems in a matrix[15] consisting of a knowledge base of facts and heuristics and an inference engine that manipulates the information in the knowledge base. Examples of expert systems in medicine are disease analysis programs; examples in geology include simulations of how geologists find mineral deposits.

Finally, most recent ongoing research in AI is aimed at designing self-modifying computers, that is, computers that can learn from their own mistakes, much as humans do. A very ambitious project called "Cyc" should lead to the next advances in AI research in the area of machine learning. This complex project, under the leadership of Douglas Lenat in Austin, Texas, is focused on equipping a computer with the background knowledge or heuristics to read and comprehend a one-volume encyclopedia. The goal is to build an artificial mind by helping the computer understand language so that it can learn by itself. Lenat describes such a computer as an "intelligence amplifier."

What is the future of artificial intelligence? It is obvious that the human brain and mind are marvelous, mysterious, and complex and that humans make decisions and comprehend language using more than facts and rules. What computer could ever have common sense or emotions or understand the subtle meanings of cultural and gender differences? Finally, will a computer ever be able to pass the Turing test? ◆

COMPUTER SCIENCE PRETEST

Select words from this list and write them in the blanks to complete the sentences.

algorithm digital morphemics
ambiguity heuristics network
analog interactive neuron
binary matrix robotics
cybernetics modeling syntax

1. A formal procedure for any mathematical operation is called a(n) _____.

2. A(n) _____ is a nerve cell of the brain that conducts impulses.

3. The science or technology that deals with robots is called _____.

4. A lack of clarity is a(n) _____.

5. An array of circuit elements designed to perform a particular function in a computer is called a(n) _____.

6. _____ is the way in which words and phrases of a sentence are arranged to show how they relate to one another.

7. "Composed of two different parts" describes something that is _____.

8. _____ is the representation of solid form or the production of designs.

9. _____ is the comparative study of human and animal nervous systems and certain mechanical systems to better understand communication.

10. Having to do with the minimum meaningful elements of language is called _____.

11. _____ is the study or use of the discovery procedure in science.

12. Having to do with or using any one of the numbers 0, 1, 2, 3, 4, 5, 6, 7, 8, and 9 characterizes a system that is called _____.

13. _____ is any system of lines that cross.

14. _____ describes the process of acting on each other.

15. The representation of a physical variable or quantity is called a(n) _____.

Answers to this pretest are in Appendix B.

Unless your instructor tells you to do otherwise, complete the exercises for each word that you missed on the pretest. The words, with their meanings and exercises, are in alphabetical order. The superscript numbers indicate where the words appeared in the reading selection so that you can refer to them when necessary. There are several types of exercises, but for each word you will be asked to write a sentence using context clues. (See Chapter 4 if you need information about how to create context clues.) You are also asked to perform some activity that will help you make your concept of the word personal. *Complete the activity thoughtfully, for creating a personalized concept of the word will help you remember it in the future.*

Answers to all the exercises are at the end of the exercise segment.

COMPUTER SCIENCE EXERCISES

Algorithm[3]

al|go|rithm (al′gə ri#ᴛH əm), *n.* a formal procedure for any mathematical operation: *the division algorithm.*
al|go|rith|mic (al′gə rith′mik), *adj.* of an algorithm; having to do with or according to algorithms: *Human methods of solving problems* fall into two categories; in one, an exhaustive examination of all possible solutions is undertaken; the other relies on shortcuts or inspired guesses. The first method is called algorithmic and the second heuristic (F. H. George).

1. What might be an example(s) of an *algorithm?*
   _____ a. multiplication _____ c. syntax
   _____ b. semantics _____ d. division

2. *Algorithm* is from what field of knowledge?
   _____ a. geology _____ c. mathematics
   _____ b. biology

3. Check the characteristics of an *algorithm.*
   _____ a. step-by-step _____ c. successive
   _____ b. global

4. Write a sentence correctly using *algorithm.* (Be sure to include context clues to show you understand the meaning of the word.)

   _____

   _____

5. *Algorithm* generally refers to a procedure or process for solving problems. How do you solve problems? What is the difference between the terms *algorithm* and *heuristics?*

   _____

   _____

Ambiguity[12]

am|bi|gu|i|ty (am′bə gyü′ə tē), *n., pl.* **-ties. 1** the possibility of two or more meanings: *The am-biguity of the speaker's statement made it hard to tell which side he was on.* **2** a word or expres-sion that can have more than one meaning: *An-swer me without ambiguities.* **3** lack of clarity; vagueness; uncertainty. [< Latin *ambiguitās < ambiguus* ambiguous]
am|big|u|ous (am big′yü əs), *adj.* **1** having more than one possible meaning; permitting more than one interpretation or explanation. The sentence "After John hit Dick he ran away" is ambiguous because one cannot tell which boy ran away. SYN: equivocal. See syn. under **obscure. 2** not clearly defined; not clear; doubtful; uncertain: *He was left in an ambiguous position by his friend's failure to appear and help him.* SYN: vague. **3** of doubtful position or classification: *an ambiguous character.* [< Latin *ambiguus* (with English *-ous*) < *ambigere* be uncertain, wander < *ambi-* in two ways + *agere* drive] —**am|big′u|ous|ly,** *adv.* —**am|big′u|ous|ness,** *n.*

1. Which of the following words describe *ambiguity?*

    _____ a. decisive   _____ d. unmistakable   _____ g. clear

    _____ b. puzzling   _____ e. confusing   _____ h. vague

    _____ c. uncertain   _____ f. unequivocal   _____ i. doubtful

2. The following sentence contains *ambiguity.* Identify the *ambiguous* fac-tors by selecting its two possible meanings from those given below. "The swimmer dives into the spray and waves."

    _____ a. The swimmer is also a diver.

    _____ b. The swimmer dives into the ocean spray and waves to us.

    _____ c. The swimmer is strong and experienced.

    _____ d. The swimmer dives into the ocean spray and into the ocean waves.

3. The *ambiguity* in Exercise 2 occurs because some words in English can serve as more than one part of speech. For instance, in (b.) the words *dives* and *waves* are both what part of speech? _____ In (d.) *dives* is a _____ and *waves* is a _____ .

4. Write a sentence correctly using *ambiguity.* (Be sure to include context clues to show you understand the meaning of the word.)

    _____

    _____

5. Imagine that your friend has given you a birthday gift that you do not like. You don't want to hurt the friend's feelings, but you also hate to tell a lie. Using *ambiguity,* write a statement that would permit you to achieve both goals.

    _____

    _____

Analog[8]

an|a|log (an′ə lôg, -log), *n., adj. U.S.* analogue.
analog computer, an electronic calculating ma-chine or automatic control which deals directly with physical quantities, such as weights, volt-ages, or lengths, rather than with a numerical code.
an|a|logue (an′ə lôg, -log), *n., adj. — n.* **1** an analogous word, thing, circumstance, or situation.

syn: parallel. **2** an organ or part analogous to another organ or part (distinguished from *homologue*). **3** a substance which interferes in a biochemical reaction because of its structural similarity to one of the normal reactants. — *adj.* of or having to do with analog computers:

The analogue machine is just what its name implies: a physical analogy to the … problem (Scientific American). [< French *analogue* < Greek *análogos* proportionate, analogous] **analogue computer,** = analog computer.

1. The etymology of *analog* shows that the word comes from the French *analogue* and the Greek *analogos* (proportionate, analogous), which also means

   _____ a. "different."   _____ c. "parallel."

   _____ b. "separate."

2. Select the part(s) of speech of *analog*.

   _____ a. adverb   _____ c. verb

   _____ b. noun   _____ d. adjective

3. An *analog* computer operates with

   _____ a. digits.

   _____ b. physical quantities.

4. What is the difference between an *analog* computer and a digital computer? Would a thermometer be an example of an *analog*? Why or why not?

   _____

   _____

5. Write a sentence correctly using *analog*. (Be sure to use context clues to show you understand the meaning of the word.)

   _____

   _____

Binary[2]

bi|na|ry (bī′nər ē), *adj., n., pl.* **-ries.** — *adj.* consisting of two; involving two; dual: *a binary number, a binary choice such as yes or no.*
— *n.* **1** a set of two things; pair. **2** = binary star.
[< Late Latin *bīnārius* < Latin *bīnī* two at a time]

1. The etymology of *binary* shows that the word comes from the Latin *bini* (two at a time). Use this information, your imagination, and your background knowledge to match the following:

   _____ a. bicameral   aa. having two leaves

   _____ b. biennial   bb. criminal offense of marrying one person while still legally married to another

   _____ c. bifoliate   cc. having two points, as the crescent moon

   _____ d. bigamy   dd. composed of two houses, chambers, or branches

   _____ e. bicuspid   ee. lasting or living for two years

2. Complete the verbal analogy.
triad : three :: *binary* : _____
a. one   b. two   c. four   d. five

3. In which of the following sentences is *binary* used correctly?
_____ a. There is a separate binary system for each piece of hardware.
_____ b. A binary requires three numbers to function.
_____ c. "Bit" is a short way of saying "binary digit."
_____ d. Computers use binary numbers to store and manipulate information.

4. Write a sentence correctly using *binary*. (Be sure to include context clues to show you understand the meaning of the word.)

_____

_____

5. Describe the *binary* system. Do you think that each computer uses the same *binary* code as its machine language? Why or why not?

_____

_____

Cybernetics[5]

cy|ber|net|ics (sī'bər net'iks), *n.* the comparative study of the human and animal nervous system and certain mechanical systems in order to better understand communication and control of impulses and responses in both types of systems. [coined in 1948 by Norbert Wiener, 1894-1964, an American mathematician < Greek *kybernē-tikós* of a pilot < *kybernētēs* pilot < *kybernân* to steer]

1. *Cybernetics* is an approach linking intelligence in both humans and machines to
_____ a. communication.   _____ c. input.
_____ b. feedback.

2. Who coined the term *cybernetics*?
_____ a. Norbert Wiener   _____ c. Joseph Weizenbaum
_____ b. Marvin Minsky

3. With what is *cybernetics* concerned?
_____ a. the nervous system   _____ c. communication
_____ b. the brain   _____ d. the interrelationship of all three

4. What do you think is the future of *cybernetics*? Would you like to study *cybernetics*? Why or why not?

_____

_____

5. Write a sentence correctly using *cybernetics*. (Be sure to use context clues to show you understand the meaning of the word. _____

_____

Digital[1]

dig|it|al (dij'ə təl), *adj., n.* —*adj.* **1** of, having to do with, or using a digit or digits: *Digital tele-phone numbers, such as 941-2898, are replacing the old letter and number combinations, such as WI 1-2898.* **2** having digits. **3** like a digit or digits. **4** of, having to do with, or based on the principle of a digital computer: *a digital code.* **5** or having to do with the recording of sound by means of electrical signals coded into binary digits: *digital recording, digital sound.*
—*n.* **1** a finger. **2** a key of an organ, piano, etc., played with the fingers. —**dig'it|al|ly,** *adv.*

1. Complete the verbal analogy.
   discrete : continuous :: *digital* : _____
   _____ a. binary   _____ c. heuristics
   _____ b. expert   _____ d. analog

2. *Digital* as used in the context of the reading selection refers to
   _____ a. morphemes.   _____ c. syntax.
   _____ b. numbers.   _____ d. electrical signals.

3. Which of the numbered dictionary definitions of *digital* best fits the word's use in the reading selection? _____

4. Write a sentence correctly using *digital.* (Be sure to include context clues to show you understand the meaning of the word.)

   _____

   _____

5. Define the term "*digital* computer." What digits does this computer use?

   _____

   _____

Heuristics[4]

heu|ris|tics (hyù ris'tiks), *n.* **1** the study or use of discovery procedures in science. **2** a heuristic approach or procedure: *The rules are not necessarily rules of logic; various strategies, or heuristics, may be available for different types of problems* (Scientific American).

heu|ris|tic (hyù ris'tik), *adj.* serving to find out or discover; leading to or stimulating investigation or research: *heuristic teaching. What methods will lead students to become more inquisitive, flexible, heuristic, which, in turn, would lead to scientific creativity?* (New York Times). [< Greek *heur-,* root of *heurískein* to find + English *-ist + -ic*] —**heu|ris'ti|cal|ly,** *adv.*

1. In which of the following sentences is *heuristics* used correctly?
   _____ a. The teacher used an approach in the classroom that was modeled on heuristics, which really motivated the students.
   _____ b. Heuristics can't be considered until the project is completed.
   _____ c. Heuristics is necessary in establishing models of human intelligence.
   _____ d. The scientist was unable to locate the heuristics before she assigned the problem.

2. Select the uses of *heuristics*.

_____ a. clarification   _____ c. discovery

_____ b. problem solving   _____ d. experiential learning

3. Which approach to learning most probably does *not* apply to *heuristics?*

_____ a. rote memorization   _____ c. questioning techniques

_____ b. group interaction

4. What classes have you taken or are you currently taking that utilize *heuristics* as a form of instruction?

_____

_____

5. Write a sentence correctly using *heuristics*. (Be sure to use context clues to show you understand the meaning of the word.)

_____

_____

Interactive[10]

in|ter|ac|tive (in′tər ak′tiv), *adj.* acting on each other.

1. What might be an example(s) of an *interactive* situation?

_____ a. chemicals   _____ c. human

_____ b. computer and human   _____ d. all of them

2. Select the characteristics that describe the word *interactive*.

_____ a. cooperate   _____ c. connect

_____ b. collaborate   _____ d. design

3. According to the reading selection, what are some examples of *interactive* computer programs?

_____ a. ELIZA   _____ c. perceptron

_____ b. SHRDLU

4. Write a sentence correctly using *interactive*. (Be sure to include context clues to show you understand the meaning of the word.)

_____

_____

5. Have you ever worked on an *interactive* computer? If so, describe the situation. If not, what might be some types of *interactive* experiences that you would like to see become software programs to be used on the computer?

_____

_____

Matrix[15]

ma|trix (mā′triks, mat′riks), *n., pl.* **-tri|ces** or **-trix-es**, *v.,* **-trixed** or **trixt, -trix|ing. — *n.* 1** something that gives origin or form to something enclosed within it: **a** a mold for a casting. **b** the rock in which crystallized minerals, gems, or fossils are embedded: *By etching away the limestone matrix in dilute acid, the silicified fossils, which are not affected by the acid, are freed from the rock* (Raymond Cecil Moore). **c** *Figurative: The tradition of the Renaissance still hung about Marx and Engels: they had only partly emerged from its matrix* (Edmund Wilson). **2** *Printing.* a mold for casting type faces. **3** = womb. **4a** *Anatomy.* the formative part of an organ, such as the skin beneath a fingernail or toenail. **b** *Biology.* the intercellular substance of a tissue. **5** *Mathematics.* a set of quantities in a rectangular array, subject to operations such as multiplication or inversion according to specified rules. **6** *Statistics.* an ordered table or two-dimensional array of variables: *Dr. Warner's group has ... set up "matrix"—a device for statistical analysis—that comprises some thirty-five different disease entities and fifty-seven symptoms known to be associated with congenital defects* (New York Times). **7** an array of circuit elements designed to perform a particular function in a computer: *The diodes on each character unit are connected to a matrix of seven horizontal wires ... In this way, any one diode can be switched on individually by applying a voltage across selected horizontal wires and vertical wires in the matrix* (Science Journal). **— *v.i., v.t.*** to arrange or organize in a matrix: *The four channels can be recorded separately as four tracks on a disc, or any one of a number of matrixing techniques can be used to combine two or more channels on a single track* (New Scientist and Science Journal). [< Latin *mātrīx, -īcis* womb, breeding animal < *māter, mātris* mother]

1. Which of the numbered dictionary definitions of *matrix* best fits the word's use in the reading selection? _____

2. Select the synonym(s) of *matrix*.
   _____ a. analog   _____ c. pattern
   _____ b. mold   _____ d. model

3. The etymology of *matrix* shows that the word comes from the Latin *mater, matris* (mother). Use this information, your imagination, and your background knowledge to match the following:
   _____ a. matriarchy   aa. wife or widow
   _____ b. matron   bb. wedlock or married life
   _____ c. matrimony   cc. act of killing one's mother
   _____ d. matricide   dd. government by women

4. Have you ever worked with a spreadsheet on a software program? If so, why is that an example of a *matrix*? What courses have you taken in which you discussed, used, or designed a *matrix*?

   _____

   _____

5. Write a sentence correctly using *matrix*. (Be sure to include context clues to show you understand the meaning of the word.)

   _____

   _____

Modeling[6]

mod|el|ing (mod′ə ling), *n.* **1** the act or art of a person who models: *Miss Carter ... said she would like to take up modeling as a profession* (Baltimore Sun). **2** the production of designs in some plastic material, such as clay or wax, especially for reproduction in a more durable material, such as marble or bronze. **3** the representation of solid form, as in sculpture. **4** the bringing of surfaces into proper relief, as in carving. **5** the rendering of the appearance of relief, as in painting.

mod|el (mod′əl), *n.*, *v.*, **-eled**, **-el|ing** or (*especially British*) **-elled**, **-el|ling**, *adj.* — *n.* **1** a small copy: *a model of a ship or an engine, a model of an island.* **2a** an object or figure made in clay, wax, or the like, that is to be copied in marble, bronze, or other material: *a model for a statue.* **b** a design or representation of anything made to scale: *a model of the DNA molecule, a model of a stage set.* **3** the way in which a thing is made; design; style: *an airplane of an advanced model. Our car is a late model. I want a dress like yours, for that model is becoming to me.* **4** any formula, diagram, or scheme used to explain or describe relationships: *a mathematical model of communications, the mechanistic model of the universe. A tree is often used as a model showing the relationship between languages.* **5** *Figurative.* a thing or person to be copied or imitated; exemplar: *a model of courage. Make your father your model, and you will become a fine man.* **6** a person who poses for artists and photographers: *Nearly every individual of their number might have been taken for a sculptor's model* (Herman Melville). **7** a person, especially a woman, who wears new clothes in a clothing store, at a fashion show, or the like, in order to show customers how the clothes look; mannequin.
— *v.t.* **1** to make, shape, or fashion; design or plan: *Model a horse in clay.* **2** to follow as a model; form (something) after a particular model:

(*Figurative.*) *Model yourself on your father.* **3** to wear as a model: *to model a dress.* **4** (in drawing or painting) to give an appearance of natural relief to: *Model the trees by shading.*
— *v.i.* **1** to make models; design: *She models in plaster as a hobby.* **2** to be a model; pose: *She models for an illustrator.* **3** (of the portions of a drawing in progress) to assume the appearance of natural relief: *The trees model as you add shading.*
— *adj.* **1** just right or perfect, especially in conduct; exemplary: *She is a model child.* **2** serving as a model: *a model house. A model home is being prepared for display by the middle of June* (New York Times).
[< French *modèle* < Italian *modello* (diminutive) < *modo* mode[1] < Latin *modus* measure, manner] — **mod′el|er**, *especially British*, **mod′el|ler**, *n.*
— *Syn.* *n.* **5** **Model**, **example**, **pattern** mean someone or something to be copied or followed. **Model** implies especially a quality of conduct or character worth copying or imitating: *The saint was a model of unselfishness.* **Example** implies especially action or conduct, good or bad, that one is likely to follow or copy: *Children follow the example set by their parents.* **Pattern** applies particularly to any example or model that is followed or copied very closely: *The family's pattern of living has not changed in generations.*

1. Complete the verbal analogy.
   digital : binary :: *modeling* : _____
   _____ a. meaning   _____ c. successive
   _____ b. learning   _____ d. pattern

2. Which of the numbered dictionary definitions of *modeling* best fits the word's use in the reading selection? _____

3. Select the synonym(s) of *modeling*.
   _____ a. shape   _____ c. design
   _____ b. clarify   _____ d. matrix

4. Write a sentence correctly using *modeling*. (Be sure to include context clues to show you understand the meaning of the word.)

   _____

   _____

5. Why do computer scientists use *modeling*? What is the relationship of the term "artificial intelligence" to *modeling*?

   _____

   _____

Morphemics[13]

mor|phe|mics (môr fē′miks), *n. Linguistics.* the systematic study of the minimum meaningful elements of language and their characteristics in living speech.

mor|pheme (môr′fēm), *n. Linguistics.* the smallest part of a word that has meaning of its own. Morphemes may be words, prefixes, suffixes, or endings that show inflection. In the word *carelessness*, the morphemes are *care*, *-less*, and *-ness. A morpheme does not necessarily* CONSIST *of phonemes, but all morphemes are statable in terms of phonemes* (H. A. Gleason, Jr.). [< French *morphème* < Greek *morphē* form; patterned on French *phonème* phoneme]

1. Complete the verbal analogy.
   cybernetics : feedback :: *morphemics* : _____
   _____ a. language   _____ c. syntax
   _____ b. reasoning

2. *Morphemics* is concerned primarily with what area(s) of research in the field of artificial intelligence?
   _____ a. information processing   _____ c. robotics
   _____ b. expert systems   _____ d. cybernetics

3. What are the *morphemic* element(s) in the word "uneventful"?
   _____ a. un   _____ c. ful
   _____ b. event

4. What is the relationship between *morphemics* and syntax? Between *morphemics* and a semantic network?

   _____

   _____

5. Write a sentence correctly using *morphemics*. (Be sure to include context clues to show you understand the meaning of the word.)

   _____

   _____

Network[14]

net|work (net′wėrk′), *n., v.* —*n.* **1** any system of lines that cross: *a network of vines, a network of railroads.* (*Figurative.*) *Their law is a network of fictions* (Emerson). **2** a group of radio or television stations that work together, so that what is broadcast by one may be broadcast by all: *Mr. Burgard mentioned two instances in which his corporation advised networks that it was withdrawing as a participating sponsor because of objections to scripts* (New York Times). **3** *Figura-* tive. anything that snares or catches, as a net does: *a police network.* **4** work or a piece of work having the texture of a net; netting; net: *The network of the spider web hung across the broken window full of flies and gnats.* —*v.t. Especially British.* to broadcast (a program) over a radio or television network: *Thirteen programmes on international economics . . . will be networked nationally in January* (London Times). [< net[1] + work]

1. Which of the dictionary definitions of *network* best fits the word's use in the reading selection? _____

2. In which of the following sentences can *network* be correctly placed in the blank?
   _____ a. My _____ of friends helps support me when I have problems.
   _____ b. It is important to _____ in one's profession.
   _____ c. The _____ is not attached correctly to the computer.
   _____ d. A modem allows computers to _____ over distances.

3. Select the synonym(s) of *network*.
   _____ a. grid   _____ c. problem
   _____ b. extension   _____ d. system

4. Write a sentence correctly using *network*. (Be sure to include context clues to show you understand the meaning of the word.)

_____

_____

5. Do you have a *network* of friends? Who are they? What kinds of activities or experiences comprise this *network*?

_____

_____

Neuron[7]

*neu|ron (nûr′on, nyür′-), *n.* one of the cells of which the brain, spinal cord, and nerves are composed; nerve cell. Neurons conduct impulses and consist of a cell body containing the nucleus, and usually several processes called dendrites, and a single long process called an axon. *To excite or "fire" a neuron, the nerve impulse has to cross the synapse, and it is probable that two or more impulses have to summate in space and time in order to "fire" a neuron* (George M. Wyburn). Also, **neurone.** [< New Latin *neuron* < Greek *neûron* sinew, nerve]

*neuron

1. Complete the following sentence:
   "*Neuron* refers to the _____."
   _____ a. reproductive system.   _____ c. nervous system.
   _____ b. digestive system.

2. The etymology of *neuron* shows that the word comes from the Latin *neuron* (sinew, nerve). Use this information, your imagination, and your background knowledge to complete the following:

   _____ a. neurosis   aa. chemical substance that transmits impulses between nerve cells

   _____ b. neuromuscular   bb. surgery of the nervous system

   _____ c. neurotransmitter cc. mental or emotional disorder

   _____ d. neurosurgery   dd. having to do with the relationship of nerves to muscles

3. An example of a *neuron*-like element that AI scientists have developed is a(n)
   _____ a. algorithm.   _____ c. perceptron.
   _____ b. network.

4. Why are scientists in the field of artificial intelligence interested in studying a *neuron?*

_____

_____

5. Write a sentence correctly using *neuron.* (Be sure to include context clues to show you understand the meaning of the word.)

_____

_____

Robotics[9]

ro|bot|ics (rō bot′iks), *n.* the science or technology that deals with robots: *There has been some excellent progress in robotics—the study of computer-controlled robots . . . programmed to "see" (some things), to "hear," and even to "speak" (some sounds)* (Alan J. Perlis).

1. Complete the following sentence:
   "Scientists working in *robotics* are concerned with _____."
   _____ a. pattern recognition.   _____ c. picture processing.
   _____ b. problem solving.   _____ d. all of them.

2. Select the characteristics of *robotics.*
   _____ a. remote   _____ c. humanlike
   _____ b. mechanical   _____ d. all of them

3. In which of the following sentences is *robotics* used correctly?
   _____ a. The field of medicine is one of the fields that has utilized robotics.
   _____ b. Robotics refers to computer-controlled devices that are fitted with sensors and activating mechanisms.
   _____ c. Robotics is an extension of the work done with analog computers.
   _____ d. The use of robotics is in the realm of science fiction.

4. Write a sentence correctly using *robotics.* (Be sure to include context clues to show you understand the meaning of the word.)

_____

_____

5. Pretend that you are a computer scientist. In what fields of work or situations in the future could *robotics* be applied? Why would *robotics* be useful in these areas?

_____

_____

Syntax[11]

syn|tax (sin′taks), *n.* **1a** the way in which the words and phrases of a sentence are arranged to show how they relate to each other; sentence structure: *In syntax and vocabulary the message of the written record is unmistakable, and it exerts a tremendous effect upon the standard language* (Leonard Bloomfield). **b** the patterns of such arrangement in a given language: *The team wants to analyze the syntax of one pair of languages* (*German and English*) *in terms of mathematical symbolism* (Newsweek). **c** the use or function of a word, phrase, or clause in a sentence. **d** the part of grammar dealing with the construction and function of phrases, clauses, and sentences: *The object in syntax is still to discover the relations between the parts of the expression* (Joshua Whatmough). **2** *Obsolete.* an orderly or systematic arrangement of parts or elements; connected order or system of things: *Concerning the syntax and disposition of studies, that men may know in what order ... to read* (Francis Bacon). [< Late Latin *syntaxis* < Greek *sýntaxis* < *syntássein* < *syn-* together + *tássein* arrange]

1. Which of the numbered and lettered dictionary definitions of *syntax* best fits the word's use in the reading selection? _____

2. Complete the verbal analogy.
   Semantics : meaning :: *syntax* : _____
   _____ a. characteristics   _____ c. theories
   _____ b. rules   _____ d. memory

3. Select the sentence that answers the following question:
   "Which is more important in comprehension and communication—*syntax* or semantics?"
   _____ a. Syntax is more important, because one needs to know the rules of language.
   _____ b. Semantics is more important, because one needs to know the meanings of words.
   _____ c. They are equally important, because they interrelate and influence each other.

4. Write a sentence correctly using *syntax*. (Be sure to include context clues to show you understand the meaning of the word.)

   _____

   _____

5. How does *syntax* influence your comprehension of printed text? What textbooks that you are currently using are difficult for you due to the *syntax?*

   _____

   _____

ANSWERS TO CHAPTER 22 EXERCISES

Algorithm: **1.** a, d **2.** c **3.** a, c
Ambiguity: **1.** b, c, e, h, i **2.** b, d **3.** verbs; verb, noun
Analog: **1.** c **2.** b, d **3.** b
Binary: **1.** dd, ee, aa, bb, cc **2.** b (definition) **3.** c, d
Cybernetics: **1.** b **2.** a **3.** d
Digital: **1.** d (antonym) **2.** b, d **3.** 4
Heuristics: **1.** a, c **2.** a, b, c, d **3.** a
Interactive: **1.** d **2.** a, b, c **3.** a
Matrix: **1.** 7 **2.** b, c, d **3.** dd, aa, bb, cc
Modeling: **1.** d (characteristic) **2.** *n.* 4 **3.** a, c, d
Morphemics: **1.** a (concerned with) **2.** a, b **3.** a, b, c
Network: **1.** l **2.** a, b, d **3.** a, b, d
Neuron: **1.** c **2.** cc, dd, aa, bb **3.** c
Robotics: **1.** d **2.** a, b, c **3.** a, b
Syntax: **1.** la **2.** b (definition) **3.** c

If you missed any of the items in the exercises, return to the exercise and to the dictionary definition to see where you went wrong. Remember: If you get something right, you only affirm that you knew it. If you get something wrong and understand why, *you have learned something.*

COMPUTER SCIENCE POSTTEST

Fill in the blanks with the words from this list.

algorithm	digital	morphemics
ambiguity	heuristics	network
analog	interactive	neuron
binary	matrix	robotics
cybernetics	modeling	syntax

1. _____ refers to the rules of grammar in the comprehension and communication processes.

2. Characteristics of a process using _____ include problem solving and discovery.

3. _____ is the study of meaningful word segments or linguistic units.

4. A term coined by Norbert Wiener that describes the link between intelligence in both humans and animals with the feedback process is
_____.

5. A _____ is a fundamental unit of nervous tissue.

6. _____ is a field of research that utilizes machines that can perform some of the complex acts of a human.

7. Another word for _____ is *vagueness.*

8. *Shape, design,* and *matrix* are synonyms of _____.

9. A(n) _____ computer does not use a binary system for its operation.

10. *Array* and *table* are synonyms of _____.

11. _____ refers to a step-by-step procedure as a problem-solving approach.

12. *Dual* and *pair* are synonyms of _____.

13. An example of a(n) _____ would be a group of people who work together with common goals.

14. Words that might describe _____ are *collaborate, cooperate,* and *connect.*

15. _____ has to do with a numerical code and has a different meaning and function than analog.

Answers to this posttest are in the Instructor's Manual.

If you missed any of the words, you may need to return to the exercises and to the dictionary entries to see why your concepts for some words are incomplete.

APPENDIXES

APPENDIX   A
GREEK AND LATIN WORD FORMS

APPENDIX   B
PRETEST ANSWER KEYS

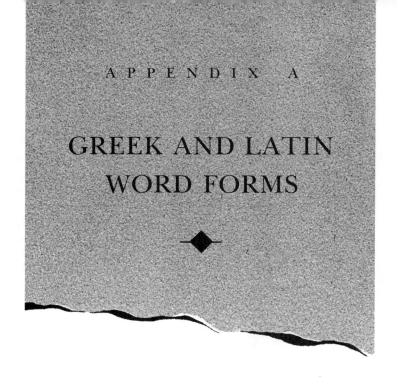

APPENDIX A

GREEK AND LATIN WORD FORMS

This appendix presents the combining forms—roots and prefixes—that make up the words introduced in this book. Where several words share the same combining form, all are included with the pertinent root or prefix. Since suffixes are primarily useful to denote the parts of speech, they are not emphasized here.

Below you will find an alphabetical listing of the prefixes and roots, including origins and meanings, the words introduced, and where they can be found in the text. For example,

aequus   (L.)   *equal*   equity   **20,** 6

indicates that the root *aequus* is of Latin origin, means "equal," and is in the "family tree" of the word *equity,* which is word number 6 in Chapter 20.

You will note that prefixes *assimilate.* That is, they vary depending on the root they combine with so that the words can be pronounced. A good example of this is *ad,* meaning "to, toward," which combines variously to form such words as *accessible, adversary, affiliation,* and *assiduous.* Remember, too, that nouns and verbs have various forms, so you may notice what seem to be inconsistencies.

Abbreviations for the languages from which the combining forms are borrowed are the following: **Ar.,** Arabic; **D.,** Dutch; **F.,** French; **G.,** Greek; **L.,** Latin; **M.E.,** Middle English; **Med.L.,** Medieval Latin; **O.E.,** Old English; **O.F.,** Old French; **P.,** Portuguese; **It.,** Italian; **T.,** Turkish. Similar English meanings are separated by commas, and dissimilar meanings by semicolons.

PREFIXES

Word Element	Origin	Meaning	Word	Chapter, Word Number
a	(G.)	*not, without*	amorphous	**9,** 15
ab	(L.)	*off, from, away*	abstract	**7,** 9
ad	(L.)	*to, toward*	accessible	**7,** 11
			adagio	**19,** 10
			adhere	**5,** 13
			adjacent	**7,** 10
			adjunct	**7,** 5
			admonitory	**16,** 8
			adversary	**21,** 14
			aggregate	**12,** 5
			amortize	**20,** 11
			arbiter	**18,** 15
			assets	**20,** 4
			assiduous	**7,** 2
			assimilate	**5,** 8
			assumption	**6,** 10
			attenuate	**13,** 15
ambi	(L.)	*both, two ways*	ambiguity	**22,** 12
anti	(G.)	*against, opposite*	antipathy	**18,** 4
co	(L.)	*intensive*	cognition	**14,** 9
			consumption	**12,** 13
			covert	**16,** 9
co	(L.)	*with, together*	coagulation	**11,** 11
			cogent	**5,** 11
			cohesive	**15,** 12
			compendium	**7,** 4
			competence	**5,** 9
			composite	**10,** 3
			concerto	**19,** 15
			condensation	**9,** 11
			contiguity	**14,** 8
			contingency	**21,** 13
			copious	**7,** 13
contra	(L.)	*against*	counterpoint	**19,** 4
de	(L.)	*completely;*	deduction	**6,** 9
		from, down, away	delineate	**17,** 7

Word Element	Origin	Meaning	Word	Chapter, Word Number
			depreciation	**20,** 9
			derivative	**10,** 13
			deviant	**15,** 10
			distillation	**9,** 9
dis	(L.)	*undoing, reversing, apart*	defamation	**16,** 11
			denouement	**17,** 3
			diffusion	**8,** 9
			diligent	**5,** 2
			discern	**5,** 6
			disclosure	**20,** 15
			dissension	**18,** 7
			diversified	**16,** 2
			diversion	**16,** 14
en	(M.E.)	*to cause to be*	ensconced	**21,** 2
epi	(G.)	*on, upon*	episode	**14,** 12
			epithet	**17,** 15
			epitome	**17,** 8
ex	(L.)	*out, out of, forth*	elite	**13,** 8
			eloquent	**17,** 10
			eradicate	**13,** 14
			erudite	**5,** 1
			evaporation	**9,** 10
			expedite	**7,** 12
			expenditure	**12,** 15
			explicit	**6,** 7
			exponent	**10,** 5
in	(L.)	*intensive*	innovative	**21,** 10
in	(L.)	*in, into; not, without; on*	entitlement	**21,** 12
			impediment	**5,** 12
			implicit	**6,** 11
			incentive	**21,** 8
			indictment	**13,** 6
			induction	**9,** 2
			inference	**6,** 8
			inflationary	**12,** 8
			inherent	**18,** 3
			innate	**14,** 1
			inquiry	**6,** 6
			intangible	**20,** 10
			integral	**10,** 14
			inverse	**10,** 15
inter	(L.)	*between, among*	entrepreneur	**12,** 11
			interactive	**22,** 10

Word Element	Origin	Meaning	Word	Chapter, Word Number
non	(L.)	*not*	nonpareil	**18,** 11
ob	(L.)	*in the way, toward*	ostensibly	**16,** 10
para	(G.)	*side by side*	paradigm	**14,** 7
per	(L.)	*through, by, thoroughly*	percolation	**11,** 5
			permeable	**8,** 3
pre	(L.)	*before*	precipitation	**11,** 4
pro	(L.)	*forward, forth*	procaryote	**8,** 1
			proclivity	**6,** 14
			procrastinate	**5,** 4
			prodigality	**16,** 4
			profound	**17,** 14
			propagation	**15,** 3
re	(L.)	*back, again*	recession	**12,** 7
			redress	**21,** 6
			remuneration	**21,** 11
			repartee	**17,** 5
			replicate	**7,** 14
			requisition	**20,** 13
			retrieval	**5,** 3
			revenue	**12,** 14
sub	(L.)	*under; up to*	sublimation	**9,** 13
			subsistence	**15,** 1
syn	(G.)	*together*	photosynthesis	**8,** 7
			symbiosis	**8,** 15
			syntax	**22,** 11
			synthesis	**6,** 12
trans	(L.)	*across*	transaction	**20,** 8
			transpiration	**11,** 3

ROOTS

aequus	(L.)	*equal*	equilibrium	**9,** 12
			equity	**20,** 6
aer	(G.)	*air*	aeration	**11,** 10
ager, agri	(L.)	*field*	agrarian	**18,** 10
agere, actum	(L.)	*to drive*	ambiguity	**22,** 12
			coagulation	**11,** 11
			cogent	**5,** 11

Word Element	Origin	Meaning	Word	Chapter, Word Number
			interactive	**22,** 10
			prodigality	**16,** 4
			transaction	**20,** 8
agio	(It.)	*ease*	adagio	**19,** 10
alacrer, alacris	(L.)	*brisk*	allegro	**19,** 12
alienus	(L.)	*another*	alienation	**15,** 15
analogos	(G.)	*proportionate*	analog	**22,** 8
			analogous	**18,** 6
ancilla	(L.)	*handmaiden*	ancillary	**7,** 1
andare	(It.)	*to walk*	andante	**19,** 11
aperire, aperatum	(L.)	*to open*	overt	**16,** 3
aqua	(L.)	*water*	aqueduct	**11,** 7
			aqueous	**9,** 6
			aquifer	**11,** 6
archein	(G.)	*to lead*	hierarchy	**15,** 13
			oligarchy	**15,** 14
aristos	(G.)	*best*	aristocracy	**13,** 9
artic	(L.)	*a joint*	articulate	**5,** 10
artrare, aratum	(L.)	*to plow*	arable	**15,** 5
audire, auditum	(L.)	*to hear*	audit	**20,** 14
augere, auctum	(L.)	*to increase*	augment	**16,** 6
avere, avidum	(L.)	*to desire, long for*	avid	**7,** 6
axios	(G.)	*worthy*	axiom	**21,** 3
baetere, baetum	(L.)	*to go*	arbiter	**18,** 15
ballein	(G.)	*to throw*	metabolism	**8,** 10
bini	(L.)	*two at a time*	binary	**22,** 2
bios	(G.)	*life*	symbiosis	**8,** 15
canare, cantatum	(L.)	*to sing*	cantata	**19,** 7
			incentive	**21,** 8
caput	(L.)	*head*	capitalism	**12,** 6
			precipitation	**11,** 4
cedere, cessi	(L.)	*to go, yield, withdraw*	accessible	**7,** 11
			recession	**12,** 7
cernere, cretum	(L.)	*to separate, distinguish*	discern	**5,** 6
certare, certatum	(L.)	*to strive*	concerto	**19,** 15

Word Element	Origin	Meaning	Word	Chapter, Word Number
charta	(L.)	*leaf of papyrus*	cartel	**12,** 1
chein	(G.)	*to pour*	alchemy	**9,** 1
chloros	(G.)	*pale green*	chlorination	**11,** 14
			chloroplast	**8,** 6
chroma	(G.)	*color*	chromosome	**8,** 12
claudere, clausum	(L.)	*to close*	disclosure	**20,** 15
clivus	(L.)	*a slope*	proclivity	**6,** 14
colare, colatrum	(L.)	*to strain, filter*	percolation	**11,** 5
congruere, congruentum	(L.)	*to correspond with*	congruent	**10,** 11
crastinus	(L.)	*tomorrow*	procrastinate	**5,** 4
credere, creditum	(L.)	*to believe*	credit	**20,** 3
currere, cursurum	(L.)	*to run*	cursory	**18,** 5
debere, debitum	(L.)	*to owe*	debit	**20,** 2
deiknynai	(G.)	*to show, point out*	paradigm	**14,** 7
deleesthai	(G.)	*to hurt, injure*	deleterious	**5,** 15
demos	(G.)	*people*	democracy	**13,** 4
			demographic	**16,** 7
densus	(L.)	*thick*	condensation	**9,** 11
despotes	(G.)	*master of the household*	despotism	**13,** 7
dicere, dictum	(L.)	*to say, speak*	indictment	**13,** 6
digitus	(L.)	*finger*	digital	**22,** 1
dividere, divisum	(L.)	*to divide*	dividends	**20,** 7
domus	(L.)	*house*	domain	**10,** 7
dresser	(O.F.)	*to arrange, straighten*	redress	**21,** 6
ducere, ductum	(L.)	*to lead*	aqueduct	**11,** 7
			deduction	**6,** 9
			induction	**9,** 2
dynasthai	(G.)	*to be powerful*	dynamics	**19,** 13
eidos	(G.)	*form, shape*	eidetic	**14,** 11
essentia	(Med.L.)	*essence, substance*	quintessential	**18,** 8
ethnos	(G.)	*nation, custom*	ethical	**14,** 3

Word Element	Origin	Meaning	Word	Chapter, Word Number
			ethnicity	**15,** 8
eu	(G.)	*good, true*	eucaryote	**8,** 2
externus	(L.)	*outside, outward*	externality	**12,** 12
facere, factum	(L.)	*to make, do*	facet	**18,** 14
			factor	**10,** 4
			fiat	**21,** 1
			liquefaction	**9,** 4
			ramification	**21,** 7
fama	(L.)	*rumor, report*	defamation	**16,** 11
ferre, latum	(L.)	*to carry*	aquifer	**11,** 6
			inference	**6,** 8
			proliferation	**21,** 15
filtrum	(Med.L.)	*felt*	filtration	**11,** 13
fiscus	(L.)	*purse, woven basket*	fiscal	**12,** 9
flare, flatum	(L.)	*to blow*	inflationary	**12,** 8
formidare, formidatum	(L.)	*to dread*	formidable	**7,** 3
fundere, fusum	(L.)	*to pour*	diffusion	**8,** 9
fundus	(L.)	*bottom*	profound	**17,** 14
fungi, functum	(L.)	*to perform*	function	**10,** 9
genus, generis	(L.)	*race, stock, kind*	generic	**6,** 2
gnoscere, gnitum	(L.)	*to know*	cognition	**14,** 9
graphein	(G.)	*to draw, write*	demographic	**16,** 7
grex, gregis	(L.)	*flock*	aggregate	**12,** 5
haerere, haesus	(L.)	*to cling, stick*	adhere	**5,** 13
			cohesive	**15,** 12
			inherent	**18,** 3
heuriskein	(G.)	*to find*	heuristics	**22,** 4
heiros	(G.)	*sacred*	hierarchy	**15,** 13
hodos	(G.)	*way*	episode	**14,** 12
homo	(G.)	*same*	homophony	**19,** 6
hydro	(G.)	*water*	hydrologic	**11,** 2
hypo	(G.)	*under*	hypotenuse	**10,** 12
			hypothesis	**14,** 2
ideo	(G.)	*form, notion*	ideology	**13,** 13
intrinsecus	(L.)	*inwardly*	intrinsic	**6,** 3
jacere, jactum	(L.)	*to throw*	adjacent	**7,** 10

Word Element	Origin	Meaning	Word	Chapter, Word Number
jungere, junctum	(L.)	*to join*	adjunct	**7,** 5
karyon	(G.)	*nut, kernel*	eucaryote	**8,** 2
			procaryote	**8,** 1
kinein	(G.)	*to move*	cytokinesis	**8,** 13
			kinetic	**9,** 3
kolophos	(G.)	*a blow, slap*	coup	**13,** 12
kratos	(G.)	*rule*	democracy	**13,** 4
			aristocracy	**13,** 9
kritikos	(G.)	*critical*	critique	**6,** 4
kybernetes	(G.)	*pilot*	cybernetics	**22,** 5
kytos	(G.)	*hollow vessel*	cytokinesis	**8,** 13
			cytoplasm	**8,** 5
legere, lectum	(L.)	*to choose, gather*	diligent	**5,** 2
			elite	**13,** 8
liber, libri	(L.)	*book*	libel	**16,** 12
libra	(L.)	*balance*	equilibrium	**9,** 12
licgan	(O.E.)	*to lie*	ledger	**20,** 1
ligare, ligatum	(L.)	*to bind, fasten*	liability	**20,** 5
			ligature	**17,** 2
limen	(L.)	*limit, threshold*	sublimation	**9,** 13
linea	(L.)	*line*	delineate	**17,** 7
lingua	(L.)	*tongue, language*	linguistic	**5,** 5
liquere, liquet	(L.)	*to be fluid*	liquefaction	**9,** 4
littera	(L.)	*letter, learning*	literacy	**6,** 1
logy	(M.E.)	*science, system, study*	hydrologic	**11,** 2
			ideology	**13,** 13
			methodology	**13,** 2
loqui, locutum	(L.)	*to speak*	eloquent	**17,** 10
			soliloquy	**17,** 11
lucrus	(L.)	*gain*	lucrative	**21,** 5
mandare, mandatum	(L.)	*to order, command*	mandate	**13,** 11
mater	(L.)	*mother*	matrix	**22,** 15
meabilis	(L.)	*passable, penetrating*	permeable	**8,** 3
medius	(L.)	*middle*	mediate	**14,** 10
meion	(G.)	*less*	meiosis	**8,** 14

Word Element	Origin	Meaning	Word	Chapter, Word Number
meta	(G.)	*change, beyond*	metabolism	**8,** 10
methodos	(G.)	*method*	methodology	**13,** 2
minasthai	(G.)	*to remember*	mnemonic	**14,** 14
minutus	(G.)	*small*	minutiae	**21,** 4
miscere, mixtum	(L.)	*to mix*	miscible	**9,** 5
mitos	(G.)	*thread*	mitosis	**8,** 11
modus	(L.)	*measured amount*	modeling	**22,** 6
monere, monitum	(L.)	*to warn, remind*	admonitory	**16,** 8
			monitor	**6,** 15
monos	(G.)	*single*	monopoly	**12,** 2
monter	(O.F.)	*to mount*	montage	**17,** 1
morphe	(G.)	*form, shape*	amorphous	**9,** 15
			morphemic	**22,** 13
mors, mortis	(L.)	*death*	amortize	**20,** 11
movere, motem	(L.)	*to move*	motif	**17,** 6
munus, muneris	(L.)	*gift, duty*	remuneration	**21,** 11
myrias	(G.)	*countless, ten thousand*	myriad	**7,** 8
narrare, narratum	(L.)	*to relate, tell*	narrative	**17,** 12
nasci, natum	(L.)	*to be born*	innate	**14,** 1
			nascent	**18,** 13
nett	(O.E.)	*net, mesh*	network	**22,** 14
neuros	(G.)	*nerve, sinew*	neuron	**22,** 7
nodus	(L.)	*knot*	denouement	**17,** 3
novus	(L.)	*new, innovative*	innovative	**21,** 10
oligos	(G.)	*few*	oligarchy	**15,** 14
			oligopoly	**12,** 3
operire, opertum	(L.)	*to cover*	covert	**16,** 9
ops	(L.)	*resources*	copious	**7,** 13
optimus	(L.)	*best*	optimum	**5,** 7
orare, oratum	(L.)	*to plead*	oratorio	**19,** 8
ordu	(T.)	*camp*	horde	**15,** 4
organos	(G.)	*instrument, body organ*	organelle	**8,** 4
osis	(M.E.)	*a condition*	mitosis	**8,** 11
			meiosis	**8,** 14

Word Element	Origin	Meaning	Word	Chapter, Word Number
osmos	(G.)	*pushing, thrusting*	osmosis	**8**, 8
palatus	(L.)	*sense of taste*	palatable	**11**, 8
pangere, pactum	(L.)	*to make fast*	propagation	**15**, 3
par, paris	(L.)	*equal*	nonpareil	**18**, 11
			peer	**15**, 11
parcere, parsurum	(L.)	*to spare*	parsimony	**14**, 6
pars, partis	(L.)	*part, side*	repartee	**17**, 5
pater	(L.)	*father*	patron	**17**, 13
pathos	(G.)	*feeling*	antipathy	**18**, 4
pecu	(L.)	*money, cattle*	pecuniary	**21**, 9
pendere, pensum	(L.)	*to weigh, hang*	compendium	**7**, 4
			expenditure	**12**, 15
personne	(O.F.)	*person*	personify	**17**, 9
pes, pedis	(L.)	*a foot*	expedite	**7**, 12
			impediment	**5**, 12
petere, petitum	(L.)	*to seek, drive forward*	competence	**5**, 9
phanein	(G.)	*to show forth*	phenomenon	**18**, 1
phone	(G.)	*sound*	homophony	**19**, 6
			polyphony	**19**, 5
photos	(G.)	*light*	photosynthesis	**8**, 7
plaga	(L.)	*snare, net*	plagiarize	**7**, 15
plassein	(G.)	*to form, shape*	chloroplast	**8**, 6
			cytoplasm	**8**, 5
plicare, plicatum	(L.)	*to fold*	explicit	**6**, 7
			implicit	**6**, 11
			replicate	**7**, 14
point	(O.F.)	*a mark*	counterpoint	**19**, 4
polein	(G.)	*to sell*	monopoly	**12**, 2
			oligopoly	**12**, 3
polemikos	(G.)	*war*	polemic	**18**, 2
polis	(G.)	*city*	polity	**13**, 3
polys	(G.)	*many*	polyphony	**19**, 5
ponere, positum	(L.)	*to put, place*	composite	**10**, 3
			exponent	**10**, 5
postulare, postulatum	(L.)	*to demand*	postulate	**10**, 10

Word Element	Origin	Meaning	Word	Chapter, Word Number
potare, potatum	(L.)	*to drink*	potable	**11,** 1
prassein	(G.)	*to do, act*	pragmatic	**16,** 5
prehendere, prehensum	(L.)	*to take*	entrepreneur	**12,** 11
pretium	(L.)	*price*	depreciation	**20,** 9
prex, precis	(L.)	*prayer*	precarious	**15,** 2
primus	(L.)	*first*	prime	**10,** 2
proles	(L.)	*offspring*	proliferation	**21,** 15
proximus	(L.)	*nearest, next*	proximity	**5,** 14
publica	(L.)	*public*	republic	**13,** 5
quaerere, quaesitum	(L.)	*to seek, inquire*	inquiry	**6,** 6
			quest	**6,** 5
			requisition	**20,** 13
quinta	(Med.L.)	*fifth*	quintessential	**18,** 8
radix, radicis	(L.)	*root*	eradicate	**13,** 14
ramus	(L.)	*branch*	ramification	**21,** 7
ranger	(O.F.)	*to array*	range	**10,** 8
regere, rectum	(L.)	*to rule, straighten*	regime	**13,** 10
res, rei	(L.)	*matter, thing*	republic	**13,** 5
reserver	(O.F.)	*to reserve*	reservoir	**11,** 15
rivus	(L.)	*stream*	derivative	**10,** 13
rudis	(L.)	*rude, unskilled*	erudite	**5,** 1
saeculus	(L.)	*age, span of time*	secular	**19,** 9
sanctus	(L.)	*holy*	sanction	**15,** 9
satus	(L.)	*sufficient, enough*	assets	**20,** 4
schans	(D.)	*fortification*	ensconced	**21,** 2
scheme	(G.)	*figure, appearance*	schema	**6,** 13
schizein	(G.)	*to split*	schism	**18,** 9
secare, sectum	(L.)	*to cut*	sector	**12,** 1
sedere, sessurum	(L.)	*to sit, settle*	assiduous	**7,** 2
			sedimentation	**11,** 12
semainein	(G.)	*to show by a sign*	semantic	**14,** 13
sentire, sensum	(L.)	*to feel*	dissension	**18,** 7
simulare, simulatum	(L.)	*to imitate*	assimilate	**5,** 8

Word Element	Origin	Meaning	Word	Chapter, Word Number
skandalon	(G.)	*offense*	slander	**16**, 13
skopein	(G.)	*to behold, consider*	scope	**13**, 1
solus	(L.)	*alone*	soliloquy	**17**, 11
solvere, solutum	(L.)	*to dissolve, loosen*	solute	**9**, 7
			solvent	**9**, 8
soma	(G.)	*body*	chromosome	**8**, 12
sonare, sonatum	(L.)	*to sound*	sonata	**19**, 14
specere, spexi	(L.)	*to look at, examine*	specificity	**14**, 15
spirare, spiratum	(L.)	*to breathe, be alive*	transpiration	**11**, 3
stare, staturum	(L.)	*to stand*	status	**15**, 7
			subsistence	**15**, 1
stilla	(L.)	*drop*	distillation	**9**, 9
stringere, strictum	(L.)	*to draw tight*	stringent	**7**, 7
sumere, sumptum	(L.)	*to take up*	assumption	**6**, 10
			consumption	**12**, 13
tangere, tactum	(L.)	*to touch*	contiguity	**14**, 8
			contingency	**21**, 13
			intangible	**20**, 10
			integral	**10**, 14
tarif	(Ar.)	*information*	tariff	**12**, 10
tassein	(G.)	*arrange*	syntax	**22**, 11
teinein	(G.)	*to stretch*	hypotenuse	**10**, 12
temnein	(G.)	*to cut*	epitome	**17**, 8
tendere, tensum	(L.)	*to stretch*	attenuate	**13**, 15
			ostensibly	**16**, 10
theorein	(G.)	*to observe, look at*	theorem	**10**, 1
			theory	**14**, 5
tithenai	(G.)	*to put, place*	epithet	**17**, 15
			hypothesis	**14**, 2
			photosynthesis	**8**, 7
			synthesis	**6**, 12
titulus	(L.)	*title, claim*	entitlement	**21**, 12
tonos	(G.)	*vocal pitch*	tone	**19**, 2
trahere, tractum	(L.)	*to pull, draw*	abstract	**7**, 9
trouver	(O.F.)	*to find*	retrieval	**5**, 3

Word Element	Origin	Meaning	Word	Chapter, Word Number
turbidus	(L.)	*agitated, muddy*	turbidity	**11,** 9
tympanon	(G.)	*kettle drum*	timbre	**19,** 1
valere, valiturum	(L.)	*to be strong*	validity	**14,** 4
vapor	(L.)	*vapor, steam*	evaporation	**9,** 10
varius	(L.)	*variegated*	variable	**10,** 6
vastus	(L.)	*immense, empty*	vast	**16,** 1
venire, venturum	(L.)	*to come*	revenue	**12,** 14
vertere, versum	(L.)	*to turn*	adversary	**21,** 14
			diversified	**16,** 2
			diversion	**16,** 14
			inverse	**10,** 15
via	(L.)	*way*	deviant	**15,** 10
vicis	(L.)	*a turn, change*	vicarious	**16,** 15
virtus	(L.)	*virtue*	virtuosity	**19,** 3
viscus	(L.)	*birdlime*	viscosity	**9,** 14
vocare, vocatum	(L.)	*to call*	voucher	**20,** 12
weorc	(O.E.)	*work*	network	**22,** 4

The following words are not listed in the combining forms table:

Word	Source	Location
algorithm	A "person word" referring to the 9th century Arab mathematician Muhammad ibn-Musa al-Khwarizmi	**22,** 3
deus ex machina	A naturalized foreign phrase	**17,** 4
draconian	A "person word" referring to the 7th century Athenian legislator Draco	**18,** 12
robotics	From the Czech word for "worker," used by Karel Capek in his 1923 play *R.U.R.*	**22,** 9
hallmark	A "place word" from Goldsmith's Hall, London, seat of Goldsmith's Company, by whom the stamping of gold was legally regulated	**15,** 6

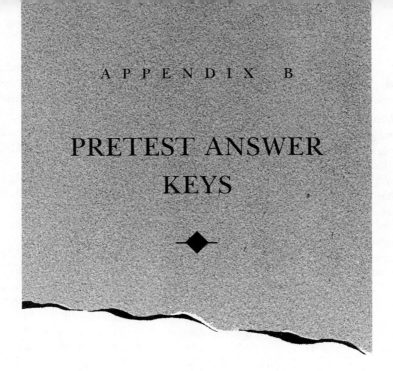

APPENDIX B

PRETEST ANSWER KEYS

◆

CHAPTER 5 PRETEST ANSWER KEY
---

1. competence
2. assimilate
3. erudite
4. linguistic
5. proximity

6. diligent
7. adhere
8. impediments
9. retrieval
10. procrastinate

11. discern
12. deleterious
13. articulate
14. cogent
15. optimum

CHAPTER 6 PRETEST ANSWER KEY
---

1. implicit
2. critique
3. inquiry
4. explicit
5. quest

6. intrinsic
7. assumption
8. generic
9. synthesis
10. schema

11. inference
12. deduction
13. literacy
14. proclivity
15. monitor

CHAPTER 7 PRETEST ANSWER KEY

1. compendium	6. accessible	11. copious
2. myriad	7. replicate	12. abstract
3. avid	8. adjunct	13. formidable
4. assiduous	9. stringent	14. ancillary
5. plagiarize	10. adjacent	15. expedite

CHAPTER 8 PRETEST ANSWER KEY

1. eucaryote	6. permeable	11. chloroplast
2. diffusion	7. meiosis	12. photosynthesis
3. mitosis	8. metabolism	13. symbiosis
4. organelle	9. procaryote	14. cytoplasm
5. osmosis	10. chromosome	15. cytokinesis

CHAPTER 9 PRETEST ANSWER KEY

1. aqueous	6. alchemy	11. amorphous
2. induction	7. condensation	12. kinetic
3. miscible	8. equilibrium	13. liquefaction
4. sublimation	9. viscosity	14. evaporation
5. solute	10. solvent	15. distillation

CHAPTER 10 PRETEST ANSWER KEY

1. function	6. postulate	11. factor
2. exponent	7. range	12. domain
3. prime	8. inverse	13. hypotenuse
4. derivative	9. composite	14. congruent
5. variable	10. theorem	15. integral

CHAPTER 11 PRETEST ANSWER KEY

1. aeration
2. hydrologic
3. sedimentation
4. turbidity
5. potable
6. coagulation
7. aquifer
8. percolation
9. reservoir
10. aqueduct
11. precipitation
12. palatable
13. chlorination
14. transpiration
15. filtration

CHAPTER 12 PRETEST ANSWER KEY

1. sector
2. monopoly
3. oligopoly
4. aggregate
5. tariff
6. fiscal
7. recession
8. inflationary
9. externality
10. capitalism
11. entrepreneur
12. consumption
13. revenue
14. expenditure
15. cartel

CHAPTER 13 PRETEST ANSWER KEY

1. democracy
2. attenuate
3. scope
4. eradicate
5. methodology
6. mandate
7. republic
8. polity
9. despotism
10. ideology
11. coup
12. indictment
13. aristocracy
14. regime
15. elite

CHAPTER 14 PRETEST ANSWER KEY

1. innate
2. hypothesis
3. theory
4. parsimony
5. mnemonic
6. semantic
7. paradigm
8. specificity
9. contiguity
10. cognition
11. episode
12. mediate
13. ethical
14. eidetic
15. validity

CHAPTER 15 PRETEST ANSWER KEY

1. arable
2. ethnicity
3. subsistence
4. hierarchy
5. precarious
6. oligarchy
7. alienation
8. deviant
9. peer
10. sanction
11. cohesive
12. hallmark
13. propagation
14. horde
15. status

CHAPTER 16 PRETEST ANSWER KEY

1. covert
2. demographic
3. admonitory
4. vast
5. prodigality
6. overt
7. augment
8. diversion
9. pragmatic
10. libel
11. vicarious
12. ostensibly
13. defamation
14. diversified
15. slander

CHAPTER 17 PRETEST ANSWER KEY

1. deus ex machina
2. personify
3. motif
4. ligature
5. patron
6. denouement
7. delineate
8. eloquent
9. repartee
10. montage
11. narrative
12. profound
13. soliloquy
14. epitome
15. epithet

CHAPTER 18 PRETEST ANSWER KEY

1. analogous
2. cursory
3. nascent
4. arbiter
5. phenomenon
6. agrarian
7. schism
8. dissension
9. nonpareil
10. antipathy
11. draconian
12. polemic
13. inherent
14. quintessential
15. facet

CHAPTER 19 PRETEST ANSWER KEY

1. virtuosity
2. tone
3. allegro
4. concerto
5. polyphony
6. counterpoint
7. secular
8. timbre
9. andante
10. sonata
11. dynamics
12. oratorio
13. adagio
14. cantata
15. homophony

CHAPTER 20 PRETEST ANSWER KEY

1. ledger
2. debit
3. equity
4. assets
5. dividend
6. liabilities
7. transaction
8. credit
9. depreciation
10. intangible
11. amortize
12. voucher
13. requisition
14. audit
15. disclosure

CHAPTER 21 PRETEST ANSWER KEY

1. entitlement
2. innovative
3. ensconced
4. ramification
5. lucrative
6. adversary
7. pecuniary
8. fiat
9. contingency
10. redress
11. incentive
12. proliferation
13. axiom
14. remuneration
15. minutiae

CHAPTER 22 PRETEST ANSWER KEY

1. algorithm
2. neuron
3. robotics
4. ambiguity
5. matrix
6. syntax
7. binary
8. modeling
9. cybernetics
10. morphemic
11. heuristics
12. digital
13. network
14. interactive
15. analog

INDEX

Note: Vocabulary words appear in bold. Numbers in bold indicate pages where the word definitions can be found.